IDEOLOGY AND PRACTICE

IDEOLOGY AND PRACTICE

THE EVOLUTION OF CHINESE COMMUNISM

JAMES CHIEH HSIUNG

中共思想之淵源

及其演變

PRAEGER PUBLISHERS
New York · Washington · London

To My Family

62,843

PRAEGER PUBLISHERS
111 Fourth Avenue, New York, N.Y. 10003, U.S.A.
5, Cromwell Place, London S.W.7, England

Published in the United States of America in 1970
by Praeger Publishers, Inc.

© 1970 by Praeger Publishers, Inc.

All rights reserved

Library of Congress Catalog Card Number: 69–15748

Printed in the United States of America

CONTENTS

ACKNOWLEDGMENTS

I AM grateful to the Arts and Science Fund, Graduate School of Arts and Science, New York University, for a research grant which supported part of the research for this book. I also owe an intellectual debt, as immense as it is unrepayable, to the many scholars whose studies of various facets of the Chinese Communist ideology and modern Chinese intellectual history have blazed a trail for some of the major concerns of the present study. My NYU students have contributed a great deal, perhaps more than they realize, to the thinking in the book, portions of which grew out of my classroom lectures and discussions.

Needless to say, my colleagues at NYU and Columbia have provided the inspiration that motivated the study. Professor Te-kong Tong, until recently curator of Chinese-language collections at the East Asian Library, Columbia University, has always been a source of help on research materials. Richard Sorich, Research Associate of the East Asian Institute, Columbia University, and a noted bibliographer on Communist China, has lent untiring assistance on the more recent materials from the mainland. In the embryonic stage of the research, my interest was sustained by the enthusiasm of Professor James P. Harrison of Hunter College, New York City, who, in addition to his interest in the history of Chinese Communism, has a long-standing interest in my topic as well. A heavy debt is owed to Dr. Donald E. MacInnis, Director of the China Program, National Council of Churches, who read a large portion of the manuscript and made many constructive suggestions. I alone, of course, remain responsible for the final work.

My thanks go to Barbara Moutsatsos, who typed the manuscript during a hot summer in an office without air conditioning. My editor, Miss Mervyn W. Adams, has rendered more than editorial help. Her contribution to the improvement of the quality of the manuscript is so enormous that I sometimes think that she is almost a co-author of the final product. Unquestionably, her careful and untiring editing has made the manuscript much more readable than before. Finally, the rigorous task of research and writing would not have been possible if not for the patience of my wife and three children, who, except for an occasional complaint, took their temporary eclipse with great grace.

J.C.H.

New York City
May, 1970

IDEOLOGY AND PRACTICE

INTRODUCTION

In ancient times, King Wen ordained
  That a royal shrine rise in his domain.
Benign and serene, he would not demand
  Forced labor on his royal land,
Yet eager subjects came to gild the tower
  (Such was the aura of his moral power).
Within the royal park, his beloved does rested
  Or roamed, sleek and content, while white cranes nested
In the reeds around his pond, or took wing,
  As fish jumped before the watching King.

"LING T'AI," TA YA,
Book of Odes (free translation)

THIS POEM from the *Book of Odes*, which eulogizes King Wen's benevolent rule in antiquity (*c.* 1100 B.C.) by portraying the enthusiastic response of the masses and the idyllic contentment among creatures in his park, could easily be mistaken for the modern adulation of Chairman Mao Tse-tung. The times are different, however, and so are approaches to human problems. Today, an ancient civilization is being transformed; the Chinese people are being mobilized by the new Communist state. The golden age, once discerned in antiquity, now lies in the millennial future. Yet the political ideals of a "sage-king" and of "spontaneous" mass support for his charismatic rule persist. The song that honors Mao—*The East Is Red*—took the place of the national anthem during the Cultural Revolution. It begins with these lines:

3

> The East is red; the sun rises;
> China has brought forth a Mao Tse-tung.
> He works for the people's welfare.
> *Hu erh hai yu* [Hurrah! Hurrah!].
> He is the people's great savior.

Whether such dithyrambs make sense to us in the West, or whether we would prefer to see the Chinese value constitutional rule more than "benevolent" rule, is beside the point. What is relevant here is that certain legacies do survive radical change. Anyone attempting to understand Communist China without an adequate knowledge of its political culture, therefore, is like the fabled blind man trying to "see" the whole elephant by feeling its trunk or leg.

This book attempts to interpret the Chinese Communist phenomenon by examining its intellectual roots. It is guided by the belief that past and present, old and new, and Chinese and Marxist are interrelated in a complex, organic whole and cannot be compartmentalized. It proposes to examine not only the conceptual composition of Peking's ideology but also its practical functions, and to do so within the larger context of cultural continuity and change.

As part of modern China's prolonged process of cultural change, Chinese Communism has encountered the same set of problems that previously confronted other imported ideas and ideologies. They include *justification* (the need for cultural change), *equivalence* (the maintenance of psychological equilibrium amid cultural borrowing), *congruence* between old and new, and *absorption* of borrowed elements into the indigenous culture, to name a few. These problems weighed heavily as China surveyed Western civilization during most of the nineteenth and the early twentieth century in the hope of finding a new ethos, new goals, and new solutions. They have continued to preoccupy the Communist elite and greatly affected their thinking and action. Two primary concerns appear to shape the way in which Chinese Communism has evolved as a new body of first principles: (1) the extent to which old and new cultural elements are conceptually and functionally compatible and (2) the way the new complements the old, or vice versa.

The question of compatibility and complementarity in cultural change as such remains relatively unexplored. There are vast areas in which elements of China's cultural legacy may be compared with the tenets of Marxism-Leninism. A thorough comparison would require an across-the-board review, ranging from metaphysical assumptions to sociological roots, utopian ideals, dialectical traditions, and political ideals. So immense a task is beyond the scope of this book. We shall, however, address ourselves to a number of basic questions: Why did Confucianism "fail" modern China? What did Marxism-Leninism have to offer to radical Chinese intellectuals? How did Mao grow as a Marxist thinker and leader of the Chinese Communist movement? How did Chinese Communism evolve under Mao? What are the intellectual roots and practical functions of Peking's ideology? What is the meaning of the "thought of Mao"? What are the ideological roots of the Cultural Revolution? What is the ideological state of Communist China today, and what is the outlook for the immediate future? We shall deal with a few notable examples where traditional culture and Marxist ideals are found to reinforce each other. One such example is the parallel between the traditional concept of *hsin* (mind, or human will power) and the Communist emphasis on *szu-hsiang* (thought, or prime mover of human action). Another is the possible effect of *yin-yang* dialectical thinking upon Mao's interpretation of the Marxist theory of contradictions (inherited from Hegel).

Because "ideology" is an extremely broad term, a brief definition is necessary here. Political ideologies are defined by Philip E. Converse as belief systems characterized by high constraint, great range, and a centrality of political items. They provide conceptual and terminological channels into which political events can be diverted and managed.[1] While Converse stresses the cognitive character, Robert E. Lane defines ideology as a system of values that provides standards by which political events may be evaluated. Ideologies, to Lane, are "normative, ethical, moral in tone and content." [2] In a more comprehensive approach, Richard M. Merelman incorporates both views. He sees ideology as involving (1) constrained political ideas, (2) an evaluational and prescriptive system (political preferences), (3) persistence, (4) deductive consistency, (5) activist directives, and so forth.[3]

These represent current definitions of ideology among Western political analysts. Their Western cultural bias is often overlooked. The authors discuss diverse "political ideologies" of social classes and groups. Quite typically, in their frame of reference the political process is an *upward* extension from part to whole—from the primary conflict of diverse ideologies (or articulated interests), to their mutual accommodation (interest aggregation) through a higher level of institutionalization (such as political parties), and eventually to the formulation of public policy. Though ideology in Communist China is also cognitive, evaluational, and prescriptive, *an* ideology is never conceived of as having emanated from any segment below; *the* ideology is always imparted by the "center," from above. The progression is from the whole to the part. The Communist elite transmits a single, all-unifying prescriptive system downward to the nation at large, to be "internalized" and translated into reality by social mobilization. Ideology, in Maoist tradition, represents the "general will" to which all particular wills (or "political ideologies," to Western analysts) must bend. It is the spiritual force behind the Communist elite's cultural management, which seeks to modernize China by reshaping its national character. Ideology here is regenerative as well.

In his monumental work *Ideology and Organization in Communist China,* Franz Schurmann comes close to this paradigm. But he subsumes ideology under organization, defining ideology as "a systematic set of ideals with action consequences serving the purpose of creating and using organization." [4] I believe that ideology under Mao takes precedence over organization. Ideology is the central purpose; organization is the means to effect it. Mao leads by ideology (prescribing goals) but uses organization to achieve his goals. Schurmann's premise is quite natural to the Western sociologist, whose primary concern is organization and who tends to see everything else as but an adjunct. In view of China's political culture and Peking's current practice, it is a mistake to place organization before ideology in importance.

In Mao's usage, the word "ideology" is coterminous with "culture," as the latter is understood by most Chinese, and has anthropological connotations. Culture, to anthropologists, is "made of the energy systems, the objective and specific artifacts, the organizations of social relations, the modes of thought, the ideologies, and the total range of customary behavior that are transmitted from one generation to another by a social group and that enable it to maintain life in a particular habitat." [5] In Communist China, ideology has a comparably wide range of application, in the sense that it seeks to establish a new culture, a new way of life, through purposeful, collective means. It is all-inclusive. It offers society an apocalyptic vision, a spiritual force, a philosophy of life, a goal structure, a value system, a body of concepts and vocabulary for communication, and a methodology.

Communist ideology has replaced the Confucian *li*; it has taken over the latter's function as the culmination of what we in the West term social conscience, morality, religious faith, and constitutional law. In the metabolism of Communist China, a new combination of revolutionary nationalism, socialist collectivism (comradeship), and Party discipline has supplanted the traditional combination of culturalism, familism, and bureaucratism. The old assumption that reality had been explained for all time has given way only to a new faith that attempts to order the present and divine the future by certain postulated universal principles. Instead of thumbing through the classics, the Chinese now must read Marx, Lenin, and Mao. The *content* of the prescriptive system has changed, but its *function* has not.

Just as the mind (*hsin*) was traditionally believed to determine people's behavior and expand the individual's psychic consciousness, ideology (*szu-hsiang*, or thought) is now believed to have a comparable function. "Correct thought is the key to correct action." This favorite saying of Mao's is as old as neo-Confucianism, if not older, though the specific content of "correct thought" is now filled by Marxism. Similarly, Mao's belief that the problem of production is more "political" than economic ("politics in command") was not only anticipated by Sun Yat-sen, Tseng Kuo-fan, and Wang An-shih but can be traced back to Mencius. These traditional precepts have merged with new concepts borrowed from Marxism, such as class struggle.

Mao has set for his revolution the specific task of altering negative traits in the Chinese character. For example, passivity must be replaced by productive energy, and personal loyalty must be diverted from family to state to create one citizenry out of a collectivity of kinships. Among other things, Peking has made dramatic use of ideological persuasion and class struggle to achieve those goals. To a certain extent, all Chinese Communist leaders share the concern that, if they can properly guide the thinking of the masses and mobilize their productive energies, China can overcome material obstacles to development. Since at least 1955, however, differences have developed within the top leadership as to the best strategy and the degree of emphasis that should be placed on ideological discipline. With time, the differences became magnified into "contradictions" that could not be easily resolved and that finally culminated in the Great Proletarian Cultural Revolution.

Not just a power struggle, the Cultural Revolution recalls the religious feuds of the medieval West. The conflict between Mao's and Liu's lines of thought on how best to translate Communist ideals into reality is an extension of the perennial debate over cultural adaptation and synthesis that has dominated China since the 1840's. The Confucian tradition has shown a remarkable ability to absorb new ideas and renew itself until the modern age posed a totally new set of problems. Under the impact of modernization, China struggled but failed to unbind its feet. The Chinese Communists boldly set out to do the unbinding, but the cloth turned out to be longer than expected. The Party has been searching for a universal consensus to resolve the problem of what to do with the entangled cloth of China's civilization and what to make of its unbound people. The fact that Mao's thought has triumphed in the Cultural Revolution holds tremendous significance for the immediate future, in that Mao's independent strategy of development, relying equally on human will power and material resources, will now prevail in the effort to achieve Communist goals. Ideological indoctrination, or spiritual mobilization, will remain important, and may be stressed even more than in the past.

This study does not pretend to break new theoretical ground. Rather, its purpose is to reinterpret the Chinese Communist ideology in the new light shed upon it by revelations during the Cultural Revolution. It attempts to show what the ideology is and what it does. For the uninitiated, the book has compressed a wide range of material that would otherwise have to be obtained from a great many monographs and documentary sources. To the specialist, it offers more than just a supplementary text to recommend to students; it proposes for his consideration a few new interpretations, such as the changing significance of Mao's class struggle with the passage of time and an analytical distinction between ideological and organizational leadership.

Existing approaches to the study of Communist China in general and its ideology in particular can be classified into four schools: (1) the "complete break" theory, which denies any continuity whatsoever with the past; (2) the "recurrence of history" theory, which views the Communist regime as the latest turn of the dynastic cycle; (3) the "textual study" approach, which compares Mao's writings with those of Marx and earlier Marxist writers, and the actual conditions of the Chinese revolution with the basic tenets of orthodox Marxism-Leninism; and (4) the "originality" approach, which is closely akin to textual study and seeks to determine whether "Maoism" contains original elements or merely rephrases earlier Marxist-Leninist positions.

While each of the four analytical techniques has merit, each has deficiencies. The "complete break" view is too simplistic: It overestimates the Communists' ability to wipe out everything "old" and create a "new" nation totally divorced from its past cultural matrix. On the other hand, the "recurrence of history" theory overemphasizes continuity from the pre-Communist past: It tends to ignore new problems and their solutions in a new age. Scholars who engage in textual research are often so preoccupied with their efforts to apply Marxist historical or political categories to Chinese history or the Chinese revolution that they are liable to neglect Chinese realities. In the 1920's, Chinese Communist leaders were guided, or misguided, by their eagerness to apply the Marxist theory of revolution in China; they did not always consider whether conditions were appropriate for a revolution by the industrial proletariat. Eventually, they were compelled to interpret Marxist tenets creatively. Mao's emphasis on the revolutionary role of the peasantry, rather than China's minute industrial proletariat, is a case in point. Strict textual analysis often results in insensitivity toward doctrinal reinterpretation in practice.

Those who concentrate excessively on Mao's "originality" may fail to differentiate between the initial impetus of Marxist theory and its subsequent development through practice. For Mao has reinterpreted Marxism-Leninism to fit China's situation, has reversed the Marxist emphasis on the working class in order to stress China's vast peasantry, and has incorporated compatible Chinese concepts into his development of Marxist-Leninist theory.

Throughout Chinese intellectual history, value has always been placed on synthesis rather than originality, which is essentially a concern of the West. Confucius specifically disclaimed originality and cast himself in the role of a great synthesizer. No Chinese thinker has departed from that tradition, not even Mao. Chinese Communist propaganda praises Mao only for his "gift" of creative "development" and "application" of Marxism-Leninism. The "originality" approach not only attributes to Mao what not even his propaganda claims but also, more serious, fails to recognize that, strictly speaking, there is no such thing as true originality. Even Marx was not original, if we view his thought as a creative synthesis of the ideas of Hegel, Ricardo, and others.

A more balanced—and valid—study of Chinese Communism should take into account the "environmental factors," such as cultural background and historical forces, should maintain an awareness of the interaction between actors and events and between ideas and practice, and should bear in mind the intellectual roots and 'normative values of ideology. Instead of debating whether or not Chinese Communism is unique, one should examine the extent to which old and new, Chinese and Marxist, are compatible and complementary, the ways in which they have been blended, and the evolution of Mao's thought over time, in response to changing circumstances. Although Mao has remained loyal to Marxist first principles, in different periods he has given new meaning and new emphases to concepts like class struggle, the mass line, or democratic centralism.

The study of Chinese Communism can benefit from an interdisciplinary approach. Social science can shed light on the practical functions of ideology, while cultural anthropology suggests that an exclusively Western frame of reference can distort our interpretation of Chinese Communism. Similarly, political philosophy can help provide an epistemological analysis of the Chinese Communist thought system. A broad sense of history helps to place events in perspective. Linguistic analysis is useful in eliminating some of the hazards of cross-cultural study that arise from inadequate translation. Although an integrated approach to the study of Chinese Communism is an enormously challenging task, to which this study is but a prelude, I believe that it offers much promise for the further development of the field.

PART ONE

The Historical Perspective

I

THE DISINTEGRATION OF A TRADITIONAL ORDER

The Confucian Background

PREMODERN CHINA enjoyed a relatively placid and coherent social order. But it would be untrue to say that, before the Communist revolution, the country's only major political or social upheavals were dynastic changes and peasant revolts. In its long history, China has undergone at least five periods of revolutionary change: the unification of China by Shih Huang-ti, the first emperor of the absolutist Ch'in dynasty (221–209 B.C.); the attempt to create an aristocratic culture during the Six Dynasties era (A.D. 222–589); the Sung dynasty attempt to substitute an educated plebeian elite for the aristocratic ruling class (960–1279); the T'aip'ing Rebellion, an effort to set up a theocratic-socialist state (1850–64); and the pre-Communist nationalist movement, beginning with Dr. Sun Yat-sen's 1911 Revolution and ending with the May Fourth Movement of 1919, the cultural apostasy that preceded the emergence of Chinese Marxism.[1]

However, except for such movements as the abortive anti-Confucian T'aip'ing Rebellion, during the two milleniums before the Communist rise to power Confucianism was the most resilient and the predominant system of thought. No dynasty since the Ch'in had claimed such a sweeping break with Confucian tradition as did the modern Communists. Confucianism, renewing itself as dynasties changed and other philosophies and religions were absorbed into the Chinese tradition, provided a pervasive and constant ethos for an ordered society through most of the past centuries. The Chinese Communist revolution is, undoubtedly, the first revolution successfully to oppose the Confucian tradition.

Ironically, both Confucianism and Marxism assumed, though on different premises, that history was self-generating. Confucianism saw man as living in three worlds at once, the spiritual (symbolized by the concept of *t'ien*—heaven, or universal order), the natural (*ti*, earth or terrestrial order), and the human (*jen*, or social order).[2] All three worlds coexisted within an all-embracing, self-perpetuating cosmos (*tao*, literally "the way"), in which order was inherent and not imposed by any transcendent force. Marx, substituting his dialectical materialism for Hegelian reason, believed that the social pattern of history was determined by economic conditions and that each successive stage of society —tribal, slave, feudal, capitalist, and Communist—would arise as a new synthesis from the contradiction between old and new principles of social organization in the preceding stage.[3] Marx was unquestionably speaking from the empirical data of Western European historical development. In fact, both Marx and Engels viewed the situation in China somewhat differently, although their specific evaluations showed slight variations at different times. As a whole, they characterized nineteenth-century China as an inherently static order in which change would have to depend upon an external cause, one superimposed by the inroads of the capitalist West.[4] Presumably, Mao was in accord with this view in 1939, when he alluded to the need for an external catalyst when no internal one existed.[5]

Although Marx did not rule out external forces in history, it is nevertheless true that the primary focus of the Marxian theory of historical development is on the "immanent" process, largely defined by a society's modes of production. Yet the new stage set by the Chinese Communist victory in 1949 was due, at least in part, to an external cause, i.e., Marxist-Leninist ideology, that was not inherent in the Chinese frame of reference and was unrelated to the material base. It is important to note that to Marx the external causes for social change, such as the impact of the Western capitalistic economy (imperialism), were not divorced from the material base. To the extent that it reflects the impact of an alien ideology, the Chinese Communist victory is in itself an implicit challenge to the theory that a society's history is, by its material force, self-generating.

It is also ironic that Confucianism, traditionally self-renewing, was unable to meet the new challenges of the nineteenth and twentieth centuries. Of course, to say that Confucianism failed to survive the test of modernization over the past century is one thing; to jump to the conclusion that Communism was by necessity the next stage in China's history is quite another. A brief review of China's long history, focusing on the nation's intellectual response to sociopolitical problems, may cast light on this problem.

Confucianism had gained and sustained its predominance among competing systems of thought in traditional China because its eclecticism made its appeal nearly universal. It had shown a remarkable capacity for self-renewal, both by absorbing new ideas and by maintaining an internal coherence. No other system of thought, not Taoism and not Buddhism, had been able to replace it permanently.[6] Confucianism arose during a troubled period of Chinese history. The Chou dynasty (1142–249 B.C.) was crumbling; hostility among former feudatories was rising. With anarchy threatening, Confucian ethics emphasized the importance of a harmonious balancing of society and state. But the Chou dynasty fell nevertheless, and was followed, for a brief interlude, by the absolutist Ch'in dynasty (221–209 B.C.), whose legacy was the indelible imprint of an idea of empire. The official Legalist ideology of the Ch'in dynasty and its authoritarian system of ethics were then absorbed into the humanist ethics of classical Confucianism. When this modified Confucianism was made the state cult in 136 B.C., as advocated by the famous Han dynasty scholar Tung Chung-shu (c. 179–104 B.C.), it became an instrument for those whose concern it was to maintain the new imperial order.

Tung's authoritarian outlook recommended his Confucian ideology to the Han emperors, but there were factors in it that tended to check the ruler. For one thing, Tung postulated that the ruler must have the "mandate of Heaven," a principle established as early as 1120 B.C., by which the ruler justified his right to govern.[7] But, according to Tung, the will of Heaven was to be discovered not by an astrologer (to whom the king may dictate) but by *portents*, which by ancient tradition were accepted as expressions of the natural cosmic forces of *yin* (the negative) and *yang* (the positive). In the final analysis, it was Confucius who understood the origin of things, of which both portents and human and natural events were manifestations. It was Confucius who taught *jen*, compassion or benevolence, which was rooted in Heaven.* Thus, under this cult, the final power of interpreting right or wrong (the will of Heaven) rested with the Confucian scholars.[8]

There was both give and take in this theory. The Han rulers accepted Confucianism because it taught the people to accept authority. The Confucian scholars supported imperial power because their wisdom and knowledge, as tested in the nascent imperial examination system, earned them a privileged status in the governmental process.

The examinations began as the key to social mobility, but, with time, they gradually came to stress formality, rote learning, and the flowery "eight-legged essays." As a result, there was a potent tendency within the system to downgrade technical com-

---

* The term Heaven is a direct translation of the Chinese word, *t'ien*, a loose concept often employed to denote the supreme power that governs all creation. It represents a cosmic moral-natural order, possessing intelligence and will, that guides impartially not only the destinies of men but the proper order of the universe. It is a secular idealization of an idyllic state of nature in which all creation and forces exist and operate in harmony.

petence and stifle creative thinking. Under later dynasties, the system led to intellectual sterility and an ossified bureaucracy primarily concerned with its own vested interests. The original idea—that the high culture and personal virtue of the Confucian "literocrats" would temper their exercise of administrative power —was gradually lost in practice. The Çonfucian emphasis upon harmony and upon individual submissiveness within an established hierarchy of human relationships hardened increasingly into a justification for the dynastic *status quo*. Because Confucianism in practice favored the elite at the expense of the peasant masses, the Confucian intelligentsia became part of the fabric of the existing imperial order and could hardly fulfill its ideal role of serving as arbiter between imperial power and the mostly illiterate populace.

Nevertheless, the official supremacy of Confucianism was maintained for more than 2,000 years—until the civil service examination system was formally abolished in 1905. From the third through the ninth century A.D., Confucianism survived the challenge of Buddhism as a competing system of thought, emerging in the reinvigorated form of Neo-Confucianism. Alien dynasties, the Yuan, or Mongol (A.D. 1280–1368), and the Ch'ing, or Manchu (1644–1912), were absorbed. It was not until 1840, under a new challenge from the West, that the Confucian social order began to crumble. Until then, the Confucian literocrats functioned as its preservers as well as its beneficiaries.[9]

When the British confronted the Chinese in the Opium War in 1840, China was in a downward swing of the dynastic cycle. Since 1644, the Manchus had ruled China as ·a garrison state. Because of their alien origin, they were in constant fear of being overthrown by the Han Chinese majority. The Manchu emperors' policy of freezing the political *status quo* to assure the longevity of their rule created social and political sterility. This, plus the cumulative effect of natural calamities, rebellions, epidemics, and bureaucratic corruption, led to widespread poverty. Government authority was further emasculated by the onslaught of the Western powers, which opened China by military and diplomatic force. Western pressure forced the Chinese to sign a series of "unequal treaties," giving Western nations the right to trade in a growing number of treaty ports. The influx of cheap Western commodities dealt a deadly blow to the weak domestic industry. The growth of urban comprador centers and the narrowing of traditional avenues of social ascent increased the gulf between rich and poor.[10] The great T'aip'ing insurrection, which dragged on from 1850 to 1864, further sapped the strength of the country. Under unrelenting pressures, a façade of dynastic continuity, maintained until 1912, concealed a shift of power from the center to regional military leaders. From the revolution of 1911 until the consolidation of Communist power in 1949, warlord politics posed a continuing threat to the stability of the Republic of China. Political order disintegrated with the dissolution of the social order. Neither Confucianism nor imported Western ideas and institutions proved capable of maintaining the whole system. Without a broadly supported authority that could rally the nation to purposeful action, none of the regionally fragmented power centers could provide the stability and leadership that a revitalized China would desperately need.

The Confucian ethos of traditional China had provided the society with a normative system known as *li*, a sophisticated code of conduct as pervasive and inclusive as Western legality and Christian ethics combined. It laid greater emphasis on persuasion and the prevention of antisocial behavior than on the punitive and remedial functions of law as understood in the West. But such a morally based normative order was a product of the traditional agrarian society, with its tranquil stability and wide, unquestioning consensus regarding social goals and values. Since the primary purpose of the *li* was the maintenance of the *status quo*, its intrinsic concern was with means—that is, the observance of proper procedures, ceremonies, and social decorum.[11] As the crisis in China's confrontation with the invading West deepened, the social matrix of Confucianism and the consensus regarding

goals and values disintegrated. The predominant concern of Confucianism with the observance of traditional patterns of behavior
could no longer meet society's need for revised ends. Initial
cracks in the Confucian system became great intellectual chasms,
which had to be filled by a new ethos.

The search for a new ethos was an agonizing experience. It
involved stubborn resistance by the traditionalists and over-cor-
rection by the radicals. As a result of Chinese contact with the
West through war and diplomacy, overseas education of Chinese
students, translations of Western literature, and revised curricula
in Chinese schools, a wide range of Western ideas filtered into
the consciousness of increasingly Westernized Chinese intellectuals. In the late nineteenth and early twentieth centuries, Darwin's
theory of evolution, Kropotkin's mutualism, Schopenhauer's
idealism, Dewey's pragmatism, Bergson's vitalism, Russell's logical analysis, and, finally, Marxism influenced Chinese intellectuals.[12] It was the age of great intellectual confusion.

The Quest for a New Ethos

For two decades after the outbreak of the first Opium War,
China's traditionalist leaders sought to ignore the Western challenge. They believed that the universal ethos of Confucianism
could survive changing times, possibly with minimal Westernization ("self-strengthening"). Grand Secretary Wo-jen, a powerful
voice in the Manchu court, completely rejected any capitulation
to Westernization. Despite the entrenched conservatism, the
great debates on how to modernize China began in the 1860's.
Tseng Kuo-fan (1811–72), the orthodox Confucian leader who
put down the T'aip'ing Rebellion, understood the dangers inherent in either accepting or rejecting Westernization. He was
nevertheless willing to study Western armaments and technology.
In the 1890's, Viceroy Chang Chih-tung (1837–1909), a reformer
after Tseng's heart, sought to maintain a balance between Confucian values and Western technical skills. He made famous the

t'i-yung maxim: Chinese learning as the "foundation," and Western technology for "use." "To save China," another phrase that gained increasing currency among intellectual leaders toward the beginning of the present century, expressed the desperate character of the search for a solution to China's chronic ills and to the "melon-cutting" of China by the Western powers (and Japan, after 1894). By the end of the nineteenth century, the constitutional monarchist reformers led by K'ang Yu-wei (1858–1927) and Liang Ch'i-ch'ao (1873–1929) were favoring more sweeping changes, not in the name of Westernization but on the grounds that Confucianism, originally progressive by nature, had been perverted by the interpreters of the classical Confucian texts.[13]

In their attempts to reform within the Confucian frame of reference, however, the traditionalists failed to perceive that Confucianism posited a universal empire with China at its center, whereas the world of the nineteenth century was one of nation-states, with power centered in the West. China would have to become a modern nation-state in a non-Chinese universe. The intellectuals of the period, educated in the Confucian tradition, still maintained the universalist Confucian perspective. They did not, and could not, view China's conflict with the West and Japan as a contest between native particularism and a modern outside world. Instead, they saw Western rational values as a particular challenge, which could be absorbed and accomodated within the centuries-old Confucian framework, as Donald Lowe has so aptly noted.[14]

By the turn of the present century, Chinese intellectuals, who came increasingly from urban backgrounds, had had more exposure to Western education. Their greater sensitivity enabled them to view the Chinese struggle in a larger context. Nationalists, such as Liang Ch'i-ch'ao in his youth and middle years (1899–1919) and Sun Yat-sen (1866–1925), sought to remold China after the Western nation-state model. They disagreed only on whether the means should be evolutionary or revolutionary.

The first fifteen years of the twentieth century marked the transition from the old Confucian order to a modern perspective. The next stage was that of the "New Culture," an attempt by Western-oriented radicals to remodel China after the industrial culture of the modern West. The attempt, despite its failure, helped prepare the ground for the climactic May Fourth Movement of 1919, during which many future leaders of Chinese Communism first emerged.[15]

The first proponent of the New Culture, in 1915, was Professor Ch'en Tu-hsiu (1879–1942), of Peking University. Ch'en maintained that because traditional Chinese culture had been conceived in an atmosphere of agrarian tranquility, it had nothing to contribute to modern civilization, that it had to be destroyed completely and replaced with the modern democratic and scientific culture of the West.[16] Ch'en's view, however extreme, was shared by most leaders of the New Culture Movement. Among them was Hu Shih (1891–1962), the celebrated Columbia University–trained philosopher, who vehemently denounced China's inferiority in every respect.[17] The more poetic, though pungent, attack on the "madman's" culture of traditional China by the illustrious writer Lu Hsün (1888–1936) swelled the chorus of denunciation.[18] All the New Culture leaders attributed Chinese social and political ills to defects in China's culture and way of thinking. Political remedies offered little hope, in their eyes. The development of a new culture and a new way of thought would require the re-education of the entire nation.

The Confucian traditionalists, in their effort to reassert Chinese superiority over the West, had attempted the impossible. In seeking to maintain China's equivalence with the West, both evolutionary and revolutionary nationalists had been unrealistic. But in proclaiming China's inferiority to the West, the New Culture radicals adopted a psychologically untenable position. A Chinese radical, regardless of his good intentions, would eventually have to resolve the problem of his Chinese roots. Equivalence, or psychological equilibrium, would require either the renovation of Chinese thought or new concepts to deal with the physical and cultural aspects of the challenge of Western civilization. In the May Fourth era, which was emotionally charged with anti-imperialism, Hu Shih resorted to the unrewarding task of intellectual renovation as the means for East-West reconciliation. Ch'en Tu-hsiu and his colleague Li Ta-chao (1888–1927) saw in Marxism the great equalizer between China and the West.[19] The greatest attraction of Marxist theory, despite its Western roots and transmission through the Bolshevik experience, was that it could simultaneously claim rational universal application and criticize the nonprogressive West on its own terms. To the Chinese Marxists, the resolution of the problem of China's equivalence ultimately depended upon realization of the Marxist revolutionary promise in China.

Models for Modernization

The traditional Chinese imperial order, the *t'ien-hsia*, which was based on the assumption of the universality of Confucianism, has generally been regarded by scholars as the period of "culturalism." Alien rulers, who were willing to be Sinified and absorbed into the Confucian system, could be accepted by the Chinese and belong in the *t'ien-hsia*. Traditional Chinese culturalism impeded the development of nationalism, which emerged belatedly in response to the incursions of the West. A major cause of Chinese nationalism, as Joseph R. Levenson has noted, was the alienation of the intellectuals and politically important segments of the population from traditional Chinese culture when it proved unable to surmount the Western challenge.[20] It is not surprising that the shift from the Confucian to the Western orientation in the Chinese intellectual climate during the first two decades of the twentieth century coincided with the dissolution of culturalism and its replacement by nationalism. It is ironic, however, that the intellectual alienation from tradition and the growth of nationalism was accompanied by an uncompromising hostility to the Western culture that had precipitated these developments. Such hostility can be explained by the difficulty of resolving the contradiction between the role of the West as teacher and its role as oppressor.[21] Modernization in China involved the conscious selection of another country as a model or catalyst, but it was difficult to square such imitation with Chinese nationalism at any given time. From the latter part of the nineteenth century on, it was not the West proper but two rapidly modernizing countries, Japan and Russia, that offered alternative models to the aspiring Chinese. Japan was first mentioned in this connection in the 1860's,[22] but its image became somewhat tarnished as a result of the 1894 Sino-Japanese war. Nevertheless, the revolutionary nationalists, (such as Sun Yat-sen, continued until 1905 to look to Japan for inspiration and example.[23]

In the 1890's, Russia began to catch the fancy of the Chinese constitutional monarchists such as Liang Ch'i-ch'ao. After the Russian Revolution of 1905, Russia gradually replaced Japan as the model for revolutionary nationalists in China, whose ascendancy signaled the decline of the constitutional monarchists. Though translations of Marx and Engels began to appear in Chinese publications after 1905, Chinese interest in Marxism was infinitesimal until the Bolshevik Revolution in 1917. Marxism in its pre-Leninist form seemed irrelevant, because it presupposed the existence of capitalist economic relations and a well-developed urban proletariat. There was some general interest in socialism, and this can be found in Sun Yat-sen's *min-sheng chu-yi*, "Principle of the People's Livelihood," whose main thrust was the general welfare of the people and a planned economy. However, Ch'en Tu-hsiu was still preoccupied with his "Mr. Democracy" and "Mr. Science." For Li Ta-chao, who still lived by a traditional philosophy of moral regeneration, progress was produced not so much by mechanical forces as by the inherent moral and spiritual nature of the universe (including both man and matter). This was within the bounds of an extremely ancient Chinese belief in the eternal youthfulness of the universe of both the animate and the inanimate worlds, which encompassed birth, change, and death and had a power of self-renewal on an ever higher plane. In his optimism that good pervaded reality, Li was intellectually akin to Ralph Waldo Emerson, although he did not share Emerson's exaltation of the individual. Like Henry Bergson, Li valued motion and change more than stability and spirituality. While Li's philosophical system provided a rationale for political activity, it fell far short of Marxist historical materialism. Ch'en, Li, and others showed at best a lukewarm interest in socialism at that stage,[24] for there was a noticeable decline of interest in socialism after the birth of the Republic of China in 1912.

After the Bolshevik Revolution of 1917, however, interest in Marxism suddenly flowered in China, and one source dates the founding of Li Ta-chao's Society for the Study of Marxism as early as the spring of 1918.* The society was a precursor of the Chinese Communist Party. The decline of interest in socialism after 1912 and the sudden surge of interest in Communism in 1918 suggest that the Bolshevik Revolution aroused interest in Marxism, rather than the other way around. As two separate studies indicate, Li Ta-chao and Ch'en Tu-hsiu were committed to the idea of revolution before they were committed to Marxism itself. Herein lies a sharp difference between Chinese Marxists and their counterparts in Western Europe and Russia. The latter had usually begun political action after long years of commitment to Marxist theory. In China, on the other hand, it was the emotional response to the message of the Bolshevik Revolution, rather than an ideological commitment to Marxism itself, that brought people into the Communist fold.[25]

As already noted, nationalism and the selection of a model for China's modernization were closely related. The intense

---

* This early date was suggested in Hatano Kanichi, *Saikin shina nenkan* (*New China Yearbook*) (*Tokyo*, 1935), p. 1597. Other accounts usually cite March, 1920, as the date for the founding of the Society.

interest of Chinese radicals in Bolshevik Russia was an index of rising feelings against the West after China's defeat at the Versailles Peace Conference in 1919. At Versailles, which Li Ta-chao called "the European division-of-spoils conference," the Allies cynically sanctioned Japan's takeover of former German interests in China's Shantung Province, although China's express purpose in entering World War I on the Allied side had been to recover those interests. In consequence, the Chinese intelligentsia's image of a rational, stable, and democratic West, whose scientific wisdom would be put to the service of all mankind, was shattered beyond recognition.[26] The tempestuous reaction of Chinese students and intellectuals, merchants, workers, and the general public to the Western "betrayal" was also unforeseen. The massive student demonstration in Peking on May 4, 1919, against the supine position of the warlord government was but the first of a series of violent nationalist and anti-imperialist demonstrations of the May Fourth Movement, which swept across the country like a prairie fire. Angry with both the West and their own government, many Chinese intellectuals turned their attention to Russia.

As late as March, 1919, Li Ta-chao, who had embraced Marxism the previous year, was still the lone advocate of Bolshevism and Marxism in China.[27] Even Ch'en Tu-hsiu, who had prophesied in 1917 that the Russian Revolution of February marked the dawn of a revolution against "international monarchism and aggression," had yet to show a positive interest in Marxist theory *per se*. In the aftermath of the May Fourth Movement, however, there was a surge of interest in such diverse socialist doctrines as the utopian socialism of Saint-Simon, the Christian socialist and agrarian socialist doctrines inspired by Tolstoy, the anarchist theories of Kropotkin and Bakunin, the guild socialism of Bertrand Russell and G. D. H. Cole, and the revolutionary socialism of Marx and Lenin. The widespread interest in socialist thought is an indication of Chinese antipathy toward capitalism and imperialism at that time.

Among all socialist doctrines, Marxism in its Leninist form had a special appeal to the anti-West intellectuals in China. The Leninist theory of imperialism held the world's capitalist exploiters responsible for China's plight, while the success of the Bolshevik Revolution offered tantalizing proof that the Marxist formula could work in a backward country.[28] When the Soviet Union symbolically disowned Tsarist Russia's imperialist policy toward China through the sensational Karakhan proposal,* it psychologically disarmed those Chinese intellectuals who had sought in vain to find an ally in the West.[29] Sun Yat-sen, whose many appeals to Western powers had fallen on deaf ears, had been attracted to Lenin's political philosophy even before the actual founders of the Chinese Communist Party themselves were.[30] Of course, Sun's nation-state perspective predisposed him to reject the universalist assumptions of the Marxist-Leninist world revolution.

In this anti-imperialist atmosphere, Li Ta-chao, the first Chinese Marxist, became the pioneer of the revolutionary ideology that emerged as the most important of the newly popular socialist creeds. A special issue of the *Hsin Ch'ing-nien (New Youth)* in May, 1919, edited by Li, was devoted to Marxism. Ch'en Tu-hsiu had professed to be a liberal internationalist during the New Culture period not long before, and both Ch'en and Li subscribed to the anti-imperialism of the May Fourth Movement. Even after his ideological conversion in 1918, Li's Marxism was still orthodox, pre-Leninist Marxism, in the sense that he never fully appreciated the Leninist Party. In 1920, Ch'en was thor-

---

* On July 4, 1918, G. V. Chicherin, Soviet Commissar of Foreign Affairs, declared that his government repudiated all Tsarist encroachments and privileges in China. In a famous Declaration of July 15, 1919, L. M. Karakhan, his deputy, made a startling elaboration of that statement. Many Chinese reacted with a profound sense of gratitude. But during the subsequent negotiations, Karakhan modified his position and was unwilling to return Russian rights over the Chinese Eastern Railway, though concessions were made on other scores. When the final agreement was reached in 1924, China did not gain all that Moscow had promised a few years earlier. Cf. Robert C. North, *Moscow and Chinese Communists*, 2d ed. (Stanford, Calif.: Stanford University Press, 1962), pp. 45–52.

oughly converted to Marxism.[31] The next year he became the first Secretary-General of the new Chinese Communist Party (CCP).

Although a minor figure in the early 1920's, Mao Tse-tung followed a similar intellectual path of conversion to Marxism. A nationalist first, like Ch'en and Li, he became interested in revolution and, finally, in Marxism. On the eve of the May Fourth Movement, an emphasis on military strength and heroism and vigorous nationalism seemed particularly to mark Mao's character, as Stuart Schram has so well documented it.[32] Although a growing Maoist legend now claims that Mao had mastered the fundamentals of dialectical materialism in 1918, Mao himself has admitted to his early *idealist* dispositions. At the First Normal School in Ch'angsha, in his native Hunan Province, Mao had received a powerful dose of idealism from his teacher, Yang Ch'ang-chi, his future father-in-law. A disciple of the English philosopher T. H. Green, Yang used as a textbook Friedrich Paulsen's neo-Kantian *System der Ethik*, which had been translated into Chinese by Tsai Yuan-p'ei, the German-educated anarchist and president of the National University in Peking. In a well-written essay in 1918, "Power of the Mind," Mao showed how deeply he had been imbued with the ethical idealism of his teacher, which was rooted in both Western and Chinese traditions, and how far he had to go to become a materialist:

> I say: the concept is reality, the finite is the infinite, the temporal is the intemporal, imagination is thought, I am the universe, life is death, death is life, the present is the past and the future, the past and the future are the present, the small is the great, the yin is the yang, the high is the low, the impure is the pure, the thick is the thin, the substance is the words, that which is multiple is one, that which is changing is eternal.[33]

It is extremely important to note Mao's reasoning within the traditional Chinese *yin* (negative) and *yang* (positive) categories in a way reminiscent of Taoist thinking. The *yin* and *yang* principles are supposed to be present in mutually complementary form in all beings at all times. A very idealist form of Chinese dialectics, the *yin-yang* antinomy differs from Hegelian dialectics in that *yin* is not an antithesis to *yang* but its temporary deflection. Progress is couched in terms of a return from this deflection to the perfect state represented by *yang*. A cyclical notion of progress (i.e., "return") is supported by this reasoning, which is clearly outside the Hegelian logic of a linear progressive development to *higher* stages through thesis, antithesis, and synthesis.

Although there was a note of activism in Mao's early thinking, such as in his article "A Study of Physical Education," published in *Hsin Ch'ing-nien* in August, 1917, Mao clung to his deep emotional roots in Chinese culture. This can be seen in Mao's profound admiration for his country and its inhabitants, especially the Han people, who constitute the overwhelming majority of the Chinese nation. Examples can be found in the manifesto that Mao wrote for the first issue of his magazine *Hsiang-chiang P'ing-lun* (*Hsiang River Review*) in July, 1919, and his article, "The Great Union of the Popular Masses," published in the next three issues of that periodical. In fact, Stuart Schram finds that the "nationalist reflex" represents what he calls "an astonishing continuity of thought" in Mao, whereas certain other ideas of Mao have undergone considerable change over time.[34]

At the same time, Mao's realization that China urgently needed cultural regeneration motivated him to found, in 1918, the Hsin-min Hsüeh-hui (New Nation Study Society). By his own account, his interest in Marxism developed during 1918–20 "under Li Ta-chao," for whom he worked as a library assistant in Peking University. To be sure, Mao's writings of the May Fourth period showed scant knowledge of Marxism. It is for this reason that Schram argues that Mao, like Li Ta-chao, was drawn first to the idea of revolution and only later made his commitment to Marxism as an intellectual system. According to Mao himself, his final conversion to Marxism took place in 1920 during his second visit to Shanghai, when he discussed with Ch'en Tu-hsiu various questions that had occurred to him in reading about Marxism. "Ch'en's own assertion of belief had deeply impressed me at what was probably a critical period in my life," Mao related years later to Edgar Snow.[35] Thus, Mao's Marxist career owes something to both Li and Ch'en.

A sense of the urgent need for change, a nationalistic urge to prove China the equal of the West, anti-imperialism, and the inspiration of the Bolshevik Revolution were major motivations when men like Li, Ch'en, and Mao became Communists. During the next years, they sought to translate their revolutionary ideals into action and to make an alien ideology relevant to the Chinese revolutionary scene.

2

FROM INTELLECTUAL COMMITMENT TO REVOLUTIONARY ACTION

Pragmatism and Marxism

ALTHOUGH THE success of the Bolshevik Revolution and the anti-imperialist sentiments of the May Fourth Movement helped to convert many Chinese radicals to Marxism, the conversion was not just an emotional affair. It involved an intellectual commitment. The 1919 debate between Li Ta-chao, the Marxist, and Hu Shih, the pragmatist follower of John Dewey, revealed something of the appeal of Marxist solutions to Chinese problems. Both men were then opposed to the solutions offered by the Kuomintang (KMT), but they disagreed on how China should approach its pressing problems.

In the summer of 1919, during Professor Dewey's lecture tour in China, Hu Shih issued a call for "more study of problems and less of isms." From the pragmatic perspective of his former professor at Columbia, Hu Shih urged Chinese intellectuals to direct more attention to individual, practical social problems. Foreign "fanciful, good-sounding isms" might not fit the Chinese context, he warned, and doctrines that advocated all-embracing and fundamental solutions were irrelevant and might even hinder the finding of real solutions to China's social problems.[1]

Li Ta-chao picked up the gauntlet in defense of his own Bolshevik and Marxist beliefs. In a long letter to Hu, Li strove to show, first, the nation's need for a "common movement" to combat social problems and, then, the urgent necessity of an all-embracing "ism" that would provide a "common direction." Li therefore urged the intellectuals to lead the political and social movement. Hu, on the other hand, had asserted that the intellectual should abandon political action and devote full time to studying social problems and finding their solutions. The disagreement between the two men involved not the role of theory as such but, instead, different perspectives toward the means by which China's social problems could be resolved.[2]

Drawing upon Max Weber's distinction between the "ethic of ultimate ends" and the "ethic of responsibility," Maurice Meisner suggests that Hu would probably have preferred the former for its primary commitment to high standards of personal morality. But Hu's belief that the intellectual should withdraw from political activity in order to function only as an impartial guide and observer made it impossible for him to further those ultimate ends, however much he may have cherished them in private.

On the other hand, a political activist like Li not only would have to follow the demands of his own conscience but also, more importantly, would need to work for the needs of society (ethic of responsibility). He must accept responsibility for whatever means he uses in, and whatever incidental evil results from, his attempts to attain presumed good ends for the society as a whole. In becoming a Marxist, Li Ta-chao finally committed himself to the ethic of responsibility as he perceived it.[3]

For Li and his colleagues, there was more in the Marxist ideal than the "cry of pain, sometimes of anger, uttered by men who feel most keenly our collective malaise," which Durkheim detected in all socialist doctrines.[4] Marxism did offer a total answer to all the social problems for which they were seeking solutions. Years later, in 1949, Mao Tse-tung was to write that, after finding the "universally applicable" Marxism-Leninism, China's face was drastically changed.[5]

As a pragmatist, on the other hand, Hu Shih denied that any

political or social program had universal applicability. He favored an empirical search for solutions. Li Ta-chao, in his pre-Marxist days, was attracted to the Marxist vision of the future but still hoped that a revival of faith in the power of the universe to renew itself would instill the Chinese people with a new confidence in their own capacity to bring about China's moral, social, and political regeneration without outside material help. As Li saw it then, the agency for change was spiritual regeneration; later, as a Marxist, he saw it instead in the self-consciousness of the alienated man and the social revolution. Marxism's call for the revolutionary destruction of society and its subsequent reconstruction appealed to Li but was anathema to Hu, whose focus on discrete social problems bore the imprint of his training under Dewey in the American philosophical and sociological tradition. That tradition, as Meisner has perceptively observed, had grown out of the experience of a stable and progressive society; it assumed that the whole would take care of itself, hence that social problems could be viewed and tackled individually.[6]

In China, however, a process of social, political, and cultural disintegration had been accelerating, particularly following the 1911 revolution. The most pressing problems were to re-establish a viable social and political structure and to formulate a new ethos within which the system could operate again. To talk about social reforms by "inches and drops" was to miss the totality of the problem. Despite Hu's good intentions, he failed, in his overenthusiasm for American pragmatism, to see that the pragmatic tradition had little relevance for the vastly different social milieu of crisis-torn China, as Meisner has pointed out.[7]

Nor did Hu's pragmatic formula have roots in traditional Chinese ways of thinking. Traditional China had had long periods of stability, but a pragmatic tradition had not developed, as it had in American society. The Chinese mental process relies more heavily on deductive thinking, proceeding from whole to part, from general to specific.[8] Because the Chinese tend to view things not as individual entities but as interrelated parts of a whole, they are predisposed (as Li was) toward a *programmatic* approach aimed at all the interrelated problems at once. The pragmatic approach, by contrast, looked quite inadequate to many of Hu's contemporaries.

The early Chinese Marxists, and others who came later, justified their ideological commitment on rational grounds. They believed that Marxist theory and practice would benefit China. What elements in Marxism-Leninism most appealed to its Chinese adherents?

A major appeal of Marxism was its claim to be a universally applicable scientific theory. Arnold Brecht has denied the scientific validity of Marxism on two grounds. First, Marx and Engels claimed an ability to predict the general course of human history with certainty, but they did so by projecting past experience into the future on the scientifically untenable assumption that the relationship between cause and effect in human and social affairs is as direct and simple as it is in inanimate nature. Second, Marx and Engels postulated that the economic base of society determines the form of its "superstructure" of ideas and values. They expressed both positive and negative value judgments on the ideas of others but did not recognize that those value judgments might also be based on personal or relative considerations, or might be inappropriate for other times and places.[9]

Such flaws in logic, if they perceived them, did not deter the Chinese who became Marxists. In traditional Chinese thought, there is a predilection for divining the future by the experiences of the past. Almost all past reformers, from Confucius and Wang An-shih to K'ang Yu-wei, tended to look back to antiquity for inspiration and justification for their reforms. Thus, the Marxist claim to predict the course of history on the basis of the past was not incompatible with traditional patterns of Chinese thought; at least it made Marxism more acceptable to those Chinese who became Marxists.

On the other hand, where Chinese thinkers had perceived a dialectical pattern in nature (*yin* and *yang*) and a cyclical pattern in history, Marx and Engels postulated that the dialectical inter-action of past and present would lead to successively higher stages of development in the future until the achievement of Communism. This new element in Marxism—the higher stage of development—complements Chinese dialectical thought but promises to carry it one stage further. This complementary quality would also have appealed to the Chinese Marxists.

Thirdly, even if Marx and Engels had denounced the value judgments of others on subjective grounds, they had nevertheless provided a methodological tool for criticism of the West and had presented socialism as a higher expression of human justice.' Marxism thus offered leftist Chinese intellectuals a means to resolve the problem of China's equivalence with the West and a beacon of hope for the future.

There were other elements in Marxism-Leninism that appealed to Chinese intellectuals. First, the Marxist idea of alienation had relevance for social conditions in China. Alienation, in the Marxist sense, describes the fragmentation of man's work in the industrial process, his loss of identification with its products, and his resultant inability to realize his full human potential. For Marx, the fragmentation of man's work and the sale of labor as a commodity set men against each other in an unnatural form of social relations. Such relations are engendered by the compul-sions of political economy—the interaction between political and economic processes—and are most sharply manifested in the exploitation of the worker by the capitalist class. Marx thus saw two forms of alienation, social and economic, as the product of the system of private property in which the producer or worker is subordinate to, or exploited by, the nonproducer, or capitalist.[10] Although private capital and the merchant class have been held in low esteem in China since the Shang dynasty (c. 1200–1122 B.C.), China has never had a formal theory regarding exploitation. The Marxist theory of alienation, supplemented by Lenin's the-ory of imperialism, filled an intellectual vacuum for many Chi-nese who found no explanation within their own tradition or that of the West for the social anomalies of what Mao later described as "semifeudal," "semicolonial," and, by implication, "semi-industrial" China.

In his theory of "self-consciousness," Marx described how the very dehumanization of the worker, and his increasing awareness of it, would induce him to take the steps necessary to lead mankind from the realm of "prehistory" to a "truly human history." [11] Admittedly, the small size of the industrial working class in China would have made it difficult for the Chinese worker to lead the revolution—unless one adopts Trotsky's classic inversion of 1906, which viewed the proletariat of the backward countries as *potentially* more revolutionary than that of the industrial states. But the dilemma was resolved by Lenin, who specified that an elite of revolutionary intellectuals would have the historical duty to inject consciousness into the spontaneous movement of the proletarian masses.[12]

Nothing in traditional Chinese thought really resembles the Marxist concept of the worker's "self-consciousness" regarding his alienation. The terms *t'ien-yi* (will of Heaven) or *t'ien-chi* (scenario of Heaven), have a more metaphysical connotation. The phrase *t'ien chu jen chu* (heaven helps one who helps himself) is still far from the Marxist idea. If any similar concept has ever developed in traditional Chinese thought, it should have appeared among the elite class of Confucian scholars, who were the most detached from labor but were believed to have the sole responsibility for universal liberation. Lenin's emphasis on the role of revolutionary intellectuals may, however, have provided a bridge between China's elite scholarly tradition and the Marxist stress on the importance of developing proletarian self-consciousness. In any event, the awareness of the importance of arousing the consciousness of the masses is a Chinese debt to Marxism-Leninism, even if the bulk of the masses belongs to the peasantry rather than to the industrial proletariat.

The goals of the Chinese Communist revolution will be discussed in more detail in a later chapter. It should only be noted here that, for the anti-West Chinese radicals, Marxism-Leninism promised unique solutions to a number of economic and social problems. If other revolutionary programs sought to oust the existing government, the Chinese Communists also wanted to overthrow the social class (the traditional elite) that dominated society. If other authoritarian ideologies prescribed the strengthening of state power as the first step to social reform, the Communists were probably the most sensitive to the gulfs between state and society and sought to bridge them. Although Communist theory regarding the eventual disappearance of state power may be utopian, it expresses the desire of class-conscious revolutionaries to make society commensurate with state, to merge the masses and the elite in one classless society. The Marxist demand for the total restructuring of society—its class structure, value system, and state power—made such theories as those of alienation or self-consciousness appear more relevant to the radical Chinese. It is also true that Marxism stressed the popular cause of anti-imperialism. However, since other revolutionary ideologies, such as Sun Yat-sen's *San Min Chu I*, also offered an anti-imperialist nationalism, the appeal of Marxism-Leninism to the Chinese Communists must have derived from a good deal more than its anti-imperialist stance.

Joining the Communist Revolution

To become a revolutionary in China in the 1920's, Marxist or otherwise, was no easy decision for Chinese intellectuals. Whatever the depth of their disillusionment with contemporary Chinese politics, by becoming revolutionaries they cut their ties to traditional society and usually risked their own lives, if not those of their families as well. Revolts and dynastic revolutions occurred in traditional China, of course, and it is true that some of them were led by Confucian scholars. It nevertheless remained a Confucian ideal that, in times of great political and social turmoil, the intellectual's duty was to withdraw from the political arena in order to remain above partisan considerations and to protect his intellectual integrity. Hu Shih's position of "ivory tower" intellectualism in 1919 thus had its Chinese roots along with its more positive purpose. But escapism was possible in traditional times only because the established social structure could withstand major upheavals. More cynically, Mu Fu-sheng has pointed out that escapism was the only recourse open to dissident intellectuals in earlier times. In the traditional stable social system, he adds, "there was no question of changing the society, but only that of staying away from it." [13] In the early twentieth century, however, withdrawal to monastic life was both meaningless and impossible. The deepening of the crisis in China and the need for action made revolutionaries of the dissatisfied intellectuals.

The social turmoil in twentieth-century China presented problems, however, for the intellectual elite as a whole, and not just for its malcontents. With the fall of the Ch'ing dynasty in 1911 and its replacement by the Republic in 1912, previous avenues of social and political ascendancy were irreparably disrupted. Nevertheless, the traditional division—following the formulation of Mencius—between labor by brain and labor by brawn continued to have its hold on the minds of the people as the norm for social stratification. The unemployed or underemployed intellectuals did not feel they could engage in manual labor or jobs that were "beneath their dignity." [14] If they did not wish to lead the life of a Taoist recluse, activists among the intellectuals had only a few options open to them. They could join one or another warlord faction, seek an accommodation with the Kuomintang (as Hu Shih finally did), or seek to overthrow the existing system and establish a new social order—a task for which neither the warlords nor the KMT was equipped. Li Ta-chao, Ch'en Tu-hsiu, Mao Tse-tung, and other Chinese Marxists were among the revolutionary radicals who took the third road.

Although personal ambition and Soviet support doubtless played a role in their decision, there is no doubt that a number of Chinese leftists became Marxists out of what was to them a genuine concern to "save" China and build a new social order. One historian succinctly refers to the Chinese Communist movement as the attempt of "a small group of intellectuals in search of a quick and effective solution to modern China's problems of poverty, internal political disorder, and foreign encroachments" to follow the Bolshevik model of Marxist revolution.[15]

A century of social turmoil, compounded by internal warfare and foreign encroachment, had resulted in a deep-seated callousness to pain and suffering among the people and a widespread sense of futility about improving life in China. Revolution may have seemed the only solution. An incident vividly described by Lu Hsün, the famous leftist author, conveys this popular feeling. While a student of medicine in Japan, Lu Hsün saw a newsreel about the Russo-Japanese War of 1904. In one scene, a Chinese crowd in Manchuria was surrounding an impassive Chinese man whose hands were tied. The narrator stated that the Chinese prisoner had worked as a spy for the Russian army during the war and was to be executed by the Japanese army. To Lu Hsün, his fellow Chinese in the crowd seemed to be cheering and milling around as if they were there to "enjoy . . . the spectacle." Sickened by the picture, he realized that what China needed most was not the physical health he was being trained to provide but the restoration of a healthy mentality and a national sense of self-respect.[16] The experience drastically changed Lu Hsün's career. He gave up the study of medicine and became a social protest writer who sought to awaken his compatriots to the need for radical social change and cultural regeneration.

Lu Hsün himself never formally joined the Communist Party. But his sentiments were shared by other leftist writers, many of whom did become Communists out of revulsion against social apathy and injustice, an empathy for the vast sufferings of their fellow Chinese, and a conviction that the masses had to be aroused to take common action. To them, the Communist revolution promised a new future. Because Lu Hsün had expressed these common sentiments, Mao Tse-tung praised him in 1940 as China's greatest revolutionary writer,[17] and in 1967 the Maoists described him as "our forerunner of the Cultural Revolution."[18]

It is not hard to understand Mao's tribute to Lu Hsün. In 1918, the young Mao had founded the Hsin-min Hsüeh-hui, which was dedicated to the regeneration of China as a "new nation" through physical education, patriotism, and moral re-education of youth.[19]

Chinese Communism Before Mao: Strategic Problems

The Chinese Communist Party, which was established in 1921 with the assistance of the Communist International (Comintern), set for itself the goal of seizing power in China. The struggle it entered involved the CCP, the Kuomintang, and the Soviet Communists in a complicated triangular relationship. Our concern here is not with the general history of the Chinese Communist movement, about which several fine works are available,[20] but with the evolution of the Communist ideology in China and its relationship to the CCP's initial reverses and eventual victory.

It was not until 1935 that Mao Tse-tung emerged as the head of the Chinese Communist Party. Between 1921 and 1935, the Chinese Communist movement, under a series of leaders, tried several different roads to power. Its leaders sought to apply, in varying degrees, Marxist theory, Soviet experience, and Comintern instructions, without due regard shown, either within the CCP or in Moscow, for Chinese realities. An intellectual commitment to Marxist theory is one thing; its application to Chinese revolutionary practice is quite another. How did the Chinese Communists reconcile theory, based on *a priori* doctrines, with the constantly changing reality of the Chinese Communist revolution?

THE INDUSTRIAL PROLETARIAT AND THE PEASANTRY

During the 1920's, there were a number of serious tensions or contradictions between Comintern-imposed policies and concrete realities in China. In the first place, the Comintern, following Marxist guidelines, insisted that the Chinese revolution must be based on the industrial proletariat, but the size of that class in agrarian China was so small as to render such a policy inapplicable. Moreover, the focus of attention on a minute industrial proletariat naturally caused most of the CCP leadership (in which Mao was not yet very important) to neglect the revolutionary potential of the vast discontented peasantry. Secondly, Comintern coalition tactics required the CCP to enter an alliance with the Kuomintang on the assumption that the bourgeoisie would lead the first phase of the two-stage revolution. Since most KMT leaders either were landlords themselves or came from landlord backgrounds and were unwilling to yield their vested interests, the absorption of the CCP into the KMT apparatus deprived the CCP of any effective means of exploiting rural discontent in order to start a peasant revolution against landlord domination. (Although many CCP leaders had similar class backgrounds, persons like Mao opposed the vested interests of their own class in their attempts to reshape Chinese society according to Marxist-Leninist ideals.) A third error in Comintern strategy in China was its characterization of the KMT as representing *all* classes. That description undermined any CCP claim to be the sole party representing the proletariat and peasantry. Furthermore, it was in Moscow's immediate interest to banish Western and Japanese influence from China. To accomplish that strategic aim, Moscow was willing to rely on the stronger KMT and to postpone the building of a peasant army under the CCP. Mao's eventual success was due to a reversal of these policies.

THE CCP COALITION WITH THE KMT

Between 1921 and 1927, the CCP leadership, with some reluctance and serious misgivings, followed rather closely the Comintern line formulated at the Second Comintern Congress in 1920. The theses that the Congress adopted on the "national and colonial question" represented a compromise between the conflicting views of Lenin and M. N. Roy, the Indian Communist leader. Although both men accepted the basic Marxist theory of a two-stage revolution, i.e., a bourgeois-democratic revolution followed by a socialist revolution, they differed as to which class should lead the first stage in colonial and semicolonial countries. In the original Marxist formulation, the bourgeoisie would come to power in the first stage after revolting against feudalism and the monarchy; only in the second stage would the revolt of the proletariat result in its dictatorship over the bourgeoisie.[21]

Although Lenin's views changed somewhat over time, he had more regard for the Chinese bourgeoisie than for its Russian or European counterparts. Lenin concluded after the 1905 uprising in Russia that "the proletariat must in its own interest assume the leadership" of the bourgeois-democratic revolution in Russia.[22] He therefore played down the role of the Russian bourgeoisie. Expressing similar disdain for the bourgeoisie in Europe, Lenin asserted that it was "in a state of decay and already confronted by its grave-digger—the proletariat." However, Lenin referred to the Chinese bourgeoisie, under the leadership of Sun Yat-sen, as "still . . . capable of championing sincere, militant, consistent democracy, a worthy comrade of France's great enlighteners and great leaders of the close of the eighteenth century." [23] Under certain circumstances, Lenin was ready to leave leadership of the first stage of the revolution in the colonies to the indigenous bourgeoisie until such time as the proletariat, i.e., the Communists, could take charge. His formula for revolution in the colonies was closer to orthodox Marxism than was his formula for Russia and Europe, but it was unacceptable to M. N. Roy.

Roy insisted that the proletariat must assert its hegemony in the revolutionary movement from beginning to end—a position reminiscent of Lenin's in regard to Russia. Although Lenin was sympathetic to Roy's views in theory, he could not accept them in practice. Lenin's concern about international pressures to reverse the October Revolution in Russia and his desire to weaken the European "imperalists" through revolts in their colonies, as well as his regard for the revolutionary potential of the bourgeoisie in Asia, may partially explain his differences with Roy in regard to revolution in the backward areas. True to his "oriental" perspective, Roy insisted that the national revolution in the colonies must be made the *sine qua non* for proletarian revolution in Europe. Lenin was willing to assign equal weight to Asia and Europe, but he would not concede that European workers should passively await the initiative of the East before pressing forward with their own proletarian revolution.

As a result, the "Theses" finally adopted at the Second Comintern Congress merged Lenin's concept of revolution from above with Roy's of revolution from below. Three main themes emerged: First, the bourgeois-democratic revolution in the colonial and semicolonial countries would be *national* in form, not just social as it had been in Europe. Second, although the proletariat, in coalition with the peasantry, should assume primary leadership, the Communist Party, which represented their interests, should form an alliance with those elements of the existing native bourgeoisie who were prepared to fight against foreign domination. Third, circumstances permitting, the bourgeois elements within the alliance could be permitted to lead the "national-revolutionary" movement.[24] The Congress, as a concession to Roy, substituted the words "national-revolutionary" for Lenin's "bourgeois-democratic" formulation.

The resolution of the Lenin-Roy dispute at the Congress, however, was largely verbal, rather than substantive. The disagreement reappeared in 1926–28 in the Stalin-Trotsky dispute over the timing of the formation of soviets in China. Moreover, a policy of alliance between the CCP and the KMT, as the spokesman for bourgeois interests, could not resolve fundamental conflicts between the goals of the two parties and the interests they represented. Chinese Communist efforts to implement the alliance policy almost led to the extinction of the CCP in 1927.

The First Manifesto of the CCP, in June, 1922, followed the

Comintern line and characterized China as feudal and semicolonial, dominated by militarists and bureaucrats at home and
imperialists abroad. It called for an alliance between the CCP
and the KMT in a "united front of democratic revolution" to
"struggle for the overthrow of the military and for the organization of a real democratic government." [25] This spirit persisted
in the Manifesto of the Second CCP Congress, in July, 1922,
which was noted for its pledge to "forge a democratic united
front of workers, poor peasants, and petty bourgeoisie." [26] The
same tone was maintained in the Third National Congress Manifesto of June, 1923, and the Fourth CCP Manifesto of January,
1925.[27] Following the January 26, 1923, agreement between Sun
Yat-sen, on behalf of the KMT, and A. A. Joffe, on behalf of the
Communists, the nature of the CCP-KMT alliance changed somewhat.[28] Prior to the agreement, the united front had been an
alliance between two disparate parties, under a "bloc without"
formula. Under the new arrangement, known as the "bloc within"
formula, members of the Communist Party could, as individuals,
also acquire membership in the KMT.

In March, 1927, Chiang Kai-shek staged a coup in which he
arrested and killed large numbers of Communist Party members in
an attempt to eliminate the CCP as a rival political force in
China. Despite Chiang's break with the Communists, the CCP
Fifth Congress two months later neither disavowed the policy of
alliance with the KMT nor chose to exploit agrarian unrest in
the countryside. Its call for a reorientation of the CCP's revolutionary movement [29] was indicative of the Party's timid response to the crisis. Moreover, as a result of Comintern pressure,
Ch'en Tu-hsiu's proposal to retreat to areas in remote northwest
China, in an attempt to salvage CCP strength, was voted down.
Its adoption would presumably have meant an open break with
the KMT. Although Trotsky had insisted on an immediate CCP
break with the KMT, Stalin, for reasons involving his domestic
feud with Trotsky, instead ordered surviving CCP members to
proceed from Shanghai to Wuhan and to join the KMT left wing

there.[30] In midsummer, however, the KMT left wing, in a dramatic reaction to Stalin's authorization of an independent CCP peasant army, expelled the Communists from the coalition. Even after that, the Emergency Conference of the CCP leadership, which was convened on August 7 by Ch'ü Ch'iu-pai under close Comintern supervision, sought to avoid, any provocation of the KMT that might jeopardize the possibility of continuing the coalition. "Under the present conditions," its Resolutions declared, "unless we achieve hegemony within the KMT, we shall not be able to achieve the hegemony of the Chinese proletariat. We must reorganize the KMT and make it a genuine mass organization of the urban and agrarian toiling masses." [31]

Soviet insistence on a CCP-KMT alliance in the 1920's reflects the interest of the U.S.S.R. in a stable, albeit KMT-dominated, China to counterbalance the power of Japan and the Western nations. That policy subordinated the nascent Chinese Communist movement to the international strategic concerns of the Soviet Union. It was not until September, 1927, that the Comintern abandoned that coalition policy. When the signal for change finally came from Moscow, Stalin's infallibility was maintained by blaming Ch'en Tu-hsiu for the failure of the alliance policy. He was accused of Trotskyist tendencies and removed from office as head of the CCP.

BRIEF EXPERIMENT WITH ARMED INSURRECTIONS

Toward the latter half of 1927, with the authorization of the Stalinist group in Moscow, the CCP began a brief period of experiments with armed insurrection: at Nanch'ang in August, in Hunan (led by Mao Tse-tung) in September, and at Canton in December. The new policy was reflected in a resolution enacted in November, 1927, by the plenum of the CCP Central Committee.[32] However, when the armed uprisings had all been put down, a resolution introduced by Stalin and passed unanimously in February, 1928, by the Ninth Plenum of the Executive Committee of the Comintern (ECCI), blamed the failure upon the CCP

leadership, now under Ch'ü Ch'iu-pai. "To play with insurrections," said the ECCI resolution, "instead of organizing a mass
uprising of the workers and peasants is a sure way of losing the
revolution." [33]

The new ECCI line imputed the CCP's failure to coordinate
worker and peasant uprisings to a tendency on the part of the
CCP leadership to skip the bourgeois-democratic stage of the revolution. "The characterization," the ECCI declared, "of the
present stage of the Chinese revolution as one which is already a
socialist revolution is false." [34] Absorbing Comintern criticisms,
the CCP Sixth National Congress, held in Moscow late in the
summer of 1928, adopted a Political Resolution, which specifically stated: "The present stage of the Chinese revolution is bourgeois-democratic." It outlined two immediate tasks for the Party:
the overthrow of imperialism and the promotion of agrarian revolution. It designated sovietization, or "setting up a democratic
dictatorship of workers' and peasants' soviets under the leadership of the proletariat," as the means by which to achieve the
two tasks. Since the national bourgeoisie of China, i.e., both
wings of the KMT, had "betrayed the revolution and joined the
counterrevolutionary camp of the imperialists, gentry, and landlords," it could no longer be considered a dependable force in
China's revolution. "Therefore," the Resolution concluded, "the
sole source of power [of the Chinese revolution] lies, at the
present bourgeois-democratic stage, in the Chinese proletariat
and peasantry." [35]

This revised CCP line, which was carried out by Li Li-san between 1928 and 1930, abandoned the old policy of national democratic alliance. As James P. Harrison points out, the CCP would
thereafter openly compete with the KMT in an attempt to use
a rural-based military force to gain an urban base for the Communist revolution in China. Enigmatic and ambivalent as it was,
Moscow's new formulation expressed its theoretical commitment
to the urban proletariat and its practical, although reluctant,
realization of the importance of the peasantry in the revolution.

Li Li-san was under orders to instigate armed insurrection and to recapture an urban base for the proletarian revolution.[36] But when the urban insurrections failed in 1930, Li was accused of "opportunism and putschism." His leadership was described as "contrary to the line of the Comintern" and "Trotskyist in nature," and he was also accused of "denying the place of the democratic-bourgeois stage of the revolution in Lenin's theory of the transformation of the revolution." [37]

There were several reasons for the failure of CCP policies before 1930. First, Comintern policies were not always relevant to Chinese conditions. Second, the Comintern and CCP definition of the KMT's class character and revolutionary role was neither orthodox nor in accord with reality. According to Marxism, political parties merely concentrate the political power of given economic classes at the superstructure level. In 1922, when Maring, the Comintern representative, urged the CCP under Ch'en Tu-hsiu to ally with the KMT, he said, according to Ch'en's account some years later, that the KMT "was not a bourgeois party but a coalition party of all classes." [38] Ch'en's reference to Maring's responsibility for the failure of the CCP policy of alliance with the KMT may not be totally reliable, since it was made after Ch'en's expulsion from the Party, hence possibly made in self-defense; but official CCP documents of the period incorporated the same notion of the multiclass character of the KMT. In January, 1925, for example, the Fourth Manifesto of the CCP enumerated certain demands in the interests of "our oppressed soldiers, peasantry, workers, small merchants, and intelligentsia" and then stated quite explicitly: "Our Party recognizes that the support of these demands is the responsibility of our *whole* people and of its representatives—particularly the responsibility of the KMT." [39]

The idea that the KMT represented a coalition of all classes ran counter to the orthodox concept of the organic relationship between party and class. As Trotsky sarcastically remarked in May, 1927, "The classes come and go, but the continuity of the

Kuomintang goes on forever." [40] If the KMT could claim to represent the whole people, how could the CCP, at the level of abstraction, claim the right to represent any class, even the proletariat?

The disparity between Chinese conditions and official Comintern-CCP policies disturbed certain members of the CCP who held different views in private. There were three broad lines of private dissent, represented, respectively, by Mao Tse-tung (whose views will be discussed in the next chapter), Ch'en Tu-hsiu and his close associate P'eng Shu-chih, and Li Ta-chao.

The Private Views of Ch'en and P'eng

When Ch'en Tu-hsiu became a Marxist in 1920, it was with the hope that China might skip the capitalist stage of development and become industrialized by way of socialism. The example of Bolshevik Russia suggested that the transition from feudalism to socialism could be swift. As Benjamin Schwartz aptly puts it, Ch'en was "a Trotskyist by instinct before Trotskyism had emerged as a distinct phenomenon and without Trotsky's ingenious theoretical rationalizations." [41]

As the head of the CCP from 1922 to 1927, Ch'en was obliged to support, at least outwardly, the official Comintern policy of alliance with the national democratic forces. Although he became reconciled to this policy, Ch'en showed some initial resistance to it and a different ideological orientation. In justifying the coalition, Ch'en fell back on orthodox Marxist formulas. Revolution, he emphasized, was produced not by subjective desires but by objective economic and social conditions. Since the "objective strength" of the proletariat—still a very weak force in China—would expand with the expansion of the bourgeoisie, the growth of capitalism in China was not so undesirable after all. [42]

But Ch'en privately maintained that, despite its alliance with the KMT, the CCP must remain an independent party (i.e., "the bloc without"), with a distinct identity with the proletariat. By 1924, his follower, P'eng, was already saying that the Chinese

bourgeoisie had become counterrevolutionary and that the peasantry could not be expected to have a Marxist revolutionary
spirit. P'eng concluded that only under independent proletarian
leadership could the Chinese revolution achieve victory.[43] If
there is no evidence that Ch'en backed P'eng's stand in 1924, he
certainly did so in 1929, after Ch'en had been relieved of his
official CCP duties. Writing in December, 1929, he ascribed the
failure of 1927 to misjudgments about the class composition of
the KMT and about the possibility of bourgeois revolution. He
pleaded for a soviet-type alliance of the proletariat, the petty
bourgeoisie, and the impoverished masses in the cities and the
countryside.[44] His bold confidence in the proletariat and the
collective model recalls the pre-1923 period. Although critical of
the mistakes of the official Comintern-CCP alliance policy, Ch'en
and P'eng nonetheless failed in their private utterances to come
to grips with the reality of nonindustrial, peasant China.

The Li Ta-chao Line

Also opposed to the official CCP line in 1925–27 was Li
Ta-chao, whose focus on the peasantry anticipated Mao Tse-tung.
In 1919, Li had expressed his concern about the isolation of
the intelligentsia from the peasant masses by calling upon young
intellectuals to bring modern culture to the villages. Predicting
that the Chinese revolution would be a peasant revolution, he had
identified the liberation of China with that of the peasantry, which
made up most of the laboring class of agrarian China. His conception of the peasant revolution recalled that of the Populist
movement in Tsarist Russia in that his passionate faith in the
spontaneous energies of the peasant masses was accompanied by
the conviction that the revolutionary intellectual must bring en-
lightenment and leadership to the peasant movement.[45]

After his conversion to Marxism, Li had at first hoped that
the Chinese nation as a whole would bring about the revolution.
He had supported the Communist alliance with the KMT in
1923 in the hope that the KMT might become a "universal

national" (*p'u-pien ch'üan-kuo*) organization that could serve as the agency for the national revolution. Disillusioned with, the KMT, especially after 1925, he shifted his attention back to the peasantry.[46]

In 1926, the year before Mao Tse-tung was to write his now famous "Hunan Report" on the peasant movement, Li Ta-chao, in his "Land and the Peasants," was already assigning the major role in the Chinese revolutionary movement to the peasantry: "In economically backward and semicolonial China, the peasantry constitutes more than 70 per cent of the population; among the whole population *they occupy the principal position,* and agriculture is still the basis of the national economy. Therefore, when we estimate the forces of the revolution, we must emphasize that *the peasantry is the important part.*" [47]

Li's orientation toward the peasant force in the Communist revolution stood in contrast not only to the European Marxist contempt for the "idiocy of rural life" but also to Lenin's views on the revolutionary role of the peasantry. Though his views on the peasantry changed in different times, Lenin consistently maintained that the peasant force would participate in the revolution as a *subordinate* ally of the urban social classes (either the bourgeoisie or the proletariat), and that the agrarian revolution, as part of the general revolutionary process, must be infused with the socialist consciousness of the Communist Party.* On the other hand, there is no suggestion in Li's writings between 1925 and 1927 (the last years of his life) that the agrarian revolution was to be subordinate to political developments in the urban sector. Li did not even pay lip service to the Comintern doctrine that the urban bourgeois-democratic revolution should precede the socialist revolution. Nor is there any suggestion in his writings

* Lenin's attention was drawn to the revolutionary potential of the peasants after the 1905 peasant uprising in Russia. In a work written in 1907, Lenin went so far as to define the bourgeois-democratic revolution in Russia as a "peasant revolution." See *Agrarian Program of Social Democracy* (November–December, 1907), in Lenin, *Selected Works,* Vol. III (New York: International Publishers, n.d.), 258.

that the Party must develop an elitist consciousness, or that it might be able to manipulate the peasantry.

Li's theory of agrarian revolution also ran counter to the policies of the Comintern and the CCP Central Committee. This was most striking in regard to the character of the peasant secret societies, such as the Red Spears. Li saw them as a genuine and spontaneous expression of the peasant revolutionary forces, whereas the CCP Central Committee viewed them—particularly the Red Spears—as "basically reactionary." At a time when the Comintern and the CCP Central Committee were attempting to curb the "excesses" of peasant uprisings in order to avoid jeopardizing the precarious alliance with the KMT left, Li was advocating an intensification of agrarian revolution. As Meisner has noted, Li's conviction about the importance of agrarian revolution derives from his compulsion to seek out the elemental forces of the Chinese nation. Li identified the peasantry as the most genuine repository of the vital energies and national traditions of China and as a great revolutionary force. Although Li shared Trotsky's belief in the revolutionary potential of the masses, he did not see their nationalism as a potential reactionary force and so did not share Trotsky's internationalism. An internationalist or Western-oriented Marxist like Ch'en Tu-hsiu saw the urban proletariat as the focus of the Chinese revolution because, apart from Marxist ideological reasons, the proletariat, regardless of its nascent strength, had been forged in the image of the West.[48] For all his difficulties in maintaining doctrinal orthodoxy, Li, the nationalist-Marxist and advocate of agrarian revolution, anticipated Mao Tse-tung, whose added mastery of Party organizational skills and whose ability to reconcile Marxist theory with Chinese revolutionary practice were to make him the "red sun of the east."

3

MAO'S EVOLUTION
AS A CHINESE MARXIST, 1917–34

EACH OF the various Communist positions discussed above—the Comintern-directed CCP policy, the private views of Ch'en and P'eng, and even Li Ta-chao's emphasis on the peasantry—failed to reconcile Marxist-Leninist doctrine with Chinese reality. Ironically, Mao Tse-tung, the architect and leader of the Communist revolution in China, is scarcely an orthodox Marxist theoretician. In practice, he is both a nationalist and a revolutionary. He has sought to transform China in the image of Marxist revolution, but he has also revised Marxist theory to suit the particular demands of revolutionary China. In retrospect, Mao's success prior to 1949 seems to contrast sharply with his style of leadership since then. His drastic efforts to overhaul China's economic, political, and social structure during the Cultural Revolution suggests that, since 1949, he has had considerable difficulty reconciling the goals of Communist revolution with the reality of governing China.

It is tempting to infer from the Communist victory in 1949 that Mao alone understood, and had always understood, what the correct revolutionary line should be at any given time. In fact, Mao's theses on the Chinese revolution and the Party's role in it were developed between his expulsion from the CCP Politburo in November, 1927, after the failure of the Autumn Harvest uprising in Hunan, and his assumption of Party leadership at

Tsun-yi in 1935. In the intervening years, Mao moved into the Chingkang Mountains along the border between Hunan and Kiangsi, where he established a guerrilla base area. There he was able to experiment with agrarian revolution and to develop his ideas independently of, and in opposition to, the urban-based Politburo.

In 1945, a Maoist reinterpretation of the Party's history at the Seventh Plenum of the Central Committee characterized the period between 1927 and 1935 as one plagued by three erroneous lines. These were the lines followed by the CCP Politburos under Ch'ü Ch'iu-pai (November, 1927, to April, 1928), Li Li-san (June, 1929, to September, 1930), and Wang Ming, Po Ku, and other "Returned Students" (January, 1931, to January, 1935). According to John Rue, the sharp Maoist criticism of past Party leadership suggests how great the tension must have been between Mao and the CCP Politburo during that period.[1] By attacking those who had criticized his views in the past, Mao may have been seeking to show that his own views prior to 1935 were consistent with the theory of "new democracy," which he developed in 1940. Yet the very fact that Mao felt obliged to defend his earlier positions may throw some light on the extent of Mao's own deviations from the official Party line between 1927 and 1935.

If Mao succeeded where the Comintern-CCP policy had failed, it was because his years in opposition had alerted him to the need to adapt the universalist principles of Marxism-Leninism to the particular demands of the Chinese revolution. What has been consistently labeled in Western literature as "Maoism" grew out of that experience. Comintern policy, on the other hand, failed because it sought to fit the Chinese particularity into the universalist framework of Marxism-Leninism.

Both by disposition and by the compulsion of circumstances Mao was more a doer than a theoretician during his years in opposition. He was, in fact, an iconoclast, nationalist, and revolutionary before he became a Communist. After turning to Communism in the 1920's, he was much too involved in revolutionary activity to master the fundamental Marxist tenets. His pre-Marxist rebellion against parental and political authority foreshadowed his difficulty in subordinating his strong personality to strict Party discipline, as required by Leninist democratic centralism. His independence may explain his three expulsions from the Central Committee and his eight reprimands by the same organ before 1935.[2] Mao's nationalist focus on the need to assure the victory of Communism in China also made it difficult for him to subordinate the interests of the Chinese revolution to those of the Soviet state or the international Communist movement, as perceived by Stalin. Even after he had gained a fuller understanding of democratic centralism and other Marxist principles, Mao retained his independent outlook and nationalist perspective.

Mao's keen sensitivity to the need to arouse and involve the masses—an important aspect of his high regard for practice—predated his Marxist period. His 1917 essay, "A Study of Physical Education," indeed a neglected subject then, expressed Mao's concern for the physical, as well as moral and intellectual, health of the individual. Physical education was described as the basis for individual activism and initiative, but Mao argued that such action must be taken in union with the masses, a theme on which he expanded in his 1911 article, "The Great Union of the Popular Masses."[3] In both articles, Mao called for the mobilization of the masses to transform Chinese society. Such views were significant in a nation where a girl's "sickly beauty" was considered an asset (Lin Tai-yü, in Dream of the Red Chamber, personifies this concept) and where an intellectual's hands, as a badge of scholarly gentility (and aloofness from the masses), "do not even have the strength to tie up a chicken."

Mao's growth as a Chinese Marxist falls into six stages, which are closely related to the growth of the Communist movement in China: (1) the initial Marxist period, from his conversion in 1920 to approximately 1926; (2) the formative Maoist period, beginning with his emphasis on a peasant-based revolution in 1927 and ending with the consolidation of his leadership within the CCP by 1935; (3) the mature Maoist period, from 1935 to his enunciation of his theory of "new democracy" in early 1940; (4) the civil-war period, 1940–49; (5) the post-victory period, from 1949 to approximately 1962; and (6) the period of the Great Proletarian Cultural Revolution, from 1962 on.[4]

The post-1949 period will be discussed in the last part of the present volume. This chapter and the next will provide an overview of the essential elements in Maoism in the period prior to 1949. Although necessarily somewhat arbitrary, the periodization is designed as a matter of convenience to help trace the intellectual growth of Mao as a Chinese Marxist.

The Initial Period (1920–26)

In the six years between his conversion to Marxism and his expulsion from the CCP Politburo, Mao showed himself to be more of a revolutionary than a sound Marxist. In a letter to Ts'ai Ho-sen written in November, 1920, Mao denied that education could move the nation from capitalism to Communism, as Bertrand Russell had maintained in a lecture in China. Although there was an orthodox Marxist base for his position, Mao's reasons still were not quite Marxist in character. Noting first that the financial control of education by the bourgeoisie made Communist propagandizing impossible, Mao then went on to refer to the "mentality of the adherents of capitalism." "How," he asked, "can one hope that [the bourgeoisie] will repent and turn toward the good?" Like the Marxists, Mao did not believe that education could "change the consciousness of the propertied classes," but his words suggest the disillusionment of an idealist rather than the Marxist concept that the material base of society will be reflected in its philosophical superstructure. Furthermore, citing historical experience, Mao argued that "no despot, imperialist, and militarist throughout history has ever been known to leave the stage of history of his own free will without being over-

thrown by the people." Capitalism was doomed, since the proletariat, "two-thirds of humanity," was "discontented," and "a
demand for Communism has arisen and has already become a
fact." [5] Mao's eagerness to see the people overthrow the existing authorities suggests that he was committed more to revolution as such than to Marxism. From the premise that revolution
was necessary, he jumped to the conclusion that Communism
was the only correct type of revolution for China.

During the 1920's, Mao's background in Marxist theory was
weak. He was therefore willing to follow, in practice, the Comintern policy on CCP-KMT coalition, under the assumption that
the KMT represented the bourgeois-democratic classes. In 1923,
for example, Mao assigned a predominant role to the "merchant"
class in China's national revolution. All classes would ally "to overthrow the militarists and foreign imperialism," with each assuming a share of the responsibility, but

> because of historical necessity and current tendencies, the work
> for which the *merchants* should be responsible in the national
> revolution is both *more urgent* and *more important* than the
> work that the rest of the people should take upon themselves.[6]

The fact that current editions of Mao's *Selected Works* exclude
practically all of his pre-1927 writings attests to his later low
regard for his intellectual development prior to 1927. The sole
exception is Mao's 1926 *Analysis of the Classes in Chinese Society*
(hereafter, *Analysis*), which was entirely revised before its inclusion
in the 1951 edition of his works.[7] In the original text of this
essay, Mao showed his difficulty in grasping the Marxist class
distinction between the bourgeoisie and the proletariat, for which
the Chinese terms are *tzu-ch'an chieh-chi* (propertied class) and
wu-ch'an chieh-chi (propertyless class), respectively. Mao's knowledge of Marxism was derived from works in Chinese, since, by his
own admission to Edgar Snow, he knew no foreign languages.
Whether because he had understood these two terms in their
literal Chinese sense or because of his own beliefs, Mao appeared

to possess a peculiar conception of classes. For one thing, he seems to have assumed that the attitudes of Chinese social classes were identical with the attitudes of the classes in Europe toward the social revolution. Mao's discussion here focuses on the social aspect of the revolutionary ferment in China in the early 1920's. More important, he seems to assume that class, in both China and Europe, could be defined according to a graduated scale of property ownership, whereas in Marxism classes are defined in regard to relative ownership of the means of production.

In an article published in the January, 1926, issue of *Chung-kuo Nung-min*, Mao endeavored to analyze "the various classes of the Chinese peasantry and their attitudes toward revolution." If there can be various classes within the peasantry, the "classes" here must refer to various strata. The concrete meaning of the Chinese term for class, *chieh-chi*, or stages and steps, as of a ladder or staircase, may well have colored Mao's understanding of the meaning of class. In Mao's early works, the term connoted social strata, as determined by varying degrees of property ownership and social station. The following property ownership scale was introduced in Mao's second article dealing with "all the classes in Chinese society" (February, 1926) but was deleted from the 1951 edition of his works:

> In any country anywhere, there are three categories of people: upper, middle and lower. If analyzed in more detail, there are five categories: the big property class, the middle property class, the small property class, the semi-propertyless class, and the propertyless class.[8]

Having defined class structure in these unorthodox terms, Mao then indiscriminately applied his five-class spectrum to both rural and urban segments of Chinese society, although orthodox Marxism separates the proletariat and the peasantry. He also divided the Chinese population into two primary groups: the 395 million who had little or no property and the 5 million big, middle, and small property owners. Moreover, he believed that the comparative numerical strengths of the various classes, as defined by his five-class scale, would determine the future of the revolution.[9] *

If this elaborate scale expressed Mao's early enthusiasm for a revolution in which the dispossessed majority would overthrow the prosperous minority, it was not long before he stopped openly using such pseudo-Marxist categories. Even in his *Analysis* of 1926, Mao was aware that his Marxist description of the industrial proletariat as "the main force of the revolution" was at odds with reality, since the Chinese industrial proletariat was only one-tenth the size of the "agrarian propertyless." Did Mao's unorthodox interpretation of Marxism result from his conscious intention, or was it due to his difficulty in understanding an alien ideology? Both factors may have played a role.

There were two major themes in Mao's writings in this period. The first, as noted above, was his belief in the unity of revolutions in China and the West. Even Roy, at the Second Congress of the Comintern, had not gone so far. Thus, in Mao's words, "all contemporary revolutions are basically one, and their goals and means are identical. The goal is an anti-imperialist one, and the means depends upon the coalition war of oppressed nations and classes." [10] The claim of unity may derive more from Mao's urge to fit the Chinese revolution into the Marxist pattern than from Lenin's anti-imperialism.

The second theme was Mao's concern with the revolutionary and counterrevolutionary forces in China, as he perceived them. His writings show that he recognized the force of popular discontent and the need for mass support of the Chinese Communist revolution, although his arguments did not quite fit within the Marxist framework of class struggle. The numerical division of society into friendly and hostile classes noted above, although not grounded solidly in Marxist theory, was indicative of Mao's concern for reality.

* The Chinese translation of Communism, *kung-ch'an chu-yi*, literally means "sharing-property-ism."

The Formative Period (1927–34)

From 1927 on, Mao increasingly embarked upon a full-scale experiment with a model of revolution that has since been identified with his name: the seizure of political power by a Party-led peasant army, operating from the countryside. Perhaps because he was fully occupied with his peasant-based revolutionary movement during the period, Mao spent little time on Marxist theorizing. His writings nevertheless expressed a keen sense of the ferment in China. His 1927 "Report on an Investigation of the Peasant Movement in Hunan" ("Hunan Report") was enthusiastic about the prospects for agrarian revolution in his country, although the Comintern-imposed CCP line was not directed toward agrarian revolution at that time. On the basis of his investigation, Mao predicted that "within a short time, hundreds of millions will rise in Central, South, and North China, with the fury of a hurricane; no power, however strong, can restrain them." In a bold rhetorical question, Mao urged that the Communists lead the massive peasant uprisings and transform them into a national agrarian revolution: "Are we to get in front of them [the peasants] and lead them, or criticize them behind their backs, or fight them from the opposite camp?" Mao's own response was clear:

> An agrarian revolution is a revolution by the peasantry to overthrow the power of the feudal landlord class. If the peasants do not apply great force, the power of the landlords, consolidated over thousands of years, can never be uprooted. There must be a revolutionary tidal wave in the countryside in order to mobilize tens of thousands of peasants and weld them into this great force.[11]

In the "Hunan Report," Mao was criticizing the restraints placed on peasant "excesses" by the National government at Wuhan, a coalition of the KMT left and Communists under the direction of the Comintern. At the time of the "Hunan Report," the CCP was under Comintern orders to support both the Wuhan KMT regime and the peasants. As Roy, the Comintern enforcement agent, later admitted, it was an impossible policy because support of Wuhan, whose leaders were drawn mostly from the landlord class, entailed the curbing of "peasant excesses." [12] The Comintern did not reverse its alliance policy until after the breakup of the Wuhan coalition in July, 1927. Though Mao did not openly criticize Comintern policy in China, his impassioned championship of the poverty-stricken peasantry was in opposition to the "Thesis on the Chinese Situation" passed by the Seventh ECCI Plenum in December, 1926. Its keynote was that "the proletariat is the only class . . . in a position to carry on the radical agrarian policy which is a condition for the . . . further development of the revolution." [13]

It is true that Lenin's "Agrarian Program of Social Democracy" (November–December, 1907), which was written after the 1905 peasant uprising in Russia, had called attention to the revolutionary force of the peasantry. Lenin even referred to the bourgeois-democratic revolution in his country as a "peasant revolution." The importance of Mao's peasant orientation lies not in its originality but in its timing and scope. First, Mao's espousal of the peasant cause came just when the central leadership of his own Party was following the Comintern policy of alliance with the bourgeoisie, even at the expense of immediate peasant interests. Second, without openly opposing the Comintern-CCP official line, Mao gave as much emphasis as he could to the peasants as an independent force equal, and not subordinate, to the proletariat. As Brandt, Schwartz, and Fairbank have argued, "no previous writer of the Marxist-Leninist school had ever conceived of the peasantry as anything but an auxiliary to the revolutionary proletariat of the cities." Mao's "Hunan Report" was thus the first indication of an inchoate "Maoism." While the term "revolutionary vanguard" invariably stands for the urban proletariat in Marxist-Leninist parlance, in Mao's "Report" its equation with the poor peasantry is just beginning to be perceptible.[14] If the germ of Maoism, the practical reliance on the peasantry as the main force of the revolution, was already present in early 1927, its full development took place only between 1928 and 1935, during Mao's years "in opposition." As late as April, 1929, in fact, Mao still maintained that *"proletarian* leadership is the sole key to the victory of the revolution" (italics added), even though he was also emphasizing the creation and expansion of rural soviets and the Red Army as major conditions for promoting a revolutionary high tide in the cities.[15]

Mao's concept of the peasantry, though influenced by Li Ta-chao, does not show Li's bias against the proletariat. Li had greater faith than Lenin in the force of the peasantry but failed to appreciate, as both Lenin and Mao did, the importance of Party organization and the role of proletarian leadership. Although Mao's emphasis on the peasantry deviated from the Leninist dogma enjoining the hegemony of the urban proletariat within the various revolutionary forces, Mao's line evolved gradually in response to the shifting realities of power within China and to the counterrevolutionary forces outside. "Maoism," as it developed through the years, never ruled out the role of the proletariat.[16]

The year 1927 was important for other reasons, however, than the publication of Mao's "Hunan Report." It was also the year that the CCP-KMT alliance disintegrated, and Mao's interpretation of the event, which differed from the Comintern-CCP line, has received insufficient attention. In Mao's view, the fiasco was due not so much to betrayal by the bourgeoisie, as the official Comintern-CCP line maintained, as to the betrayal of the bourgeois-democratic revolution by the "comprador-gentry" regime of Chiang Kai-shek.

After the CCP had been expelled from both the right and left wings of the KMT, in March and June, 1927, respectively, the August 7 Emergency Conference of the CCP declared that the *"national bourgeoisie* has separated itself from the democratic revolution and has gone over to the camp of counterrevolution." [17] Mao was present at the conference and was elected to the Politburo, only to be expelled from it three months later. Mao's own position during the conference remains unknown, but in late 1928 he expressed views that differed not only from the official Comintern-CCP doctrine but also from his own previous views.

In his *Analysis* of 1926, when he was more fully in tune with the Comintern, Mao did foresee the possibility of a split within the middle bourgeoisie (which he sometimes equated with the national bourgeoisie), with "some sections turning left and joining the ranks of the revolution, and others turning right and joining the ranks of the counterrevolution." [18] But this formulation probably echoed Stalin's 1925 prediction of a split of the "national bourgeoisie . . . into a revolutionary and an antirevolutionary wing in backward countries." [19] Until 1928, therefore, Mao seems to have accepted the Comintern view that the KMT represented the national bourgeoisie. In late 1928, however, Mao insisted that the KMT represented only the comprador-bureaucratic bourgeoisie and not the national or middle bourgeoisie. He also maintained that in 1927 the KMT had betrayed not only the proletariat and the peasantry but the Chinese bourgeoisie as well. It remains unclear how Mao reconciled his 1926 and 1928 views, but, by distinguishing between the national bourgeoisie and the compradors and bureaucratic capitalists of the KMT,[20] he anticipated a theoretical justification for his 1940's coalition of four classes (the proletariat, the peasantry, and the national and petty bourgeoisie) against the comprador and bureaucratic-capitalist class led by the KMT.

Like Leninism, "Maoism" is not only a set of principles but also a strategy for seizing and holding power under any particular circumstances. Its development occurred only after Mao had established peasant-based soviets, first in the Chingkang Mountains in November, 1927, and after August, 1929, in neighboring Kiangsi Province. Throughout the early 1930's, before the Long March to northwest China in 1934, Mao, as head of the Kiangsi Soviet Region, fought off five campaigns by Chiang Kai-shek's forces. Although the failures of the Nanch'ang and Hunan uprisings and the Canton Commune in late 1927 belied Mao's initial optimism about the prospects for early success of an agrarian revolution, his experience with the Chingkang and Kiangsi soviets between 1928 and 1934 sharpened his sense of reality about the peasant problem.

During that period, as noted above, Mao's revolutionary practice was in opposition to the official Party line and probably left him little time for theoretical pronouncements. In what appears to be his most theoretical writing of this period, Mao emphasized the need to educate Party members and cadres in the Marxist method of political and class analysis, to base tactics upon actual investigation of social and economic questions, and to prevent idealism from contaminating the Party.[21] His interest in the organization and discipline of the Party—an approach that is more Leninist than Marxist—bespeaks his practical preoccupation. Not surprisingly, Mao evolved a strategy of gradual victory, a departure from his previous adventurist inclinations. His new gradualist approach was revealed in four writings: "Report of the Front Committee to the Hunan Provincial Committee" (dated October, 1928, and available in abridged form), "Report of the Front Committee to the Central Committee" (November 25, 1928), a letter written in April, 1929 (as quoted in the next chapter), and a letter to Lin Piao in January, 1930.

Mao's new strategy envisaged a protracted revolution that would pass through several stages and require many years to complete. It was based on his awareness of the unique collusion in China between the feudal warlord forces and the imperialist forces and on his realization that the CCP was not yet strong enough to seize regional power in the provinces as a first step toward national power. Mao's strategy was in conflict with the pre-1927 assumptions of Lenin and Stalin. Moreover, his policy of establishing soviets on a small scale and without further delay was in marked contrast to Comintern policy after August, 1927, which counseled lengthy preparation, and to Trotsky's position, which urged the immediate formation of soviets all over China.

There were also differences between Mao's strategy of gradual revolution and Trotsky's concept of permanent revolution. As Shanti Swarup has noted, Trotsky advocated the *continuous (qualitative) deepening* of the revolution, in a single linear process, from the bourgeois-democratic stage to the socialist stage, with proletarian leadership from beginning to end. On the other hand, as Swarup points out, Mao's strategy called for the *continuous (geographical) extension* of peasant-based soviet government from a small region to other parts of the country.[22]

Mao's relative caution was probably due to the general state of demoralization within the CCP membership after 1927. More than once, Mao had to try to instill confidence in his fellow Communists about the prospects for his peasant-based revolutionary strategy. In his draft resolution for the Second Party Conference of the Hunan-Kiangsi Border Area (October 5, 1928), Mao cited several factors to justify his strategy: (1) feuding among the warlords within the "white political power," with different factions at different times gaining the support of imperialist and/or comprador-gentry (KMT) forces; (2) the revolutionary experiences of 1926-27 in many rural and urban areas of Central and South China; (3) the persistence of revolutionary ferment in those areas; and (4) the presence of a strong Red Army and a well-organized Communist Party.[23] In his report of November 25, 1928, to the Central Committee, Mao added that the existence of a solid mass base, a sound Party, a Red Army of adequate strength, a terrain strategically favorable for military operations, and a self-sufficient economic base provided the necessary support for his armed insurrection program.[24]

In the letter of January 5, 1930, to Lin Piao, who was then in agreement with the urban-based CCP leadership, Mao argued that, "although the *revolutionary* forces of the Chinese revolution are weak, the *counterrevolutionary* forces are also weak; therefore the revolution in China will certainly approach a rising wave much faster than in Western Europe."[25] Although not quite consistent with Marxist theory, this dichotomy reveals Mao's concern for specific practice and his faith in the peasant revolution, despite the initial setbacks suffered by the Party.

Between 1920 and 1926, Mao was more attracted by the specific model of the Bolshevik Revolution than by the general appeal of Marxism and believed that the experience of the Russian Revolution was relevant for China. However, Mao's experience with the peasant-based soviet areas in China between 1928 and 1934 changed his perspective. He discarded his previous insistence on the identity between social classes and revolutionary conditions in China and those in Europe. Moreover, he became keenly aware of the revolutionary potential of the peasantry, the strategic importance of a highly disciplined Red Army, under the leadership of the Party, and the tactical advantages of the base areas to the survival and viability of the Chinese Communist movement. Mao's practical experience in the base areas enabled him to be more realistic about revolutionary strategy than either the official Comintern-CCP establishment or other private dissenters, such as Ch'en Tu-hsiu and P'eng Shu-chih. But Mao still lacked sophistication in Marxist theory, and the problem of reconciling Soviet theory with Chinese realities remained unsolved.

4

MAO'S EVOLUTION
AS A CHINESE MARXIST, 1935–49

Mao's Mature Period (1935–40)

THE MOST fruitful period of Mao Tse-tung's intellectual growth came between his ascent to effective CCP leadership at the Tsun-yi Conference in 1935 and the crystallization of his concept of the "new democracy" in early 1940. During that period, he was under greater pressure as a Marxist theoretician than before. The grim fact of having to start all over again at Yenan, the added burden of his new office,* and the Sino-Japanese War of 1935–45—all compelled him to approach the Communist revolution from much broader perspectives.

Underlying most of his writings of the period was a standing concern to unify theory and practice. For example, in December, 1936, in a discussion of the particularities of China's revolutionary war, Mao transcended the immediate issues, which would have preoccupied him in the preceding period. Instead, he differentiated in broad terms between the laws of revolutionary wars and those of wars in general, and between revolutionary wars and China's particular war. He sought to understand military principles, as well as those in other spheres, as the theoretical re-

---

* Although Mao was elected at Tsun-yi as the Chairman of the Politburo, he actually wielded more power than Chang Wen-t'ien, the new Secretary-General of the CCP. See Jerome Ch'en, *Mao and the Chinese Revolution* (Oxford University Press, 1967), p. 189.

flection of objective reality. In so doing, he became keenly aware of the need to resolve the contradiction between the subjective and the objective, the revolutionary and the counterrevolutionary. Applying this theoretical concern to the practical plane, Mao abandoned his previous belief that the Soviet model (both as revolutionary strategy and as a form of government) could be applied to China if properly harnessed to peasant discontent, and called for solutions based on China's peculiar experience. He said, for instance, that "there are a great number of conditions special to the Chinese revolution and the Chinese Red Army" not shared by the Soviet Union or any other country.[1] Thus, he prescribed, among other things, protracted war for China. His whole theory of protracted war attested to his consciousness of the unity of theory and practice. It is, not surprisingly, a product of the period. Of course, as suggested above, his initial understanding of the protracted nature of the Chinese revolution can be traced back to 1928, when he adopted a gradualist approach.

After the war broke out with Japan in 1937, Mao began to reclassify China in a unique status as "a large semicolonial country." It was different from both the industrial countries, e.g., Britain, the United States, France, Germany, Japan, and, by implication, the Soviet Union, on the one hand,[2] and small semi-colonial countries, such as Ethiopia and Morocco, on the other.[3] In neither of those two groups of countries, though for different reasons, was it possible to pursue a protracted peasant war that would first win the countryside and then, by encirclement, the cities. "But a large semicolonial country such as the China of today can prosecute this type of war." [4]

Regardless of the fruitless debate in the West as to whether Mao's "On Practice" and "On Contradiction" were actually written in the 1930's or were works of a later date that were attributed to the earlier period,[5] there were at least certain clues to the two topics in a few scattered essays that Mao indisputably did write in the 1930's. In his "Strategic Problems of China's Revolutionary War," he was alert to the contradiction between the revolutionary and counterrevolutionary forces, as noted above. His intense concern for practice and practice-oriented knowledge characterized most of his utterances during those years.

In his "On the New Stage," a report to the Central Committee of the CCP in October, 1938, Mao declared that "we must not study the *letter* of Marxism and Leninism, but the *viewpoint* and *methodology* of its creators, with which they observed and solved problems." The task of studying Marxism-Leninism was, among other things, "to understand *our historic inheritance* and to evaluate it critically by the use of the Marxist method," because "the history of our great people over several millennia exhibits *national peculiarities* and many precious qualities." [6] Mao added, "There is no such thing as abstract Marxism, but only concrete Marxism. What we call concrete Marxism is Marxism that has taken on a national form, that is, Marxism applied to the concrete struggle in the concrete conditions prevailing in China, and not Marxism abstractly used." After criticizing "talks of Marxism apart from Chinese peculiarities" as "an empty abstraction," Mao urged "the Sinification of Marxism—that is to say, making certain that in all of its manifestations it is imbued with Chinese peculiarities, using it according to these peculiarities." [7]

As Donald Lowe has noted, *On the New Stage* represented a turning point in Mao's thinking. Although Mao had become increasingly conscious, after 1937, of the contradictions between Marxist claims of universality and the special realities of China, this report constituted his first public statement that Marxism must be "Sinified." He meant that the *history* of the development of Communism in China must be the link between the abstractions of Marxist theory and the practice of the Chinese revolution. This formulation represented neither sound history nor good theory, but it was, nevertheless, a reconciliation of the conflicting demands of the two.[8]

In several other writings, Mao dealt with the relevance of Chinese history for the current revolution. He sought "to understand our historic inheritance and to evaluate it critically by the use of the Marxist method." In "The Chinese Revolution and the Chinese Communist Party" (December, 1939), Mao tried to periodize Chinese history within the framework of historical materialism by tracing its course from an "egalitarian, classless primitive Communist society" to a "slave society" and a "feudal society." Under the impact of Western capitalism, China's feudal stage assumed such semicolonial, semifeudal characteristics as: (1) the end of a naturally self-sufficient economy; (2) the joint exploitation of the people by landlords in the countryside and by compradors and usurer-capitalists in the cities; (3) the rule of warlords and bureaucrats in place of the monarch; (4) a weak national bourgeoisie with links to foreign capitalism and domestic feudal remnants; and (5) the impoverishment of the peasantry under feudal-imperialist oppression. The enemies of China's "new democratic" revolution were foreign imperialism and domestic feudal survivals in league with big landlords and the comprador-capitalists. The proletariat, according to Mao, would not be able to win the revolution by itself. It should make alliances with other classes with the following understanding: "The peasantry [mainly middle and poor peasants] is the firm ally of the working class; the urban petty bourgeoisie [the intelligentsia, the urban poor, the functionaries, the handicraftsmen, the professionals, and the small merchants] is a reliable ally; and the national bourgeoisie [the middle bourgeoisie, which has a 'dual character'] is an ally during certain periods and to a certain extent." [9]

The concept of the "new democratic" revolution in China was elucidated in Mao's "On New Democracy" in January, 1940. While Mao placed the Chinese revolution within the context of world revolution, he also argued that China's unique historical background made it a special case. Tracing the course of the bourgeois-democratic revolution in China since the Opium War of 1840, Mao claimed that, after World War I and the Bolshevik Revolution, it had ceased to be the "old" type of revolution, characteristic of the West, which had been led solely by the bourgeoisie.

Anti-imperialism had transformed it into a "new democratic" revolution whose purpose was "the setting up of a new democratic society, a new state of the joint dictatorship of *all revolutionary classes.*" (Italics added.)

The concept of joint dictatorship, which allows a supporting role for the bourgeoisie (both petty and national), also set China apart from the Soviet revolutionary model, in which the weak revolutionary character of the Russian bourgeoisie, due to the fact that Tsarist Russia was itself an imperialist power, disqualified that class from any leadership role in the bourgeois-democratic revolution.[10] In the same essay, Mao tried to conceal the importance of the CCP, although it was already an independent force with an army strong enough to contend with the KMT. Since the CCP had reached agreement in 1937 with the KMT government to form a united front against the Japanese invasion, Mao understandably sought to minimize any provocation of KMT resentment.

Mao's "new democracy" is not wholly new. For instance, his four-class alliance recalls the concept of a "united dictatorship of several classes," with which the Stalinist group had justified the CCP's entry into the Wuhan KMT government in 1927, an act opposed by Trotsky. Moreover, the resolutions of the Seventh Plenum of the ECCI in 1926 also noted the centrality of the peasant problem. The importance of Mao's "new democracy," however, lies not in its originality but in its definition of the role of the proletariat. Where the Kremlin had always insisted upon "proletarian hegemony" in the revolution, Mao quibbled. Not only is his statement in "On New Democracy" as vague as possible, it is also negatively phrased: "Without the workers, the Chinese revolution will not be able to succeed, for it is they who are the most revolutionary section of the people." [11]

Mao's sensitivity to the interaction between particular reality and general theory appeared again in his "Dialectical Materialism" of March, 1940.[12] Dividing all philosophy into the two schools of idealism and materialism, Mao portrayed the struggle between

the two "armies of philosophy" in terms of the place each ac-
corded to "reality" and general theory in the thinking process. He
attacked the idealists for relying solely on "the activity of consciousness" as the source of knowledge and for neglecting the
"materialist truth [that] consciousness is limited by matter."
Claiming that only dialectical materialism correctly "points out
that thought arises from social practice and at the same time
actively shapes practice," Mao proclaimed as invincible truth "the
unity of knowledge and action." Ironically, Mao's views on the
unity of knowledge and action are not very different from the
official ideology of the KMT, as laid down by its foremost
ideologue, Ch'en Li-fu, in a series of lectures under the title
Hsing te che-hsüeh (A *Philosophy of Action*) delivered at the
KMT's Central Political [cadres] Institute in 1933. In fact, in
1918 Sun Yat-sen was the first in the KMT to stress the supreme
importance of unifying knowledge and action. But, insofar as
Mao followed Marxist thinking on "the social origins of idealism
and materialism," he is more indebted to Marxism than to Chinese tradition. Mao explicitly acknowledged this Marxist debt:
"The distinguishing characteristic of Marxist philosophy—i.e., dialectical materalism—is its effort to explain clearly the class nature of all social consciousness (including philosophy). It publicly
declares a resolute struggle between its own *proletarian* nature
and the idealist philosophy of the *propertied* class." [13] However,
as Stuart Schram has remarked, the "pedestrian character" of this
and other explicitly theoretical writings of Mao is matched only
by the "vivacity of his exposition when he speaks of the link
between theory and action." [14] If Mao owes his epistemology
to Marx, his acute awareness of the interplay between reality and
theory recalls the traditional Chinese attitude toward the empirical
nature of true scientific propositions. [15]

Between 1935 and 1940, Mao realized that a new framework
was needed to incorporate both Chinese reality and Marxist theory. The strategic concerns involved in the defense of China
against the Japanese invasion and China's particular social structure

and internal situation led him to reject the Soviet model as automatically applicable in China and to adopt his "new democracy" formula. (Chang Kuo-t'ao had also opposed the adoption of the Soviet model first in 1932 and then at the Tsun-yi Conference of January, 1935; he had found it unsuited to contemporary China in that nationalization of land simply ran counter to the peasant hunger for land.[16])

Mao's "new democracy" envisaged a four-class coalition that would include the petty and national bourgeoisie. Under the old formula of the Kiangsi Soviet period, the alliance had been limited to workers, peasants, and soldiers. The broadening of the class coalition was in keeping with the wartime united front policy adopted at the Mao-erh-kai Conference on August 1, 1935. Since 1926–27, Mao had been claiming that his revolution was aimed at imperialism as well as the KMT. When the Japanese invasion in 1937 stirred powerful national emotions in China, Mao was able to support these claims by appealing for a four-class coalition against Japanese imperialism and for the subordination of particular class interests to the national cause. Although his "new democracy" formula marked a break with the past in that Mao abandoned the soviet form of government for Yenan, there was also strong continuity in the deepening current of nationalism in Mao's thought.

The Civil War Period (1940–49)

Civil war maneuvers by both parties began long before the end of the Sino-Japanese war was in sight. Although this was a critcal period for China, it was an intellectually barren one for Mao, preoccupied as he was with immediate issues. As his preface to "Village Investigation" (March 17, 1941) shows, he was no longer relating theory to practice but was overwhelmingly concerned with practice itself. He no longer stressed the study of Marxism but urged the investigation of real-life conditions of the various social classes.[17]

The practical need to avoid extremism led to his attack on three types of "subjectivism" * that were plaguing the Party: lack of interest in practical investigation; lack of interest in the study of history; and lack of interest in the practical application of Marxism-Leninism.[18] The attack on "subjectivism" was not a denial of Marxist theory—that would have resulted in "empiricism," or the excessive dependence upon experience to the exclusion of theory. Mao inveighed against both "empiricism" and "dogmatism," the latter being an excessive reliance upon abstract theory, but regarded dogmatism as the greater evil. Two other aspects of subjectivism—sectarianism and "eight-legged" formalism—were also criticized as showing an inadequate grasp of realities and priorities. The desire to rid the Party of the evils of "subjectivism" motivated the *cheng-feng* (Party reform) movement of 1942.[19] It is true that Mao's writings in the *cheng-feng* movement should be viewed against the background of the increasing shortage of ideologically trained cadres due to (1) wartime casualties; (2) the need for more personnel in the expanding guerrilla areas; and (3) a sudden influx of new Party members. But, more importantly, Mao was also responding to some of the more doctrinaire Party members (e.g., Wang Ming), who were increasingly disturbed by the shift from the previous Comintern policy and by the apparent discrepancies between Marxist texts and the actual practices of the CCP under Mao. The discrepancies were particularly striking in two areas: relations between the proletariat and the peasantry and the conflict between Communist theory and a growing Chinese nationalism fed by the Sino-Japanese war.

Concerned about doctrinaire tendencies within the Party and about the need for rectification, Mao reiterated the importance of the Sinification of Marxism in his important lecture, "Correcting Unorthodox Tendencies in Learning, the Party, and Literature and Art," delivered at the opening day ceremonies of the Party

---

* "Subjectivism" (*chu-kuan chu-yi*) here refers to thoughts and ideas that are detached from reality. See also note 25, Chapter 3.

Academy on February 1, 1942.[20] The role of Mao's thought in the Party's decision to launch the rectification movement is suggested by the title of a document adopted by the Propaganda Bureau of the Central Committee (CC) of the CCP on April 3, 1942, "The Decision of the CC's Resolutions and Comrade Mao Tse-tung's Report Concerning the Correction of Three Unorthodox Tendencies." [21]

Practical experience in conducting the 1942 *cheng-feng* (rectification) movement strengthened the CCP's conviction that a "leading core"—an elite, which "must maintain a close relationship with the masses who participate in the learning process"—was indispensable if the goals of the movement were to be fulfilled.[22] The criteria for members of this "leading core," as specified by the CC in June, 1943, were close relationship with the masses, ability for independent work, unlimited devotion, and observation of discipline.[23] By insisting on the submission of the individual to the Party, the CC reasserted the primacy of the Party. All four criteria, however, reflected the Leninist stress on the elite character of the Party membership and on Party organization itself. To the extent that the CCP official documents reflected Mao's thinking, it appears that, although Mao diverged from Marxist texts in some areas, he did not seem to differ with Leninist dictates concerning Party organization. Nevertheless, with due deference to theory, practice was fundamental for Mao, and theory must be linked to practice. In the same spirit, he condemned "art for art's sake" and called upon artists and writers to "whole-heartedly go among the masses of workers, peasants and soldiers . . . [and] go into fiery struggles." [24]

In evaluating the political forces at work in China, Mao saw the revolution as a competition between two minority groups, the urban and rural proletariat, represented by the CCP, and the landlord-capitalist class, represented by the KMT, with both groups vying for the support of the broadest group of intermediate classes. Without openly violating the spirit of the wartime "united front" with the KMT, Mao equivocated on the issue of the directorate of the revolution: "We should also cooperate with those elements within the landlord and capitalist classes who are still resisting the Japanese, but we must not forget that they oppose a *broadly based democracy* for the Chinese people." [25] The CCP, Mao claimed in April, 1945, represented "not only the proletariat . . . but also simultaneously the broadest peasantry, petty bourgeoisie, intellectuals and other democratic elements. . . . Any government which excludes the Communist Party can accomplish no good—this is the fundamental charateristic of a China entering the new democratic stage of history." [26]

Here one sees a shrewd maneuver by Mao to exert pressure for a coalition government on the KMT by portraying the CCP as having a broad class base. But some years later, when his position was much more secure, Mao argued that a coalition government must exclude the KMT (and the big bourgeoisie it represented) because only the CCP, which represented several classes, could be identified with "broadly based democracy." Still later, though, all passages claiming that the CCP represented various classes were deleted from the 1951 edition of Mao's *Selected Works*.

Other remarks were subject to the same kind of later revision. In "On Coalition," a report to the CCP Seventh National Congress in April, 1945, Mao challenged the Chinese people to choose between "a dictatorial fascist rule" under the KMT and "a state of the *united front of democratic alliance* based on the overwhelming majority of the people." [27] But in the 1951 edition of Mao's *Selected Works*, "under the leadership of the working class" was inserted after "people," lending a more orthodox cast to Mao's program.[28]

There are two likely explanations for such ideological addenda and corrigenda: First, in actual practice, Mao may have been carried away by his enthusiasm, leaving many non-Marxist or pseudo-Marxist loopholes to be patched up in later, more sober years; second, Mao *purposely* deviated from the Marxist-Leninist ideology during a time when the CCP rather desperately needed all possible support in its deepening struggle with the KMT for national leadership. While the latter hypothesis sounds more likely, one hesitates to reject altogether the possibility that Mao may really have believed many of the quaint things he said during that period. In either case, Mao was not unwilling to deviate from orthodox Marxism when the situation seemed to call for it.

As World War II drew to a close, all the issues that had divided the KMT and CCP since the 1920's finally culminated in civil war. There were sharp differences between the two camps. The political style of the KMT top leadership was moderate and conservative in character; its political power was based on the support of a military elite and the armed forces they controlled; the appeal of its ideology, from 1928 on, was its combination of traditionalist nationalism with a revival of the Confucian ethics of Tseng Kuo-fan.[29] Mao's Communist movement, with its mass base and peasant Red Army, claimed to offer a weary population a new ideology for a new era and hope for reconstructing war-devastated China. The victory of the CCP in 1949, if less unexpected than the Bolshevik victory in 1917, gave substance to the claim that Mao had creatively applied Marxism-Leninism in the Chinese context.

The civil war period saw the recurrence of Mao's "new democracy" concept. It was his belief that this new formulation—a reaction to the conflicting demands of theory and practice in the pre-1949 period—would justify and guide revolutionary action in the years ahead.

As we have seen, Mao's thought evolved from stage to stage in response to past mistakes and new demands of changing times. However, Mao was also capable of using ideology for manipulative purposes. Between 1937 and 1945, Mao sought to use Chinese anti-imperialist sentiments in two ways: first, to stir up Chinese nationalism for the struggle with Japan; and second, to weaken popular support for the KMT by charging that the KMT was linked to feudalism and imperialism. Mao's technique was to

arouse Chinese hostility toward an external force, then to direct
the hostility against his domestic rivals by charging them with
collusion with China's external enemies. In 1946, when the war
with Japan ended, Mao strove to maintain a high pitch of emo-
tion throughout the nation against "American imperialism" and
for the "socialist democratic bloc" and postulated that the two
were locked in an open international struggle.[30]

In the next year Mao sought, by describing the KMT government as a "stooge" of "U.S. imperialism" and the U.S.-KMT
alliance as the successor to "Japanese imperialism and its running
dog, Wang Ching-wei," to convince the masses that the civil
war was not merely a CCP attempt to seize power but a just war
to defend the Chinese nation against a foreign-supported "fascist
dictatorship."[31]

Once the Communists had emerged victorious in the civil
war, Mao exuded a hearty optimism in regard to the future. In
September, 1949, on the eve of the proclamation of the People's
Republic, he pronounced "the bankruptcy of the idealist conception of history." Why had the Chinese Communist movement
achieved victory? He gave three important reasons: Marxism-
Leninism answered a crushing need in China's social setting;
theory had been united with revolutionary practice; and the
Chinese people had "grasped" Marxism-Leninism. Had it not
been for those factors, even Marxism-Leninism, that "most precious thing," would have had no effect in China. "We believe,"
he said, looking ahead, "that revolution can change everything
and that before long there will arise a new China with a big
population and a great wealth of products, where life will be
abundant and culture flourish. All pessimistic views are utterly
groundless." [32]

Summing Up

The traditionalists of the nineteenth century, who remained
loyal to the Confucian universalist framework of *t'ien-hsia*, were

ill equipped to solve China's modernization problems. The "self-strengtheners" were realistic about the need to face the problem of modernization, but they insisted that China was unique and continued to resist the new world system of nation-states. For their part, the Westernizing radicals adopted a psychologically untenable position by rejecting much of their Chinese heritage. Evolutionary nationalism did offer a long-term solution for China's problems, but China's needs were too urgent. Both revolutionary nationalists and Communists wrestled with the problem of rapidly modernizing China while maintaining an equivalence with the West. Although the KMT's revolutionary nationalism after 1928 gradually refined a traditionalistic Confucian ideology allegedly based on the Tseng Kuo-fan model, the Communists used Marxism-Leninism both as an ideological weapon against the capitalist West and as the replacement for a discredited Chinese tradition. For its adherents, Communism not only prescribed solutions for China's internal needs, it also seemed to solve the problem of equivalence by offering a methodological tool for the critique of the West and by promising that socialism would permit backward China to overtake the capitalist West.

Although Marxist-Leninist doctrine prescribed a revolution by the proletariat, China's industrial proletariat, during the interwar period, was infinitesimal. Whereas Marxist-Leninist doctrine conceived of revolution primarily in social terms, China was dominated by foreign powers and needed both a national and a social revolution. The Comintern line advocated a two-stage revolution, its first stage led by the bourgeoisie, and therefore enjoined a policy of coalition with the KMT upon CCP leaders from Ch'en Tu-hsiu to Li Li-san. But this policy blocked the social revolution. There were some CCP leaders whose landlord background resembled that of most KMT leaders, but men like Mao, Chu Teh, and others were willing to renounce their own class background and to exploit the discontent of the peasant masses. So long as the Comintern's coalition policy remained in effect, however, their hands were tied, for a peasant revolution against the landlords would have alienated landowning KMT leaders and probably ended the alliance.

Eventually, the line Mao had developed during his period in "opposition" turned out to be more in accord with Chinese realities. Although he adopted the two-stage revolution formula, he insisted that it must be led, from the first stage on, by the CCP with its peasant base, with only a supporting role for the bourgeoisie. At the same time, Mao undertook to build a peasant Red Army, despite the initial objection of the Central Committee leadership.

Mao's revolutionary strategy also differed from Lenin's in several ways. In Lenin's formulation, the proletariat had primacy and the peasantry played a supporting role; Mao, on the other hand, assigned equal importance to both in theory, but in actual practice the huge size of the Chinese peasantry made its role crucial. Again, Mao did not accept Lenin's belief that the bourgeoisie could play a leadership role in the "backward" countries that it could not play in Russia. Moreover, in an effort to increase the national appeal of the CCP, Mao redefined the bourgeoisie in quite unorthodox terms. He divided it into two groups, a small coterie of big bourgeoisie or comprador-gentry, allegedly represented by the KMT, which would need to be overthrown, and a much larger group of national and petty bourgeoisie, which Mao absorbed into his four-class coalition. Chinese Communist participation in the Sino-Japanese war of 1937–45, as well as the CCP's earlier opposition to Japan's incursions on Chinese territory prior to 1937, further strengthened Mao's claim that his revolution was both national (anti-imperialist) and social.

Although Mao's practical modification or Sinification of Marxist-Leninist doctrine eventually prevailed, his thought evolved slowly through a long process of trial and error. Between 1920 and 1926, like other CCP leaders, Mao followed the Comintern line, which applied Moscow's policies without due regard for Chinese conditions. From 1927 to 1935, Mao still sought somehow to equate the Chinese agrarian revolution with the Soviet model of revolution—an attempt that he only gradually abandoned. Mao's prescriptions for China were finally adopted by the Party in 1935, upon his formal election to leadership. The launching of the 1942 rectification campaign against subjectivism within the CCP—the preoccupation with dogma as opposed to reality—signified the triumph of Mao's thought as the "unity of theory and practice."

In the post-1949 period, Mao tended to apply guerrilla strategies that had worked in the Yenan period to the resolution of the nation's social and economic problems. Mao has a tendency to be more Marxist in thinking about China's historical past than in dealing with its present and future economic and political problems. His revolutionary realism prior to 1949 gradually gave way to doctrinaire impulses of an idealist sort as his Communist regime sought to govern and modernize China. Troubles seemed to multiply as bold practice overcame prudent thought. Nor has the equivalence problem yet been fully solved. Is there, perhaps, in China's competition with the Soviet Union for the ultimate ideological leadership of the world Communist movement a recurrent sense of inferiority and a need to compensate for China's earlier debt to Marxism-Leninism and Soviet experience? It may be that the Cultural Revolution is an aging Mao's last campaign to Sinify Communist ideology and to create, through a long-range process of re-education, a new proletarian culture, one that the Maoist-Chinese could accept as their own and regard as superior to Soviet "revisionism."

PART TWO

The Ideological
Perspective

5

THE GOALS OF MAO'S REVOLUTION

DESPITE THE frequency of revolutions in human history, students of politics have yet to agree on a definition of the phenomenon, which involves the shift of power from one locus of authority to another within a political system and accompanying changes of various sorts. Each revolution must be understood within its own social context and in the light of the changes it seeks to bring about.

The present chapter is concerned with a number of questions: (1) What is the nature of revolution? To what extent does the Chinese Communist revolution resemble other revolutions and to what extent is the Chinese experience unique? (2) How relevant is Marxism-Leninism to the Chinese Communist revolution? Is it a means or an end? (3) What is the basis for the Chinese Communist Party's claim to legitimacy? (4) What are the objectives or goals of the Chinese Communist Party's leadership under Mao? (5) What ideological problems do these goals entail for Mao's revolution, as he emphasizes revolutionary commitment over material incentives?

The Nature of Revolution

In a study of the sociology of revolution, Chalmers Johnson defines revolution as a continuation of politics at the level of violent physical struggle. Three conditions form the syndrome of

85

a revolution. First, the society's own mechanisms for social change break down or fail to respond properly to the pressures to alleviate social problems (dysfunction). Second, when social problems cease to be isolated in particular areas but spread like cancer throughout the whole system, the chances of nonviolent change greatly decline. The resultant metastasis (multiple dysfunction) can be fatal to the entire system. Third, expanding pressures for change may not automatically produce revolutions; instead, change may very gradually permeate the society. But the presence of "accelerators of dysfunction"—occurrences that accentuate or catalyze the already revolutionary level of dysfunctions—may trigger the explosion.[1]

The historical background of the Chinese Communist revolution reveals several of these conditions. There was "multiple dysfunction" in Chinese society during the half-century that followed the T'aip'ing Rebellion; there were also "accelerators of dysfunction," e.g., the impact of the West, internecine fighting among the warlords, and, most important, the Sino-Japanese war. But where Johnson's formula stresses the sociopolitical aspects of pressures for change, the Chinese revolution had an additional dimension: the breakdown of Confucian culture under the new challenges of the nineteenth and twentieth centuries. Before a new society and nation could emerge, a new ethos would have to be forged.

After its establishment as the state cult in 136 B.C., Confucian morality became not merely the superstructure of the old society but its very foundation. It represented for Chinese society what the combination of constitutional law, Judeo-Christian values and ethics, and social conscience is for Western society. The collapse of the Confucian *li* was a most crippling phenomenon, accompanied as it was by sociopolitical disintegration. At the same time, the appeal of Marxism-Leninism and the Bolshevik revolutionary model may have served as an "accelerator" of China's cultural-ideological dysfunction, deepening a cultural revolution that was already under way and has yet to subside.

If so, what Johnson's sociology of revolution has only touched upon in passing—the cultural-ideological aspect—must be doubly stressed in China's case. Communist China's thought reform programs, indoctrination efforts, and socialist education campaigns constitute a cultural-ideological revolution aimed at creating a new "socialist man" and a new system of thought and culture. That cultural-ideological revolution, however, is also an integral part of the "permanent revolution" Mao has sought to bring about in China.

In a definition given in 1927, Mao said that "revolution is not a dinner party . . . [but] an *insurrection*, an act of violence by which one class overthrows another." [2] If revolution is no more than that, then the Chinese revolution should have ended with the Communist victory in 1949. However, the Maoist call from 1958 on for "permanent revolution" shows that revolution has taken on a new meaning. "China," Mao wrote in 1958, "is forging ahead in her socialist *economic* revolution . . . as well as in her *political, ideological, technical* and *cultural* revolution." [3] Thus, not only is Mao's revolution "not a dinner party," but it is even more than "an act of violence."

REVOLUTIONS: A COMPARATIVE APPROACH

Crane Brinton, in a stimulating study of the English, American, French, and Russian revolutions, identifies certain common characteristics in their development. They progress, for example, through several stages—"predrome," "fever," and "crisis" (often accompanied by a "delirium")—before reaching "convalescence." [4] Similar stages can be identified in the series of revolutions that China has undergone in the last century or so. But the Chinese revolutionary experience also included some unique factors such as foreign "imperialist" exploitation,[5] which had no counterpart in the four revolutions Brinton studied. In China, the collapse of the Hundred Days' Reforms in 1898 highlighted a predrome that had been under way since the 1830's. The period was characterized by Brinton's "very bitter class antagonisms," "transfer of allegiance of the intellectuals," and the clear inefficiency of the *ancien régime*. As conditions deteriorated between 1898 and 1908 with the intervention of the arch-conservative Empress Dowager, China experienced the first of many fevers. The overthrow of the Manchu rule in 1911 marked the first crisis stage, which was characterized by the "emergency centralization of power" in the hands of President Yüan Shih-k'ai (1912–16). Convalescence ensued, however, during the anarchic warlord period (1916–27) following Yüan's death, but this period can also be viewed as a new fever leading to another crisis stage, which culminated in Chiang Kai-shek's successful campaign of national unification and his establishment of the Nanking government in 1928.

The centralization of power in the Nationalist government was both encouraged and endangered by Japanese expansionist thrusts and the outbreak of war in 1937. But, to the extent that increasing bureaucratization nibbled away at the earlier revolutionary élan of the Nationalist Government, a new convalescence crept in. The rapid disintegration of the Civil War period, a new fever, led to a new crisis period in 1949. Since then, the Communist leaders have carried centralization of governmental power to unprecedented heights. If "delirium" can describe the Communist rule, particularly during the Cultural Revolution of 1966–68, this stage has lasted far longer in China than in any of the countries Brinton studied. In fact, the Maoists have been trying hard to forestall a convalescence period. This is probably the most singular aspect of the Chinese experience.

In Brinton's scheme, convalescence is a natural stage following a crisis and is marked by the relatively rapid return to most of the simpler and more fundamental courses of life obtaining under the old regime. He described the fall of Robespierre as the beginning of the convalescence period of the French Revolution. Although he does not cite one dramatic event as the advent of convalescence in Russia, Brinton does place that onset within Lenin's own lifetime. He compares the new class of entrepreneurs who emerged in the Soviet Union after the launching of the New Economic Policy (NEP) in 1921 with a similar class of French profiteers who came to the fore after the fall of Robespierre and the abandonment of price-fixing. The rejection of the NEP and Stalin's emphasis on central planning and collectivization after 1928 were held to be "no more significant than Napoleon's apparent repudiation of the corruptness and moral looseness of the Directory once he had achieved secure power by the coup d'état of the 18th Brumaire." The reappearance of the necktie at a national youth congress, a fashion show in Moscow, lipsticks and other cosmetics in shops patronized by working girls, crime and human-interest stories in newspapers, movies portraying human beings rather than abstractions of Socialist Man —all these led Brinton to conclude that the dictatorship of the proletariat in interwar Russia "was by no means the dictatorship of virtue we have seen prevailing in the crisis periods of our revolutions." [6]

SPECIAL CHARACTERISTICS OF THE CHINESE REVOLUTION

Mao distinguished the Chinese revolution from other revolutions on the basis of two criteria: class leadership and the presence or absence of imperialist oppression. In the West, the bourgeois-democratic revolutions were led by the bourgeoisie; the Chinese revolution was led by an alliance of the proletariat and the peasantry under the guidance of the CCP. In the case of the Bolshevik Revolution, Tsarist Russia, unlike China, had never been a victim of imperialism but was itself an imperialist power.

The collapse of the Chinese empire in 1911, after decades of Western inroads on Chinese soil, was accompanied by a deepening crisis of national survival. None of the four revolutions Brinton studied had been subject to such outside pressures. Instead, the dissolution of the Chinese imperial system, like that of the Holy Roman, Ottoman, and British empires, posed a problem of nation-building or rebuilding. By definition, nation-building entails the establishment or re-establishment of national autonomy, and it finds its ideological manifestation in nationalism. Although the transition from empire to nation in China entailed less territorial fragmentation than was the case for the other empires, China passed through a similar process in which a new nation-state, the *kuo-chia*, emerged from China's former imperial shell, the *t'ien-hsia*.

The intense desire for national autonomy in twentieth-century China explains the anti-imperialist tenor of China's revolutionary movements as well as their fierce opposition to the old order. Revolutionary leaders such as Sun Yat-sen, Chiang Kai-shek, and Mao Tse-tung had one thing in common: anti-imperialism. The fact that three men with quite different views on China's future shared this feeling is an indication of the widespread and profound popular resentment of "imperialist" domination. Anti-imperialism was thus a widespread phenomenon in China before the arrival of Communism; it could also be effectively used to enlist the masses in the process of nation-building—an essential task in a country that had been dominated for centuries by the belief that civil responsibility was the exclusive domain of the elite.

Adam Ulam has argued that Lenin's primary interest was not in directing a Marxist revolutionary movement against the evils of capitalism but in adapting Marxism to serve as the ideological basis for intensive, militant efforts to industrialize and modernize Russian society.[7] Can the same be said of the Maoist revolution?

The task of mobilizing the masses for meaningful participation must begin with the correction of social and economic inequities and the destruction of sociopolitical barriers between the elite and the masses. The economic and social pillars of the old elitist structure (sizable land ownership and a bureaucratic career) must be leveled, and the value of manual labor must be extolled to release the energies of the masses and to persuade the old elite to step down, psychologically speaking, from its traditional exalted status and join hands with the masses. In the final analysis, the Chinese Communist leaders envisaged their task as the sweeping destruction of much of the *ancien régime* and the reconstruction of a very different new order. Mao put it brutally in "On New Democracy" in 1940: "Without destruction there is no construction, without damming no flowing, and without disruption no motion . . ."

The destruction lies first in removing the many barriers separating the elite-dominated "state" and the mass-based "society," though the lines of division were fuzzier and more complicated than the Marxist scheme of class struggle would have us believe. As in many other transitional societies in Asia, these barriers caused various forms of "immobility," such as economic immobility (peasant impoverishment and landlord affluence), civil immobility (lack of mass participation), status immobility (due to an orientation toward ascription rather than achievement), and psychic immobility (due to superstition and tradition-bound inertia).[8]

The constructive part of the Communist program lies in measures to achieve national reintegration and to build a new ethos, a new value system, new patterns of social organization and human relationships, a new sense of identity, and new skills commensurate with the tasks of modernization.[9]

In Communist jargon, the domestic task was called the "struggle against feudalism" and the international task was equated with "anti-imperialism." Thus, in "The Foolish Old Man Removed the Mountains" (1945), Mao Tse-tung called "feudalism" and "imperialism" the two arch-enemies of the Chinese Communist revolution.

Historians are generally agreed that China did not have a "feudal" society, as defined in the Marxist scheme of historical development. Although this is very true, the term used for "feudalism" in Chinese, *feng-chien*, can also mean old-fashioned, if not reactionary. For example, after the Western concept of the love-marriage had penetrated China, parents who still believed in the old practice of arranged marriages would invariably be called *feng-chien* (feudal) parents. The term "feudal" in Chinese is also a convenient label that iconoclasts apply to anything that they consider reactionary. For example, the 1950 Marriage Law stipulates that the pre-existing "feudal marriage system" must be abolished. According to Article 1 of that law, a "feudal" marriage is one that is "compulsory," that is "based on the superiority of man over woman," and that "ignores the children's interests."

The struggle against "imperialism" and "feudalism," and later "bureaucratism," characterized the Chinese Communist revolution and helped make Marxist-Leninist ideology relevant to the CCP leaders. Mao has made it clear that China's urgent need to fight these chronic ills led to the discovery of Marxism-Leninism through the Bolshevik Revolution, rather than the reverse.

Marxism-Leninism in China's Revolution: Means and Ends

The place of Marxism in the Chinese Communist goal structure was succinctly stated in Mao's "Reform Our Study," which was first delivered as a lecture before a cadres meeting in May, 1941. Addressing himself to the correlation between Marxism and the Chinese revolution, Mao used a metaphor: "The 'target,' " he said, "is the Chinese revolution; the 'arrow' is Marxism-Leninism. We Chinese Communists look to this 'arrow' for no other reason than to shoot the 'target' of the Chinese revolution and the Eastern revolutions. *If not for this 'target,' the 'arrow' itself would be no better than a plaything, without the slightest usefulness."* [10]

For Mao, Marxism was thus a means to an end, and he implied that the target, the Chinese revolution, existed quite independently of Marxism. The italicized statement above was subsequently deleted from the official *Selected Works* (1951). Although the deletion may represent an attempt to modify the impact of his rather pseudo-Marxist argument, the remaining sentences still suggest the need for a re-evaluation of the place of Marxism within the goal structure of Mao's revolution.

Chalmers Johnson's study of the peasant nationalism that the CCP was able to arouse behind enemy lines during the Sino-Japanese war supports the view that the Chinese Communists saw Marxism as a theoretical tool to achieve Chinese revolutionary goals rather than as an end in itself. "In essence," Johnson concluded, "the Party is . . . the leader of a war-energized, radical nationalist movement; while the Chinese Communist version of Marxist-Leninist ideology is . . . an *adjunct* to Chinese nationalism." [11]

However, what Johnson observed and Mao's statement above represent a wartime mentality at a critical stage (1940–45), when the immediate task was to rally maximum domestic support to save China from Japanese conquest and when the victory of the Communist revolution seemed very remote. In view of what Mao has been trying to accomplish since 1949, and especially since 1958, it would be difficult to maintain that Communism was only a means and not an end in itself. In his "On New Democracy," Mao quotes from Marx to stress the interaction between theory and practice. The same interaction between means and ends also seems to apply to Mao's revolution. During the insurrectional stage, Marxism served as the means to bring about the Chinese revolution, but the overthrow of the previous sociopolitical power structure was expected to lead to the establishment of Communist values, organizations, and programs. Thus, the distinction between means and end is blurred at best; each reinforces the other.

The Problem of Revolutionary Legitimacy

If, as Mao suggested in 1941, Marxism-Leninism is a means to an end, what then is the source of the Party's legitimacy as leader of the revolution? The CCP makes two claims: First, it is the vanguard of the proletariat and thereby expresses the revolutionary interests of the class that best expresses the collective interests of society as a whole; second, it can overthrow the nation's class enemies. As Mao declared in 1940:

> It is quite evident that whoever in China can lead the people to overthrow imperialism and feudal influence will win the people's confidence, because the mortal enemies of the people are imperialism and the feudal forces, especially imperialism. Today, *whoever can lead* the people to drive out . . . imperialism and bring about a democratic government *will be the savior of the people*. . . . Therefore, under all circumstances, the proletariat, the peasantry, the intelligentsia, and other sections of the petty bourgeoisie in China are the basic forces determining her fate.[12]

In 1949, Mao argued that the bourgeoisie cannot lead the Chinese revolution, because that class cannot "lead any genuine revolution to victory" in the imperialist era; moreover, "the Chinese national bourgeoisie had led the revolution many times and each time had failed." Instead, "the people's democratic dictatorship needs the leadership of the working class, because the working class is the most far-sighted, just, and unselfish and is imbued with thorough revolutionary commitment." [13]

In the classic Marxist view (*Theses on Feuerbach*), the legitimacy of the "dictatorship of the proletariat" rests on the assumption that the complete dehumanization of the worker makes the working class the most acutely conscious of its mission in historical redemption. Mao's theory, in contrast, implies that the Party's claim to legitimacy is based on its service to the working class and its commitment to the latter's "liberation." Undoubtedly, this theory echoes Lenin's elitism, as enunciated in *What Is To Be Done?* But Mao has insisted that the Party must do more than arouse the consciousness of the masses; it must be more than a vanguard and a leader; it must learn from the masses and join with the masses in seeking to achieve revolutionary goals. If it fails to do all this, as the Maoists alleged in 1966–68, the Party's "handful of power-holders" must be forced to abdicate (see Part III of this book).

Since the legitimacy of the Party, in Mao's view, is largely based on its "altruistic" service to the proletariat and to the revolution, and since both short- and long-term goals are involved, there can be no let-up of effort. The Party's interests, according to this doctrine, are identical with those of the masses, and a Communist's responsibility to the Party and his responsibility to the masses are said to be indistinguishable.[14]

As James Townsend has observed, the CCP maintains that collective interests have primacy over and above those of any class, including the proletariat. During the Yenan period, the Party claimed legitimacy for its leadership on the basis of the organizational help it could offer to the masses in resisting the Japanese invader. Since then, the CCP has similarly asserted that the dictatorship of the proletariat aims at goals of such importance to the people as a whole that they eclipse all other political interests. The basic objective of the attainment of socialism is not cast in the nature of any class interest but is projected as the highest national interest, much as resistance to the Japanese invasion was during the war.[15]

Although Maoists once again regarded the interests of the proletariat (in fact, the peasantry and the workers) as supreme in 1966–68, during the Cultural Revolution, Townsend's observation still seems valid. The renewed focus on the "proletariat" was, as we shall see later, meant to correct what Maoists contended was favoritism toward an emergent privileged class (e.g., cadres, professionals, and intellectuals) on the part of Liu Shao-ch'i's administration. Nevertheless, the principle that collective interests take precedence over those of individuals or particular classes was maintained.

Unquestionably, overemphasis on collective interests often results in encroachment on private interests. The disregard for private interests in a socialist state, even in time of peace, is often more extensive than in a democracy under wartime emergency conditions. But one must not overlook major differences between China's situation and that faced by many Western democracies. As a backward country struggling to develop rapidly, China must deal with the conflict between macro-development and micro-development. Mao's solution, however objectionable to us, is to sacrifice individual personal rewards (micro-development) for the time being, in the belief that this will ensure a more rapid march to modernity (macro-development).

The clash between collective and individual interests is not new in human history. Hannah Arendt has tried to find an explanation for the atrocities committed during the French Revolution in the name of the Republic of Virtue. She postulates a conflict between solidarity and pity. While the latter contains compassion for individuals, the former is a commitment to a collective being, which blurs the image of any single individual. A revolutionary movement propelled by solidarity, although devoted to the collective good, may show no pity toward the plight of the individual.

> For solidarity, because it partakes of reason, and hence of generality, is able to comprehend a *multitude* conceptually, not only the multitude of a class or a nation or a people, but eventually all mankind. But this solidarity, though it may be aroused by suffering, is not guided by it, and it comprehends the strong and the rich no less than the weak and the poor; compared with the sentiment of pity, it may appear cold and abstract, for it remains committed to "idea"—to greatness, or honor, or dignity—rather than to any "love" of men.[16]

However, can Mao's advocacy of the supremacy of the poor and the lower-middle peasants and his praise of personal sacrifice as the key to the attainment of the collective good be equated with Robespierre's glorification of the poor and praise of suffering as the spring of virtue? It is true that both men found a justification for revolutionary action and that neither seems solely motivated by the lust for power. Robespierre's empathy was, according to Arendt, "sentimental in the strictest sense of the word." Mao's conception of China's revolutionary goals and how to achieve them through the mobilization of the masses, however, seems to impart more rationality than sentimentality.

There is always a larger purpose in rallying the masses. Lu Ting-yi, a former CCP propaganda chief, asked, "What do we unite [the masses] for?" And he replied: "To build a new, socialist China and combat our enemies both at home and abroad." [17] Ironically, because the Party claims to serve the larger interests of the Chinese nation, it sees little, if any, difference between its interests and those of the nation as a whole.

The Goals of Mao's Revolution

In his report to the Seventh Party Congress in April, 1945, Mao outlined his conception of China's future as "an independent, free, democratic [min-chu], unified, prosperous and strong [fu-ch'iang] new nation." [18] This concept of a "new China" was repeated in two editorials written for the New China News Agency, dated July 12 and 19, 1945. As Stuart Schram correctly points out, the term fu-ch'iang is an ancient concept: "to enrich the country and make it strong militarily" (fu-kuo ch'iang-ping). [19] However, the word min-chu (literally, people being the master) should be translated as "oriented toward the people," rather than "democratic."

Mao further defined the goals of his revolution in a report to the Second Plenum of the Seventh Central Committee on March 5, 1949. He called for the construction of "a great socialist state" by transforming China "steadily from an agricultural to an industrial state." [20] In "On People's Democratic Dictatorship" (June, 1949), Mao laid down the immediate tasks ahead: (1) the strengthening of the "people's state apparatus"; (2) the elimination of the landlord class and the bureaucrat-bourgeoisie"; (3) the remolding of the national bourgeoisie; (4) the education of the peasantry; (5) the construction of a "new democratic" society "under the leadership of the working class and the Communist

Party" to prepare for the ultimate socialist and Communist society; and (6) the socialization of agriculture and industry to advance the economy to the industrial stage.[21]

In 1949, Mao was not examining the effect that changes in the social structure would have upon the course of his revolution once socialism had been established. But after 1956, Mao differed with Soviet and Chinese "revisionists" in his insistence that ideological purification must be continued after the achievement of socialism. His underlying assumption that a socialist structure does not of itself guarantee the complete shedding of "bourgeois ideology" will be discussed in other contexts. The point here is that Mao did not believe that the construction of socialism was the only goal of the Chinese revolution, nor did he believe that that revolution ended with the establishment of a socialist society.

As Benjamin Schwartz has suggested, the will to exert "totalitarian" control of political power is rather an inadequate explanation of the Party's goals. He sees, instead, a convergence of Mao's revolution with China's historical process of modernization and nation-building.[22] "One might say," Schwartz writes, "that for the whole course of human history power has always been 'function' . . . If the Chinese Communist Party is conceived of as the sole effective instrument for achieving a certain vision of the good society or for making China a great world power or for consummating the process of modernization, then the general goals and power considerations may actually reinforce and enhance each other." [23]

Since both ideology and political power have a functional significance, as means more than ends (or as well as ends), it remains now to summarize the main goals of Mao's revolution, in the light of what the regime has sought to accomplish since 1949:

1. the restructuring of Chinese society to create a new system of authority, new institutions, new roles, and a new hierarchy of relationships most conducive to social-political reintegration as conceived by the CCP leaders;

2. the reorientation of social values and patterns of behavior through a ceaseless process of indoctrination, re-education, and acculturation, to create a Marxist ethos;

3. social mobilization, accompanied by a new working consensus, to bring "state" and "society" into a new polity, the "people's democratic dictatorship";

4. transfer of loyalty and associational sentiments from the traditional primary groups (essentially family-oriented solidarity units) to the nation-state, the Party, and new work-relationship groups;

5. the formation of a new identity, both national and personal, forged in the "proletarian" spirit;

6. the improvement of skills through selective adoption of traditional and modern methods;

7. the socialization of the economy to spur rapid development by collective means;

8. the building of a powerful modern nation free of real or imagined foreign domination or intimidation.[24]

In sum, CCP leaders do not seem to have embraced Communism purely for its own sake, nor are they motivated by the lust for power pure and simple. It appears then that Mao's revolution and the nation-building drive of modern China converge. The general goals of modernization have been absorbed in the Marxist revolution—the agency by which, CCP leaders believe, these goals can be attained. Adam Ulam's point about the Leninist revolution (see above) seems likewise applicable to Mao's revolution: Marxism provides the ideological basis for intensive and militant industrialization and modernization.

Chinese and Soviet Ideology in Practice

The Chinese Communists and the Soviet Communists have both used revolutionary goals for manipulative purposes. To induce self-sacrifice, both Parties define their goals in an open-ended continuum, ranging from short-run to long-run and low-priority to high-priority objectives. Both maintain stress at points along the continuum so that continued sacrifice can be induced by persuasion or, if necessary, by coercion. The degree of stress, however, must not be so overwhelming that the masses become apathetic or antagonistic to the pressures exerted by the regime. At the same time, the goals must be both specific enough to be readily recognized by the masses and ambiguous enough for the leaders to make whatever shifts and adjustments changing conditions may suggest.[25]

THE PROBLEM OF INCENTIVES

In China, for example, the initial agrarian reform was relatively successful because the Party cushioned its call for self-sacrifice with a land redistribution program that benefited the poorer peasants. In later years, however, Mao sought to substitute "spiritual" (revolutionary) incentives for material ones and upset the precarious equilibrium between the state's demands and private rewards.

Since 1955, Mao's theories on incentives and those of the Soviet leadership have increasingly diverged. The Soviet Union has perhaps reached a stage of development at which it can afford more generous rewards for the Soviet people than it could in earlier periods. Mao, however, does not believe that China's present stage of development permits it to offer its people material incentives on a comparable basis or to abandon the regime's continued stress on utopian goals. In a very real sense, Mao's objection to Liu Shao-ch'i's alleged "economism" was generated by Mao's fear that his revolution would die a premature death.

The establishment of a socialist economy is not enough; China must also be prosperous and strong, but without demanding too much of its resources. Mao is therefore desirous of prolonging the revolutionary spirit beyond the socialist stage and postponing material incentives in the present by promising greater future rewards. Personal sacrifice will continue to be demanded.

"To abandon revolution on the pretext of avoiding sacrifices," the official *Peking Review* declared, "is in reality to demand that the people should forever remain slaves and endure infinite pain and sacrifice." [26] Sacrifice at the present stage is thus presented as an investment in a millennial future; only by making sacrifices now can a great future be assured. What we call sacrifice is to Mao a much more positive concept than passive abstention or self-deprivation in despair. Mao demands a ceaseless struggle to overcome both internal and external obstacles with determination, courage, and will power and, above all, in a spirit of defiance.

CLASS STRUGGLE

For Mao, class struggle is a means of overcoming internal and external obstacles. Orthodox Marxist theory defined classes in relation to the material base of society and assumed that class struggle would no longer be necessary in the progressive society of socialism. Mao's new interpretation of the term is inward-directed in two senses: First, it is aimed against those among the Party cadres and the working masses whose special privileges have made them a new class of "labor aristocracy" [27] and, second, against any remaining influence of bourgeois ideology and undesirable traditions within each individual, regardless of his social background.

For Mao, the significance of class struggle extends far beyond the socio-economic realm. The concept expresses his belief that the reshaping of society requires the transformation of people's minds through ideological purification and rebirth. It also expresses Mao's growing conviction that ideological purity, not Communist social structure, can eliminate the inequities of bourgeois society and can free the masses from exploitation.

Because the Maoist interpretation of class struggle has added internal and ideological dimensions to the orthodox meaning of the term, and because class struggle, in his view, remains necessary in a socialist society, Mao's interpretation is sometimes described as contrived class struggle. The theoretical foundation for this concept lies in Mao's theory of contradictions. A major expression of this theory is "On the Correct Handling of the Contradictions Among the People" (1957).

THE THEORY OF CONTRADICTIONS

Mao accepts the basic Hegelian notion, endorsed by Marx and Lenin, that contradiction within everything is the primary cause of self-movement, but he has given greater emphasis than his ideological mentors to a different kind of contradiction, that between two things. The latter, which was no more than "interconnections" in Lenin's discourse on contradiction,[28] is elevated by Mao to the position of "secondary cause" of all change and development.[29]

Mao's conception of the duality of contradictions—both within a thing and between two or more things—recalls a fundamental principle of *yin-yang* philosophy: that antinomy (or contradiction) is found between two entities (one *yin* and one *yang*) as well as within a given entity. Even more striking is Mao's insistence that without contradiction "each aspect loses the condition of its existence." [30] This reminds one of the famous Chinese dictum dating from Confucius but showing the influence of *yin-yang* thinking: *wu ti-kuo wai-huan che kuo heng wang* (a state without an adversary and external threat is apt to perish). The notion expounded by Mao here is much more than "a logical deduction," as Arthur A. Cohen alleges, from Lenin's statement that "every thing (phenomenon, process, etc.) is bound up with every other." [31] Mao's illustration is revealing. Answering a rhetorical question—"Can each aspect exist by itself without its counterpart?"—Mao states:

> Without life, death is nonexistent; without death, life is nonexistent. When there is no top, there is no bottom; where there is no bottom, there is no top. If not for the existence of bad fortune, nothing can be known as good fortune; if not for good fortune, nothing can be known as bad fortune.[32]

The statement is but a paraphrase of a famous saying by Lao Tzu, to the effect that "it is upon bad fortune that good fortune leans, upon good fortune that bad fortune rests." Mao has often quoted the saying and once explicitly ascribed it to Lao Tzu.[33] The *yin-yang* reasoning has probably influenced Mao's theory of contradictions as much as Marx and Lenin have.

A key difference between *yin-yang* dialectics and its Hegelian counterpart is that *yin* is not the antithesis of *yang* but its natural complement and alternate. If Mao drew from orthodox Marxism his concept of antagonistic contradictions, it is quite possible that his theory of nonantagonistic contradictions owes much to the *yin-yang* heritage of Chinese thought. Like the *yin-yang* antinomy, Mao's nonantagonistic contradictions are not between truly antithetical polarities; such contradictions may continue to exist after the passage from capitalism to socialism. Yet Mao, in a way reminiscent of Hegelian thought, sees the final resolution of all contradictions not in the circular motion from *yin* to *yang* but in an advance toward a higher stage of development.

"REVOLUTIONARY IMMORTALITY"

The practical significance of Mao's theory of contradictions is that it takes issue with the Soviet approach to the building of Communism. Since Stalin's death, the Soviet Union has begun to offer more material incentives, on the grounds that its socialist society has transcended contradictions and class struggle. Mao objects to such a relaxation; he believes that, under socialism, contradictions merely exist at a higher level. Regarding material incentives as a return to capitalism and exploitation, Mao insists on recharging the revolutionary spirit and will power. In his view, that is the only way to keep the revolution alive and to maintain, as one writer has put it, a "revolutionary immortality" long after his own disappearance from the scene.[34]

In other words, unlike Stalin, Mao is concerned about the *future* of his revolution. As Stuart Kirby has observed, Stalin "apparently did not particularly care about posterity, simply continuing his introvert autocracy until he died." Mao, on the other hand, "is deeply concerned about who should be his 'inheritors,' their fitness and their commitment not merely to continue Communism, but very specifically Mao's own form of Communism." [35] It may be that Mao is consciously or subconsciously seeking to avoid the fate that befell Stalinism after 1954. But a larger concern is implicit in Mao's view that the Party's mandate to lead derives from its ability to achieve the goals of the revolution. His fear that the revolution might fall short of its goals if the Party and the people rush to enjoy immediate material rewards and cease to invest in the future has apparently made Mao exceedingly anxious about the quality of his successors and future generations.

As he became even more apprehensive in the 1960's about what he perceived as the rise of "revisionism" within China, Mao felt increasing justification for his long-held belief that class struggle must be perpetuated in all phases of social development. His strong reaction to the phenomenon of "revisionism" at home and abroad explains his urgent call for redoubled class struggle. On the other hand, Mao's support for the Cultural Revolution and its violent efforts to overthrow opposition within the Party raises the question of whether or not Mao still believes, as he did in 1957, in the nonantagonistic nature of contradictions in a socialist society.

Since 1953, Mao has seen the Chinese Communist revolution as different from the Bolshevik model for two primary reasons, First, China's century-long revolutionary ferment (from the 1840's on) had an anti-imperialist element that was missing in the Russian case. Second, Mao has been highly critical of the "revisionism" of the present generation of Soviet leaders, charging that their position on revolution has softened since the passing of the Stalinist era. Recent events in China have demonstrated Mao's determination to eradicate any possible growth of "revisionism" in his own country by whatever means were at his disposal.

On balance, however, there is little difference between the goals Mao has set for China and those of the Soviet Union. Both regimes have sought to build a strong, prosperous, and egalitarian society through collectivistic means and under state and Party patronage. The harsh measures taken by the Communist leaders of both countries probably in part bespeak the immensity of the problems that China and Russia have experienced in a turbulent century. What divergencies there are lie, first, in the fact that the two nations are now in different stages of development and face a different set of economic and geopolitical problems; [36] and, second, in Mao's different assessment of human nature and of what can be done to make it commensurate with the gigantic tasks of modernization. It is clear that agreement on the goals of the revolution does not imply an agreement on the specific means to attain them. This is true of the relations between Communist China and the Soviet Union and the relations among CCP leaders themselves.

6

IDEOLOGY IN NEW PERSPECTIVE

The Chinese Communist Ideology and Its Content

THE IDEOLOGY of the Chinese Communist system is difficult to define, as noted in the Introduction, not only because its content is vast but also because, in application, it is so closely related to questions of political power, organization, leadership, policy, and social ethics. It is at once the source of morality and authority and the basis for a social order and a political program. As one writer puts it, "The Communist ideology offered a solution to ethical and aesthetic problems, an ontology, a theory of history, an epistemology, a pretension to philosophy of science, and a universal formula or 'law' of thought, the Dialectics, very much like the old Chinese formula of *yin* and *yang*." [1]

This is a sweeping statement, but it contains more than a grain of truth. The separation between morality and politics, or church and state, that we know in the West is foreign to the Chinese tradition. In the West, the long struggle between church and state during the sixteenth and seventeenth centuries had two political results: The church was obliged to give up the idea that it could realize religious principles on the political plane; and the absolute sovereigns of the time could no longer claim a religious principle, i.e., the Divine Right of Kings, as the moral justification for their personal right to rule. They had to find a new basis of legitimacy in the public sector, the preservation of order. The church's loss of political authority did not mean the loss of its moral authority, however. It remained a separate, institutional channel through which criticism of the political system could be expressed and pressure exerted. More important, it retained its influence as a source of personal and social morality. At the same time, the sovereign's loss of religious authority resulted in a partial separation between the law he established and the morality accepted by the society, between external and internal matters, and between the public and the private sector. In other words, in much of the West the political system is secular; there is a constant dialogue between the political and moral spheres of authority, but they remain distinct.

In China, however, no such distinction has ever existed. Under the Communist regime, as in the past, morality and authority are inseparable, as if church and state were one. The Communist regime not only dictates laws in the public sector, it also seeks to "legislate" the private morality of its people. In imperial China, the Confucian *li* prevailed in both state and society, as noted in Chapter 1. Today, Communist ideology, as interpreted by Mao, exerts a similar influence. In practice, the Communist regime serves as a "guardian" of public and private morality and as society's judge and legistlator. Like the dynasties of imperial China, the Communist regime is not to be criticized or its authority challenged, an exemption it enjoys as long as its performance lives up to the expectations created by the official ideology. If that performance appears to fall short, as in 1957 and 1966–68, forces within the Party or the society may question the mandate of the regime. The accumulation of repressed grievances was responsible for the convulsive character of the Hundred Flowers Movement and the Cultural Revolution. Those events had elements that resembled the dynastic crises of traditional times.

In China, the real locus of authority is not in the conscience of the individual but in the affairs of the nation. The basis for the legitimacy of CCP leadership is the Party's revolutionary program, which, it claims, will bring power and wealth to the Chinese nation. Despite the Party's claims to authority, the myth of Chinese Communist infallibility seems subject to the tests of reality. The Party's reverses during the Great Leap Forward have elicited lingering doubts. Since 1962, the thought of Mao Tse-tung has been cited as the ultimate authority. While this looks at times like simple personal aggrandizement, it may have begun as a tactical device to deflect support from the "revisionist" line followed by the "handful of Party leaders taking the capitalist road." In the first analysis, dictatorship is practiced in the name of utopian goals. Personal identification with the values of the regime must be created so that the Chinese people will accept the excesses and sacrifices imposed by their central authorities. The regime seeks to justify its program in terms of its revolutionary goals and its ability to achieve them; only when it does so can it expect to retain the loyalty of the masses.

Ideology and Organization

Chapter 5 focused on the ambitious goals of the Chinese Communist revolution and the place they occupy in the whole political system. To attain their goals, the Chinese Communists have taken it upon themselves to establish a special kind of dialogue between the leadership and the people in order to mobilize the masses for the fullest participation in the nation's social and political life. The dialogue is based not on a consensus emanating from the masses but on a set of values, ideals, and ethics formulated by the leaders, allegedly "for the good of the masses" and for adoption by the masses.

Because organization of the people is a technique of extraordinary importance for goal attainment, the responsibility for leading the mass organizations resides with the cadres and Party leaders. Thus, the training and education of cadres must always "occupy first place in the general educational program." [2] Precisely because leadership or responsibility brings with it the demand for discipline, the Party leaders and cadres are expected to be hard on themselves, as they are hard on others. Mu Fu-sheng reports the following incident:

> Hundreds of trained political workers were sent to work among the aborigines soon after the Communists entered Yunnan. The aborigines lived in a primitive form of society based on slavery and they would not be interfered with. Hundreds of political workers were butchered, but the Party ruled that there should be no reprisals and hundreds more were sent.[3]

In the execution of national policy, Mao is known to be very hard on himself, his family, and his close associates. His own son, An-ying, was killed in combat during the Korean war.[4] The Cultural Revolution provides examples of Mao's willingness to dismiss even his closest associates when their actions, in his view, do not exemplify his vision of the good society and his conception of how to attain it.

In the existing literature, problems of ideology and organization in Communist China have been quite extensively explored.[5] Our concern here and in subsequent chapters is with the way ideology functions in Maoist China as a catalyst in the process of socialist transformation and construction. The functional importance of ideology cannot be overstressed. Since 1949, the issue causing the greatest dissension within the Politburo has been the pace and strategy for China's socialist development. At the same time, the greatest challenges to Mao's leadership have occurred in response to his crash programs, notably the campaign to form agricultural cooperatives in 1955–56 and the Great Leap Forward in 1958–59. Almost all the anomalies involved in the Cultural Revolution were in one way or another related to dissensions over developmental strategies. These questions will be elaborated upon in later chapters, but they provide the backdrop against which the present discussion of ideology will be presented.

Although the goals that the Party has defined provide a common direction for the entire country, the Party still needs to build a consensus on the ways to achieve those goals and an effective organization to provide stability, cohesion, and the necessary institutional basis for operation. Because ideology breeds commitment and helps create a consensus on proper modes of action, it represents the soul of the whole system, while organization is its body.

Political power in China tends to be distributed in proportion to the responsibility borne by component units of the system. As greater responsibility brings greater rewards in the form of security, trust, prestige, and the sense of participation in decision-making, so it also demands greater discipline. The entire system is one in which power radiates out from a central policy-making core in the top Party hierarchy, through the interlocking directorates of Party and state cadres and the institutions they staff, to the mass of the people, with the level of responsibility, power, reward, and discipline diminishing in proportion to distance from the center. (This principle does not apply to the ostracized classes, which, until rehabilitated, are the most remote from responsibility and yet subject to the greatest measure of control.)

Six Major Functions of Ideology

The ideology of Communist China is thus both the source and the legislator of morality and authority, and in this it is like the Confucian *li* it has replaced. In any comparative study of traditional morality and Communist ideology, one must bear in mind the fundamental distinction between content and function. Whereas the *content* of China's ideology may change, it does not follow that its *function* must also change. The Confucian *li*, the all-pervasive and resilient morality or ethos under which the traditional society operated, has been replaced,[6] but the new Communist ideology functions today in ways reminiscent of the Confucian *li* before 1949, although the regime disposes of modern means of communication to give its application greater range and effectiveness. Let us now examine six major functions of ideology.

(1) The first function is to offer hope to the millions of living Chinese who have endured decades of war, hunger, sickness, and loss. The CCP ideology promises that, after the final overthrow of domestic and foreign evil forces, the righteous nation will live in peace and prosperity in a renovated social order, free from all forms of bourgeois exploitation. As Mao proclaimed with compassion upon the founding of the People's Republic of China on October 1, 1949: "The people throughout China have been plunged into *bitter sufferings and tribulations.* . . . Now, the war of the people's liberation has been fundamentally won, and the majority of the people throughout the country have been liberated." [7]

(2) Ideology offers the Chinese Communist regime a new intellectual framework for interpreting historical processes and, for that matter, a new philosophical system. The system is founded on the assumption that human thought is divided into two schools, the metaphysical and the dialectical. Mao's "On Contradiction" expounded this theme:

> Throughout the history of human knowledge, there have been two conceptions concerning the law of development of the universe, the *metaphysical* conception and the *dialectical* conception, which form two opposing world outlooks. . . . In China, another name for metaphysics is *hsüan-hsüeh.** For a long period in history, whether in China or in Europe, this way of thinking, which is part and parcel of the idealist world outlook, occupied a dominant position in human thought. In Europe, the materialism of the bourgeoisie in its early days was also metaphysical. As the social economy of many European countries advanced to the stage of highly developed capitalism, as the forces of production, the class struggle, and the sciences developed to a level unprecedented in history, and as the industrial proletariat became the greatest motive force in historical development, there arose the Marxist world outlook of materialist dialectics.[8]

* It is interesting that Mao equates "metaphysics" with the Chinese term *hsüan-hsüeh*, a broad and vague term for all forms of occult philosophy. Here Mao means idealism as opposed to materialism.

In comparing the two world outlooks, Mao finds that the Marxist philosophy of dialectical materialism is superior, first because it seeks *internal* causes of development in the nature of things (i.e., modes of production), whereas the metaphysical school holds to the theory of external causes (e.g., ideas); and, second, because the metaphysical world outlook sees things as isolated, static, one-sided, and immutable. This dialectical approach underlies the Communist interpretation of human history:

> Changes in society are due chiefly to the development of the *internal contradictions* in society, that is, the contradiction between the productive forces and the relations of production, the contradiction between classes, and the contradiction between the old and the new; it is the development of these contradictions that pushes society forward and gives the impetus for the suppression of the old society by the new.[9]

As a "scientific" system, the Communist ideology, based on Marxist dialectical materialism, claims to offer the only correct interpretation of history. The Chinese Communist leaders, like their Russian counterparts, believe that the "scientific" validity of the Marxist ideology sanctions their leadership role.

The critique of the metaphysical school and pre-Marxist materialism logically leads to a glorification of "practice," another key element in the CCP's official ideology. To know is to do, and knowledge is inseparable from practice, as seen from the Marxist viewpoint. As Mao puts it in "On Practice":

> *Before Marx*, materialism examined the problem of knowledge apart from the social nature of man and apart from his historical development, and was therefore incapable of understanding the dependence of knowledge on social practice, that is, the dependence of knowledge on production and class struggle. . . .
> *Marxists hold that man's social practice alone is the criterion of the truth of his knowledge of the external world.* What actually happens is that man's knowledge is verified only when he achieves the anticipated results in the process of social practice (material production, class struggle, or scientific experiment).

If a man wants to succeed in his work, that is, to achieve the anticipated results, he must bring his ideas into correspondence with the laws of the objective world; if they do not correspond, he will fail in his practice.[10]

With this new system of knowledge, dialectical in outlook and practice-oriented, the Maoist ideology could boldly claim its superiority over the Chinese philosophical heritage, including Confucianism itself.[11]

(3) Ideology in Communist China provides a set of national goals, institutions, and programs. As noted above, the "scientific" validity of Communism, the revolutionary goals of the Party, and its ability to lead the country to achieve those goals are the source of the Party's legitimacy. There must also be a theoretical foundation for the institutions established after the revolution has overthrown the old regime.

The American Declaration of Independence invoked the "Laws of Nature" and "Nature's God" to entitle the American people to a separate republic. To secure the "inalienable rights" of men, "Governments are instituted among Men, deriving their just powers from the consent of the governed." Although the Declaration of Independence probably exaggerated existing wrongs, its real significance, from the standpoint of political theory, is that it summed up the political ideals and principles of government of the time and provided a cogent theoretical foundation for the political institutions to be established in the new republic.

In the case of Communist China, Marxism-Leninism supplied the theoretical foundation for the institutions that the Chinese Communists established. The CCP bill of wrongs charged that the "imperialism, feudalism, and bureaucratic capitalism" of the "old society" justified a revolution to bring about the new era of the "People's Democratic Dictatorship." The "New Democracy," consisting of the four-class alliance, was "the political foundation for the national construction" of the new China. The new state was to be "led by the Communist Party" and founded

on the "united front" of the four classes,* because that relationship had been formed during the revolutionary struggle to establish the new republic.[12]

The abolition of private ownership of the means of production
was the most sweeping change introduced by the Communists,
but major changes were envisaged in a great many other political
and social institutions as well. Several important principles underlie these changes: (a) The regime is a "people's democratic state
led by the working class and based on the alliance of workers and
peasants"; (b) the regime, "by relying on the organs of state
and the social forces, and by means of socialist industrialization
and socialist transformation, ensures the gradual abolition of systems of exploitation and the building of a socialist society";
(c) "all organs of state must rely on the masses of the people";
(d) the regime "suppresses all treasonable and counterrevolutionary activities . . . [and] deprives feudal landlords and bureaucratic capitalists of political rights for a specific period of
time according to law"; (e) the state also professes to protect a
long list of "rights" of the "people" (those belonging to the specified four classes); and (f) the state "directs the growth and
transformation of the national economy through the economic
planning to secure constantly increasing production, thus enriching the material and cultural life of the people and consolidating
the independence and security of the country."[13]

These principles run through all Chinese Communist political
and social institutions. For instance, the interdiction of political
activity by counterrevolutionaries and the dispossessed classes
was upheld in the regime's Electoral Law of 1953.[14] In another
instance, the regime's attacks on feudalism find expression in the
Marriage Law of 1950. "The arbitrary and compulsory feudal marriage system, which is based on the superiority of man over
woman and which ignores the children's interests, shall be abolished."[15]

The laws and decrees of the regime are rooted in ideological

---

* Workers, peasants, [urban] petty bourgeoisie, and national bourgeoisie.

principles. The Common Program and the Organic Laws of 1949, the Constitution of 1954, and the supporting laws all derive from Mao's ideological policy statements and reports. Among these are: (a) "On New Democracy" (1940); (b) "On Coalition Government" (1945); (c) "Report to the Second Plenary Session of the Seventh Central Committee of the Communist Party of China" (March 5, 1949); (d) "Address to the Preparatory Committee of the New Political Consultative Conference" (June 15, 1949); and (e) "On People's Democratic Dictatorship" (June 30, 1949).

In the Cultural Revolution, during the course of Mao's ideological rectification and purification campaign, the normal operations of the structures set up under the Constitution of the People's Republic of China were suspended, as were the Party's standing procedures and organizational lines of command. Those two developments signified the supremacy of ideology over organization and over statutory law. To the extent that Peking's ideology serves as moral legislation for the entire nation, its role and importance eclipses that of law itself. Though this is a common phenomenon in a socialist state, the Chinese Communists have carried the practice to such lengths that the Soviet Union has been unable to restrain its disapproval. In 1964, for example, *Izvestia* charged:

> Violation of socialist legality became a practice of state activity in China. Distorting Marxist-Leninist teaching on the role of the Party in the system of the dictatorship of the proletariat, the Chinese leaders assigned to Party organs not the role of organizers and teachers of the masses, but the role of a 'commanding force' determining and regulating all activities of local organs of power, of the courts and the procuracy. The persistently repeated conceptions that 'politics is the commanding force' and that the Party official is 'the commander of production' are served up as a kind of *theoretical justification* of such practices.[16]

The *Izvestia* phrase, "politics is the commanding force," is a reference to the Chinese (or Maoist) slogan, "politics takes command" (*cheng-chih kua-shuai*), an important concept that conveys little concrete meaning in its English translation. *Cheng-chih*

means concern for and governance of public affairs, with implications of the macro-interest of society as opposed to the
micro-interest of the individual. Since the Great Leap Forward
in 1958, the term, as used by the Maoists, has increasingly meant
the subordination of immediate personal benefits to collective
interests. It implies that all considerations, whether economic,
social, or organizational, must be subordinate to Mao's conception of macro-development. Mao's development strategy, which
relies on psychological as well as social mobilization, calls for
individual austerity and places a low priority on the production of
consumer goods. The "revisionist" line, which would permit
greater personal incentives, less economic austerity, and less ideological pressure, was condemned by the Maoists in 1966 for
putting "economics in command." In the final analysis, "politics
takes command" means that ideological considerations—ultimately the thought of Mao—govern policy and prevail over purely
economic considerations and other particularistic interests.

(4) Ideology furnishes Chinese society with a new set of basic
moral values by which individuals and the community as a whole
are to judge all thought and behavior. If totalitarian states
throughout history have demanded certain standards of behavior,
the Chinese Communist leaders seek to impose, on a national
basis, a uniform set of values and sentiments, and a single, "socialist" personality structure. In the broadest sense, the new value
system prescribed by the Party is at the heart of what Mao calls a
"new culture" or "proletarian culture," which replaces the old
"imperialist" and "semifeudal" culture. The foremost values of
the "new culture" are nationalism, scientism, and popularism,
which are meant to combat three evils from the culture of the
past: imperialist and comprador-capitalist influence, superstition
and metaphysical knowledge (i.e., occult philosophy and "idealism"), and feudal snobbishness and exploitation.[17] Many of
those traits had developed in the past as psychological and social
defense mechanisms against authoritarian rule and foreign pressures. Some were carried over from the Ch'ing dynasty, when the

Manchu rulers actually encouraged their Chinese subjects to withdraw into scholarly pursuits, or even hermit life, in order to reduce opposition to their dynasty.

Ideology establishes not only a set of basic moral values but also a system of priorities by which cadres and masses can judge the relative emphases to be placed upon various essential policies. For instance, under Mao's "four firsts" formulation, man has priority over weapons; ideological work is more important than political work, and political work than other kinds of work; and living ideas in the mind take precedence of those in books. In a special directive of March 7, 1968, Mao proclaimed the "four firsts" principle and the "three-eight" working style * as the correct methods for revolutionizing China's school system in the wake of the Cultural Revolution.[18]

The Maoist ideology prescribes a similar hierarchy of values for resolution of the practical problems of everyday life. For example, an individual can achieve contentment in life by attaining goals or by suppressing aspirations. Traditional Chinese folk philosophy favored the latter course. Today, the Chinese Communists encourage achievement, but it must be oriented toward the goals they prescribe for society as a whole and not toward purely individual aspirations.

The ideology particularly stresses a spirit of personal self-sacrifice. As Tung Chi-pung, an ex-diplomat who fled to the West, recounted:

> For the first decade and more of the Communist regime in China, we were exhorted to work hard, make sacrifices and obey the leaders on the constantly repeated promises of fantastic prosperity. We were told over and over again that materialism—the goods and services with which the degree of living standard could be marked—was the basis of all social progress and that socialism

---

* The "three-eight" working style was originally introduced by Mao in the People's Liberation Army during the Civil War. It consists of (1) three phrases: correct political direction, a simple and arduous working style, and flexible strategy and tactics; and (2) four two-character phrases meaning unity, alertness, austerity, and liveliness.

under Communist Party leadership was best because with it this progress was made faster.[19]

After the failures of 1958–59, the regime continued to stress the spirit of cheerful sacrifice for the public good rather than the hope of immediate socialist salvation. No one ever suffered as much as the fictionalized figure named Lei Feng—or enjoyed it more.[20] Throughout the 1960's, the "spirit of Lei Fing" and of other heroes was extolled to keep the faith alive. In the midst of economic disarray and peasant discontent, when hunger, disease, and death seemed more persuasive than Radio Peking or the nearest cadre, Mao opposed Liu Shao-ch'i's liberalization policy and redoubled his own ideological exhortations to sacrifice. The "thought of Mao Tse-tung," which in the 1960's practically eclipsed Marxism-Leninism in the Chinese press, was romanticized as a "spiritual A-bomb." The foremost political qualities urged upon the nation were "political consciousness, bravery, and sacrifice." [21]

There are three primary means by which these values are to be inculcated: (a) The superiority of dialectical materialism over the "metaphysical" philosophies of the West and traditional China must be emphasized, as already discussed. So that the "new culture" based on dialectical materialism can flourish, all traces of the old culture founded on metaphysics must be eradicated. (b) Rationalism must be stressed, and parochialism, idolatry, and other irrational practices must be suppressed through mass-education efforts. Superstitious practices such as geomancy (feng-shui) * must be discontinued.[22] (c) Class struggle must be stressed. This is a unifying concept that deserves elaboration because it has replaced the traditional Confucian focus on harmony and mutual adjustment. The Communists believe that progress results from a dialectical process of "unity, struggle, and again unity."

---

* The selection by divination of proper sites for houses, graves, etc., in relation to surrounding natural forces. The practice is often deemed expensive in terms of financial resources and land use.

Class struggle is not just directed toward the former ruling classes. It aims at three broad goals, all having direct relevance to the new value system. First, class struggle is employed to eliminate all rival centers of enculturation of the society, such as the family and the church, which may impart values opposed to those upheld by the Party's ideology. The family (or clan) system had inculcated particularist values and pursued family-oriented interests, instead of the universalistic type of political and social order that the regime sought to establish. To the Chinese, the family had been the primary agent of socialization, providing both education and social training. By deprivng the family elders of authority—including the authority to teach the young —the Communists could undermine the entire institution of filial piety, the very foundation of the family system. To the CCP, there was no better device for penetrating the hard shell of family solidarity than class struggle, which alone could humiliate the family elders and alienate family members from each other and from the kinship system. The use of class struggle is known to have seriously weakened clan solidarity by introducing a non-kinship criterion of group interest. As C. K. Yang, who was on the spot until 1951, observed:

> The peasants' struggle against the landlords, the disclosing of hidden ownership of land to the Communist cadres, the tenants' accusation of cruelty and exploitation against rent collectors, the victims' charges of injustice and oppression by 'local bullies,' the activists' efforts in ferreting out counterrevolutionaries—all these turned many close kin against each other. . . .
>
> Our observations in Nanching confirmed the impression that the clan was unlikely ever to recover its traditional importance in the operation of village life, and that the whole kinship framework of collective action, supported by its traditional status system, would diminish in strength while the *universalistic type of political and social order would increase its influence*.[23]

The second broad goal of class struggle is to release peasants from all forms of "feudal" bondage in thought and in action, so that all productive forces can be freed. "The land ownership system of feudal exploitation by the landlord class shall be abolished," the Agrarian Reform Law declared, "and the system of peasant land ownership shall be introduced *to set free the rural productive forces*." [24] Class struggle was more important to the Party than the actual improvement of peasant living standards, because the Party was willing to sacrifice immediate rewards for the present generation in order to increase productivity for the benefit of many generations to come. In Mao's view, class struggle, rather than the immediate improvement of living standards, is the only way to release and fully utilize all the latent productive forces. After almost every production setback, Mao's remedy is always more, not less, class struggle. Although a period of relaxation in 1960–61 followed the failure of the Great Leap Forward, it ended abruptly after the Tenth Plenum of the Central Committee. The new line urged much sharper class struggle. As the *People's Daily* put it in March, 1963:

> The main demonstration of the class struggle and the two-road struggle in the countryside is the struggle between the collective economy and the spontaneous capitalist leanings of small producers. The surviving old ideas, deeply ingrained in the minds of the peasant masses and the habits and customs left over from the old society cannot be wiped out overnight. The class struggle still remains . . . in the countryside.[25]

The third broad goal of class struggle is to overturn a value system that had traditionally regarded leisure and nonactivity as superior to manual labor. Known as the *shih-ta-fu hsi-ch'i* or, literally, the "habit and aura of the gentry-literati," it was expressed in various ways—an abhorrence of manual labor, a hypersensitive concern for "face," overt conformity but covert deviation, a dual standard of behavior toward in-groups and out-groups, outward geniality and internal suspiciousness, withdrawal from civic spirited activity, neglect for personal and public hygiene, and so forth.[26]

The fact that class struggle is intended to help remold the thinking of the old *shih-ta-fu* is borne out by the regime's practice of sending large numbers of college professors and students to the countryside during the land reform program in 1950. They were made to participate in struggle meetings and public trials of landlords. They were also asked to join in abusing and attacking the landlords so that they might overcome their own "bourgeois sentimentalism" and acquire proletarian sentiments. During the Socialist Education Movement of 1962–65 and during the Cultural Revolution, intellectuals, students, and cadres were again sent to the countryside, factories, and outlying grazing lands to join actual production labor as part of an ideological reform program. What is most offensive to the Chinese Communist regime, with all its production zeal and stress on hard work, is a persistent traditional disdain for manual labor and a kind of lingering passivity ("lethargic mentality").[27] The latest tendency to withdraw from "struggle between the proletariat and the bourgeoisie" has emerged among—of all people—the youth. Some young people have responded negatively to the pressures to conform to the Party's utopian image of socialist man, and Mao has been forced to combat this trend.[28]

Class struggle is a standard remedy for various tendencies the regime opposes. As a standing policy, the Party condemns inactivity as equivalent to opposition. The Maoists criticize "lethargic mentality" because it leads to underestimating the enemy, indifference to class struggle, and apathy toward subversive actions, and also because it weakens the revolutionary ranks.[29] At different times, the Maoist leadership has related "lethargic mentality" to "rightist tendencies," "remnant capitalist thinking," and "wanderers" among the youth who enjoyed new opportunities to travel and evade discipline and responsibility during the confusion of the Cultural Revolution.

Although class struggle is a standard technique, the content of the term and the targets of the regime have changed over time. Until about 1960, class struggle was an ideological struggle *between* classes, with the peasants and workers on one side and the bourgeoisie on the other. But since 1960, bourgeois thought has been seen as an infection that contaminates all classes. Although in Mao's usage in the past class struggle did have the connotation of a struggle between conflicting ideologies as well as between the classes that generated them, the emphasis definitely shifted to the ideological aspect of the struggle in the 1960's. The new emphasis has arisen from the intra-Party fight between Maoists and "revisionists." In current usage, the term means the struggle *within* each person, irrespective of his class background, between proletarian thinking and remnant bourgeois thinking. This new and quite unorthodox version of the Marxist concept may best be described as contrived class struggle.[30]

(5) Ideology sets up a body of concepts, terms, and ideas by which people interpret the world around them and communicate with one another. It serves to unify the thinking of the Party and the masses by establishing a uniform language for the discussion of national goals. As Franz Schurmann has shown, a major vehicle for such communication is the Chinese press, whose function is not just propaganda or indoctrination but broad political communication.[31]

Communication between the Party and the masses, however, is subject to the intrusion of misconceptions about the meaning of Marxist terminology and its application to the outside world. The Chinese Communist leaders were trained to use the Marxist vocabulary, but the subconscious influence of Chinese thought probably persists. The leaders ostensibly use Marxist categories in their thinking and pronouncements and refer to economic interests, social classes, and class struggle. They claim that different class backgrounds determine individuals' responses to social issues. In "On People's Democratic Dictatorship," Mao Tse-tung stated: "Sun Yat-sen had a world outlook different from ours and started from a different class standpoint in studying and tackling problems." [32] But the Chinese Communists' understanding of the outside world is often limited by a preconceived ideological perspective, the lack of direct personal experience outside of China, and an inadequate grasp of Western history and philosophy. (Mao, for example, has never been abroad, except for brief visits to the Soviet Union after 1949, and knows no foreign language.) For these reasons, Chinese Communist leaders have difficulty in understanding the essentially Western conception of politics as the arena for the settlement of differences among individuals and groups under rules that have been formulated to protect the individual as well as the community, the minority as well as the majority. Communication therefore suffers from a somewhat distorted world view.

The process of political communication in China is known as "ideological work." By its doctrine of historical necessity and redemption, the Communist ideology has been transformed from academic speculation into an action program demanding positive commitment from its adherents. The Communist elite must not only mobilize itself; it must also establish channels of political communication with the masses in order to mobilize the population at large.

In its ideological work, the Party must arouse the political consciousness of the nation and transmit its own aspirations, anxiety, and experience vertically to the masses and horizontally to the non-Party elites. Because the masses are so vast and because it is difficult to reform the thought of the non-Party elites (as the 1957 Hundred Flowers campaign demonstrated), the Party places a higher priority upon its vertical communications than upon its horizontal ones. Sensitively attuned to the importance of political communication, the Party has always been seriously concerned with bridging the psychological and ideological distance between the Party and the public.[33] Richard Solomon has studied how the Chinese Communists exploited the weak communication links, due to both emotional and structural gaps, between the peasantry and the established elite in the pre-1949 society. He has also shown how the Party managed to transform peasant passivity into positive support for the Communist regime during the Civil War.[34] Other severe communications barriers in pre-1949 Chinese society divided one generation from the other and the masses from the government. The Communist regime has sought to demolish those barriers by placing political interests above family interests and by opposing any aloofness from the masses on the part of the Party.

The Communist stress on political communication underlies the Party doctrine of the "mass line" (ch'ün-chung lu-hsien). The mass line is a broad statement of Party policy, expressed in ideological terms, and a principle of leadership and organization holding that Party cadres must not merely proclaim their dedication to the Party's cause of serving the masses but must merge with the masses in a spirit of solidarity and lead them in implementing the Party's program. This is epitomized in the phrase "from the masses, to the masses." As will be discussed later, Mao also regards the mass line as an indispensable means of furthering productivity.

Social integration, a central goal of the Chinese Communist Party, requires a unity of purpose, which a common vocabulary and system of thought can help create. The Maoists also believe that the process of political communication and social integration requires an unrelenting struggle to root out old and revisionist ideas, to purify the mind, and to remold humanity. But the exhortation to "study and apply creatively the thought of Mao Tse-tung"—a constant refrain of the Socialist Education Movement and the Cultural Revolution—reflects the difficulty Mao has encountered in achieving unity.

(6) Ideology provides a set of methodological tools for "dialectical analysis." Although the Maoist ideology prescribes many analytical and practical methods, "one divides into two" (yi-fen wei-erh) is probably the most sophisticated. This "Marxist method of dialectical analysis" was formulated for the socialist struggle against "revisionist" tendencies, following Mao's reassertion of effective ideological command at the Tenth Plenum of the Central Committee in 1962. Chou Yang, head of the CCP's Propaganda Department until the Cultural Revolution, gave the concept prominent play in his statement of October 26, 1963.[35]

According to the official CCP interpretation, the principle means that one must look at a person or at a work from two sides, examining the good features, which should be no cause for complacency, and the deficiencies, whose correction demands unrelenting struggle.

Applied to the international scene, the principle provided a rationale for a formal split in the world Communist movement, since the example of the Soviet Union furnished concrete evidence of the perpetuation of good and bad side by side and demonstrated the inevitable need for "permanent revolution." On the domestic scene, the same rationale can explain the appearance of "revisionist" tendencies. The Mao-Lin group has been particularly concerned about the revolutionary credentials of the succeeding generation and has used the "one divides into two" principle as a means of identifying and correcting errors. One of their five criteria for the next generation of leaders is the ability to use the principle as a method of self-criticism. In application, it means constant reflection upon one's own strong points and deficiencies and the willingness to be both part of the revolutionary force and a target of the revolutionary struggle. "Revolution will fail if one does not revolutionize oneself" by the dialectical method of "one divides into two." [36]

7

THE STRUCTURE OF THE
CHINESE COMMUNIST IDEOLOGY

BECAUSE OF its multiple functions, the ideology of Communist China is a structure of many dimensions, drawing upon a wide range of sources. In addition to its Marxist-Leninist heritage, it has roots in predispositions inherited from China's past and in the imperatives of the nation's objective situation.[1]

Problems of Terminology

The very terms that the Chinese Communists use can serve to illustrate the complex structure of CCP ideology. In the first place, "ideology" at the most abstract or philosophical level is known in CCP parlance as *kuan-nien hsing-t'ai*, which literally means "forms of concepts" but implies a way of conceptualizing the outside world, or a body of conceptual tools for analysis and for gaining knowledge. Man's acquisition of knowledge consists of two related but separate processes, involving varying degrees of consciousness: the perceptual and the conceptual.[2] As Spengler suggests, it is not differences in our perceptual order but those in our conceptual order that make people different and are responsible for the cultural diversity of the world.[3] The importance of the conceptual order lies at the heart of the Kantian epistemology, which distinguishes sharply between the things of our experience (phenomena), which can be fitted into categories of our understanding, and things-in-themselves (noumena), which the intellect cannot actually fathom. The "categorical imperative" (the set categories in our minds) gives meaning to things we perceive. Different ways of conceptualizing the same data, in other words, may result in different understanding, and this has been borne out even in the study of physics and biology.[4]

In "On Practice," Mao specifically maintains the distinction between the perceptual and the conceptual processes. In a key section in "On New Democracy," he equates "culture" (used in the anthropoligical sense, to mean a way of life, a methodology, and an ethos) with *kuan-nien hsing-t'ai*. How a people approaches and conceives of reality is the key to its culture, but its culture is subject to the influence of the class structure of the society in which it lives. Mao suggests that a given culture not only is a concrete manifestation of a people's way of conceiving or conceptualizing the outside world but also reinforces or perpetuates it. To change one entails the change of the other.[5]

In "On Contradiction," Mao suggests that dialectical materialism (as opposed to both idealism and mechanistic materialism) is the correct cosmology for a true Communist to adopt. Using the term *yü-chou-kuan* (cosmology, or way of viewing the universe), Mao makes it amply clear that dialectical materialism is more than a theory of history.[6] The use of the word *kuan* (view, or way of looking at things) both in this phrase and in *kuan-nien hsing-t'ai* suggests a concern with the "correct" way of perceiving and conceiving the world. The major components of dialectical materialism outlined in Mao's discussion, which follows the general lines of orthodox Marxist thinking, are matter, principle of the whole, principle of contradictions, and the dialectical concept of transformation and change. When this body of first principles (*kuan-nien hsing-t'ai*) is applied to the historical process, a theory of historical materialism (linear development) results. Thus, ideology as a conceptual order and ideology as theory are two separate things, the latter derived from the former.

In both the 1945 Constitution and the 1956 Constitution of

the CCP, Marxism-Leninism was given the epithet *li-lun*, theory. The designation means that, as "theory," Marxism-Leninism is the outgrowth of dialectical materialism (a conceptual system) but offers a program for changing the existing social order by conscious action. The Chinese revolutionary struggle is, therefore, the actual "practice" that translates Marxist-Leninist "theory" into action. Since theory should not remain an exercise on paper, practice is its indispensable sequel.[7]

Franz Schurmann, in his fascinating book, *Ideology and Organization in Communist China*, has drawn the distinction between "pure ideology" (Marxism-Leninism) and "practical ideology" (the thought of Mao Tse-tung).[8] While the distinction has been very useful for purposes of analysis, I have adopted a more elaborate scheme in this chapter, for two main reasons: First, in the new CCP Constitution adopted by the Ninth Party Congress in April, 1969, the "thought of Mao Tse-tung" is elevated to a position of parity with Marxism-Leninism, forming the "theoretical basis of [the Party's] thinking." * Mao's thought, therefore, should now be classified as part of the CCP's "pure ideology," if we follow Schurmann's original division. This, then, would leave the component of "practical ideology" in doubt. Second, if we take into consideration the implications of ideology as a conceptual system (*kuan-nien hsing-t'ai*), as "theory," and then as "thought" (*szu-hsiang*), the structure of the CCP's ideology has a triple, rather than dual, division. We shall elaborate further by dwelling upon the significance of "thought" as it is used in Chinese.

What is often called "Maoism" in English actually has no Chinese counterpart. The term in Chinese is the "thought" of Mao. The significance of the cryptic phrase should not be underrated. In traditional China, it was a centuries-old belief that man's thought was the source of all his psychic activity, behavior, and action. The Chinese Communists have paid equal attention to thought. As the official *People's Daily* puts it: "Work is done

* See Chapter 15 for a discussion of the new CCP Constitution and its meaning.

by man, and *man's action is governed by his thinking* (szu-hsiang). A man without correct political thinking is a man without a soul. If politics does not take command—i.e., if proletarian thinking does not take command—there can be no direction." [9]

Western scholars have sometimes asked why one cannot change the rather meaningless English phrase, the "thought of Mao Tse-tung," to "Maoism." [10] While the term "Maoism" may be desirable in English, it has two defects: First, it fails to take into account the Chinese concept of "thought" as the determinant of all action. In Communist China today, all successful endeavors, from atomic weaponry to manure collecting, are invariably attributed to the guidance of correct "thought." If the underlying significance of "thought" is disregarded, such allusions would be all but ludicrous. Second, the term "ism" in Chinese has special connotations.

"Ism" in Chinese (*chu-yi*) is used normally in three categories of terms: (1) translated terms, including Communism (*kung-ch'an chu-yi*); [1] (2) terms for rather peculiar tendencies or idiosyncrasies; and (3) terms associated with the idea of a "principle."

Before the twentieth century, the word for "ism," *chu-yi*, did not exist in the Chinese language. The earliest appearance of the word was probably associated with the translation of Western ideas into Chinese, such as Darwinism, socialism, parliamentarianism, etc. The use of *chu-yi*, a combination of two characters meaning "principal" and "tenet," respectively, may well have been modeled on the Japanese word *shugi* which uses the same two Chinese characters.

Many other Chinese terms ending in *chu-yi* denote quite peculiar tendencies or idiosyncrasies. A few examples: *tu-shen chu-yi* (celibacy—an oddity in a society in which a prime obligation of filial piety is the continuation of the family line); *ko-jen ying-hsiung chu-yi* (self-seeking heroism); *ming-ling chu-yi* (commandism); *wei-pa chu-yi* (tailism); and, more recently, *ching-chi chu-yi* (economism, or an emphasis on economic in-

centives at the expense of political goals, a "crime" charged to
Liu Shao-ch'i). The Chinese terms for "commandism" and "tailism" are in themselves also translations from the Russian.[12]

Chu-yi also has the connotations of the English terms "principle" and "action program." For example, Sun Yat-sen's *San-min
Chu-yi*, or *Three People's Principles*, is not translated as San-
min-ism or Sun Yat-sen-ism, because it is a body of three separate
principles and a program for action. Although they represent the
essence of Sun's ideology the three principles are only part of
what Sun stands for. Significantly the ideology or thought of Sun
in its entirety is known as the "theory" of Sun Yat-sen (Sun Wen
hsüeh-shuo), which suggests a scope much broader than *chu-yi*.
Another example is Mao's *Hsin min-chu chu-yi* (New Democracy), which is also an adaptation of the Chinese translation of
the English word "democracy." [13]

There are thus three reasons why the Chinese term for "Maoism"
is not used for the "thought of Mao Tse-tung": First, it is not a
translated term; second, any possible pejorative connotation must
be avoided; and, third, "Maoism" meaning "the principle(s)
of Mao," is too narrow to convey the Chinese concept of
"thought."

The Chinese concept of ideology is also related to the Chinese
view of "theory." Although the Communists use *li-lun* for the
"theory" of Marxism-Leninism, and the Nationalists refer to
hsüeh-shuo for the "theory" of Sun Yat-sen, the terms have other
connotations as well. *Hsüeh-shuo* is an older word, used normally for a school of thought, most often a school of interpretation. The teachings of Confucius himself, an original body of
thought, are known as *K'ung chiao* (not K'ung-tzu *chu-yi*, as
the word Confucia*nism* suggests in English). The schools of academic interpretation of his thought by Chu Hsi and Wang Yang-
ming are called *chu-tzu hsüeh-shuo* (the school of Chu Hsi) and
Wang Yang-ming *hsüeh-shuo* (the school of Wang Yang-ming).
The two schools have often been lumped together in Sinological
studies under the general label "Neo-Confucianism." But in none
of these cases is the component "ism" present in the original.

It is quite pertinent to refer to the "theory" of Sun Yat-sen as *hsüeh-shuo,* insofar as the term applies to his interpretation of adopted Chinese and Western ideas, as distinct from his Three Principles.

The other term for theory, *li-lun,* is used in regard to Marxism-Leninism, instead of either *hsüeh-shuo* or *chu-yi.* Obviously, *hsüeh-shuo* is much too closely associated with academic interpretation for the kind of action- and organization-oriented "theory" of Marxism-Leninism. Nor does the word *chu-yi,* in the sense of principles, convey the full import of Marxism-Leninism as a brand of philosophy. *Li-lun* actually suggests "a body of theorems," with scientific overtones. Its use is not without reason in view of Communists' claims regarding the scientific validity of their ideology. For these reasons, the term *Ma-k'o szu lieh-ning li-lun* is officially used in CCP documents to express Marxism-Leninism.

Another epithet often used for Marxism-Leninism is *chen-li,* "truth." In "On People's Democratic Dictatorship" (1949), Mao spoke of the Chinese "discovery" of Marxism-Leninism as the discovery of "truth." [14] The frequent appearance of the epithets *li-lun* and *chen-li* in CCP documentary literature is meant to set action-oriented and "scientific" Marxism-Leninism apart from other types of theories.

Li-lun (as an action theory) thus dramatizes Marxism-Leninism's tie with *shih-chien* (practice). The true significance of the thought of Mao-Tse-tung is that it is the very synthesis of theory and practice and the ultimate force that welds the two together. A correct understanding of the place of Mao's thought must be sought not in the cult of personality but in the meaning of thought, *szu-hsiang,* which will be further explained below.

To recapitulate, the three basic dimensions of the CCP's ideological structure are (1) *kuan-nien hsing-t'ai* or conceptual order, the epistemological part of ideology; (2) *li-lun,* the theoretical part of ideology, which is associated with the application of Marxist thought to the interpretation of social development or, more concretely, Marxist historical materialism and Leninist organizational techniques; and (3) *szu-hsiang*, or thought, the absolutely indispensable link between theory and practice. *Szu-hsiang* is the process of internalizing an external theory and creatively applying it in changing circumstances.

Despite vast changes within the Party and nation in recent years, this ideological structure remains valid today, although *szu-hsiang* has been elevated to a prominence it has never before enjoyed. The three dimensions meet needs of different phases of historical development and different levels of sophistication. The Communists need a composite armory of ideological weapons to deal with a new China undergoing unprecedented changes. They must (1) define a new world view, (2) formulate a strategy for revolution and organize its execution, (3) provide a total critique of traditional social values and societal institutions, (4) bring about a complete reconstruction of society and humanity within the Chinese setting, and (5) instill in the people a faith that the reconstruction can be done and will be good for them.

Marxism supplies the world view, as well as a critique of social values and institutions; Leninism offers the best strategy and organization for revolution. Together, they provide a broad framework, a world view from which to comprehend and measure all things, a standpoint from which to approach a situation or problem, a direction to follow, a body of effective organizational skills, and a promise of historical redemption.[15]

However, only the "thought of Mao Tse-tung," the Maoists claim, can rally the masses to the Party's efforts to rebuild man and society in China. Mao's "thought" generates "correct" thought (*szu-hsiang*), breathes relevance into the actual practice of Marxism-Leninism, maintains situational flexibility within rigid operational principles and schemes, translates doctrines into reality, and can sustain the people's faith in the darkest hours. The purpose of the rectification of *szu-hsiang* is, in large measure, to release the latent productive capacities of the masses by overcoming psychological inhibitions and by psychic mobilization for the vast job of development. *Szu-hsiang* was also relied upon to sustain popular faith in the Communist future during the post-1958 spiritual depression. Its overwhelming importance has been reconfirmed during Mao's Cultural Revolution.

The Thought of Mao Tse-tung

Since Yenan days, the "thought of Mao Tse-tung" has been officially exalted as the synthesis of Marxist-Leninist theory and Chinese revolutionary practice. "The Chinese Communist Party," the CCP Constitution of 1945 declared, "takes as its guide for all action the *thought* [*szu-hsiang*] of Mao Tse-tung—the thought that unifies the theory of Marxism-Leninism and the practice of the Chinese revolution—and is opposed to any dogmatic or empiricist deviation." [16] Mao's thought, rather than Marxism-Leninism pure and simple, has been established as the official ideology of the Party; its ability to unify theory and practice seems to be the basis for its claim to such prominence.

The status of Mao's thought as the ultimate official CCP ideology was, however, interrupted for a decade (1956–66). The phrase, "the thought of Mao Tse-tung," was dropped from the Party's 1956 Constitution.[17] Until 1966, people outside of China assumed that the omission had been made in the spirit of collective leadership to counter any tendency toward "independent kingdoms," such as had transpired during the 1954 Kao-Jao purge.* Those who supported that assumption could easily point to the publication of Mao's "Historical Experience of the Dictatorship of the Proletariat" (1956) [18] and Peking's initially receptive attitude toward Khrushchev's diatribes against the Stalin cult of personality.[19]

Information that came to light during the Cultural Revolution reveals that an opposition group within the Party's Central Com-

---

* Kao Kang, head of the Party in Manchuria, and Jao Shu-shih, organization chief of the Central Committee, were accused of running "independent kingdoms" and of belonging to an "anti-Party bloc." The purge began in February, 1954, when their work was suspended, and was completed in April, 1955, when both were officially expelled from the Party. Kao reportedly committed suicide.

mittee, led by Marshal P'eng Te-huai, apparently with the support of President Liu Shao-ch'i, was responsible for the deletion of "the thought of Mao Tse-tung" from the Party Constitution at the Eighth Congress of the CCP in 1956.[20]

The eclipse of Mao's thought was only temporary. Significantly, its re-emergence after 1962 in important Party documents heralded the Cultural Revolution. The Communique of the Eleventh Plenum of the Eighth Central Committee, dated August 12, 1966, celebrated Mao's role:

> Comrade Mao Tse-tung is the greatest Marxist-Leninist of our era. Comrade Mao has inherited, defended and developed Marxism-Leninism with genius and creativity in an all-round way and has raised Marxism-Leninism to a new stage. The thought of Mao-Tse-tung is Marxism-Leninism of the era in which imperialism is heading for total collapse and socialism is advancing to worldwide victory. It is the *guiding principle* for all the work of our Party and country.[21]

Once again, Mao's thought is serving as the Party's "guiding principle" and is projected as a "development of Marxism-Leninism in the new era." Extravagant claims like this in the past were often challenged by Mao's detractors in the West on the ground that Mao could not claim originality.[22] However, those who had doubts as to whether Mao's contribution should be judged purely by its originality tended to see the use of a psychological factor (nationalism) in the effort to glorify Mao's thought: By claiming that Mao's thought was a Chinese "development" of Marxism-Leninism, the CCP made it easier for mainland Chinese to accept an otherwise foreign ideology.[23] While that is true, it is also possible, as the Cultural Revolution suggests, that these extravagant claims represented efforts by beleaguered Maoists to subdue ideological opposition within the Party and to reassert the supremacy of Mao's thought. In any case, the practical impact of Mao's thought on the people's life in mainland China today cannot be overstressed. Increasingly, his thought has been elevated to a popular creed of religion.

As an Indian scholar once put it, a horse-drawn buggy, to the Chinese, is made up of more than just a horse and a buggy. There is a third dimension, i.e., the relationship between the two, which makes them into a larger whole. The example suggests the existence of a third element—a horse-buggy-ness—which is often missed. Any attempt to approach the study of Mao's thought as a "practical ideology," patterned after but derived from the "pure ideology" of Marxism-Leninism, tends to overlook this third element. Marxist-Leninist views on "consciousness" and "matter" underlie the dualism of theory and practice in that ideology.

The Marxist concept of history sees social conditions, rather than ideas or thought, as the motive force shaping human activity. In the absolute sense, the materialist view is opposed to Hegelian idealism. Hegel, reacting to the horrors of the French Revolution, had conceived the history of nations as the movement of "ideas" and systems of ideas. The ideas, according to Hegel, evolve and rise to prominence in history, are challenged and fought by opposing ideas, and are finally superseded by a compromise between old and new—until the new compromise is challenged in turn by the rise of further new ideas. This method of interpretation (comprising thesis, antithesis, and synthesis) is known as dialectical idealism. Marx, a generation later, borrowed the Hegelian dialectics but substituted material conditions for ideas; hence, dialectical materialism. Marx, however, never spoke of the dialectics in nature: He was always concerned with the sociohistorical realm. To Marx, "the phantoms formed in the human brain are . . . sublimates of the *material life process*. . . . Life is not determined by consciousness, but consciousness by life." [24] In his *Theses on Feuerbach*, Marx emphasized practice rather than theory, just as he had put matter over consciousness: "The question whether objective truth can be attributed to human thinking is not a question of theory, but is a practical question." [25]

Lenin continued to maintain the same basic Marxian premises.

In his discourse on thought (knowledge), Lenin described thought as "the reflection of Nature on the part of man." [26] While admitting that this process involved "a series of abstractions, formulations, the framing of conceptions, laws, etc.," [27] he assigned no independent existence to thought. "Truth (knowledge of reality) is a process. Man advances from subjective idea to objective truth by way of 'practice' (and technology)." [28] There is certainly an element of activism in Marx and particularly in Lenin. The activist strain is evident in the *Communist Manifesto*, with its call to revolution, and in the frankly utopian spirit of *Civil War in France*, a commentary on the Paris Commune of 1871. Lenin even drew upon the Hegelian origins of the Marxist tradition to reinforce his faith in the powers of the human will and the conscious and purposeful activities of men, especially the elite. Despite his concern with subjective consciousness, Lenin's reasoning remained within the dualism of theory and practice, consciousness and matter.

It therefore seems safe to conclude that Marxism-Leninism, regardless of its activism, conceives of theory as essentially rooted in practice, with consciousness (thought) arising as a sublimate or reflection of matter. Its analysis does not go beyond the socio-historical realm, and it recognizes no independent variable that bridges consciousness and matter, unifies theory and practice, and extends beyond the human world. *Szu-hsiang* is such an independent variable in the usage of the Chinese Communist ideology.

The Nature of Szu-hsiang

The first important thing about *szu-hsiang* is its independent status; it must be understood outside the existing theory-practice framework. Its independence is clearly expressed in this reference to *szu-hsiang*, Communism, and the Party: "Those people who in their *szu-hsiang* have not entered the Party carry in their heads many dirty things of the exploitative class. They know nothing about what proletarian *szu-hsiang* is, what *Communism* is, and what the *Party* is." [29] Conversion to Communism (theory) and membership in the Party (practice) do not guarantee the "right" *szu-hsiang*, according to this view.

Furthermore, since *szu-hsiang* has an independent existence, it can no longer be understood within the Marxist concept of superstructure. In "On the Correct Handling of Contradictions Among the People" (1957), Mao suggested that ideological contradictions would continue beyond the achievement of socialism.[30] The implication is that *szu-hsiang* does not necessarily conform to the prevailing economic base and that socialism does not automatically entail the creation of a proletarian *szu-hsiang*. The Chinese Communist concept of *szu-hsiang* is thus a departure from the Marxist view that ideology is but a superstructure of the economic base or substructure. As a result, proletarian *szu-hsiang* must be fostered by frequent ideological purification campaigns. The doctrine was expounded in 1966 by *Chieh-fang chün-pao* (*Liberation Army Daily*): "The struggle to *foster* what is proletarian and liquidate what is bourgeois . . . is an important aspect of class struggle." [31] The implication that, despite the official advent of socialism in 1956, purposeful struggle was still necessary to erase the past bourgeois ways of thinking and to generate a new, proletarian way of thinking is worth noting. Maoists stress the notion that one's mentality determines one's membership in this or that social class. A formerly rich man who has been converted to Marxism may be considered an irreproachable proletarian. Conversely, a worker or poor peasant who clings to old customs falls into the bourgeois or even feudal category.* The belief that a person's mentality is not solely determined by

---

* Admittedly, former "exploiters" or property-owners are more likely than poor peasants or workers to retain "bad" ideas and customs from the past and to be cool to the new socialist order. But there are exceptions, as K. S. Karol has noted in his *China: The Other Communism* (New York: Hill and Wang, 1966), p. 184. On the other hand, a "labor aristocracy" could very easily emerge in the socialist society of contemporary China, should "bourgeois" thinking take hold of members of the proletariat. Cf. *Peking Review*, May 10, 1968, p. 3.

his relation to the actual production process demonstrates the independent existence of *szu-hsiang*.

Another important characteristic of the cult of *szu-hsiang* is its voluntarism, which extends even to the realm of nature. A volume on the study of Mao's thought during the Great Leap declared:

> Many living examples show that there is only *unproductive thought* [*szu-hsiang*], there are no *unproductive regions*. There are only poor methods for cultivating the land, there is no such thing as poor land. Provided only that people manifest in full measure their *subjective capacities* for action, it is possible to modify natural conditions.[32]

These bold assertions about the ability of human will power to conquer the natural world far exceeded Lenin's faith in the power of human will to transform the social and political world. If Stalin also entertained extravagantly ambitious ideas about the possibility of transforming deserts into gardens, he still never suggested that deserts existed only in the mind.[33]

The Chinese Communist definition of the right *szu-hsiang* as "subjective capacities" that are capable of overcoming all material hazards has two important aspects. First, overreliance on the power of such subjective capacities has had economic repercussions arising from the overtaxing of human resources and also raises theoretical questions about Mao's Marxist credentials. Schram has described this excessive voluntarism as revolutionary "romanticism." [34] Second, the belief that one's subjective capacities define the character of natural conditions and can modify them seems to place *szu-hsiang* in the same category as *hsin* (heart or mind) in Confucian and Neo-Confucian thought. Here one is reminded of a Chinese tendency to perceive some kind of bridge or matrix that integrates man and nature.

Szu-hsiang and Hsin

Szu-hsiang and *hsin* are not the only elements of Chinese Communist and traditional Chinese thought that merit comparison, but it is not possible to do full justice to the others within the limits of this study.

A comparison of the Communist *szu-hsiang* and the *hsin* of Confucian and Neo-Confucian thought does not necessarily imply the existence of causal relations or links of continuity between *szu-hsiang* and *hsin*, although such a possibility should not be summarily ruled out. Chinese Communist leaders on occasion make use of terms used in Confucian and Neo-Confucian writings. Mao himself has alluded to *hsin* in terms reminiscent of his characterization of *szu-hsiang*. In his famous "On Protracted War" (May, 1938), Mao laid down the golden rule: "War is a contest of *jen-li* (human power) and *jen-hsin* (human mind or, literally, human heart)." A few pages later, Mao invoked an ancient adage to illustrate his point: "The ancients had it: 'The art of varying tactics resides in one's *hsin*.'"[35] The connotations of *hsin* in Chinese are so broad that one must stretch the meaning of the usual English translation, "mind." *Hsin* connotes wisdom, will power, morale, indomitable spirit. In other words, it serves as a synonym for *szu-hsiang*.

If almost all traditional Chinese philosophers were concerned with the union of man and nature (*t'ien jen ho yi*), the bridge or matrix for such union was, with necessary differences of interpretation, *hsin* (human mind) itself. Nowhere can this be better illustrated than in Neo-Confucianism—a synthesis of Confucianism, Buddhism, and Taoism—which is part of twentieth-century China's philosophical heritage.

Among the leading exponents of Neo-Confucianism is Chu Hsi (1130–1200) who headed one of its two main schools. In a discourse on *hsin*, he discussed the universal existence of *li* (principle) and *ch'i* (material force) and their "mutual pervasion." In his reasoning, Chu consciously drew upon the ancient *yin-yang* antinomy, which postulates that the universe is made of *yin* (negative) and *yang* (positive) elements. The two forces are complementary, rather than antithetical, and flow into each other. In Chu's exposition, the ultimate unifying matrix of principle and material force is *hsin* (mind) itself. In *hsin* are found both *yin* and *yang,* expressed in the forms of tranquility and activity, respectively. *Hsin* is the Great Ultimate; it has no opposite (such as *yin is to yang*).[36]

An earlier chapter suggested that the *yin-yang* philosophy had been an important part of Mao's thought before his conversion to Marxism. In his Marxist stage, Mao's theory of "contradictions" reflects this heritage. His theory that contradictions manifest not only "mutual contention" but also "mutual complementarity" (*hsiang-ch'eng*) and that contradictions may be nonantithetical as well as antithetical recalls the "mutual pervasion" (complementarity) of *yin* and *yang*. At the same time, in Mao's view all contradictions are rooted in ideological (*szu-hsiang*) conflicts. His solution—ideological rectification—indicates the central importance he attaches to *szu-hsiang* and his faith in the perfectibility of man.

Chu Hsi, for his part, believed that man's weaknesses could be overcome by the "investigation of all things (*wu*)" to derive right knowledge or consciousness of the principle (*li*) inherent in them, and by self-cultivation to bring one's conduct into conformity with the principles thus discovered. Prior to such self-cultivation, *hsin* was no more than *jen-hsin* (human heart) and could be led astray. But when rectified by consciousness of the principles that comes through the "investigation of all things," *hsin* is purified and becomes *tao-hsin* (moral heart).[37]

The things to be investigated in Chu's formulation included matters of conduct, human relations, and political problems. Full understanding of them could be achieved through the practice of the supreme virtue of *jen* (Confucian morality based on human-heartedness). It is through *jen* that the individual overcomes his selfishness and partiality, sheds his tiny ego, and unites himself with the mind of the universe, which is love and creativity itself.[38]

In current Chinese Communist thinking, man's *szu-hsiang,* like Chu's "human heart," can be led astray, and Mao's thought resembles the new *jen* through which the individual can purify his own thought, shed his selfish bourgeois mentality, and steep himself in the collective proletarian ethics. This is perhaps the main rationale for the emphasis placed on Mao's thought during the Cultural Revolution. Mao's thought is to inspire and guide the nation's all-out struggle to cleanse itself of the remnant "poisonous weeds" of bourgeois ideology.

Although *hsin* unites Chu Hsi's subjective (*li*) and objective (*ch'i*) worlds, the philosopher nevertheless maintained the separate identity of both worlds. On the other hand, Wang Yang-ming (1472–1529), the chief exponent of the other main school of Neo-Confucianism, asserted that "principle" (*li*) no longer exists in the outside world but is equivalent to *hsin* (the mind) itself. All things are contained in *hsin*, and the objective world is the same as the subjective world. The universal moral law is not to be sought externally but exists in man's innate sense of right and wrong (*liang chih*).

Two strands of thought in Wang Yang-ming find striking parallels in Chinese Communist thought. By de-emphasizing the search for objective truth or principle (*li*), Wang made it possible to argue that man's perfection, or sagehood, is open to all, humble peasant as well as learned scholar. The Buddhist ideal of universal salvation may have reinforced this view. An egalitarianism maintained by ideological self-discipline finds expression in CCP ideals as well.

The second strand is Wang's call for unity of knowledge and action. Wang deplored the fact that, in the intervening two centuries, Chu Hsi's search for objective truth had degenerated into irrelevant academic exercises on the part of many Confucian scholars. As a remedy, he offered a doctrine unifying knowledge and action. True knowledge does not emanate from "investigation" alone but must have practical consequences, just as valid action must be based on or guided by knowledge. "Knowledge is the beginning of action; action is the completion of knowledge." [39] To combat the overemphasis on book knowledge at the expense of practice, he revived a definition of knowledge dating back to Chinese antiquity.[40]

Like Chu Hsi, Wang firmly believed that man *can* control his mental and psychic being and that, since his mental process, however defined, constitutes his bridge with the outside world, the way to universal order is through self-discipline. The Wang Yang-ming school, nevertheless, differed from the Chu Hsi school in that it placed self-discipline ("rectification of the mind") before the acquisition of knowledge ("investigation of all things"); Chu Hsi, believing that only with knowledge could one properly order one's mind, had reversed that order of priority. In restoring self-discipline to first place, Wang Yang-ming revived the original Confucian belief that only a properly ordered mind can acquire correct knowledge.[41]

The Chinese Communist leaders have made similar pronouncements about what self-discipline through correct *szu-hsiang* can do to change objective circumstances. In a volume on how to learn from the thought of Mao, it is argued that, by changing one's "subjective world," it is possible to change the "objective world." Practice (*shih-chien*) does not automatically change one's subjective world. A conscious "subjective exertion" (*chu-kuan nu-li*) is necessary, and the success of practice very much depends on it.[42]

Although Mao's concept of *szu-hsiang* embodies this "subjective exertion," it is not a simple reincarnation of the New-Confucian *hsin*. There are major differences. For one thing, *szu-hsiang* implies no system of metaphysics, as *hsin* obviously does, but is a means of linking the individual to the Party in a cause larger than both. In Confucian parlance, the basic moral sense of the universe is contained within *hsin*, whereas Mao's *szu-hsiang* is a means of attaining ideological "purity" and assuring its creative and zealous application. Moreover, the purpose of the self-discipline of *hsin* is to maintain the unity and harmony of man and nature (i.e., a harmonious ordering of man's moral universe), while the purpose of the Communist *szu-hsiang* is to alter the natural and social environment by means of struggle ("subjective exertion").

Just as Neo-Confucian thought tended to idolize *hsin*, Chinese

Communist ideologues have romanticized *szu-hsiang* as the source of what amounts to a superhuman power. Correct *szu-hsiang* expresses total devotion to Communism and the Party, an indomitable spirit, and inexhaustible strength, with the result that "stupidity gives way to intelligence, the difficult becomes easy, the dangerous path becomes smooth, and [the individual becomes] capable of achieving distinction and being outstanding in any kind of work." [43] This romanticized view was advanced in 1947 by Ch'en Po-ta, who for years served as Mao's ghost writer and in 1966 became director of the Central Cultural Revolution Group in Peking. Its similarity to Neo-Confucian thought is so striking that David Nivison was prompted to remark that "we perceive at once that Ch'en [Po-ta], like Chiang [K'ai-shek], like Sun [Yat-sen], is singing of the age-old mysteries of 'sincerity,'" the epitome of rectified *hsin*.[44]

Chinese Communist Thought and Other Schools of Chinese Philosophy

The Chinese Communist thought process also shows elements resembling that of traditional Chinese philosophy. F. S. C. Northrop has defined two major types of concepts, one achieved by *intuition* and the other by *postulation*. The former "is one which denotes, and the complete meaning of which is given by, something which is immediately apprehended. 'Blue' in the sense of the sensed color is a concept by intuition." On the other hand, "a concept of postulation is one the complete meaning of which is designated by the postulates of the deductive theory in which it occurs. . . . 'Blue' in the sense of the number of a wavelength in electromagnetic theory is a concept by postulation." [45]

Northrop classifies both Confucianism and Taoism, the two main forms of Chinese philosophy, as belonging to the aesthetic-intuitive archetype, though with their variations.[46] Fung Yu-lan, still one of the greatest living Chinese philosophers despite his difficulties with the CCP leaders, has extended Northrop's discussion. In the aesthetic-intuitive continuum, the Columbia-trained scholar states, there is no demarcation between the subject and the object. That is why, in his view, epistemological problems —such as whether the world we see is real or illusory— are not to be found in Chinese philosophy, except in Buddhism, which was imported from India. Indeed, in the aesthetic-intuitive continuum, "the knower and the known are one whole." [47] Such an approach seems to underlie almost all Chinese philosophies. While space does not permit a detailed explication, two central questions have occupied the interests of various schools of thought in China's history.

The first is a universal concern for the unity of man and *t'ien*, or nature. The concept of *t'ien* (literally, heaven or universe) was passed down from antiquity (*c*. 1120 B.C.).[48] Inheriting that tradition, Confucius (551–479 B.C.) and his elaborator, Mencius (372–289 B.C.?), advocated following man's innate good as the best way to elevate humanity to the level of *t'ien*. The ultimate goal or ideal of every *chün-tzu* (Confucian "gentleman," or model of virtue) is to arrive at a communion with nature.[49] Whereas Confucius never elaborated his views on *t'ien*, Mo Tzu, a utilitarian totally different in disposition from Confucius, regarded the Emperor as the symbol or agency of man's moral quest for union with the natural order. Obedience to the Emperor, the "Son of Heaven," is described as a sure way to avoid "punishments of Heaven," such as violent storms and other natural disasters. Although Mo Tzu put it in utilitarian terms, the ultimate ideal beyond obedience to the "Son of Heaven" is conformity with the "will of Heaven." [50]

The Taoist School, another competing school, founded by Lao Tzu, accepted the concept of *t'ien* but made *tao* (the way) a higher order, which even regulated *t'ien*. Taoists, however, believed that man should approach this ultimate cosmic order through *wu-wei* (doing nothing, or not happening), because too much human or social activity, or too much happening (as manifested in civil strife, cut-throat competition, etc.) would eclipse the pre-existing natural order, *tao*. The idea of the return to equilibrium through the effortless absorption of every individual and entity into a benign order of nature remains the highest ideal of Taoism.[51]

The Taoist idea of effortless absorption was continued by a Confucianist, Hsün Tzu, who regarded human nature as basically evil (in stark contrast to Mencius, another Confucian disciple, who believed that human nature was basically good but subject to the corruption of objective circumstances). Hsün Tzu reasoned that man should "not contest with Heaven" but should follow its will; he saw man as forming a triad with Heaven and earth.[52] His inclusion of earth may reflect the influence of Taoism, which holds that *tao* (the way) is larger than both Heaven and earth. But the idea of the unity of the human world (the knower) and the world beyond (the known), as opposed to a cleavage between them, also guides the thinking of Hsün Tzu.

The only ancient school that did not give much credence to the idea of *t'ien* is the radical Legalist school, whose principal spokesman, Han Fei Tzu (d. 233 B.C.), insisted on government by rewards and punishments (the "two handles"). Han Fei Tzu's advocacy of harsh laws by the prince, in place of rule by social virtue, shows a distrust of the moral and intellectual capacity of the common man and a contempt for the ideal of natural harmony.[53] To a certain extent, the Legalist premise that man's nature is basically evil and requires harsh laws was anticipated by Hsün Tzu. The Legalists' desire to see rationality prevail over superstition probably explains why they avoided the concept of *t'ien*, although their approach also recalls Mo Tzu's utilitarian focus. In any case, the various schools of thought should not be compartmentalized, since there was considerable interchange among them. Although the Legalist school did differ drastically from other schools, at least in regard to man's relation to *t'ien*, it shared with them a common interest in the correspondence between actuality (*shih*) and name (*ming*).

That correspondence constitutes the second central question of interest among the various schools of Chinese thought. Although Confucius's concern with the "rectification of names" (*cheng-ming*) focused attention on the problem, it was almost universally shared by the various ancient philosophical schools in China, including the Legalists. Put in the simplest terms, the idea of *cheng-ming* presupposes the existence of a perfect state of being, of which everything in actuality is but an imperfect or deviant version. It vaguely recalls the Platonic "idea of ideas," according to which the "idea" of chair is more "chair-ish" than the actual chair itself. The assumption is that, if actuality could be made to resemble "name" (the state of perfection) more closely, there would be great harmony and order.[54] Quite amazingly, the ideal was endorsed by the various schools, although for different purposes: The Confucianists stressed the ethical and social meaning of the theory of *cheng-ming*; the Taoists, the metaphysical and aesthetic aspects; the Logicians (the School of Names), the logical aspect; and the Legalists, its utilitarian value from the point of view of political control. The Legalists believed that sociopolitical disorder would cease to exist if the actual behavior of the citizenry could be made to correspond faithfully to the *ming* (the original pure essence) of the laws.[55]

The ideal of achieving full correspondence between actuality and name, much like that of harmonizing man with *t'ien* or, to use the Taoist term, *tao*, shows a process of thought that, as Fung Yu-lan has suggested, does not divide man and Heaven, actuality and name, or horse and buggy, but strives for their union. This explains the value the Chinese have always placed on synthesis, rather than creativity or originality.

The Chinese Communist concept of *szu-hsiang* seems in a very real sense to partake of the same characteristics, insofar as *szu-hsiang* is the meeting ground of theory and practice. The *szu-hsiang* perspective conceives of man (the subjective world) and his environment (the objective world) as forming an integral whole. The substructure, or economic base, and the superstructure, or ideology, as used in the original Marxist framework, are no longer separate categories but form a continuum whose boundaries are very much blurred, if they exist at all. Any analysis that separates ideology in its "pure" form from ideology in practice fails to capture the true spirit of *szu-hsiang*.

8

RAMIFICATIONS OF
SZU-HSIANG IN PRACTICE

THE UNIQUE underlying assumptions of the cult of *szu-hsiang*
quite naturally entails certain ramifications or implications. They
can be broadly described as: (1) the substitution of ideological
purity for objective reality; (2) a new interpretation of the relationship between ideology and social structure; (3) the fanat-
ical belief that mass indoctrination is essential to the achievement
of the goals of the regime; and (4) the belief that the Chinese
experience constitutes the model for revolution in the underdeveloped countries.

Ideological Purity and Objective Reality

Certain parallels between Neo-Confucian and Chinese Communist thought were noted in the last chapter. Both systems also
share a common assumption about "truth" and "reality," if truth
is defined as an ideal or as a concept of the fundamental nature of
things, which transcends perceived experience, and if reality is understood to mean something that exists independent of the ideas
concerning it. The terms are related but often not synonymous.
Although Chu Hsi urged the "investigation of all things" in order
to discover truth, he did not really suggest that truth has an
existence independent of man's perception of it. In fact, like other
Neo-Confucianists, he was interested in finding concrete manifes-

tations of truth in certain fundamental principles that man's enlightened mind regards as truth. Wang Yang-ming, in his interpretation of Neo-Confucianism, went much farther and explicitly stressed that man must use his innate sense of right or wrong to find universal moral law, suggesting that truth may be found within man himself. Wang believed that "principle" may be discovered through practical experience with reality, but it is still man who makes the discovery on the basis of his practical experience; truth or principle is not independent of man. Wang thus made a fundamental assumption, equating the highest truth man can perceive with reality; man's mind or consciousness becomes the bridge or matrix uniting the two.

A similar assumption is reflected in Mao. In "On New Democracy," he states that "a scientific attitude is one of 'searching for truth and reality and sees reality as a manifestation of an *a priori* truth in actual things.'" Mao here regards man's mind as the matrix uniting truth and reality and sees reality as a manifestation of an *a priori* truth. For David Nivison, that attitude recalls both the "Marxist rejection of the bourgeois dualisms of analysis and the world (of 'truth' and 'reality')" and Wang Yang-ming's denial of the dualism of principle (*li*) and material force (*ch'i*).[1]

The assumption underlying Wang's thought (and Mao's) may have certain ominous consequences. When one investigates "reality" to discover "truth," one's thought process is still guided by an empirical spirit. But when one proceeds with a preconceived "truth" to investigate "reality," one's attitude can only be doctrinaire.

In a major passage in his "Preface and Postscript to *Rural Surveys*" (1941) Mao states:

> The only way to know conditions is to make social *investigations*, to investigate the conditions of each social class in real life. For those charged with directing work, the basic method for knowing conditions is to concentrate on a few cities and villages *according to a plan, use the fundamental viewpoint of Marxism*, i.e., the method of class analysis, and make a number of thorough investigations.[2]

It is plain that Mao's investigation does not start with an empirical study and proceed to the finding of truth; it starts with an *a priori* truth (Marxism) and seeks to find a reality that can only be understood according to the fundamentals of that truth. For Mao (and the Neo-Confucianists), this is what "searching for truth in actual things" really means.

Michael Lindsay has noted in the Chinese Communist personality a "sharp contrast between serious and scientific thinking at one extreme, and the parrot-like repetition of propaganda slogans at the other." [3] Whether it is one extreme or the other obviously depends on whether the equation is in forward or reverse gear. Quite correctly, Nivison traces the schizophrenic facets of the Chinese Communist personality to the effects of the equation of truth with reality.

The tension between realism and doctrinairism within the Chinese Communist leadership has underscored major changes of policy, as weight has shifted from one scale to the other. Theodore Chen's point is well taken:

> When Mao Tse-tung said that any popular revolution in China must first of all be a peasant revolution, and that the best way to win over the peasants is to give them what they want most— namely, land—he was being eminently realistic. When he proposed agricultural cooperation without depriving the peasants of the legal ownership of land, he was still guided by realism. But when he ordered full-scale collectivization and moved on from collectives to communes, he was led by Marxist dogma—and this could only mean trouble. [4]

The same conflict is found in the CCP's conflicting policies toward the intellectuals—the Hundred Flowers campaign and its reversal or the problem of "redness" versus "expertness." Mao's doctrinairism resulted in overreliance on will power during the Great Leap and accounted in part for his defiant attitude after its failure. Recent events tend to confirm the revolutionary "romanticism" that Stuart Schram sees in Mao. [5] In its extreme form, the trait appears in the dictum that deserts exist only in the mind and in the belief that the best way to overcome external adversities is to obliterate their images from men's minds. Revolutionary "romanticism" may be merely an extreme form of doctrinairism, fortified by a preoccupation with the power of correct *szu-hsiang* (see Chapter 7).

Szu-hsiang and Social Structure

Mao's unique approach to questions of social structure in China has led him to formulate somewhat unorthodox views on the relationship between ideology and class struggle. Three aspects of Mao's views on this relationship deserve particular mention here.

The first is Mao's frequent departure from the Marxist definition of classes in terms of their relationship to modes of production. Mao employs his own criteria, whose orthodoxy is often questioned by more punctilious Marxists. As previously noted, in the 1920's Mao drew class lines according to the extent of property ownership. In 1931, he delineated the contradictions in Chinese society as between "workers, peasants, soldiers, and toilers," on the one hand, and "warlords, bureaucrats, landlords, and capitalists" on the other.[6] That picture suggested an alignment of friendly forces against hostile ones, rather than a definition of class structure *per se*. In Marxism, the category "class" precedes "ideology." For Mao, the reverse also is conceivable: Ideology not only derives from class, but may create it.[7]

Second, because Mao tends to see the cause of separation of the classes not so much in structural barriers as in ideological differences, class coalition under the ideological hegemony of the CCP is justifiable. Were it not for this ideological definition of class structure, the idea of a joint dictatorship *after*, not before, the Communist rise to power would be close to heretical in the eyes of orthodox Marxists. However, the very vagueness of Mao's class distinctions may conceivably have made the idea of the four-class dictatorship less unpalatable to ideological purists. Although the promised joint dictatorship turned out to be more nominal than real, Mao's purposes in formulating the theory of joint dictatorship may thus be justified on ideological grounds, as Mao viewed it.

Third, because, for Mao, proletarian thinking (*szu-hsiang*) is independent of both the economic base of society and its class structure, it requires constant ideological purification through a kind of contrived class struggle. During the socialist stage, the contrived class struggle is actually *intra*class ideological struggle. Since the Cultural Revolution, the contrived class struggle has been primarily between conflicting ideologies or conflicting ways of thinking within the individual himself, irrespective of his class background. Hence, it is an inward-directed, *intra*personal struggle as well.

A visitor who returned from mainland China shortly after the outbreak of the Cultural Revolution reported encountering a "model" student of poor peasant origin whose entire training had been under the new regime. Despite her correct class background, she disclaimed qualification for membership in the Communist Youth League because, she said, "I have not yet succeeded in throwing off feudal and bourgeois ideological influences. . . . We are living in a period of acute class war, and the feudal bourgeois ideology of the old society is still very much alive. I fight it strongly, but I am not sufficiently liberated to be worthy of becoming a member of the [Communist Youth League]." [8]

The girl's remark implies that everyone in Communist China today harbors the dangerous germs of bourgeois thinking. Their eradication requires a long process of class struggle within each individual, although the struggle may have its external targets as well. By emphasizing the struggle of the majority against the handful, the Maoists seek to convey the impression that the majority have the proletarian spirit but the size of the minority remains significant. Despite correct class background and the advent of socialism, individuals are susceptible to bourgeois influences. These can be eradicated only by complete dedication to the guidance of Mao's thought and through a prolonged process of contrived class struggle.

There are Soviet antecedents for the thesis that class struggle persists in the socialist stage. Lenin once stated that class struggle *"does not disappear* . . . but merely changes its forms and in many respects becomes fiercer."[9] As early as 1929, Stalin claimed that, because reactionary forces were stepping up their struggle against socialism, Engels's famous promise of the withering away of the state had to be reinterpreted dialectically—that is, in such a way as to postpone indefinitely its fulfillment. Stalin repeated the contention at the Sixteenth Party Congress in 1930.[10]

Those and other statements by Soviet leaders have been adduced as evidence of Mao's Stalinist mantle,[11] but as Stalin defines it, class struggle seems to take place between classes along Marxist lines of social structure; it does not occur within the proletariat itself after the attainment of socialism. Unlike Mao, the Soviet leaders do not seem to conceive of class struggle as an *intra*class, *intra*personal ideological struggle.

At the Twenty-second Party Congress (1961), Khrushchev somehow modified the position he had taken at the Twentieth Congress (1956) and condoned renewed class struggle against counterrevolutionaries, perhaps because of his concern about developments in Eastern Europe. But his remark was directed at a class of anti-Party or antiproletarian elements and was confined to the period of socialist construction, that is, before the arrival of socialism.[12]

The 1961 Program of the Communist Party of the Soviet Union (CPSU) declared that "with the liquidation of the exploiting class, the [state's] function of suppressing their resistance withers away."[13] In his report on the Party Program, Khrushchev purposely drew a line between the stages of socialist construction and Communist construction (after socialism's arrival) and placed the Soviet Union in the latter stage, in which class struggle no longer existed.

The transition from capitalism to socialism is effected under conditions of class struggle. . . . It is natural . . . that the *building of Communism* [during the socialist stage] is effected by the most democratic methods. . . . *Society will no longer experience the difficulties induced by class struggle within the country*.[14]

As early as 1957, Khrushchev explicitly rejected Mao's insinuations that contradictions continued to exist in the Soviet Union.[15] On this point, Khrushchev demonstrated that his concept of class struggle was structurally defined and tied to the modes of production, whereas Mao's was more ideologically defined. If CPSU documents continued to refer to "struggle against bourgeois and reformist ideology," they were directed to the division of the world at large, not to divisions within a given socialist society. The Party Program of the CPSU of 1961 made this quite clear: "A fierce struggle is going on between two ideologies— Communist and bourgeois—*in the world today*. This struggle is a reflection in the spiritual life of mankind of the historical process of *transition from capitalism to socialism*." [16]

The Soviet usage is quite consistent; class struggle means struggle *between* classes or class coalitions, and ideological struggle is its extension to the ideological front, which is still structurally defined and does not extend beyond the "transition from capitalism to socialism." To overstate Stalin's influence on Mao is to overlook the existence of two different concepts of class struggle.

Ideological Work

Tremendous importance, to the point of fanaticism, is attached to ideological work in Communist China today.[17] The Party believes that the key to China's modernization lies in instilling correct thinking (*szu-hsiang*) in people's minds. The objective of ideological work is to create a uniformity of thought, sentiment, outlook, and psychic commitment. Several patterns for achieving that objective have been developed, including (1) thought reform, primarily administered to cadres and intellectuals; (2) propaganda (impersonal), indoctrination (personal and face-to-face), and such mass campaigns as the socialist education campaign; and (3) production-directed mass movements, combining psychological appeal ("the Party cares for me"), persuasion ("for the good of the nation"), and rational explanation ("it is good and necessary because—").

Although propaganda, indoctrination, and public information control are to varying degrees tools of all political systems (particularly those in which an elite leadership is not regularly responsible to the populace), the extent of their use in Communist China is almost unprecedented. One perceptive psychiatrist calls the phenomenon a "psychology of totalism." Ideological work in China aims to control man's "psychological milieu," so that he will not only think revolution but dream revolution. It also seeks to manipulate his emotions so that he will feel unable to escape from the power above. Mao, for instance, is referred to as "our great teacher, great leader, supreme commander, and great helmsman". Ideological work exerts unrelenting pressure to maintain purity of thought: It fires hatred for the heretic and support for his removal, incites ideological struggles, and organizes a universal ritual of criticism, self-criticism, and confession. Finally, ideological work inculcates the belief that doctrine (*szu-hsiang*) is the soul of man, so that existence comes to depend upon creed and upon total obedience and submission.[18] The measures for assuring ideological purity make the work of indoctrination in other totalitarian countries look like child's play. Their very pervasiveness attests to the power *szu-hsiang* has for the Maoists.

"To put organization in order," Mao said at the Yenan Forum on Literature and Art (1942), "we must first of all put ideology [*szu-hsiang*] in order. We need an ideological struggle by the proletariat against the nonproletariat." [19] This essay was among the first of Mao's works to be reprinted during the Cultural Revolution. Its reappearance confirms that Mao is more preoccupied with ideology than with organization, although both are close to his heart. Quite naturally, the Cultural Revolution struck first at the literary and arts circles and the Party's propaganda machine. Those were the channels through which ideology was transmitted to the masses; their functioning had a direct impact on the thinking and behavior of the people.

A consistent feature of Mao's working style is the prime importance he attaches to leading by ideology and to the issuance of encyclicals on topics ranging from guerrilla warfare to the making of atomic bombs. He has paid increasing attention to the channels of ideological dissemination, even more than to the organizational apparatus. The implicit division between *ideological leadership* and *organizational leadership*—which are only relative concepts, advanced here as tools for analysis—has been confirmed by recent revelations from mainland China. According to Mao's speech at a CCP Central Committee work conference on October 25, 1966, a division of responsibility between the "first line" (Liu and Teng, etc.) and the "second line" (Mao himself) had been in practice for more than a decade and a half when Mao terminated it in 1962.[20]

Two lessons can be drawn from this experience. First, although Mao is a good organizer (as his rise to the top of the peasant-based Party he organized attests), between 1949 and 1962 it was primarily through ideological means that he maintained his leadership. That is not incompatible with a favorite Chinese approach to leadership, *yi szu-hsiang ling-tao* (to lead by ideology), an adage followed by Sun Yat-sen, Tseng Kuo-fan, and many other leaders before them. If it is true that Stalin, on the other hand, ruled mainly by organization, operating through the state ministries and the secret police (though at the expense of the Party after the Great Purge), then Mao may be less Stalinist than has been asserted in the past. Of course, Stalin made his own contributions to Communist ideology. For instance, he supplied a rationale, apparently consistent with the theoretical writings of Lenin, for the pursuit of socialism within one country, as opposed to the Trotskyist line of world revolution, and explained why the national state not only showed no signs of withering away under

Communism but exhibited a remarkable tendency to grow in scale, authority, and degree of centralization. Nevertheless, Stalin was essentially an organization man who did not rely as heavily as Mao on ideological tools or stake his claim to leadership on ideological proficiency, as Mao certainly does.

The second lesson is that, in the Cultural Revolution, ideological conflict was in fact more important, if less dramatic, than the struggle for power among personalities, although the two phenomena were closely related. In the final analysis, the purpose of Mao's campaign, now as before, is the rectification of ideological errors, and only when such errors cannot be corrected does Mao find the physical removal of the man necessary. In Mao's view, since *szu-hsiang* is the ultimate point at issue, it makes more sense to change men's minds than to destroy them. In this light, the impact of the "confessions" of Liu Shao-ch'i and company on the thinking of the entire nation was far greater than if the principals had been physically destroyed. If this consideration, aside from Liu's own organizational strength, was chiefly responsible for the fact that he has not been executed by the Maoists*, it is but another testimony to the importance of ideology in Mao's approach to leadership. A caveat should be entered here. The pre-eminence of ideology does not necessarily make men expendable. It means that each individual is expected to make his own thinking and behavior correspond with the dictates of Mao's thought. When his thought and action conflict with Mao's thought, however, he will be subjected to corrective measures in the physical sense.

A practical implication of Mao's style of placing ideology above organization is that, although the Chinese Communist political system is organized around the principles of democratic centralism, class struggle, and the mass line—these are the constants—

---

* Liu was not officially expelled from the Party until the Twelfth Plenum of the Eighth Central Committee, in October, 1968. Although his removal as the Chairman of the Republic (President) must await the action of the National People's Congress, the Party's action means that he is not to function in that office any more.

their application is to be flexible and to follow situation-oriented variables, as Mao may define them from time to time. These principles have specific connotations in regard to ideological leadership in practice: (1) Implementation of the principle of democratic centralism requires the total submission of all interests to the "command of politics." In practice, this means that purely economic or professional interests must be subordinated to broader and more fundamental considerations, as defined by Mao's thought. (2) The principle of class struggle is to be realized in a process of psychic mobilization through ideological purification, guided by Mao's thought. (3) The ultimate aim of the mass line is the creation of the "socialist man," tailored to the designs and expectations of Mao's thought. Those purposes were clearly behind the campaign to "creatively learn and apply the thought of Mao Tse-tung." The campaign, launched in 1965, continued on an imposing scale during the Cultural Revolution.

Implications for World Revolution

Szu-hsiang also has a number of implications in regard to China's foreign policy. It appears true that Mao manipulated public opinion by first building hostility toward the revisionism of post-Stalin Russia and then redirecting it toward "China's Khrushchev" (Liu Shao-ch'i) some years later. If correct, this analysis would imply that Peking's foreign policy in the period after the Great Leap Forward was still very much Mao's policy. In retrospect, Mao seems to have wielded more power in the making of foreign policy than in domestic policy between 1959, when he stepped down as Chief of State, and 1965. To put it differently, Liu's revisionism seems to have had less effect on the nation's foreign policy than on the domestic scene.[21]

In Peking's foreign policy, as in its domestic policy, there is a strong Maoist preference for leading by ideological example. A number of scholars have sought to find in Communist China's view of the world the roots of Peking's policy differences with Moscow.

The quest is often fruitless for two main reasons. First, Peking's conception of world politics and of its own world role is only one of a wide range of factors affecting the formulation of China's foreign policy. Among the others are the Marxist-Leninist ideology, national interests, historical experience, the relationship between goals and capabilities, Peking's reputation as a revolutionary regime, and expediency. Second, our present level of knowledge is not adequate to the immense task of comprehending the cultural-psychological foundation of collective policy-making in China. Different strategic assessments, no less than different ideological assumptions, are probably behind the disagreements between Peking and Moscow in the field of foreign policy.[22] Strategy should not be confused with world view (i.e., conceptualization of an international order).

In its international application, the term Maoism is generally defined as a specific strategy, attributed to Mao, for Communist world revolution. Shaped essentially by the experience of the Communist revolution in China, the Maoist strategy is a synthesis of the classical "left" and the classical right strategy of the international Communist movement. From the obsolescent classical "left," Mao took the idea of a "united front from below." From the classical right, Mao borrowed the idea of a two-stage revolution. During the first stage, Communist-type social demands are subordinated to national and democratic goals. During the second stage, Communist goals will predominate. Like that of the classical right, the Maoist strategy in the first stage appeals to all anti-imperialist groups and classes, including the national bourgeoisie and even patriotic landlords. In addition, Mao insists that Communist hegemony must be maintained from the very first stage of the two-stage revolution, rather than wait until the second stage, as advocated by the classical right strategy.[23]

In the post-1959 Sino-Soviet dispute, a key issue of world revolutionary policy has been the Soviet tendency to follow the classical right strategy, now described as "national democracy," which permits the Communists to enter into coalition with native nationalist leaders without insisting upon Communist hegemony, as Mao advocates, from the first stage on. During the Khrushchev period, at least, that strategy sought to bring about an ideological rapprochement with nationalist leaders, especially in one-party states, by working through a united front from the top.

By contrast, the Chinese Communists have placed greater emphasis on armed struggle through a united front from below. Peking's militant attitude and revolutionary ideology are well known, but, when it comes to real action, the Chinese Communist regime has shown quite striking caution. In fact, in 1963, the Soviet Union ridiculed Peking's double standard: Despite its own restraint in dealing with the "imperialists" with regard to Hong Kong and Macao, Peking had demanded a Soviet nuclear showdown with the United States over the Cuban missile crisis.[24]

Scholars like Franz Schurmann and Harold Hinton have argued that Lo Jui-ch'ing, former Chief of Staff, was removed in November, 1965, because he had advocated preventive action in Vietnam, and perhaps also because he had designed Peking's disastrous policy in Indonesia. The same scholars see the ascendancy of Lin Piao as signifying the adoption of a Mao-Lin policy under which China would remain on the sidelines in the Vietnam War and would pursue a more subdued, pragmatic line in foreign policy, verbal saber-rattling notwithstanding.[25]

If such is the case, what is the explanation for the wide discrepancy between Peking's bold words and its sober actions? How seriously should one take Peking's claim to be the "center of world revolution"? The late Anna Louise Strong, an American Communist in Peking, probably spoke for the Chinese Communist leaders when she said that the "center of world revolution" does not mean the "center from which orders are issued." [26] She may be suggesting here that Peking is a source of inspiration and ideological leadership for the underdeveloped world rather than a center of direct organizational control or direct participation. The suggestion is borne out in Lin Piao's famous "Long Live the

Victory of the People's War" (1965), the platform on which he stands as heir-apparent to Mao Tse-tung.

In plain language, Lin is telling the revolutionary comrades in the underdeveloped areas, among them Vietnam, (1) not to fight more than one "imperialist" power at a time, (2) to follow not the Soviet national democracy strategy but the strategy of a united front from below under the leadership of the Communist Party, (3) to observe the mass line in building a people's army to ensure that it has the support of a highly conscious revolutionary people, (4) not to neglect the resources of the masses and not to rely exclusively on foreign aid (including aid from Peking) but to be self-reliant, (5) not to forget the importance of adapting Marxism-Leninism to local conditions, (6) not to neglect the role of the masses in the militia, and (7) not to give up hope in the face of reverses. Lin is also warning the "imperialists" that the repression of local revolutions will bring retaliation and resistance. The Chinese Communist revolution succeeded, Lin is saying, as a result of Mao's creative application of Marxism-Leninism to Chinese conditions and the people's primary reliance on their own efforts. Why should not the revolutionary peoples in Vietnam and elsewhere do the same? [27]

If Mao's China is viewed as a center of ideological inspiration for the world revolution, many points become clearer. For example, Mao's famous phrases "political power grows out of the barrel of a gun" and "a single spark can start a prairie fire" were reprinted in 1968 in the *Peking Review*. Both sayings were described as part of Mao's thought, which "lights the world" and benefits revolutionaries everywhere.[28] Who provides this single spark, and why were the two statements published together?

In juxtaposition, the two statements suggest that Peking's role is to offer encouragement by holding up the Chinese experience as an example of what the barrel of a gun can do in attaining political power, while the actual lighting of the prairie fire is left to the local single sparks themselves. Such an interpretation

seems to tally closely with Mao's stress on the primacy of ideological over organizational leadership. Although other interpretations are possible, it is important to recall that, while Mao has
termed the barrel of a gun the source of political power, he has
also insisted that "man [with the right ideology] is more important than weapons."

Many China specialists agree that Lin Piao's article was a
manual for revolution by Communist Parties in the underdeveloped world. As Donald Zagoria has aptly pointed out, the
article is neither Fourth-of-July oratory nor a *Mein Kampf* design for China's expansion. If *Mein Kampf* was a blueprint for
what Germany would do under Hitler, "Lin Piao's statement is
designed to tell *other* Communist Parties what *they* should do." [29]
The fact that the Chinese Communists seem more concerned
with telling other people how to conduct their revolutions than
with participating in revolution elsewhere themselves suggests
that they see their primary role as one of offering inspiration
and ideological guidance.

It is true that practical considerations, such as limited military
capabilities and the hard lessons learned from the Korean War,
may also be responsible for Peking's relative prudence at the
action level. But Mao's tendency to lead world revolution by
ideology is probably more deep-seated than is generally realized.
Precisely because of its lower stage of development, Peking is
all the more anxious to prove itself the ideological superior in its
dispute with the Soviet Communists over the correct course of
world revolution. Peking's obsession with the export of its ideology, more than with the export of material aid, should not be
taken too lightly. It is, indeed, another manifestation of Mao's
belief that correct *szu-hsiang*, applied to the international scene,
can determine the success or failure of a revolution.

Although Mao's leadership by ideology makes his commitment
to world revolution appear more positive than current Soviet
strategy, Mao's commitment is quite different from that of Trotsky in the early years of the Soviet Union. Trotsky and his fol-

lowers were committed to a monolithic and centrally directed international Communist movement, not an ideologically inspired world revolution in which each local Communist Party would carry out its own policies on the domestic scene, as Mao and Lin Piao prescribe. Trotsky abhorred nothing more than nationalism, "that national revolutionary messianic mood which prompts one to see one's own nation-state as destined to lead mankind to socialism." [30] Like his mentor Li Ta-chao many years before, Mao is committed to both nationalism and world revolution and identifies class struggle with national and racial conflict.[31] For him, the only way to reconcile the international Communist movement with revolution within one country is through an internationally inspired but locally directed revolution in each nation-state. Mao's China, in such a scheme, would do more inspiring than directing.

Mao's orientation toward ideological leadership of the world revolution entails the recognition of nationalism and the international application of the principle of the mass line, as interpreted by Mao. Domestically, the mass line opposes the notion that any elite should dictate to the masses in a way that would stifle effective mass participation; it places equal emphasis on ideological leadership from the top and on psychically mobilized participation by the masses from below. Internationally, any attempt to impose the physical presence of Peking or Moscow upon another regime or native revolutionary group would violate that principle. Peking was therefore openly critical of the Soviet invasion of Czechoslovakia in August, 1968. Peking attacked that "shameless act" on three grounds: (1) ideological issues should not be settled by forceful intervention ("big-nation chauvinism"); (2) Czechoslovak revisionism was the result of the bad example set by Soviet revisionism; and (3) Soviet invasion was no way to safeguard the fruits of socialism—it merely proved that the Soviet Union intended to dominate a new colonial empire.[32]

China's condemnation of the Soviet move is another example

of the importance Peking attaches to leadership by ideological example. Peking here assumes the existence of a moral normative order that operates at both the domestic and the international levels and in which the ideologically weak follow the example of the ideologically strong. The Chinese Communist view recalls the traditional Chinese view of the world as an ideologically defined hierarchical order based on a universal moral code.

Unquestionably, China's interest in increasing its influence on the Western flank of the U.S.S.R. was a prime motive in Peking's denunciation of the Soviet occupation of Czechoslovakia. This purpose is implicit in Chou En-lai's statement at the Rumanian National Day reception in Peking on August 23, 1968, and also in Peking press declarations on the Czechoslovak situation. Chou virtually called for a guerrilla resistance movement against the Russians in Czechoslovakia and for Rumanian preparations against the possibility of Soviet invasion. In his speech, Chou offered both countries China's support.[33] However, Peking's interest in weakening Soviet–East European ties—a long-shot policy at best—is not the only factor at work here. In a sharper version of his speech in a New China News Agency dispatch, Chou referred to the Prague regime as "the Czechoslovak revisionist leading clique" and attacked its "call on the people not to resist." In another passage, he said that, as a consequence of the occupation by Soviet revisionists, the Czechoslovaks would learn to oppose not only the Russians but their own revisionists, who, Chou implied, were selling them out to the Russians.[34]

Although the Chinese leaders obviously hoped that the Soviet move into Czechoslovakia would produce an opposition that would develop an affinity for Peking's policy line, they seemed more concerned with ideological influence than with practical power gains. They continued to express respect for nationalism and to think in terms of the need for ideological leadership of the world Communist movement, as distinct from direct organizational control or intervention by any Communist superpower. There is an ideological basis for Mao's world view, just as there is for his concept of armed struggle and his claims to Chinese leadership of the world revolution. As the Soviet occupation of Czechoslovakia has amply shown, propaganda for "peaceful coexistence" has not made the Russians any less prone to "big-nation chauvinism." Conversely, Peking's persistent advocacy of armed struggle has remained for the most part at the verbal and ideological level.

In conclusion, Mao's concept of leadership of the world revolution appears in effect more ideologically oriented than Trotskyism or the hard-line policy of the CPSU, as evidenced in the 1968 Soviet occupation of Czechoslovakia. Although there may be unforeseen and sudden shifts in future Chinese policy, Mao conceives of three major contributions for China to make in its role as leader of the world revolution in the anticolonial, anti-imperialist, underdeveloped countries: (1) a hope for and vision of the future; (2) an example of audacity and a successful policy of disdain for imperialist "paper tigers"; and (3) an encouragement to the "single sparks" in underdeveloped countries to light their own "prarie fire" and creatively adapt theory to local practice.

Mao's concept of *szu-hsiang* is central to Communist China's perception of its role in the world revolution as primarily spiritual and ideological. That perception partially explains the striking discrepancy between Peking's verbal militancy and its practical prudence in foreign relations, although, of course, material weaknesses and strategic considerations also help explain the discrepancy.

PART THREE

Ideology and Practice
Since 1949

9

FROM CONSENSUS TO DISAGREEMENT TO DISSENSION

FEW, IF any, Western observers foresaw the outbreak in 1965–66 of China's Cultural Revolution. Although some perceptive observers had become aware of the prevalence of "bureaucratic politics"—the serious competition for the allocation and management of resources among different bureaucratic groups within the state and Party hierarchies [1]—most assumed that the monolithic nature of Communist power would silence any serious dissent to Mao's leadership within the highest Party councils. Although the Cultural Revolution appeared at first to be primarily a power struggle, revelations during its course made it clear that genuine policy issues were at stake. Despite a considerable ideological consensus within the CCP leadership about China's ultimate goals, there have been major policy differences for many years as to how those goals should be achieved. The Cultural Revolution is the latest attempt by one group, the Maoists, to impose on dissenters their resolution of the tension between ideology and policy. In launching the Cultural Revolution, Mao was seeking to impose an ideological order on the economic, political, and social anomalies of a rapidly changing society. Can the massive ideological assault succeed in imposing order, changing human nature, modernizing the society, and maintaining its own Maoist identity after Mao?

The areas of ideology and policy cannot be sharply delimited.

Ideological differences may not always produce different policy preferences, and policy considerations may have an impact on ideology itself. Nor can ideology or policy be divorced from the economic, social, and political realities a country faces at a given time. It was assumed in the West, however, that CCP leaders had reached an ideological consensus roughly analogous to the acceptance in a Western democracy of the spirit and principles of a constitution, and that their ideological consensus would facilitate agreements on policy. In a Western democracy, however, minority positions can be institutionalized in political party platforms until such time as the minority can persuade the majority to adopt its views. As a result, a Western minority is often willing to abide by the political rules of the society while seeking change. In Communist China, however, policy differences within the Party are tolerated only prior to a decision by the top leadership; opposition views cannot be allowed to develop an institutional life of their own. Under democratic centralism, moreover, a numerical majority within the Party hierarchy cannot be allowed to challenge the decisions of the top Party leadership, even when they seem misguided. Once opposition elements within the Party ceased to observe those two cardinal rules governing policy differences, an ominous dissension developed into the Cultural Revolution, an event whose proportions are without precedent in the history of the Party since Mao's ascension to its leadership in 1935.

Although there is still far too little information on the history of the Party under Mao's leadership to permit any general review or reinterpretation of that history yet, it is clear that policy disagreements have existed since the regime's establishment in 1949, as before. There is no doubt that the Maoist denunciations of 1966–68 were exaggerated and implicated many more Party leaders—and more viciously—than the facts warranted. Nevertheless, the available literature does suggest some of the real policy issues that have been in contention throughout the life of the regime. The existence of such rifts and Mao's efforts to resolve them by ideological pressures mean that the Maoist ideology has become deeply involved in policy issues. A rejection of Maoist policies after his death may well raise fundamental questions about the survival of the ideology itself.

Although it is not possible to analyze policy differences in any depth here, this section will trace the erosion of a broad ideological consensus into specific policy disagreements, which, remaining unresolved, grew into deepening rifts and culminated in the Cultural Revolution. Throughout this section of the book, the central theme will be the interaction between ideology and policy in the governing of China and the implications of that interaction for China's future. The present chapter will deal with the period prior to the Great Leap Forward in 1958.[2]

Areas of Policy Disagreement

When the Chinese Communists established their regime in 1949, they faced immediate issues in all areas of government policy, with decisions needed about the structure and role of the government and the Party, the reconstruction and development of the economy, the definition of a General Line, the formulation of an appropriate foreign policy and defense program, and the creation of a new society. While Communist ideals were cherished by all Party leaders, their implementation called for an entirely different set of perspectives. The wide range of possible policies and personal preferences, reflecting different experiences and interpretations of the ideals and standards set by the Communist ideology, made it enormously difficult at times to achieve a consensus on policy that would match the consensus on goals. Several major policy debates arose as early as the 1950's.

THE KOREAN WAR

The decision to enter the Korean War was a painful one; it involved questions about the nature of China's relationship with the Soviet Union and meant the diversion of resources from other pressing national and economic goals.

According to remarks attributed to Mao in a talk before the

Central Committee in 1962, Stalin harbored strong suspicions during the early 1950's that Communist China would become another Titoist Yugoslavia. Since the CCP had come to power without much help from the U.S.S.R., Stalin's fears were not totally unfounded.[3] Mao's trip to Moscow in December, 1949, and China's later participation in the Korean War were allegedly prompted by a desire to allay Stalin's fears. "In 1945," Mao was reported to have said, "Stalin refused to [authorize] China to carry out a revolution and said to us: 'Do not engage in civil war; cooperate with Chiang Kai-shek. Otherwise, the Republic of China will collapse.' However, we did not adhere to that, and the revolution succeeded. Even after the success of the revolution," Mao reportedly continued:

> *Stalin feared that China might become a Yugoslavia* and that I might become a Tito. Afterward, I went to Moscow and concluded the Sino-Soviet treaty of alliance [February 14, 1950]. This too was the result of much struggle. Stalin did not wish to sign the treaty. He finally signed it after two months of negotiations. It was *only after our resistance* to America and our support for Korea *that Stalin finally came to trust us.*[4]

Although Mao may merely be defending the decision to go to the aid of North Korea during the war of 1950–53, his account may also illustrate the dilemma facing the CCP leadership at the time. From other sources, we do know that there was opposition to the decision to intervene. Liu Po-ch'en, Commander of the Second Field Army during the civil war (which placed him on an equal footing with Lin Piao, P'eng Te-huai, and Ch'en Yi, who commanded the other three field armies), was said to be among those opposed to China's participation in the war, on the grounds that such action would mean the diversion of resources originally committed to the taking of Taiwan and the indefinite postponement of that operation.[5]

Others are known to have feared that financing the war effort in Korea would have extremely damaging effects upon China's domestic economy. For example, Lung Yün, a former KMT leader who joined the Communists and became Vice Chairman of Peking's National Defense Council, spoke out during the 1957 Hundred Flowers campaign against the high costs of China's intervention.[6]

THE KAO-JAO CASE

The end of the Korean War, following Stalin's death, marked the beginning of more serious debates on policy matters. During that period, Party unity was again stressed, as it had been after earlier periods of internal dissension. The first signs of trouble came with Mao's campaign against the alleged "anti-Party bloc" of Kao Kang, Party leader in Manchuria, and against Jao Shu-Shih, who, as the organization chief of the Central Committee, was said to be in league with the "bloc." Kao Kang was accused of building a "small independent kingdom" in Manchuria under the influence of the Soviet Union. At least outwardly, the dispute also touched upon issues relative to the correct strategy for implementing the Communist program. Kao's organization of power in Manchuria was criticized for the extent to which it separated Party, military, government, and economic planning structures, all under the direction of a small clique at the top. Moreover, Kao's policy gave greater primacy to the technical and specialized elites, favoring greater independence of factory managers and a one-man managerial system. It endorsed a rapid industrialization program concentrated in his own region (Manchuria had an important industrial base left by the Japanese) and relied heavily on Soviet aid. As John W. Lewis points out, Party unity, mass-line operation, "investigation and research" by cadres, collective leadership, democratic centralism, and revolutionary vigor became the themes emphasized for the decade following the purge of Kao and Jao.[7]

The issue was perhaps further complicated by the Soviet role in Manchuria. In July, 1949, Kao had headed a regional delegation from Manchuria to Moscow and, in that capacity, had signed an agreement covering Soviet-Manchurian trade.[8] In any event, because of their personal stature in the Party, the Kao-Jao case was the first to involve leaders at the Politburo level. To the extent that Kao represented the interests of Manchuria, it was also the first open clash between regional and national interests on the policy plane.

MILITARY POLICY

With the end of the Korean and Indo-China conflicts, Peking's military attention was increasingly redirected from Northeast to Southeast and South Asia, because of both its desire to "liberate" Taiwan and the formation of the SEATO alliance. However, Peking's 1954 threat to attack Taiwan produced a counterthreat of nuclear retaliation from U.S. Secretary of State Dulles. At the same time, CCP leaders became painfully aware of Soviet reluctance to back the Chinese in such a military venture. The Taiwan issue exposed Peking to the realities of modern nuclear warfare and to the realization that its 1950 treaty of alliance with the Soviet Union did not mean that Moscow would support Peking's efforts to enlarge the territory under its control.

A period of top-level debate about defense politics ensued, in which a major question was whether mainland China would be subjected to a sudden attack, especially one involving nuclear weapons.[9] That issue was tied to another equally important strategic question: the relative priority of "socialist economic construction" and "national defense construction." [10] In other words, should there be more or less military spending? Determination of this question involved decisions as to whether the military should emphasize professionalism at the expense of politics or politics at the expense of professionalism—a dilemma best described by the phrase "red or expert." [11] The question also involved the relationship between the regular army—its structure and strategic doctrines—and a militia system designed to carry out a strategy of guerrilla warfare. It is not unlikely that Soviet strategic thinking during the period had some impact upon those Chinese military leaders who favored greater professionalism.[12] Marshall P'eng Te-huai, the regime's Defense Minister until relieved in 1959, was probably the chief advocate of professionalizing the Chinese army after the Soviet model.[13] Furthermore, Khrushchev's revised evaluation of the world's balance of forces, made public at the Twentieth Congress of the CPSU, also had repercussions in China. The new Soviet view that the growing strength of the forces of peace (meaning the Communist nations) had made a war with or by the "imperialists" no longer inevitable was, for example, endorsed in an article in the *People's Daily* by Chang Wen-t'ien, a Politburo member who served as Ambassador in Moscow from 1951 to 1954.[14]

The exact line or lines of division in the debate cannot be drawn with certitude, but by 1957 it had become clear that military spending had been reduced in favor of greater allocations for economic development and other purposes, although there was a continued interest in the military applications of technology.[15] Mao had openly acknowledged the growing importance of the "intermediate zone" or third camp, which included some capitalist countries not in league with the "imperialists" and non-aligned Afro-Asian states. He advocated peaceful coexistence with that intermediate zone but did not rule out the possibility of war with the "imperialists." Although Mao's continued hostility toward the latter has often been regarded as an exhortation to war, his rather cautious wording, on closer examination, suggests a fear lest an unprepared China become involved in a war with the "imperialists." Unity within the socialist camp and with like-minded revolutionaries was Mao's answer: "The strengthening of the unity of the world's proletariat will make the bellicose elements of the imperialists dare not risk [a war]. Therefore, no matter how hard the imperialists may resist these efforts [for peace], the forces of peace will eventually triumph over the forces of war." [16]

Mao's call for unity in the struggle against imperialism reflects an apprehension on his part that the Soviet Union would use the threat of U.S. nuclear deterrence as an excuse for not aiding Peking's contemplated "liberation" of Taiwan. He may also have feared that CCP endorsement of the Soviet view would jeopardize domestic morale. Block unity did not, on the other hand, mean subordination to Soviet primacy. At home, Mao wanted an ideologically purified army, supported by a ubiquitous militia system that could carry on guerrilla warfare.

It was not a coincidence that a rectification campaign was launched within the People's Liberation Army (PLA) in 1956–57, during which known advocates of military professionalism, including Liu Po-ch'en, were relieved. At the same time, the dismissal of Lo Juan-huan, Director of the PLA General Political Department, signaled a re-emphasis of ideological purity over technical competence, man over weapons, saving over spending.[17] A new call for egalitarianism and the primacy of ideology in the military was issued to correct the growing division between military commanders and political commissars, officers and men, soldiers and civilians, school education and troop training, and tactical requirements and technical training, and also to correct a spirit in which officers sought desk jobs instead of field commands. These inadequacies were said to have reached serious proportions as early as 1955.[18] The problems and debates were reflected in nonmilitary spheres as well.

FOREIGN POLICY

Although Peking's foreign policy has had alternating periods of "soft" and "hard" tactics,[19] it is even more difficult in this area than in others to ascribe a hard or soft line to a particular individual. The most striking feature of the evolution of Peking's foreign policy over the past two decades has been its shift from an initial strategy of dependence upon the Soviet Union and hostility toward the "imperialists" to an independent course of simultaneous hostility to both. Unquestionably, Peking's perception of the character of its relationship with Moscow has been the central cause of the evolution. Several basic questions have been raised in Peking's continuing debate about Sino-Soviet relations: Should China accept Soviet primacy in the Communist camp, or should it put its own interests first? Should Peking continue to seek a military solution to the question of Taiwan, or should it, in view of Soviet reluctance to support a military "liberation" of the island, attempt to negotiate a settlement with the United States? How should Peking respond to the U.S. mutual defense system encompassing Japan, South Korea, Taiwan, and South and Southeast Asia? Finally, and at a higher level of abstraction, was the world divided into two camps, as Stalin had claimed, partly to justify Soviet hegemony within the socialist bloc, or into three, which would allow greater room for independent action and maneuver by each Communist state in coping with both the nonaligned states and the "imperialists"? [20]

Without a doubt, 1954 was a crucial year for new decisions about the direction of Peking's foreign policy. Stalin had died in 1953, the conflicts in Korea and Indo-China had ended, and Peking's attention had shifted to Taiwan and Southeast Asia. The Kao Kang case was one harbinger of change. In 1948, shortly after the Comintern had expelled Yugoslavia for its independent avenue to socialism and insubordination to Moscow's leadership, Kao Kang had been outspoken in urging a selfless "internationalism" bordering on servitude to Soviet supremacy.[21] That same year, Liu Shao-ch'i also gave his unreserved support to "proletarian internationalism," stating: "We Chinese Communists are thorough proletarian internationalists." His statement, "Internationalism and Nationalism," was included, along with the speech of Kao Kang and others, in a small volume under the same title, which became required reading for all Chinese Communist Party members.[22] Mao's endorsement in 1949 of the Stalinist view that the world was divided into two hostile camps and his pro-Soviet posture of "leaning toward one side" may have been an attempt to outbid Kao Kang for Soviet favor as well as to calm Stalin's fear that Mao might become another Tito. The purge of Kao in 1954 thus indicated not only a decline of Soviet influence after

Stalin's death but also a possible rejection of Kao's brand of "internationalism." [23]

However, Kao Kang was probably not the only "traitor"; Chang Wen-t'ien's endorsement of Khrushchev's belief that war was no longer inevitable suggests that other CCP leaders may have preferred a closer alignment with Soviet policies than Mao was willing to consider after 1954. For example, one of the charges against Liu Shao-ch'i during the Cultural Revolution was that he had favored Soviet "revisionists" during the 1950's and sought to bring about a policy of greater friendship toward the Soviet Union.[24]

Whatever the implications of the Kao Kang case, several other considerations probably lay behind China's decision to pursue a softer foreign policy line in the mid-1950's. Peking's failure to change the status of Taiwan through military pressure in 1954, the rise of newly independent countries in Asia and Africa and their conference at Bandung in 1955, and the humiliation of European "imperialist" powers during the Suez crisis of 1956 may have led the CCP leadership to try to achieve through multilateral diplomacy what it had failed to achieve by military means and through reliance on the Soviet alliance. The fact that the "five principles of peaceful coexistence," which Peking applied to its relations with the Afro-Asian world, were considered by the Chinese Government to be "all the more" applicable to relations with Communist nations, suggests a de-emphasis of "proletarian internationalism." [25] Although it is not possible to examine the details of this complicated question here,[26] Mao's post-1954 advocacy of a more independent status for China apparently led to a redefinition of Sino-Soviet relations in his talks with Khrushchev in 1954 and 1958. Although the two negotiations were different in character, neither of the concluding communiques made any reference to "proletarian internationalism" (which had implications of Soviet "big-nation chauvinism" from Mao's point of view) but focused on equality and mutuality instead of Soviet primacy.[27]

The repercussions of Khrushchev's de-Stalinization speech and the Hungarian revolt in 1956 were among the foreign policy events that caused Peking to shift to a harder line in 1957–58. Although the Peking press initially endorsed Khrushchev's attacks on Stalin, a more guarded response soon followed. Although there is some evidence of support for a similar probing review within the CCP, Mao Tse-tung was probably opposed to it.[28] His reaction in "On the Dictatorship of the Proletariat" (April 5, 1956) was extremely ambivalent; he expressed a qualified approval of criticisms of Stalin's mistakes and a fear of possible damage to his own prestige at home.[29] In retrospect, this fear appears to have been justified. The Eighth Party Congress in September, 1956, adopted a new constitution in which the reference to the "thought of Mao Tse-tung," which had appeared in the 1945 Constitution, was dropped. Red Guard literature in 1966 laid the omission to an alleged anti-Mao conspiracy led by P'eng Te-huai and Liu Shao-ch'i.[30]

Mao's reaction to the Soviet intervention in Hungary, however, was emphatically negative. In "More on the Dictatorship of the Proletariat" (December 29, 1956), he described the invasion as a manifestation of "big-nation chauvinism" and qualified his support for proletarian internationalism by calling attention to the need for greater respect for the sovereignty of the weaker Communist states.[31]

Mao's ambivalence toward Khrushchev's attack on the Stalinist cult of personality was not necessarily a sign of Mao's defense of all aspects of Stalinism, however, particularly in the case of Stalin's foreign policy. In 1957, Mao rejected Stalin's earlier bipolar world view, probably in an attempt to halt domestic debates on the matter. Moreover, in his important "On the Correct Handling of Contradictions Among the People" (February 27, 1957), Mao envisioned a tripolar world in proposing three basic guidelines for Communist China's foreign policy: First, China must join in solidarity with nations of the socialist bloc. Second, it must empathize and align with the "peace-loving" Afro-Asian countries and peoples. And third, it must strive for an understand-

ing with the people in the "imperialist" countries, practice peaceful coexistence with those countries, and prevent the possible
outbreak of wars. Of course, Peking must never entertain any "unrealistic ideas" about the imperialists." [32] This reformulation
implied that Soviet supremacy within the socialist camp was no
longer justifiable (if it ever had been), that Peking would have
to rely on its own resources in any future confrontation with
American military power, and that the Soviet Union could not
be trusted to honor its alliance with China in the event of a war
between China and the "imperialists." Thus, Mao anticipated the
role of foreign policy differences in the later deterioration of Sino-
Soviet relations, although disagreements on domestic policy also
played an important role in the dispute.

THE CORRECT STRATEGY FOR ACHIEVING SOCIALISM

Many crucial problems surrounded decisions about the precise
programs for socialist transformation and eventual socialist construction. For example, how soon should socialization of agriculture follow land redistribution? How long a transition should there
be between public-private joint ownership and the final, complete
socialization of industry? To what extent should China depend upon
Soviet capital and assistance? What should China do if the Soviet
Union curtailed or terminated such aid? What role should the
technocrats play vis-à-vis the Party cadres in economic and tech-
nological development? Since a large percentage of the technocrats had a bourgeois social background and were not members of
the Communist Party, what policy should the Party adopt regarding their absorption into the system and the efficient use of their
skills and knowledge? Would the Party's dependence on the non-
Party technocrats and resultant concessions to them, such as
limited property ownership and other special privileges, compromise its socialization program? Should the planning and management of economic development, in both agriculture and industry,
be centralized in Peking or decentralized to the provincial level
and below? Would not centralization result in greater bureaucrati-

zation of the Party and a loss of its revolutionary spirit? If decentralization were adopted, how could the Party prevent any repetition of the pre-1954 phenomenon of regional "small kingdoms"? More specifically, should more resources be allocated to agriculture or to industry, to consumer goods or to heavy industry? In agriculture, should mechanization or the mobilization of human labor resources be stressed? How should the Party organize the masses to support its gigantic efforts to modernize the nation, not only technologically, economically, and politically, but also in achieving a new proletarian way of life and value system? Should development efforts be launched all at once on all fronts, or should they be directed at a selected number of targets at any given time? Should all the initial fruits of labor be reinvested into the economy, or should the people be permitted to enjoy some rise in their standard of living and, if so, how much? [33]

Although the options must have been as varied as the problems, I shall discuss them in a sort of shorthand form. The "Kao Kang" model, for example, was probably patterned on Soviet experience and relied heavily on Soviet assistance, while the "Ch'en Yün plan" seems to have favored a more balanced growth at a moderate pace.[34] Mao's ambitious policies prevailed in most cases, but their adoption in the Politburo was not without dissent and, at times, serious struggle. For example, in 1955 Mao was probably one of a few who advocated accelerating agricultural cooperativization, while many others, including Teng Tzu-hui, Vice Premier and Director of the Rural Work Department of the CCP Central Committee, and Li Fu-ch'ün, Vice Premier and Chairman of the State Planning Commission, were openly in favor of the prevailing moderate pace.[35] After Mao's policy of acceleration was finally adopted by the Central Committee in October, Ch'en Yi remarked that the report Mao had made in July to an unprecedented conference of provincial Party secretaries "had settled the *debate of the past three years.*" [36]

Mao himself called 1955 "the year of decision in the struggle

between socialism and capitalism," in which "a raging tidal wave
has swept away all the demons and ghosts." [37] The assertion anticipated the extravagant language that was to be used during the
Cultural Revolution more than a decade later.[38] Red Guard literature in 1966 accused Liu Shao-ch'i of having opposed Mao's agricultural program back in 1955.[39] While such accusations are not
entirely reliable, they nevertheless confirm Ch'en Yi's allusion to
the existence of a policy debate. When Mao's policy of acceleration succeeded, a number of erstwhile "rightists," including Li
Hsien-nien, Vice Premier and Minister of Finance, admitted past
errors of "empiricism." Others, like Po Yi-po, Vice Premier and
Chairman of the State Economic Commission, conceded that
Mao's policy had been correct.[40]

Mao's triumph of 1955 was not repeated in 1956, however, possibly because of the reluctance of the CCP bureaucracy to
accept his desire to increase the pace of agricultural socialization
in an even more ambitious twelve-year program, the "1956–67
National Program of Agricultural Development."

The difficulties that Mao had with the Party bureaucracy in
1956 need reinterpretation in the light of events a decade
later. During the Cultural Revolution in 1966–67, Mao used the
Red Guards, an extra-Party force, to overthrow opposition to his
policies within the top Party hierarchy. Is it possible that Mao
also intended to exploit the discontent of the non-Party intellectuals during the dramatic but brief Hundred Flowers campaign
in 1957, in order to exert pressure upon the Party bureaucracy
to implement his policies more energetically? The 1957 literature on rectifying the Party's "working style" also needs reap-
praisal in the light of recent history. Several points in Mao's
"On the Correct Handling of Contradictions Among the People"
(February 27, 1957) merit a new look.

In the first place, why did Mao deliver this important speech
at an enlarged session of the Supreme State Conference, an institution that supposedly bridged Party and non-Party groups, rather

than within a major organ of the Party itself? Second, why was the speech not published until June, and then only in what was generally believed to be a revised version? Had there been any serious opposition within the Party to Mao's willingness to permit criticism from outside the Party? Did the power-holders of 1957 fear Mao's invitation to the non-Party intellectuals as much as they feared his summoning of the Red Guards a decade later? Did they attempt to tone down his Hundred Flowers campaign, just as they later sought to restrain the Red Guards? In any event, when Mao's speech finally did appear in print, the invitation to outside critics was a strictly limited one, although the harshness of the criticisms that had appeared between February and June probably also made such restrictions necessary. The fact that the speech dealt with twelve topics, all of which were directly or indirectly related to the question of the "correct" approach to socialist development, confirms the importance of that issue within top Party councils. Mao's classification of all twelve topics under the rubric of the correct handling of contradictions suggests a propensity on his part to sublimate personality or policy differences by transforming them into ideological contradictions needing rectification, on the assumption that an ideological purification would resolve policy disputes. Since these contradictions existed *among* the people, rather than *between* the people and the enemy, they were "nonantagonistic" in nature and could be resolved through the peaceful process of "unity, criticism, and unity." The method drew upon the experience of the 1942 rectification campaign, as Mao explicitly stated in the speech. He claimed that the method had succeeded in unifying the Party in 1945, the year, it is to be noted, in which the "thought of Mao Tse-tung" was codified into the guiding principles of the Party Constitution. Mao's call for a return to unity through ideological purification was an implicit admission of the lack of Party unity. In 1957, unlike 1942, however, non-Party circles were allowed to express their criticisms, perhaps with the thought that a general catharsis would do everyone some good. If so, the 1957 campaign heralded similar practices during the Cultural Revolution nine years later.

In the same speech, Mao referred to a "small typhoon" blowing over the Party's (i.e., Mao's) intensified collectivization program in the countryside. In the past, observers thought that he meant peasant opposition, but it could have been actually an allusion to policy debates among CCP leaders themselves. At another point in the speech, Mao argued that "democracy" and "freedom" were not absolutes but were values relative to "centralism" and "discipline." Both, he stressed, were means to an end, but not an end in themselves; both must "serve the economic base" in the course of historical development. Mao's concern with the development of the economic base and with centralism and discipline may reflect an early measure of disillusionment with a bureaucracy that had become less obedient to his thinking and whose revolutionary spirit was declining as it sought to preserve and expand its own interests at the expense of large revolutionary goals. The widening gaps between the goals of Mao's "permanent revolution" and the backsliding bureaucracy he depended upon to carry it out were thus defined by Mao as "contradictions among the people." His efforts to revive the revolutionary *élan* and his call for continued personal sacrifice anticipated the Great Leap Forward and greater contradictions to come. The effort to impose ideological solutions on policy questions was already characteristic of Mao's governing style in the 1950's.

10

THE GREAT LEAP FORWARD AND ITS AFTERMATH

THE ECONOMIC decisions made by the Chinese Communist Party in 1956–57 had a crucial impact on mainland Chinese politics for the next decade. Maoist literature in 1966–68 linked the Cultural Revolution to dissensions within the Party that began with the Great Leap.[1] In 1956, the First Five Year Plan was approaching its end, and the search for a new plan followed two mediocre harvests in a row. The speed-up of agricultural collectivization in 1955–56 and the increased level of industrial investment during the same period had created new strains and bottlenecks calling for a more coordinated strategy. The economic problems had their sociopolitical parallels throughout the country following the failure of the Hundred Flowers movement. Ideally, the new strategy would simultaneously develop industry and agriculture without sacrificing one for the other.

During 1956–57, Peking also faced major decisions about the development of an independent nuclear program and about how the economy could set aside the enormous funds necessary for such efforts. Chinese interest had been drawn to the field of nuclear science even before 1955, but Peking did not attach much urgency to acquiring its own nuclear capability until 1957. The deteriorating Sino-Soviet discord by then had raised serious doubts in Mao's mind about Moscow's reliability as an ally and an effective nuclear guarantor.

Although a general agreement on "new technology for national defense" was signed with Moscow on October 15, 1957, and further negotiation about the details continued until June, 1959, it soon became evident that Moscow was not going to give Peking "a sample of an atomic bomb and technical data concerning its manufacture," as Peking claimed it had promised to do.[2] The crucial issues obstructing progress toward Sino-Soviet nuclear sharing probably concerned Soviet control of the warheads and other weapons it supplied, measures of joint planning and joint command,[3] the question of remodeling the Chinese People's Liberation Army (PLA) to meet the needs of the nuclear age, and assurances that Peking would not unilaterally embark upon military adventures in the Taiwan Strait, which was patrolled by the U.S. Seventh Fleet.[4]

In view of the 1968 Soviet charges ("Leninist Policy of the U.S.S.R. in Relation to China")[5] that Mao had deliberately provoked the 1958 Taiwan crisis in an attempt to precipitate a Soviet-U.S. confrontation, it seems clear that Peking's strategic thinking during 1956–58 was dominated by the problem of manipulating its alliance with the U.S.S.R. to exert pressure on the United States in the Taiwan Strait area. The Soviet refusal to back Communist China in a confrontation with the United States over Taiwan probably convinced Mao that Peking would have to rely on its own resources in "liberating" the island and may have given him one additional reason to initiate a total self-reliance program.

In was in this complex tangle of economic, sociopolitical, and military problems that the Great Leap Forward strategy was formulated. Mao, its principal architect, stubbornly greeted the dismal array of problems with the indomitable spirit that had sustained him during past guerrilla struggles. Quite typically, instead of retrenching in 1957–58, he chose to rely on the masses to move forward decisively, just as he would do again in 1966–68. Mao's faith in the potential and strength of the masses distinguished him from his colleagues.[6]

The adoption by the Central Committee of Mao's Great Leap

Forward program in August, 1958, signified the defeat of other programs that had been under consideration. Until October, 1957, a more moderate approach identified with Ch'en Yün had seemed to be in favor among members of the Central Committee.[7] Mao's triumph ten months later was probably no more easily won than his 1955 victory on collectivization. His vigorous advocacy of the Great Leap Forward could not help but result in his personal identification with the program; its dismal failure would cast long shadows on Mao's claim to be the ultimate spokesman for the CCP's ideology.

Mao's Rationale for the Great Leap Forward

The Great Leap Forward actually incorporated three separate but related campaigns, which were launched in the summer of 1958. Known in CCP jargon as the "three red banners," they comprised: (1) the "general line" for building socialism, which established a broad ideological perspective based on the concept of permanent revolution; (2) the Great Leap Forward, calling for rapid industrial progress; and (3) the People's Communes, a counterpart of the Great Leap applied to agriculture. Enmeshed in the commune program was the Everyone-a-Soldier Movement, designed to boost the strength and resources of the PLA by a ubiquitous militia system in which the peasant masses received military training during their spare time.

The program reflected Mao's total dissatisfaction and impatience with the rate of progress at home and with the Soviet economic model and Soviet aid as a solution to China's spiraling needs.[8] It also reflected a mood of optimism that greater progress could be achieved by moral-psychological mobilization and by ideological purification where material incentives were lacking. In Mao's view, Ch'en Yün's approach, which favored material incentives and decentralization of economic planning and control to the provincial level, would greatly curtail the level of reinvestment and overburden the Party bureaucracy, since provincial administration was dominated by the Party.[9] Mao wanted to skip the normal steps of economic and social advance by utilizing to the fullest China's abundant manpower and supposedly boundless enthusiasm. His strategy, in essence, substituted "spiritual" (ideological) incentives for material ones and extended decentralization down to the primary level, in order to give lower-middle and poor peasant masses greater initiative. Decentralization to the primary level would reduce the influence of the rich peasants and the Party bureaucracy and would mean that Mao's ideological directives could reach the masses without passing through the various levels of the Party's hierarchy. Mao's program thus had political as well as economic implications, a point that did not become clear until the Cultural Revolution.

In agriculture, relying heavily on mass mobilization, the Great Leap sought to achieve three principal ends: (1) an increase in productive capacity through labor-intensive investment projects, such as irrigation and soil conservation, flood control, and land reclamation; (2) an increase in agricultural unit yield through closer planting techniques, more careful weeding, and other expedients; and (3) the rapid expansion of small industry. A central feature was that the growth of the rural sector (now organized in communes) would be based largely on its own output and investment. In industry, the program stressed the simultaneous development of the more or less traditional small-scale, labor-intensive sector and the modern large-scale, capital-intensive sector. This dual approach came to be graphically described as "walking on two legs." [10]

The Program, a kind of autarky, was symbolized by the slogan *tzu-li keng-sheng*, which, though often translated as self-reliance, meant the decentralization of planning and management to the primary level. In view of later Chinese charges that the Soviet Union never fulfilled the 1957 nuclear agreement and scrapped it altogether in 1959,[11] the slogan of self-reliance had international implications and anticipated the eventual withdrawal of Soviet aid. Because of wide regional variations in the rural sector, the idea of self-reliance was tied to another principle, *yin-ti chih-yi* (adaptation to local conditions), which in practice meant roughly "the best for and out of each locality." It authorized the practice of economic "verticalization" (or "vertical integration")—the multiplication or diversification of investment by an economic unit, a commune or a super-enterprise, to achieve self-sufficiency. The practice would cut the cost of transporting goods and materials from other regions. Economic decentralization was accompanied by political decentralization under the slogan *ch'üan-li hsia-fang* (downward transfer of authority and power), to transfer initiative from a cumbersome and sometimes self-seeking bureaucracy to the masses in a gigantic mass mobilization drive. The communes were to be the institutional form for the transfer of political and economic initiative and for the all-out mobilization of human resources.[12]

Although the purposes of the Great Leap Forward were sound, it was launched too fast, with too little preparation (even within the Party itself), and with too much pressure for the overachievement of targets. Its very complexity may have been due, in part, to the need to incorporate various other development programs that had been proposed during the deliberations of the Central Committee. But there is scarcely any doubt that the stress on mass mobilization was Mao's. The successful implementation of the program, however, would have required a combination of preconditions: the enthusiasm of the masses and their willingness to submit to strict controls on their consumption for purposes of capital formation; unfailing leadership at all levels, including the provincial and primary levels; and full mobilization of the masses on an unprecedented scale, to provide the badly needed labor force. Deficiencies in any of those preconditions would endanger the program, and there were deficiencies in all of them.

Mao's optimism about the prospects for the Great Leap Forward was rooted in certain assumptions that are inseparable from his preoccupation with *szu-hsiang* as the ultimate determinant of action. The first was that ideological purification could change humanity and create the "socialist man," who requires little material incentive, leads an ascetic life, and places the interests of the community ahead of his own. Such purification would assure a universally low standard of personal consumption that would be conducive to capital accumulation.

A second assumption was that productivity could be raised not only by capital-intensive investment in the modern sector, although its importance was not denied by the Maoists, but also by labor-intensive projects involving a large number of compact production units organized and run by the masses themselves. This was at the heart of Mao's "mass line," as applied to production, and probably reflected Mao's distrust of technical and professional competence that was not guided by "correct" ideology.

Third, Mao believed that significant progress could result from a mass assault on a given number of production objectives, such as iron works, small fertilizer plants, and other enterprises, at a given time. Such a specific approach actually anticipated unbalanced growth in the short run, a pattern of growth that has sometimes been described by Western economists as an application of Mao's guerrilla war tactics to the economic sphere. It also recalls Mao's conception of the wavelike motion of socialist construction. A series of great leaps forward would be followed by periods of consolidation and adjustment. Thus, the rhythmic progression of "unity, struggle, and unity" characterized not only the resolution of contradictions in the natural and human worlds but the process of economic production as well.[13]

The most crucial of the three assumptions was Mao's faith in the power of mind over matter. Mass mobilization and the inculcation of a revolutionary ideology were, to Mao, the best ways to bring that power to bear on material conditions,[14] the implicit disdain for professional knowledge resulted in many blunders, such as the revival of the ancient practice of leaving a third of the land fallow to combat the shortage of chemical fertilizers. As a result, some 300 million mou of land lay idle, according to an official report. The enthusiastic construction of backyard blast furnaces by the masses led to the waste, misuse, and shortage of labor and fuel. These and other grandiose projects created a general labor shortage, reaching 50 per cent in some areas during the fall harvest season and resulting in great crop losses.[15] In their zeal to overfulfill the production quotas, the masses and cadres often sacrificed quality for quantity. By the Party's own admission in April, 1960, there were leaks in no less than 40 to 60 per cent of the canals constructed during the Great Leap Forward. Widespread padding of production figures paralyzed the entire statistical reporting system.[16] Even Han Suyin, with her unabashed sympathy for the Chinese Communist regime, has admitted that an overreaction to Party directives produced a kind of "mass hysteria." [17]

Although it is not possible to examine the technical details of the Great Leap Forward here, Mao's excessive reliance on psychic mobilization did have negative effects on the economy. His optimism about the potential productive capacity of the masses, when mobilized, led him to gamble on a strategy of "instant Communism." [18] The program's emphasis on simultaneous leaps on more than one front, based on the belief that a "correct" ideology could overcome material obstacles, almost sealed its fate from the start. In the end, however ironically, the strategy built upon bold assumptions regarding the power of man's will succumbed to human frailty.

The Aftermath of the Great Leap Forward

THE PURGE OF P'ENG TE-HUAI

On December 10, 1958, after Mao had offered to step down as the Chairman (President) of the People's Republic following the failure of the Great Leap Forward, the Central Committee adopted a resolution that generally reflected the prevailing mood and foreshadowed the course of events for the next few years. In the light of our present knowledge, it is apparent that the Wuhan

Resolution, as it is known, represented a compromise among conflicting opinions. The greater part of it was meant to curb or modify Mao's original excessive optimism or, in the harsh language of P'eng Te-huai, his "petty-bourgeois fanaticism." [19] The bulk of the resolution called for moderation in the pace of communalization, easing of the restrictions on private ownership, relaxation of the military discipline introduced into commune life, and stricter discipline among the cadres responsible for the execution of the Great Leap Forward programs. The Resolution covered the retreat with a masterpiece of euphemism, describing the Great Leap Forward program as "fresh as the morning sun above the broad horizon of East Asia." [20] Partly because of such flourishes, the outside world remained largely unaware of China's internal dissensions until the mid-1960's.

The most outspoken critic of the Great Leap Forward was probably P'eng Te-huai, who launched a lengthy attack on Mao's policy at the Lushan Plenum of the Central Committee in August, 1959.[21] Lacking information until the mid-1960's, Western observers often linked P'eng's subsequent dismissal to his disagreements with Mao on military and foreign policy.[22] In the light of recent revelations, however, it seems that P'eng's criticisms were much broader and were aimed at Mao's political and economic as well as military policies.[23] Among other things, P'eng attacked Mao's cult of *szu-hsiang*, as embodied in the "politics in command" formula. "Putting politics in command," asserted P'eng, who was then a member of the Standing Committee of the Central Committee's Politburo as well as Minister of Defense, "is no substitute for economic principles, still less for concrete measures in economic work. *Equal importance* must be attached to putting politics in command and to effective measures in economic work; neither can be neglected." Insinuating that Mao's hasty program smacked of "Left" deviationism, P'eng said that it would be more difficult to correct Left manifestations than Right conservative tendencies.[24]

One of the accusations against P'eng Te-huai in the Maoist

literature during the Cultural Revolution was that he had had "dealings" with Khrushchev during the 1950's.[25] P'eng may have favored closer relations with the Soviet Union for both military and economic reasons. Without the Soviet nuclear umbrella, China would have to develop its own nuclear program; and without Soviet aid, such an independent course would be extremely costly and would impose harsh sacrifices on the economy in general. Greater reliance on the Soviet Union for nuclear support as well as economic aid, on the other hand, would have avoided those hardships. If P'eng's policy had been adopted, it would have entailed the professionalization of the PLA—to make it capable of handling the nuclear armaments supplied by Moscow—and the possible absorption of China into the Warsaw Pact and COMECON systems.[26] It would also have obviated hasty measures of economic stringency and brought about a reconsideration of Mao's self-reliant military strategy, his emphasis on a militia system and preparation for guerrilla warfare. The crucial disagreement between P'eng and Mao lay, therefore, in their differing estimates of the reliability of the Soviet Union as a benevolent source of sustained economic aid and as a guarantor of China's security against nuclear attack. In this sense, the debates linked economic, political, and military considerations in a complex nexus of decision-making. P'eng may have sought Khrushchev's support in his opposition to Mao's policies, as crystallized in the Great Leap Forward. Certainly, any unauthorized contacts between P'eng and Khrushchev for this purpose would have infuriated Mao and contributed to the widening of the Sino-Soviet split, with its repercussions on the whole range of Peking's domestic and foreign policy.[27]

Although P'eng was soon dismissed from office and obliged to admit his mistakes before the Eighth Plenum of the Eighth Central Committee of the CCP in August, 1959, he may have expressed a dissent shared by many other Central Committee members.[28] Possibly in response to that dissent, the Central Committee decided on August 26, 1959, to scale down future production targets and to admit that previously announced production figures for 1958–59 had been exaggerated.[29] The purge of P'eng ushered in the 1959 "anti-rightist" campaign against Party functionaries who presumably shared P'eng's dissenting views. The main thrust of Mao's counterattack in that campaign was that the "rightists" had disparaged the efforts of the people, denied that the tasks of. "revolutionary construction" were within the competence of the masses, criticized the mass movements without participating in them, discredited the achievements of the Great Leap, magnified its drawbacks, and shirked responsibilities and tasks that were objectively possible.[30]

The dismissal of P'eng Te-huai led to Lin Piao's appointment as Minister of Defense and placed Lin in charge of the Central Committee's powerful Military Affairs Commission. Lin's selection enabled Mao to maintain control of the People's Liberation Army while his grip on the civilian Party bureaucracy was slipping. Mao's withdrawal from the presidency of the People's Republic, however, only led to a period of greater routinization under Liu Shao-ch'i, who succeeded in 1959 to the office vacated by Mao.

Liu Shao-ch'i's "NEP"

Upon assuming the Presidency in 1959, Liu began to reduce the size of the communes, place ceilings on peasant production quotas, and reintroduce personal incentives and private farm plots in a series of liberalization moves. Those measures probably had the support of many Central Committee members, although they became increasingly objectionable to Mao and his followers during the early 1960's. Anticipated to some extent by the Wuhan Resolution of December, 1958, Liu's liberalization policy was confirmed by the "Sixty Articles" adopted by the Central Committee in 1961.[31]

Between 1959 and 1962, Liu's liberalization was notable for the greater emphasis on cost-consciousness and profitability (for financial soundness) than on output goals in state enterprises, increased regional and local freedom in fixing production goals, greater material incentives for the workers, more independent managerial authority, tolerance of an "open market," and the subordination of "redness" to expertise. For a time, the more liberal policy was identified in the West as Liu's "NEP," recalling the New Economic Policy that Lenin had introduced in the early 1920's after the period of War Communism in the Soviet Union.[32] As a general rule, Liu's "NEP" was guided more by the demands of the market and the consumer than by the strong will of the planner. The emphasis on production in quantity, which had dominated the thinking of the preceding period, was now tempered with a consciousness of quality and "profit" factors. To the Maoists, however, Liu's policy of putting "economics in command" was at best distorted and at worst heretical. Whatever the Maoists said later, Liu's liberalization of 1959–61 was a matter more of expediency than of mercy. As an individual and a Party leader Liu was known for his ruthlessness, which became visible during the reorganization of the Party in the early 1960's. Although it was generally recognized that there was an urgent need to revitalize a demoralized Party bureaucracy,[33] Liu demanded strict punitive or disciplinary action against corrupt cadres, while Mao tended to stress the need for ideological rectification and to emphasize the role of the masses as a counterweight to the role of the Party.

A series of measures introduced between the end of 1960 and the spring of 1961 were directed specifically at the corrupt practices of the basic-level cadres in the communes, such as embezzlement and the appropriation of peasant belongings. Basic-level cadres were ordered to correct tendencies of "commandism," to study Party directives more conscientiously, and to subject themselves to greater Party discipline. They were also directed to defer to people with technical skills and to efface themselves generally. Just as expertise took priority over "redness," centralized discipline was placed above local discretion, reversing the decentralization of authority that had been prescribed during the Great Leap Forward.[34] Although Mao's specific role during this period is unclear, such measures were probably part of Liu's over-all effort to revitalize Party activity in cells and committees at all levels. Greater discipline was enforced with improved communication channels. While the cadres were urged to promote "democratization" in their dealings with the masses, the role of the Party secretary was enhanced from the primary level up. In 1960, the structure and functions of the Party's control commissions were expanded and the Central Committee's six regional bureaus were reinstituted to act as the eyes and ears of the Party.[35]

Party reorganization was apparently related to Liu's liberalization policies in the economic sphere. But it may also reflect Liu's stress on *organizational* discipline, i.e., greater reliance on institutional checks and controls through the Party's structural channels, in sharp contrast to Mao's emphasis on "correct" ideology and reliance on the masses. By 1962, Liu's recentralization drive appeared to have solidified his control of the Party apparatus. An enlarged "work conference" of the Central Committee in January, 1962, assembled some 7,000 Party officials, many of them from provincial and *hsien* levels. A number of them expressed harsh criticisms of the Great Leap Forward, but only Lin Piao and Chou En-lai among the top leaders were reported to have come to Mao's defense.[36]

Party directives from Peking in 1960–62 warned Party officials throughout the country that they should not subordinate organizational principles (*tsu-chih*) to ideological ones (*szu-hsiang*). In at least one instance, it was clearly implied that *tsu-chih* took precedence over *szu-hsiang*.[37] In January, 1961, the Ninth Plenum of the Central Committee authorized a new rectification campaign to continue the purge of primary-level cadres begun by Liu in 1960. Although it paid lip service to Mao's 1959 "anti-rightist" campaign, the Plenum's decision probably represented Liu's continuing effort to consolidate his organizational command. There is some circumstantial evidence for this conclusion in the rehabilitation of many "rightists" (who shared Liu's views).[38] As Liu was to admit in his "self-criticism" before a Central Committee "work meeting" on November 23, 1966, at which Mao presided, he had recommended to Chairman Mao in 1962 that Ch'en Yün, who then held no official post, be made head of the Central Committee's finance division.[39] Ch'en is known to have opposed the Great Leap Forward and to have been the principal architect of Liu's economic rationalization policies. His rejection by Mao was a foregone conclusion. The very fact that Liu, as he admitted in his self-criticism, had consulted Ch'en about the state's financial crisis in 1962 and had even attempted to appoint Ch'en to an important post seems to substantiate subsequent Maoist allegations that Liu was aiding the "rightists" who sought a review of their cases during 1960–62.[40]

It is worth noting that rehabilitation of the "rightists" was anathema to Mao because it insinuated a tacit admission that the critics of the Great Leap had been right. Their rehabilitation not only would encourage the adoption of the "rightist" policies Mao opposed but also, even worse, would force the issue of the Chairman's ideological infallibility and prescience, on which he based his claim to leadership. Liu was said to have insisted in 1961 that criticisms of Mao, aired within the Party councils, did not constitute an anti-Party crime so long as they incurred no international complications.[41] Liu was even alleged to have said in 1963 that "Marx, Engels, Lenin, Stalin, and Chairman Mao all made mistakes." [42] There is perhaps some substance also in more recent Maoist charges that Liu Shao-ch'i's omission of any reference to the "thought of Mao Tse-tung" in the 1962 edition of his one-time CCP classic, *On the Self-Cultivation of a Communist* (sometimes translated as *How to Be a Good Communist*), was a deliberate affront.[43]

The conflicts that arose out of the decision to undertake the Great Leap Forward, and the decision to retreat when the Great Leap failed, appear to have involved more than a power struggle or a personality clash. A few fundamental questions seem to have been raised: Should the initiative for social progress reside with the ideologically motivated masses or with the Party bureaucracy, or both? Should the "thought of Mao Tse-tung" take precedence over the Party apparatus, or vice versa? Should Party officials lead the masses more through institutional channels of control or through ideological motivation? Should the society be more clearly stratified according to functional roles, even at the expense of excessive bureaucratization, or should it develop a more egalitarian structure, continuing the earlier guerrilla warfare tradition? Should the Party bureaucracy be faithful to utopian goals and continue to enforce a puritanical discipline upon the masses, or should it respond more readily to their immediate material needs, even at the price of postponing the achievement of the ultimate goals of the revolution? Needless to say, such questions involved strategic decisions about the wisdom and feasibility of an independent nuclear capability (as opposed to dependence upon Soviet weapons) and economic decisions about the cost of an independent nuclear program. Beyond them lay a more abstract issue: Who should determine what for whom, by what right, for what purpose, and how? Later events suggest that Mao conceived of the answers to these questions in terms of four general formulas: (1) Ideological-psychic mobilization is more important for the nation than routinization or bureaucratization, if the rapid achievement of revolutionary goals is not to be compromised; (2) revolutionary education must be carried on in all aspects of the people's life to sustain the momentum of a "permanent revolution"; (3) common goals (including China's nuclear technology) must take precedence over the interests of any class, including the Party bureaucracy, although after 1966 the "interests of the proletariat," however defined, were increasingly regarded as synonymous with those of the society at large; and (4), since all forms of micro-development must give way to macro-development, just as economics must yield to politics and the individual to the society, a Party bureaucracy that has stopped being selflessly devoted to the attainment of the society's goals (as conceived by Mao) can no longer base its claim to status upon its professed ability to lead in goal attainment. In that case, the existing Party bureaucracy must be subjected to the scathing criticism of the society at large, for which the proletariat is to serve as spokesman, and forced to abdicate in favor of a revitalized Party that can live up to the expectations of the masses.[44]

Those four tenets, which have come to dominate Mao's view of Chinese society and the role of the Party, were not shared by other Party leaders, including Liu Shao-ch'i, after 1959.[45] The conflicts between the two principal schools of thought, rightly or wrongly identified in the current usage as Maoist and anti-Maoist, smoldered from the late 1950's through the Socialist Education Movement of 1962–65 and eventually flared into the Cultural Revolution.

11

PRELUDE TO
THE CULTURAL REVOLUTION

The Origins of the Socialist Education Campaign

DISTINCT POLICY differences broadly identified with Mao Tse-tung
and Liu Shao-ch'i, which came into sharp focus in the post-1958
era, set in motion a smoldering political struggle with ideological overtones. Against the background of those policy disputes,
other hard issues came to the surface during the 1962–65 Socialist
Education campaign. The central points of contention prior to
1962 were Liu's policy of rationalization and his emphasis on
organization in preference to ideology. Here, Liu had the support
of the Party machine he controlled; its prevailing mood was best
summed up by the Central Committee's Secretary-General, Teng
Hsiao-p'ing: "Private farming is all right, so long as it raises
output, just as it doesn't matter whether the cat is black or white,
so long as it catches mice." [1] The policy permitting private plots,
free markets, and small private enterprises and laying down production quotas (known as the "three freedoms and one guarantee") had, by 1962, given rise to a new rich-peasant economy.
That result, and the philosophy behind it, soon alarmed Mao,
whose frequent absences from Peking had apparently enabled
the Liu-Teng group to exercise considerable discretion. Mao
claimed that private ownership and independent entrepreneur-
ship had greatly weakened the collective economy and threatened

the well-being of the poor and lower-middle peasants. He charged that the "old bourgeois elements" that had survived, plus a new class of landlords and rich peasants, were engaged in usury, speculation, profiteering, and exploitation of the hired labor they had recruited from the poor and lower-middle peasant classes.[2]

When Mao returned to Peking in the summer of 1962, he sought to arrest the trend of economic individualism, to stop cadre corruption, and to reinvigorate the collective economy. The decisions adopted by the Central Committee at its Tenth Plenum in September, 1962, bore the imprint of Mao's views. The Plenum called for an all-out attack on "revisionism" and renewed emphasis on class struggle. Ideological discipline again officially took priority over organizational rigidity. To help break down that rigidity, an interchange of senior personnel between Party and state bureaucracies was ordered.[3] Mao sought to reassert his own effective command by terminating, after seventeen years, the previous two-line division of responsibility, under which he had delegated to Liu authority for day-to-day operations and retained only broad decision-making power.[4] To implement the call for class struggle, the Socialist Education Movement was launched. It represented the merging of three closely interwoven campaigns: a rural educational campaign directed at the broad non-Party masses, the urban *wu-fan* (five-antis) campaign against bourgeois elements and attitudes, and the *ssu-ch'ing* (four-cleans) campaign against rural Party cadres. These were either supported by or dovetailed with a number of other campaigns: the formation of associations of poor and lower-middle peasants, with which Mao had first experimented in 1960–62; "Learn from the PLA," started in 1963; the *chieh-pan-jen* campaign to train a new generation of revolutionary youth and thus prevent the "peaceful evolution" that Roger Hilsman, then U.S. Assistant Secretary of State, had predicted in a speech on December 13, 1963; and the "Creatively Learn and Apply the Thought of Mao Tsetung" campaign, launched in 1965.[5]

The many-faceted Socialist Education Movement thus spanned

a critical four-year period. It began with Mao's return to active public life in 1962 and ended with the publication in late 1965 of Yao Wen-yan's scathing attack on the controversial *Hai Jui Dismissed from Office*, a historical play sharply satirizing Mao's purge of P'eng Te-huai.

The multiplicity of documents issued by the Central Committee to guide the conduct of the Socialist Education campaign suggests the extent of the ideological disagreement that eventually contributed to its failure and led to the Cultural Revolution. The first such document was the "Resolution on Some Problems in Current Rural Work (Preliminary)," issued on May 20, 1963. Known subsequently as the "early ten points," it laid down general instructions regarding the Socialist Education campaign and the "four-cleans" (a drive to clean up irregularities in account books, granaries, property-holding, and the work-point system in the communes). In September, 1963, the resolution was supplemented by "Some Concrete Policy Formulations in the Rural Socialist Education Movement," which came to be known as the "later ten points." A later version, the "revised later ten points," was issued on September 10, 1964. Still another directive, "Some Problems Currently Arising in the Course of the Rural Socialist Education Movement," or the "twenty-three articles," was made public on January 14, 1965. The "twenty-three articles" repudiated aspects of the "later ten points" and the prevailing regulations on peasant associations, giving a clear impression that it was designed to correct erroneous tendencies in the earlier documents.[6]

Prior to the Cultural Revolution, students of the Socialist Education period attributed the conflicting Central Committee directives to vacillation and fluctuating opinion among Central Committee leaders. It was only after the Eleventh Plenum of the Central Committee in 1966 that the real reasons for the shifts became known. Maoists dominated that session. The Plenum's official communiqué of August 12, 1966, explicitly singled out the "early ten points" and the "twenty-three articles" as the two documents "formulated under the direction of Chairman Mao" that would continue to guide the country's "socialist revolution" during the new era ushered in by the Cultural Revolution.[7] In other words, the Maoists charged that the "later ten points" (both the preliminary and revised texts) and the other documents issued in the name of the Central Committee had been falsified by those "power-holders" who schemed to modify Mao's intent by amendment or interpretation.[8] The picture of an anti-Mao faction working in concert to oppose Mao's ideological leadership should not be overstressed, however. Undoubtedly, a majority of the high-level leaders did not share Mao's bold confidence in the productive potential of China's masses, once mobilized. But, under the rules of democratic centralism, the dissenters could not reverse Mao's policies without forcing drastic changes in the regime; they could only seek to mitigate the effect of his policies through liberal interpretation and limited application.

On the other hand, Mao should not be depicted as an iron-willed dictator, determined to defend his past errors against all criticism. It is true that Mao tried to explain the failures of 1958 as a temporary eclipse of the revolutionary forces by the forces of reaction—an eclipse that would be followed by the eventual triumph of the revolutionary forces. But, as we shall see later, Mao from 1960 on changed his views without fanfare. Nevertheless, the old disagreements or contradictions between Mao and the dissenting "power-holders" gained in complexity, while new contradictions emerged over time.

Purposes and Cross-Purposes

MAO'S INTENT

Mao regarded the Socialist Education campaign, whose purpose was to produce a new consensus and solidarity through "unity, struggle, and unity" as a continuation of previous rectification campaigns.[9] It differed from earlier campaigns, however, in that it was not to be limited to any segment of the population but was to affect equally both cadres and the masses, and in that the target of the struggle was "revisionism" as well as "rightism." The forces of "revisionism," according to Mao, had been so strong that the Socialist Education Movement could not be started until 1962.[10] An inevitable component of the movement was class struggle, by which Mao sought to stamp out remnant "bourgeois influences, the ingrained habits of the old society, and a spontaneous tendency toward capitalism among some of the small producers." [11] The purpose of the struggle, however, was "educational," not punitive. As Mao put it, "Once class struggle is grasped, miracles are possible." [12]

In the countryside, the campaign was to organize the poor and lower-middle peasants, whose associations would play an active role in such tasks as the rectification of the cadres ("four cleans") in order to "overcome mistakes that cause betrayal of the proletarian standpoint, so that our cadres and Party members can correctly provide the leadership for the great majority of the masses in carrying on class struggle and the struggle between socialism and capitalism." [13] The peasant associations, which would wield broad, quasi-autonomous power, were also hailed as an indispensable means to ensure the "dictatorship of the proletariat," the "collective economy," and the growth of agricultural production.

According to the "early ten points," the entire nation was to undergo a thorough purification campaign, appropriately labeled as "washing hands and bodies" and "taking a bath." Decentralization was the strategy for the purification campaign. The stress was upon local initiatives, especially from the poor and lower-middle peasants, supported by Party leadership where necessary. There were probably a number of reasons for selecting that strategy. First, the targets of the rural rectification campaign were remnant bourgeois elements and a new class of landlords and rich peasants, whose existence and misconduct were best known to the poor and lower-middle peasants. Hence, the new associations formed by the latter would "assist and oversee the work of the commune and brigade administrative committees (local government)." Second, the effectiveness of the Party's local cadres had declined in many areas, because of either corruption or peasant opposition to Party "commandism" during the Great Leap. Third, decentralization, by bypassing possible obstruction in the Party's higher councils, would enhance Mao's charismatic leadership. Here, the strategy reflects Mao's long-standing tendency to reach down to lower levels when difficulties developed within higher echelons. During the Great Leap Forward, when opposition to his policies had developed within the Party's central leadership, Mao had worked with the provincial level; in the Socialist Education Movement, he reached down to the new peasant associations. Fourth, decentralization would encourage egalitarianism; both cadres and masses would receive the same socialist education. The alliance of cadres, technical personnel, and poor and lower-middle peasants, which was widely acclaimed at the time, was characteristic of this egalitarian tendency. The same consideration lay behind Mao's insistence that Party cadres join the masses in actual production. Party secretaries in rural areas "should strive to be good hands in production work, to be models of labor," as well as "advanced elements in politics." [14]

Yet egalitarianism was not an end in itself. Mao saw it as a means of regenerating the Party bureaucracy, whose loss of revolutionary *élan* had alarmed him. By requiring that cadres, from primary to higher levels, must spend part of their time tilling fields or working in factories, Mao sought to restore the cadres' revolutionary spirit and to bridge the widening gulfs between the cadres and the masses. In Mao's view, the cadres' actual participation in production would, among other things, prove by deeds that they "are part of the working people," help them "retain the true qualities of the working people . . . and resist the influence of bourgeois ideology," help strengthen "class consciousness and class feeling," set a good example to "stimulate the labor enthusiasm of the masses," help create "a new social attitude which regards labor as honorable and not taking part in labor as shameful," especially among youth, and enable cadres to have a firsthand understanding of production problems.[15] Thus, both practical and ideological considerations were behind Mao's Socialist Education campaign. Mao hoped not only that an increase in production would result but also that "our cadres will be versed in politics as well as business operations, become red as well as expert . . . will no longer be overbearing, no longer bureaucrats and landlords, no longer divorced from the masses." [16] Those goals indicated that existing conditions urgently needed correction. In the Maoist jargon, the campaign's objective was to unite 95 per cent of the cadres (the remaining 5 per cent was presumably irremediably "unclean") with 95 per cent of the masses (excluding the 5 per cent who were bourgeois). Its ultimate purpose was to destroy a nascent "revisionism."

LIU'S "REVISIONISM"

The "power-holders" who had initiated the measures now branded as "revisionist" were ordered by Mao to carry out the rectification movement. They did so, but without always agreeing with Mao's policies or carrying them out to his satisfaction. Their different outlook was reflected in Party directives like the "later ten points," in which they claimed to clarify, or elaborate upon, Mao's original instructions, and in the actual conduct of the Socialist Education campaign. As in the case of the "later ten points," the differences were often subtle enough to escape the attention of the sharpest observers. It is only with the historical perspective and new documentation afforded by the Cultural Revolution that one can begin to perceive which attitudes of the Liu group angered Mao.

First, Liu's men would go along with an ideological campaign to rally the masses and oppose cadre corruption so long as it did not seek to maintain the spirit of the Great Leap Forward. They would use such a campaign to support their own policy of "re-adjustment." Those who drafted the "later ten points" spoke of two stages in the Socialist Education Movement: The first would seek the "solution to the problem of the 'four uncleans' among the cadres and the launching of struggles against the enemy"; the second would be a period of "organization and construction," in which "the Party's basic organizations, the communes . . . would be *readjusted*." [17] Their attitude toward the "four uncleans" also seems to convey a more negative approach than Mao's. Instead of promoting the "four cleans," Liu's supporters would fight the "four uncleans." In so doing, they probably meant to minimize the scope of the contradictions within the Party and between cadres and the masses. Wang Kuang-mei, the wife of Liu Shao-ch'i, was alleged to have said in late 1963 at T'aoyuan—where she was stationed to direct the local implementation of the campaign—that it was not possible to distinguish clearly between enemy and friend for the moment, because "contradictions between the enemy and us (people)" cut across the lines of the "contradictions among the people." [18] Mao was critical of her view and, in the "twenty-three articles" of 1965, specifically stated that the current conflict was not just between the "four cleans" and the "four uncleans" and denied that contradictions between "the enemy" (plus non-Party elements) and "us" (the Party) had cut across those among the people. He saw the conflict basically as the contradiction between socialism and capitalism. [19]

Second, the Liu group tended to approach the Socialist Education Movement as an organizational matter. The "later ten points" particularly stressed organization and leadership, rather than Mao's decentralized ideological purification campaign for both cadres and masses.

> The *key* to the questions of whether the Socialist Education Movement can be carried out smoothly, whether the masses can be fully mobilized, and whether the Party's policies can be correctly carried out during this Movement, lies in *leadership*. [20]

To provide leadership, a number of measures were prescribed that reflected a basic view divergent from Mao's: The cadres must "lead the 'hand-washing' and 'bathing'," setting an example for the masses to follow; leadership cadres from the provincial level on down "must personally take command at strategic points [for prolonged on-the-spot observation] in order to obtain experience, set examples, and direct and push the entire Movement" (thus underplaying any peasant initiative); in the selection of the "work teams" to be sent to the local command posts (known as "squatting points"), great attention must be paid to "quality and capability"; and their members "must be recruited through strict screening and examination." [21] The last point appeared to place higher priority on "expertise" than "redness."

In the "twenty-three articles," however, Mao again de-emphasized the leadership role of Party cadres and upheld the importance of uniting the masses, cadres, and work teams in a more or less equal relationship, or tripartite alliance.[22] He also reaffirmed the role of the poor and lower-middle peasants. On-the-spot investigation by the "work teams" must be not only conducted in depth at selected "squatting points" but also extended as widely as possible. Mao also ruled that the composition of the work teams need not be "fully and completely clean." Even "those who have committed mistakes may also participate," in order to have the opportunity for "education and transformation" and to "gain an all-round view of the movement and thus become useful workers" again.[23] As Mao viewed it, participation in the campaign was educational even for cadres, whereas Liu's view was that the cadres had nothing to do in the campaign but lead the masses.

Although the "later ten points" acknowledged a role for the poor and lower-middle peasants in the rectification movement, the resolution also called for "careful ideological education of the cadres." The addition revealed that the Liu group's appraisal of the relative importance of cadres and masses was fundamentally different from that of Mao. Red Guard propaganda explicitly attacked Liu for attempting to replace Chairman Mao's policy of "uniting the two 95 per cents" (cadres and masses) with a new policy in which "unifying the 95 per cent of the cadres" took precedence of "unifying the 95 per cent of the masses." [24]

To correct this emphasis, Mao pointedly stated in the "twenty-three articles" that the associations of poor and lower-middle peasants would *"supervise* and assist cadres of various levels within the people's communes in carrying out work." [25] In Mao's view, the Liu group's conduct of the Socialist Education Movement was not fully in the interest of the masses.[26] The "twenty-three articles" therefore flatly ruled that "the use of pretexts for opposing the masses of commune members shall not be permitted." [27]

Third, Liu's attitude toward class struggle appears to have diverged from Mao's in two fundamental ways. In the first place, Liu seems to have defined the masses' struggle with the bourgeois classes in structural terms, following orthodox Marxist thought.[28] Liu envisaged class struggle between Party and anti-Party forces and between the proletariat and the bourgeoisie only,[29] whereas Mao prescribed the application of class struggle to all, irrespective of class origin or Party membership. For Mao, class struggle is not only *inter*class, *inter*personal, and *outward*-directed but, especially during the socialist stage, also *intra*class, *intra*personal, and *inward*-directed.[30] Similarly, Liu prescribed uninterrupted "self-cultivation" as the means by which Party members should strive to maintain their personal ideological rectitude. Although Liu's "self-cultivation" suggests a form of intrapersonal and inward-directed struggle that is reminiscent of Mao's cult of *szu-hsiang*, the internal ideological strife existed for him only within the Party. In Liu's view, the Party's external struggle against the enemy and hostile forces was the true "class struggle" involving physical violence; violence was not to be practiced within the Party. The Chinese word for struggle, *tou-cheng*, can mean either "strife" within oneself or "struggle" against an enemy or adverse circumstances, or both. Liu kept the two meanings separate, hence, he used the term to mean two kinds of struggle. Mao, on the other hand, seems not to have made the differentiation but tended increasingly to stress the internal "strife" within each individual. He conceived of "class struggle" as a perpetual rectification, affecting Party members and nonmembers alike, consciously waged against bourgeois attitudes and old habits. Interestingly enough, Liu's ideas on rectification also recall the Confucian moral cultivation of *hsin*, and there are repeated references in Liu's "On Self-Cultivation" (sometimes also translated as "How To Be a Good Communist") to Confucius, Mencius, and others.[31]

The second fundamental difference between Liu's attitude toward class struggle and Mao's stems from the first. Liu followed the orthodox Marxist view that class struggle disappears in a socialist society; since China has crossed the socialist threshold, class struggle has ceased to exist. In Mao's view, that attitude was unpardonable and placed Liu in the same category as Khrushchev. Thus, Mao's attack on "revisionism" actually had domestic undertones from the very beginning, although Soviet policy appeared at first to be the primary target.[32] Liu's more orthodox views on class struggle were shared by many in the Party, including one of its senior theoreticians, Yang Hsien-chen. An elderly member of the Central Committee and head of the Advanced Party (Cadres) School from 1955 to 1961, Yang had been troubled by the discrepancy between Maoist revolutionary enthusiasm and the realities of Chinese life and had embarked upon a review of the concept of contrived class struggle. Yang and a few colleagues in the Advanced Party School presented their views as a modest elaboration or modification of Mao's basic tenets on the subject. Yang's theory, known as "two merging into one," (*ho-erh wei-yi*) argued that opposites were inseparably and permanently united, whereas Mao believed that opposites were permanently in contention and could achieve only a temporary unity.[33] Yang was said to have argued that opposites, by their very nature, were compelled to seek unity and that the problem was "precisely a study of how to identify (unify) opposites to seek common ground and let differences remain." [34] The root conflict between opposites, in this theory, tends toward resolution. Thus, unity supersedes struggle. On the level of society, class struggle results in the "gradual growth of the Communist element while the capitalist element gradually weakens, until its final elimination," according to an elaboration by two of Yang's adherents.[35]

Yang's critics charged that he had grossly neglected the necessity of uninterrupted struggle in bringing about a union of opposites. They cited Lenin's statement that "dialectics is the study of the contradiction inherent in the object." To understand and analyze social struggle, the mind must use a method that dissects the apparent unity. They therefore formulated the dictum *yi fen-wei erh* ("one splitting into two"). If contradictory elements can unite without a struggle and without one's vanquishing the other, Yang's critics argued, then the final unity must contain elements of both in what is essentially a compromise. The theory advocated by Yang and his associates would lead away from class struggle to class conciliation—a frightening thought to the Maoists, because the proletariat would then stop fighting the bourgeoisie and would accept a lasting compromise.[36]

After a period of open debate in the Communist press, the "one splitting into two" formulation and the concept of contrived class struggle were hailed as the foundation for the "general line" of socialist construction. Yang's theory was condemned as heresy.[37]

The denunciation of Yang's theory was followed by a fierce Maoist attack on the Soviet "revisionist" view that class struggle ceases to exist under socialism. The polemic, "On Khrushchev's Phony Communism and Its Historical Lessons for the World," which was released through the *People's Daily* and the *Red Flag* on July 14, 1964, is more concerned with the defense of Mao's domestic policies than with criticisms of the Communist Party of the Soviet Union (CPSU), except perhaps for the influence of the CPSU upon Chinese "revisionists." Mao's "twenty-three articles" of January 14, 1965, issued under the name of the CCP's Central Committee, firmly stated that "revisionism," or, to be more exact, "opposition to socialism," existed even in the "provincial and Central Committee departments" of the Chinese Communist Party.[38]

An Appraisal of the Socialist Education Campaign

By 1965, it was plain that the campaign to remold the nation in the revolutionary spirit of the "thought of Mao Tse-tung" and to cleanse it of "revisionism" had been no more successful than Mao's "three red banners" of the Great Leap Forward. The "power-holders" were determined to continue their course of routinization and rationalization. The available literature suggests that in 1965 Liu Shao-ch'i was contemplating the institution of a "socialist cartel" system, which the Maoists regarded as the severest form of "revisionism." Liu is said to have designed the system to fulfill a number of purposes—all following the principle of "economic management"—the improvement of technology, the diversification of production, reduction of costs, increase of labor productivity, improvement of quality, and increased attention to consumer goods. To realize those goals, Liu was further alleged to have advocated learning from the Soviet Union and even the capitalist countries, because they had richer experience in managing large enterprises. The Maoists condemned Liu's program as a "revisionist" intrigue to "restore capitalism." [39] In their view, such a policy would vitiate the emphasis that the mass line placed upon the role of the poor and lower-middle peasants and would undermine Mao's policy of "walking on two legs," which permitted small and medium-sized enterprises to coexist with large ones. Liu's stress on "economic management," at the expense of political or ideological guidelines, was the fundamental cause of the conflict between Liu and Mao.

By 1964–65, it had become clear that the economic measures Liu had introduced in the wake of the Great Leap Forward were not designed as mere temporary correctives. Moreover, economic innovators, led by Sun Ye-fang, contended that profit should be the criterion for investment and economic planning.[40] Maoists attacked such theoretical justifications for Liu's "economism" on the grounds of their excessive concern for micro-development, as opposed to macro-development.[41] Here lies the most fundamental difference between what the Maoists have called Liu's "economics in command" and Mao's "politics in command." Although Sun was dismissed in 1966 from his post as Director of the Economics Institute of the Chinese Academy of Sciences, subsequent sharp Maoist denunciations of economic liberalization and the theory of profitability indicate the extent of popular support for a more liberal economic structure.[42]

In retrospect, the Socialist Education campaign was largely a failure, except perhaps for its effect on the youth and the army. Disillusioned with the decline of morality and revolutionary enthusiasm among old-guard leaders, many of whom had been with him on the Long March and in Yenan, Mao sought to instill ideological fervor in the next generation of revolutionary leaders. The "Learn from Lei Feng," *hsia fang* (downward transfer to the village), and *yi-k'u* (recollect bitter memories from the old society) campaigns were designed to accomplish just that.[43] Although it is difficult to appraise the impact of those campaigns on the youth of China, the vitality of the Red Guard movement suggests that China's youth had been made conscious of their responsibility as the inheritors of Mao's revolution. On the other hand, the continuation of the Socialist Education Movement in the PLA under the direction of Lin Piao produced more positive results.

Mao's realization that the PLA could serve as a counterforce to the "power-holders" within the Party probably dates to the dismissal of P'eng Te-huai in mid-1959, after he had challenged Mao's leadership.[44] One of the first acts of his successor, Lin Piao, whom Mao had chosen, was to publish on National Day, October 1, 1959, a pro-Mao statement, "Hold High the General Line and the Red Banner of the Military Thought of Mao Tse-tung in Marching Forward." It reaffirmed the principle of "politics in command" in the PLA, suggesting that, though military hardware was important, man was more important than weapons. A series of successful rectification measures were undertaken first in the PLA. Many of the semifictitious heroes like Lei Feng and Wang Chieh, later held up for emulation by the nation at large and youth in particular, were drawn from PLA legends. On November 18, 1965, in the darkest days of the Socialist Education campaign throughout the country, Lin Piao advanced his "five principles for continuing to bring politics to the fore." The most important of them were "creatively learning and applying Chairman Mao's works," with the emphasis on application, and the "four firsts." The latter term meant the priority of man before material (weapons), political work before other work, ideological work before pure political work, and living ideas before book knowledge. The "five principles" were actively propagated within the PLA.[45] The success of the PLA's Socialist Education campaign was lauded in 1966 by the Eleventh Plenum of the Central Committee, which in its communique announced that "the mass movement introduced in the PLA for studying Chairman Mao's works has established a glorious example for the entire Party and the entire nation to follow." [46]

In civilian quarters, however, Mao's critics became more outspoken, and intellectuals articulated in the mass communications media their support for liberalization. By 1962, Mao had become much concerned about the "revisionist" tendencies of China's cultural circles. He was critical of the high value many intellectuals attached to bourgeois aesthetic principles (such as art for art's sake) and to the ideal of the unity of the whole people and all mankind. Mao regarded such values as a betrayal of the proletariat and a denial of class struggle.[47] The Maoists embarked upon the difficult task of overhauling the existing structure and forms of art and literature. For example, passive elements in historical plays were rewritten. The 1944 Yenan play, The White-haired Girl, which was said to be based upon a true story, was rewritten to eliminate the suicide of an old peasant, victimized by a landlord's deceit and oppression. Instead, he is killed by the landlord's men after a heroic struggle. The village peasants, angered and grieved by his death, are then recruited into the Red Army by a Communist militant, a character who had not existed in the old script. The peasant's daughter, whom the landlord had abducted and whose hair had turned white despite her youth, expresses her perpetual hatred for her landlord enemy. Her dignity and courage imbue her audience with a sense of class hatred. The climax arrives when the heroine joins the Red Army and leaves, rifle on shoulder, to fight for the total victory of the proletarian revolution.[48]

Another example of the Maoist attempt to combat "revisionism" in art and literature is Rent Collection Courtyard, a large group of life-size clay figures that was placed on permanent display in the autumn of 1965. Comprising extremely defiant and fierce peasants, the group purports to depict "the brutality and exploitation" of the landlord class and "the suffering and struggle of the peasants before the [1949] liberation." Its intent is to impart militancy and to overcome the historical passivity of the Chinese masses. The ensemble has been hailed as "another victory of the revolutionary artists who, guided by the great thought of Mao Tse-tung, have resolutely followed the line laid down by him—that literature and art should serve the workers, peasants, soldiers, and socialism." [49]

Despite fervent Maoist efforts to promote the proletarian spirit, the most serious dissident voice was from within the Party and centered in its Peking Committee. Between October 10, 1961, and July, 1964, three ranking members of the Peking administration jointly published 67 articles under the general title "Notes from the Three-Family Village," in The Front Line, a theoretical journal of the Peking Municipal Party Committee. Individually, they also published scores of other writings. These not only reflected the people's longing for private property and better living conditions but also, by transparent allusions to history and literature, even defended such desires. One of the trio, Wu Han,

Deputy Mayor of Peking, was the author of the now notorious *Hai Jui Dismissed from Office*.[50] Mao must have been particularly exasperated by the support that the "three-family village" and other exponents of "revisionism" had from the Central Committee's propaganda machine. Until 1966, P'eng Chen, member of the Politburo and secretary of the Central Committee's Secretariat, was in full charge of matters related to the "political front" (i.e., the ideological front), the intellectuals, and art and literature. Under him was Lu Ting-yi, alternate member of the Politburo and a member of the Central Committee's Secretariat, who directed its Propaganda Department, translating policy into action. Lu was assisted by Chou Yang, alternate member of the Central Committee and assistant director of the Propaganda Department, and another assistant director, Lin Mo-han. Their lukewarm attitude toward Mao's fight against "the binding spell of the dead upon the living" [51] and the perfunctory way in which they carried out his policies indicated serious disaffection. The very fact that Mao was absent from Peking in November, 1965, and had to fire the first shots of the Cultural Revolution from Shanghai suggests the depth of the opposition to his policies within the Party's central apparatus.

12

THE GENESIS OF THE CULTURAL REVOLUTION

Importance of "Culture"

THE USE of the word "cultural" in the Maoist phrase "Cultural Revolution" is significant in a number of ways. It recalls the traditional Chinese belief in the didactic function of all forms of culture and in cultural regeneration as the key to social or national regeneration. Until recent decades, Chinese culture was characterized by the pervasiveness of the traditional *li*. In the 1920's and 1930's, intellectuals like Ch'en Tu-hsiu and Hu Shih, each in his own way, sought to create a "New Culture" as an instantaneous solution to China's chronic sociopolitical problems. In his *New Democracy* (1940), Mao stressed that, while a society's economic and political base would produce a given culture, the creation of a new culture would also anticipate a corresponding stage of social development. In 1942, in his *Talks at the Yenan Forum*, Mao stated that arts and letters must fulfill a didactic function, and, under Mao, plays and sculpture were pressed into the service of socialism. Thus, in the largest sense, the Cultural Revolution was a spirited attempt to rectify the thinking of the entire nation through an all-out assault on "revisionism," capitalism, and undesirable strands of tradition, and a campaign to foster a proletarian culture.

Although the Cultural Revolution as such began in 1965–66, it was, in fact, a dramatic continuation of the more limited and unsuccessful campaign that Mao had waged since 1962 to uproot "poisonous weeds" in art and literature. Between November, 1965, and July, 1966, the targets of the Great Proletarian Cultural Revolution were primarily the writers of influential literary works like *Hai Jui Dismissed from Office*, as well as historians, university professors, and other intellectuals and performing artists. The campaign of criticism and denunciation gradually spread to Party secretaries and propagandists, including the Minister of Culture, Lu Ting-yi, and eventually to top CCP leaders. The magnitude of the campaign may or may not substantiate the Maoist charge that "revisionism" had penetrated every corner of the people's life, but it certainly shows the importance that Mao attaches to the cultural and ideological molding of men's minds.

Whether by design or by accident, the Cultural Revolution grew in intensity and violence and extended from central to peripheral issues. During its two principal years, the crusade was perhaps a "concentrated expression," to borrow a favorite Maoist phrase, of a historical trend toward a deepening revolution in modern China. As William Dorrill has aptly stated, the Cultural Revolution was not started by a dispute or disputes over either economic or military policy issues, or both.[1] No single event or policy dispute triggered the explosion. Beginning in the 1950's, especially after 1958, two (if not more) fundamental approaches developed to the choice of strategies for China's "socialist construction." Rightly or wrongly, they have come to be identified as the Maoist and (for lack of a better term) anti-Maoist approaches to socialism. The various policy differences were concrete manifestations of those crucially different interpretations of how Communist ideology should be applied in China.

No Evidence of a Master Plan

Contrary to early impressions, the Cultural Revolution does not seem to have followed any master plan. There was little logic to its series of spontaneous eruptions, and its erratic course of development suggests that even Mao did not foresee certain specific events and features. Prior to the spring of 1966, Mao probably had no definite plan to remove such Party leaders as P'eng Chen and Liu Shao-ch'i. Nor did he seem to have drawn up any clear plan for the use of the Red Guards. Certainly, he did not intend to sanction the kind of anarchism that threatened to paralyze the entire nation until it was effectively curbed in 1968.

The beginning of the Cultural Revolution has commonly been given as September, 1965, when Mao outlined his ideas before a Central Committee work conference, but what he said there remains unknown. He probably called for a general renewal of the struggle against "reactionary bourgeois ideology" and, more specifically, for criticism of Wu Han and his play, *Hai Jui Dismissed from Office*.[2] It is likely that he used that forum to voice his perennial concern for ideological renewal—a task that the apparent lack of success of the Socialist Education Movement had made urgent. In the course of his talk he probably reiterated his own utopian vision of the good society and reasserted his conviction that members of the Party bureaucracy were betraying that vision.[3]

The effect of Mao's speech is unknown, but two events suggested that its reception was less than enthusiastic. First, Yao Wen-yüan's attack on Wu Han's play—the first attack to appear in print—was not published until November 10, 1965, two months after Mao's speech, and not in Peking but in Shanghai's *Wen-hui Pao*. Second, according to later disclosures, the initial Central Cultural Revolution Group of five members was headed by P'eng Chen, who had apparently been appointed by Liu Shao-ch'i. If subsequent Maoist accusations are to be trusted, P'eng Chen was the man most responsible for frustrating Mao's earlier efforts at cultural reform during 1962–65, and his continued covert obstructionism impeded the initial phase of the Cultural Revolution until his removal around May, 1966.[4] We do not know whether Mao initially delegated the responsibility for executing the new campaign to Liu Shao-ch'i and his colleagues, or whether Mao was unable to direct the Party machine himself. It was only after P'eng Chen's removal that Mao revealed the reason for launching Yao Wen-yüan's attack on Wu Han's play from Shanghai: The Party apparatus in Peking had been "impenetrable." [5]

THE "FEBRUARY THESIS"

Nor is it clear what specific role P'eng Chen played in the months prior to his dismissal and disgrace in the spring of 1966. Some Red Guard units have published veiled charges that he was involved in a coup plot against Mao some time in February, 1966. P'eng allegedly issued an "Outline Report on the Current Academic Discussion" on February 12, 1966, on behalf of the original Group of Five, which he headed. The document came to be known as the "February Thesis." On May 16, 1966, a circular of the Central Committee announced the dissolution of the original Group of Five and the appointment of a new Cultural Revolution Group under the direct authority of the Standing Committee of the Politburo.[6] More significantly, it also revoked the "February Thesis." The Maoists were serious about the episode. A joint editorial by *Red Flag* and *People's Daily* subsequently called the circular that had revoked P'eng's "February Thesis" a "great historical document written under the personal auspices" of Mao himself.[7] Elsewhere, Mao's spokesmen alleged that P'eng Chen had publicly espoused some of the views found in the "February Thesis" as early as 1965, when he addressed a conference of provincial cultural commissars.[8]

The available evidence [9] suggests that P'eng's treatise was written with the following objectives: (1) to play down class struggle in the current stage in China; (2) to permit the expression of a broader range of ideas and views; (3) to emphasize "equality before truth" (which would immediately undermine the supremacy of Mao's thought); [10] (4) to prevent the application of class distinctions to academic, literary, and art circles; (5) to place "construction" before "destruction" (reversing Mao's sequence); (6) to criticize the "scholar-tyrants" (e.g., Maoist critics of the "Three-Family Village"); (7) to demand a rectification campaign against the "stanch left" (Mao's line); (8) to suggest that the Cultural Revolution should be conducted "under direction," "with prudence," and "with the approval of the leading bodies concerned." Despite references to Mao's contribution to the cultural and ideological front, the "February Thesis" seems to have been generally opposed to the more fundamentalist line of thought advocated by Mao. For that reason, it was condemned as a sinister move to oppose and block the Cultural Revolution, to shield the bourgeois right against the proletarian left, and to prepare public opinion for the restoration of capitalism.[11]

WORK TEAMS VS. RED GUARDS

The "February Thesis," as described in the available literature, probably reflected the views of Party leaders in 1966 and their conduct during the 1962–65 campaign. These leaders were probably seeking once again to cool Mao's ideological ardor. In the interval between P'eng Chen's removal from office and his formal purge at the Eleventh Plenum of the Central Committee in August, 1966, the Party machine under Liu Shao-ch'i and Teng Hsiao-p'ing reorganized the Peking Municipal Party Committee and, during Mao's absence from Peking, rather hastily sent out work teams whose mission, ostensibly, was to carry the Cultural Revolution to the universities and elsewhere. The team that was sent to Tsinghua University was headed by Wang Kuang-mei, Liu's wife.

It is not impossible that the work teams sent out by the Liu-Teng group were actually attempting to institute reforms that would forestall Mao's revolution and to shift the center of gravity from the masses to the cadres. The Liu-Teng group had employed such techniques during the Socialist Education campaign, and the "February Thesis" had defended their use. The work teams soon ran into opposition—often violent—from less well-organized groups of students responding to appeals for revolutionary ferment that had begun to appear in the official press (the Maoists had regained control of the press by April, 1966).[12] The groups became known as the Red Guards. Although Mao officially launched the Red Guards at an August 18, 1966 rally, and although his wife, Chiang Ch'ing, soon became their active leader, Mao's role in the creation of the units remains obscure. At a Central Committee work conference months later, Mao made it known that the Red Guards had received only his personal encouragement. He said then that he had sent a letter to Miss Nieh Yuan-tzu to congratulate her for writing the first student wall poster and had then composed a poster of his own entitled "Bombard the Command Headquarters" (dated August 5, 1966). In the same talk, Mao expressed regret that the student response to those actions had been excessive and seemed to suggest that the Party should make the best of the situation, by improvisation if necessary.[13] The title and tone of Mao's own poster suggests that he felt himself isolated, if not opposed, within the Party. If he did play an active role in the organization of the Red Guards, it may have been because he feared that his position would be untenable if he did not win new allies.

During the early phases of the movement, the Red Guards were beset with conflicting loyalties—an indication, perhaps, that they sprang from diverse origins. In Heilungkiang, for instance, the original work teams sent by the provincial Party committee in June and July, 1966, were opposed by some student groups, but were supported by the "August 8 Corps," a coalition of Red Guard groups from various provincial universities. Maoists later charged that the Heilungkiang Party (then under Liu's influence) had sent the teams to curb student zeal in implementing Mao's May 16 Circular, which called for intensified class struggle. The "August 8 Corps," which supported the work teams, was by no means pro-Mao. After the Maoists assumed control, the work teams were accused of having resorted to "white terror" in labeling the leaders of the pro-Mao groups as "counterrevolutionaries," "right-wingers," and "anti-Party" elements and of having incited their own supporters to assault the pro-Mao student groups.[14] Considering that some Red Guard units in the initial months were opposed to the Maoists, it is highly unlikely that they had been formed by Mao or his followers.

The Sixteen Articles

The famous Sixteen Articles issued by the Eleventh Plenum of the Central Committee on August 8, 1966, formally signaled a personal victory for Mao and his line of thought. At that Plenum, the Central Committee officially recognized Lin Piao's ascendancy as the Party's sole Vice Chairman and Mao's heir-designate. It also formally dismissed P'eng Chen and his Peking Party Committee and lowered the Party ranks of Liu Shao-ch'i, Teng Hsiao-p'ing, and other important Politburo members, who would be targets for vilification by the end of the year. Since the primacy of the Sixteen Articles was reaffirmed in subsequent Central Committee documents bearing Mao's imprint, its content would depict Mao's original intent far more accurately than the actual course of the Cultural Revolution.[15]

(1) After announcing the advent of a new phase of the socialist revolution, the document named as the main force for carrying out the Cultural Revolution the "masses of workers, peasants, and soldiers"; the "revolutionary intellectuals"; and the "revolutionary cadres." Only then did the document acknowledge the appearance of an army of "previously unknown revolutionary youths [who] have become courageous and daring pathbreakers . . . and who through the medium of big-character posters and great debates argue things out, expose and criticize thoroughly, and launch resolute attacks on the open and hidden representatives of the bourgeoisie." It is open to speculation why "revolutionary youth" (the Red Guards) was listed separately and given a lower priority. Apparently, the separate listing meant that the Red Guards were *not* part of the main force designated to carry

out the Cultural Revolution. Furthermore, the reference to revolutionary youth was accompanied by a rather apologetic statement that they could hardly avoid having "shortcomings of one kind or another." [16] The document suggests either that its authors had reservations about including the Red Guards or that their inclusion was an afterthought. Moreover, the role of revolutionary youth was explicitly confined to criticizing and attacking the bourgeois foe by means of wall posters and debate. Other provisions stipulated that the Cultural Revolution should be conducted by "peaceful struggle, not violent means." The fact that Red Guard violence did erupt in the course of the struggle runs counter to this interdiction and may have disturbed Mao. Mao's dismay may be a partial explanation for his silence during eight reviews of Red Guard representatives in 1966. The ban on violence and physical destruction was repeated in the Eight-Point Order issued by the Military Affairs Commission, dated January 28, 1967, which bore Mao's personal approval. The order, which instructed the PLA to stop the fighting among different Red Guard factions, explicitly denounced such popular Red Guard practices as forcing "revisionists" to kneel down and to wear humiliating signs, parading them through streets, forcing entry into their homes, and destroying or confiscating their personal effects.[17] In July, 1968, Mao was reported to have openly decried Red Guard disunity and ineffectuality in an emotional session with five of its leaders. By then, the Red Guards had been curbed, and he had begun officially to replace them with worker-peasant teams to continue the unfinished campaign.[18] In short, although the Red Guards enjoyed considerable prominence between August, 1966, and January, 1967, and were not officially restrained until July, 1968, their role was not necessarily foreseen or planned.

(2) The Sixteen Articles called for "daring" above all else and for "boldly" arousing the masses. The purpose appeared to be to loosen the control of the "power-holding" cadres and to encourage greater initiative and more spontaneous participation by the masses. The goal of educating the masses through ideological

rectification was reaffirmed. No substitute method (presumably a reference to the Party's efforts to use the work teams to convert revolution into reform and mass-orientation into cadre-oriéntation) was to be permitted.[19]

To prevent the work teams from suppressing the Maoist activists, as they had done in Heilungkiang in June–July, 1966, the document condemned any attempt to brand "revolutionary masses" as "counterrevolutionaries." It also prohibited struggle against students and the instigation of struggle between students, though it stated that cases involving any infraction of the law would be dealt with according to law.[20] As during the Socialist Education campaign, a call was issued to unite the 95 per cent of the cadres with the 95 per cent of the masses.[21]

If the Liu-Teng apparatus had stressed tighter organizational discipline, so that basic-level cadres came under the close surveillance of the *hsien* Party committee, the Sixteen Articles decreased the latter's authority and control. The remedy for all cadre misdeeds was ideological rectification, rather than structure-oriented disciplinary measures. Thus, an article declared that "good" and "relatively good" cadres were in the majority. Though some cadres had committed "serious mistakes," only a small number had become "anti-Party, anti-socialist rightists," who would be "fully exposed, repudiated, overthrown, and completely discredited, and [their] influence eliminated." At the same time, the article insisted that those same elements "should be given a chance to turn over a new leaf." [22] The ruling repeated Mao's view, expressed in the "early ten points" and the "twenty-three articles," that the purpose of rectification was not punitive but "educational," i.e., ideological reform.

(3) The Sixteen Articles also reiterated Mao's 1957 formulation of his theory of contradictions, under which two different kinds of contradictions required different resolutions. Contradictions among the people should be distinguished from those between the people and the enemy and should be resolved by "full debate." Article Six warned, however, that the views of the

minority should not be overlooked. Ironically, this argument had first been advanced after 1959 by Party leaders who wished to reinstate the "rightists" whom Mao had purged for their opposition to the Great Leap Forward. The inclusion in the Sixteen Articles of a statement about the protection of minority views may indicate that Mao felt himself isolated and surrounded by a majority that did not share his more utopian outlook.[23]

(4) The Party reasserted its class line of isolating and crushing the "handful" of the "most reactionary bourgeois rightists and counter-revolutionary revisionists." Singled out as the "main target" of the Cultural Revolution were the "power-holders within the Party taking the capitalist road." The long struggle had by now reached the level of the Central Committee and was directed at the top leadership rather than merely its adherents.[24]

The exact form for "attacking" and "criticizing" the enemy (as distinct from the people) was not spelled out. Limited violence against the class enemy was in practice tolerated until specifically banned in January, 1967. However, violence was never officially sanctioned in dealing with "contradictions among the people." "When there is a debate, it should be carried out by peaceful, not violent, means." [25] The explicit interdiction of indiscriminate violence at that relatively early stage (August, 1966) was apparently provoked by the fierce battles of June and July, 1966, the initial months of Red Guard activities.

(5) Maoists contended that students wanted sweeping reforms of the existing school system. In response to a June 6, 1966, letter to Mao from a group of students,[26] which was widely publicized as typifying student feelings, a provision in the Sixteen Articles demanded curricular reforms that would merge economic production and education in one process. Only in this way, it asserted, could education be made to serve the politics of the dictatorship of the proletariat, as Mao insisted it must. Schools were called upon in the provision to train students "morally, intellectually, and physically." [27] As Donald MacInnis has quite

pertinently pointed out, the reform measure illustrated the underlying ideal that " 'culture' is not some ivory-tower activity divorced from the rice paddy and the production line." For Mao, "culture begins with the peasant and the worker. All artistic, literary, and intellectual activity must be socially relevant, must flow *from* and *to* the people. Theory and practice are inseparable." [28]

(6) Although the rectification campaigns that Mao has launched since 1962 have subordinated production goals to ideological objectives, with some unfortunate economic consequences, his purpose in initiating such campaigns has been to increase production by means of ideological mobilization. Increased production was a measure of the success or failure of the Socialist Education campaign. This point was made by Mao in June, 1964, at a meeting of the Standing Committee of the Politburo, which was attended by the first secretaries of the Central Committee's regional bureaus. It was also embodied in the "twenty-three articles." [29]

Under the slogan, "take firm hold of the revolution and stimulate production," the Sixteen Articles of August 8, 1966, explicitly stated that the aim of the Cultural Revolution was to "revolutionize people's ideology . . . to achieve greater, faster, better, and more economical results in all fields of work." There was no contradiction between the Cultural Revolution's ideological and production objectives.[30] So long as scientists, technicians, and "ordinary members of working staffs were not against the Party and socialism and maintained no illicit relations with any foreign country," they would be subject to no more harassment than the standard ritual of "unity, criticism, and unity" required. In fact, Article 12 directed that special treatment be given to those scientific and technical personnel "who have made contributions." The article, however, also suggested that Mao did not have full confidence in the intellectuals' ideological outlook. It added that "efforts should be made to help them gradually transform their world outlook and their style of work." [31]

(7) Although the Cultural Revolution was supposed to continue the rural and urban phases of the Socialist Education campaign, its center of gravity would be in the "large and medium cities." Where the rural and urban phases of the Socialist Education campaign were "appropriate and . . . going well," the Sixteen Articles specified that they should not be upset by the Cultural Revolution. Questions of implementation that might arise in the Cultural Revolution should be put to the masses "for discussion at the proper time," in order to foster proletarian thinking and eradicate bourgeois thinking.

In other areas, at the discretion of the local Party apparatus, the Sixteen Articles suggested that the Cultural Revolution could provide a new focus and new momentum for the Socialist Education Movement and the "four cleans." The last phrase was now broadened to mean rectification in politics, ideology, organization, and economy.[32] The fact that the local Party apparatus was allowed some discretion suggests that Mao had not decided, as of August, 1966, to use the Red Guards to overthrow the Party structure.

(8) Several articles dealt with procedures for the conduct of the Cultural Revolution. Cultural Revolution groups, committees, and congresses were to be widely established as "permanent mass organizations" in industrial and mining enterprises, street communities, and the countryside, as well as in schools and offices. Membership in those organizations would be by a "universal election" procedure modeled on that of the Paris Commune.[33] It is not clear whether the same principle of election would apply to the Central Cultural Revolution Group in Peking, which appeared to have been appointed by Mao in the spring of 1966.[34] There is no evidence, however, that elections of the Paris-Commune type were ever carried out at any level.

Another provision, which displayed relative restraint, was that "criticisms of anyone by name in the press should be decided after discussion by the Party committee at the same level, and in some cases submitted to the Party committee at a higher level for approval." [35] The requirement would give the Party ultimate discretion and control. The principle was widely violated in practice, however. There were Red Guard denunciations of almost every major Party leader, with the possible exception of Mao and Lin Piao.

(9) An important measure in the Sixteen Articles, with far-reaching effects, was the separation of the military and civilian spheres of the Cultural Revolution. In the PLA, the Central Committee's Military Affairs Commission (MAC) and the PLA General Political Department, rather than the civilian Central Cultural Revolution Group, would direct the struggle. The decision to accord some autonomy to the PLA in carrying out its internal Cultural Revolution probably reflects the rise of Lin Piao and a number of other considerations. Mao regarded the PLA's level of ideological purity as much higher than that of any segment of the civilian population. The PLA's version of the Cultural Revolution had been launched in 1962. Furthermore, the PLA would have to provide stability until the Party, the backbone of the Chinese Communist sociopolitical system, had been sufficiently rectified to reassume control of the gun. Until then, the gun must be behind efforts to rectify the Party. In the strictest sense, the gun had never controlled the Party. During certain phases of the Cultural Revolution, the PLA seemed to control the Party, but the PLA itself contained its own internal Party apparatus.

Mao may have felt he had more power and more room to maneuver in the military than in the civilian sphere. As Party Chairman, Mao is generally believed to act as Chairman of MAC, with Lin Piao serving as his first deputy. His wife, Chiang Ch'ing, was appointed an adviser to the PLA on December 3, 1966, just before the PLA began to take over civil administration in the provincial capitals. In late 1967, Mao named Hsü Hsiang-ch'ien, one of his appointees to the new Politburo formed in August, 1966, head of the PLA's Cultural Revolution Group. Many current military leaders, including Hsieh Fu-chih,

Vice Premier and Minister of Public Security; Wang Hsin-t'ing, Deputy Chief of Staff; Wang Hung-k'un, Deputy Commander of the Navy; Hsü Shih-yu, Vice Minister of Defense and Commander of the Nanking Military Region; and Ch'in Chi-wei, Commander of the Kunming Military Region, had been subordinates or associates of Hsü's, and some of these associations dated back to the Oyüwan Chinese Soviet in the early 1930's. Hsü's appointment marked his reappearance after a long interval of political inactivity and probably reflected Mao's desire to provide a counterweight to leaders identified with Lin Piao. Hsü had been a senior leader of the Fourth Front Army; his appointment would please his former fellow officers, including those mentioned above.

The above interpretation, if valid, would raise doubts about the theory that Lin Piao's command of the PLA had reduced Mao to the role of a figurehead. Some writers have even suggested that the Cultural Revolution was a power struggle in which Lin Piao appropriated Mao's name. The separation of the military and civilian spheres of the Cultural Revolution does not show, however, that Mao could not or would not later restore Party control over the PLA, once the Party had been remolded. Although it is tempting to suggest that the PLA was the beneficiary of an intra-Party struggle, this is probably too simplistic an interpretation. In view of Mao's real power in the military and the historical background dating from the "Learn from the PLA" campaign to the formulation of the Sixteen Articles, it seems likely that Mao had planned to rely on the PLA in the Cultural Revolution.[36] If so, the Red Guards may have been regarded as a form of shock treatment but no more than that.[37]

(10) Conspicuous evidence that the Sixteen Articles represent Mao's greatest triumph since 1956 is the unequivocal affirmation that his thought will be the "red banner" of the new phase of the socialist revolution. The Sixteen Articles also reasserted Mao's 1958 slogan, "politics in command," inserting the word "prole-

tarian" in front of "politics." The addition recalls Mao's view that the current struggle is between the proletarian and the bourgeois roads and that "proletarian" thinking has to be fostered by conscious, contrived class struggle, because it does not necessarily coincide with society's advance to the socialist stage of development. The triumph of Mao's thought—more than two decades after its original glorification at the 1945 Party Congress in Yenan and a decade after its deletion from the Party's Constitution of 1956—came as a vindication of Mao's leadership. At the same time, Mao's writings of the 1938–42 period, such as his *Talks at the Yenan Forum,* were reissued, partly for reasons of nostalgia and partly to maintain his stress on the importance of ideology in keeping revolution alive.

The Disparity Between Plans and Events

The Sixteen Points not only assigned a relatively secondary role to the Red Guards in the Cultural Revolution and allowed a measure of discretion to local Party committees but also underestimated the prominent role of the PLA in the unfolding drama. Without going into detail here,[38] there are probably several major reasons for the disparity between the plans for the Cultural Revolution, as outlined in the Sixteen Points, and actual events. First, the increasing incompetence and even evasiveness of the Party bureaucracy in handling Mao's campaign probably exacerbated his frustration and despair and increasingly turned him against its members, especially those who seemed to him to be deliberately undermining his campaign and hence challenging his ideological leadership. Second, as the functioning of the Party bureaucracy declined in effectiveness, the Red Guards began to play an increasingly important role, particularly between September, 1966, and January, 1967. The Red Guard license to attack the "power-holders" lasted approximately until the time of the "January Revolution" (1967) in Shanghai. During that period, Red Guard fury (possibly with Chiang Ch'ing's instigation) paralyzed the Party organs and state administration in Peking and provincial capitals and throughout most of the country.[39] Third, some form of state authority had to be re-established after the Red Guards had served the Maoist purpose of "shaking up the class enemy." The task of restoring order, however, fell not to the unreformed Party machine but to the PLA. The eight-point decision to bring in the PLA to restore political and social order was announced on January 23, 1967.[40] In February, 1967, the PLA began to set up military control commissions in every province to take over the civilian administration. The Sixteen Articles do not suggest that these developments had been foreseen in August, 1966.

Although the PLA takeover of the civil administration was meant to be a transitional operation, in less than six months the PLA had modified the course of the Cultural Revolution. In the famous Wuhan Incident of July 20, 1967, Wang Li, an extreme leftist leader of the Cultural Revolution, was arrested during a visit to Wuhan by Ch'en Tsai-tao, Commander of the Wuhan Military Region. Significantly, the Wuhan Incident was resolved only after the personal intervention of Chou En-lai, whose career has been the epitome of pragmatism. Although the details of the incident remain obscure, it seems to have had three major effects. First, the extreme left faction (headed by Wang Li and others, whose political ambition was probably responsible for their clash with the PLA) within the Cultural Revolution Group in Peking lost power in the wake of the Wuhan Incident.[41] (This, incidentally, weakened the Central Cultural Revolution Group itself).

Second, the once unchallenged authority of the PLA in provincial capitals was curtailed. In September, 1967, following a personal tour of the country, Mao ordered the military commissions that had been set up since February, 1967, to transform themselves into revolutionary committees, which would be composed of members from the PLA, "revolutionary" (pro-Mao) members of the former Party bureaucracy, and Red Guard leaders.[42] The principle came to be known as the "three-way alliance." Whether or not the "three-way alliance" was a division of spoils, it certainly represented a compromise among the three main forces professing loyalty to the thought of Mao Tse-tung. The revolutionary committees, whose formation was completed in the twenty-nine main administrative divisions of the country by September, 1968, seem to have superseded the system of Cultural Revolution groups, committees, and congresses envisaged in the Sixteen Articles, just as the principle of the three-way alliance has superseded the Paris Commune type of election. By all indications, the three-way alliance seems to have been only a symbolic concession to demands of Red Guard activists for recognition—an eventuality that Mao may not have anticipated at the Eleventh Plenum. Yet, actual Red Guard representation on the tripartite revolutionary committees turned out to be not more than 15 per cent in most cases, far less than that of the other two groups.[43]

A third significant development in the aftermath of the Wuhan Incident was a discussion in the Peking press of the need to rebuild the Party, which roughly coincided with the drive to spread the revolutionary committees, beginning in September, 1967. Party-building was specifically named as a major task in the *People's Daily* editorial on New Year's Day, 1968. Consequently, the communique of the Twelfth Plenum of the Central Committee for the session of October 31 announced that "at the appropriate time," the long-overdue Ninth Party Congress would be called into session.[44]

To sum up, the overthrow of the old Liu-Teng Party machine had, in the initial stage, resulted in power struggles among the Red Guards and between certain Red Guard units and the military in many regions. The clash eventually necessitated the rebuilding of the Party as the center of power, in order to fill the political vacuum. The actual process of Party rebuilding will no doubt be long and tortuous. The purges, in February and March, 1968, respectively, of Ch'i Pen-yü, a Cultural Revolution leader identified with the extreme left, and Yang Ch'eng-wu, acting

Chief of Staff, who allegedly had executed orders from his "backstage boss" to oppose the leftist leadership of the Cultural Revolution (possibly led by Chiang Ch'ing, Mao's wife), indicated the complexity of power redistribution and the urgency of Party rebuilding.[45]

Amid this internal reorganization, Mao's propaganda channels began, on August 15, 1968, to issue new calls for the rectification of the thoughts, loyalties, and actions of the intellectuals (including Red Guard students) under the leadership of workers, soldiers, and peasants.[46] Yao Wen-yüan, whose attack in November, 1965, on Wu Han's play had formally launched Mao's Cultural Revolution, was the author of a new editorial that symbolically terminated the Red Guard mission. Apparently reflecting Mao's views, Yao praised the Red Guards for having given the reactionary forces hard blows in the early stages of the Cultural Revolution. But in the later stages, Yao continued, "certain people were again active in secret," with the result that fighting had occurred among the masses. Such fighting, he said, jeopardized the original task of purifying class ranks and the Party.[47] That task was by now placed squarely back on the shoulders of the workers, soldiers, and peasants, having been taken away from the youth, pending the eventual return of Party authority.

13

ISSUES UNDERLYING THE CULTURAL REVOLUTION—I

THIS CHAPTER and the two following will discuss some of the fundamental issues that underlie Mao's Cultural Revolution and are likely to continue beyond it. The focus of the present chapter will be primarily on the interrelated issues of ideology, leadership, education, and culture. An analysis of the various concrete, substantive issues that have preoccupied Mao since 1966 may clarify what he means to accomplish when he speaks of "construction by destruction." Among them are the crucial questions known to have come under consideration at the Eleventh Plenum in August, 1966, at which Mao presided; specific policy measures that the Maoists have attempted to introduce since 1968; and Mao's broad outlines for rebuilding the Party.

The dissensions of the 1950's, the failures of the Greap Leap Forward, the antirightist campaign, and the Socialist Education Movement of the 1960's led directly to the Cultural Revolution. By 1965, an intra-Party dispute had been transformed into what Mao called "a struggle between two roads," turning comrades into enemies and constructive intent into destructive fury. True, personal grudges, greed for power, and self-interest played a part, but they were not really the most essential issues. Personal ambitions and personality conflicts could have been subordinated to higher principles had not the system of democratic centralism broken down at the highest level, the result of a loss of consensus after 1955 as to what constituted the collective interest and how it should be interpreted and implemented.

In the late 1950's and early 1960's, policy differences increasingly touched on strategic interpretations of ideology and even on questions of ideological direction. Even in the initial stage of the Cultural Revolution, between September, 1965, and P'eng Chen's removal in the spring of 1966, Mao still seemed to look to the Party apparatus as an agent for executing his latest ideological campaign.[1] As the situation degenerated, Mao found himself obliged to abandon many of his original plans for the Cultural Revolution as outlined in the Sixteen Articles and to improvise. It became clear that even the most basic consensus regarding the general direction of the Party's program had been badly eroded by the growing differences and clashes within the Party hierarchy.

The Cultural Revolution was, in a large sense, Mao's attempt to re-establish his ideological leadership within the Party, but that attempt eventually led, in the course of events, to the destruction of the existing Party apparatus. In Mao's opinion, the widening ideological division between himself and his former heir apparent, Liu Shao-ch'i, meant that no construction would be possible without destruction. Under a different set of circumstances, Mao's "construction" would not necessarily have followed the same course.

A Philosophy of Selfless Struggle

The first thing Mao apparently wants to establish is a philosophy of struggle in the minds of the people and in their way of life. On the question of contradictions, Mao and Liu differed as to whether to place more emphasis on the contention of opposites or on their unity. Mao increasingly stressed their contention, which was expressed, at the social level, in intensified class struggle. While the idea of contrived class struggle reflected Mao's defiant reaction to the domestic reverses of 1959–61, it was based on the philosophical concept of *yi fen-wei erh* (one splits into two). This has been increasingly identified as the philosophy of the proletariat, as opposed to that of the "bourgeoisie," known as *ho-erh wei-yi* (two merge into one).[2] In plain language, the basic question was one of accepting the routinization of roles within the society—and whatever social rigidity that entailed—or of artificially inducing a struggle mentality in order to obtain greater sacrifices from the masses.[3]

Even after the Liu group had been ousted from power, Liu's philosophical outlook continued under attack. His *huo-ming* philosophy—an epithet that defies translation but connotes a self-seeking, epicurean indulgence, with hedonistic overtones— was condemned on the grounds that it opposed the socialist asceticism and selfless devotion that the Maoists professed. An article in the *People's Daily* in 1968 reasserted Mao's statement that a "change in a person's *weltanschauung* is an all-or-nothing change." One either has made the change or has not, the article suggested, and a half-revolutionary is no revolutionary at all but a fake or a renegade. The writer charged that Liu Shao-ch'i saw only a small difference of conception between commitment to and betrayal of revolution, although the two attitudes might have drastically different consequences. The Maoist writer condemned Liu's view for not recognizing the supreme necessity of a total commitment to revolution and for its defense of rightists and counterrevolutionaries.[4]

The article then eulogized the selfless spirit of Men Ho, a semi-legendary PLA hero, who was said to have sacrificed his own life for others. Such force of character, it was claimed, could only have come from unswerving devotion to the socialist revolution and, more important, from Men Ho's "twenty years of creatively learning and applying the thought of Mao Tse-tung." No small differences of conception could explain or create such self-sacrifice.[5]

Another article in the same issue of *People's Daily* pointedly compared Men Ho's self-sacrifice with Liu Shao-ch'i's *huo-ming* philosophy. Men Ho's example only showed how cheap, mean, and worthless was the philosophy embraced by "China's Khrushchev" in its "reactionary, corrupt, and exploitative" indulgence in "momentary sensual pleasure." The author then laid down a Maoist criterion for a true revolutionary: "To fear or to dare hardship, to fear or to dare death—this is the distinction between true and fake revolutionaries." The true revolutionary, he continued, armed with the thought of Mao Tse-tung, struggles ceaselessly for the final victory of the Chinese revolution and is always ready to shed his blood and life for others.[6]

To bring about this commitment to revolution, the Maoists urged each man to struggle to overcome his own selfishness, to devote himself completely to the revolution, and to destroy any "bourgeois" self-indulgence. This appears to be the true meaning of Mao's statement: "Without destruction, there can be no construction. Destruction is criticism, which is revolution. To destroy, we must talk reason. To talk reason is to construct. When we start with destruction, the germ of construction is already present." [7]

The re-emphasis on struggle during the Cultural Revolution marked Mao's return to the militant line he had taken as early as 1927. In his "Hunan Report" then, Mao had obliquely challenged the *Analects* of Confucius in stating flatly that no real revolution could be carried out "gently, kindly, politely, plainly, and modestly." The Sixteen Articles of 1966 revived that militancy, and the Red Guards adopted it.[8] The new Maoist class struggle did not need to be directed against any real "class" (structurally defined). Rather, it was directed against undesirable attitudes, ideas, or traditions and those who still held them.[9] The revolutionary philosophy that Maoists urged upon the entire nation could also, by virtue of the many connotations of the word *koming* (revolution) in Chinese, be a call to "get rid of one's own soul" as well as the soul of the foe, either literally or figuratively.[10]

When obstacles appear, the Maoist philosophy does not bend or compromise but asks the individual to make more sacrifices for the collective good. The communique of the Eleventh Plenum in 1966 pleaded that industrial enterprises "learn from the Ta-ch'ing Oil Field," that agriculture "learn from the Ta-chai Production Brigade," and that the whole country "learn from the PLA." [11] The three models were offered as examples of how the people could overcome material difficulties once they had absorbed Mao's thought and turned to selfless struggle. The Eleventh Plenum thus called on the PLA, factories, villages, schools, commercial departments, service trades, and Party and state organs to become "great schools of revolution" for imparting Mao's philosophy and insuring that all live by it. The Maoist press stressed that the entire nation must be armed with the "boundless power" of Mao's thought.[12]

The Red Guard movement also had apparently been intended to serve as a learning-by-doing school of revolution; its failure led to massive efforts, beginning in June, 1968, to send youth into agricultural and industrial production.[13] At the same time, new "worker-soldier-peasant (WSP) teams" were sent about the country to carry through the Cultural Revolution.[14] By October, Red Guard wall-poster activities had been discontinued, at the Maoists' command. The WSP teams were soon reported to have taken over the press, schools and universities, and other public institutions.[15]

While the Red Guards had sought to express and enforce the Maoist revolutionary philosophy, they tragically failed to realize that true Maoist revolutionaries must submit themselves to the same discipline that they impose upon others. The dispatch of the Red Guards from the cities to agricultural and industrial production centers was, in this sense, a corrective or therapeutic measure. Their replacement by the WSP teams meant that the task of disseminating a selfless philosophy and supervising its compliance now fell to a different group of more worthy Maoists. The demise of Red Guardism also coincided with the beginning of the stage of "construction."

Leadership Issues

Disagreements over both the philosophy and techniques of leadership have marked the dispute between the Maoists and Liu Shao-ch'i's group. The Maoists claimed that Liu was opposed to leadership by the working class. In his important editorial (possibly written at Mao's request), Yao Wen-yüan stated that "China's Khrushchev" practiced "polycentrism," "mountaintopism," and "factionalism" while endeavoring to sabotage working class leadership.[16] In Maoist usage, "polycentrism" meant "usurping" power and defying Mao's leadership.[17] Other accusations insinuated that Liu and his coterie had given special privileges and status to an elite group of Party bureaucrats, a practice that was incompatible with the mass line, had created their own "independent kingdoms" (a term once used against the Manchurian and East China Party leaders Kao Kang and Jao Shu-shih in 1954), including the "impenetrable" Peking Party committee under P'eng Chen before his dismissal, and had established the organizational and institutional framework for a return to capitalism.[18]

Bureaucratization of the same sort, as opposed to Mao's mass orientation, had emerged as an issue during the Socialist Education campaign. Mao's egalitarian policies called for greater respect for the masses, if only because both cadres and masses were or should be subject to the leadership of Mao's thought. Mao regarded the Party cadres, whose organization and leadership Liu had sought to enhance, as an element that could be interposed between the masses and Mao's own ideological leadership. Mao therefore used the Red Guards to dissolve the Party hierarchy as a source of opposition to his policies but then found himself obliged to rely on the army to restrain Red Guard interference with vital production activities. The extremist character and inexperience of the Red Guards and the undesirability of permitting

the PLA to wield political power for any prolonged period led
Mao, in the summer of 1968, to re-emphasize the role of the
masses—the workers and the poor and lower-middle peasants:

> To carry out proletarian educational revolution, the workers must
> be the leaders. . . . Worker propaganda teams must stay in the
> schools for long periods of time to participate in the tasks of
> struggle, criticism, and reform in the schools, and must lead the
> schools all the time. In the countryside, the schools will be under
> the supervision of the most trustworthy ally of the working class
> —the poor and lower-middle peasants.[19]

What are the credentials of the working class, according to the
Maoists? First, workers had had practical experience in the "three
revolutionary movements" (class struggle, the drive for production, and scientific experiment and application). Second, they
hated all words and deeds opposed to socialism and to Mao's
thought. Third, they abhorred the old educational system, with
its alleged bias in favor of children from "bourgeois" families.
Lastly, they were strongly opposed to "civil war" actions by
"certain intellectuals" (including students), which had destroyed
state property and had hindered the Cultural Revolution's tasks
of "struggle, criticism and reform." Workers also had no patience
with "empty talk" and "duplicity." "Therefore," it was claimed,
"the worker masses, in conjunction with the PLA warriors—
the main pillar of the dictatorship of the proletariat—will be
most capable of curbing all erroneous tendencies pernicious to
Chairman Mao's road of revolution." [20] In the same editorial,
Yao Wen-yüan refuted as trivial or misleading the arguments of
those whose opposition to such a prominent role for the working
class was based on the belief that workers should concentrate on
production because they lacked understanding of the educational
system and the situation in the schools.

The purpose behind the dispatch of WSP teams, as that editorial indicates, may have been to withdraw leadership from those
who had practiced "civil war," "empty talk," and "duplicity"

during the Cultural Revolution. Although the use of the WSP teams is consonant with Mao's mass line, the principle seems to have gained new meaning during the Cultural Revolution.

In the first place, the term "masses" was now defined to include industrial workers, PLA members, and the poor and lower-middle peasants. Marxist ideology has always stressed that the industrial proletariat is the main force of the revolution against the bourgeois class, but the emphasis on the army has new significance.

Although the army has occupied a unique position since the beginning of the Chinese Communist movement, the Party has always been in control of the gun. Especially after 1954, when the Ministry of Defense was established under the new Constitution, there had been a discernible effort to bring the PLA under the *administrative* jurisdiction of the civilian bureaucracy (the State Council), while, in ultimate *policy* matters, it remained under the Party's Military Affairs Commission (MAC). Yet the political (as distinct from military) importance of the PLA had been rising since the "Learn from the PLA" campaign of the early 1960's. It reached new heights after February, 1967, in response to Red Guard anarchism.

The third element of the masses in the current definition, the poor and lower-middle peasants, have always received Mao's attention. But it was not until the "four cleans" movement, from 1962 on, that Mao envisioned them as a counterweight to the cadres and gave them an unprecedented measure of independent managerial responsibility in commune government. Toward that end, Mao encouraged the formation of the associations of poor and lower-middle peasants.

Mao's renewed emphasis on the mass line appears to assign to the masses an unprecedented political significance, particularly in relation to the Party cadres. Mao's purpose, as noted, was to reverse the strong cadre orientation and bureaucratization that had characterized Liu's administration and to dislodge the "capitalist power-holders" who opposed Mao's views. The slogan now was: "You must be a pupil of the masses before you can be a teacher of the masses." [21] Although eventually, as the slogan suggests, the cadres will again become a "teacher of the masses," the privileges they had been permitted under the incentive system imputed to Liu were now abolished. Calls for "ties with the masses" and "supervision from the masses," recalling those in Mao's "twenty-three articles" of 1965, were widely stressed after February, 1967, during the formation of the Revolutionary Committees (also known as revolutionary or three-way alliances).

One purpose of the current campaign to learn from the masses is to train a new generation of Chinese Communist leaders. In the long run, the mandate that the masses confer on the Party must be accompanied by Party leadership of the masses. This relationship was one of the concerns of the Eleventh Plenum and of the new Constitution of the Party. The communique of the Eleventh Plenum, which reaffirmed the principles of democratic centralism and the mass line, referred specifically to the question of "rearing and training a new generation of leaders in the proletarian revolutionary cause."

The post-1963 campaign to train new leaders stemmed from Mao's fear that younger generations might succumb to the temptations of the heretical doctrine of "peaceful evolution" to Communism in the relaxed atmosphere prevailing under Liu's material incentive system. During the early stages of the Cultural Revolution, youth was urged to preserve the revolutionary spirit in order to take over the leadership of the revolution. In a talk before a Central Committee work conference in late 1966, Lin Piao cited five criteria for a qualified young leader. These were:

(1) a stanch belief in Marxism-Leninism and the thought of Mao Tse-tung, as a higher stage of development of Marxism-Leninism;

(2) selfless service to the people, which, in Communist doctrine, means "fighting selfishness, and devotion to the public";

(3) uniting oneself with the majority of the people (mass line);

(4) discipline in democratic centralism;

(5) analysis and correction of one's own merits and deficiencies according to the "one splitting into two" method.[22]

Lin particularly stressed the last criterion, stating that one must see oneself both as a member of the revolutionary force and its target. The revolution, he added, would die if future generations failed to apply this dialectic to self-analysis.[23]

However, perhaps in response to tendencies of irresponsibility, anarchy, and extremism in the Red Guard movement, references to the training of a new leadership generation decreased in the later stages of the Cultural Revolution. With surprising honesty, the Shanghai *Wen Hui Pao* attributed the "loss of bearing" of some youths to their inability to meet the superhuman challenges of the Cultural Revolution.[24] The re-education of the intellectuals (which in China embraces both the intelligentsia and the students) therefore became a central theme of the communique of the Party's Twelfth Plenum of October 31, 1968.

Education and Re-education

In early 1968, Mao sought to integrate education into the regular curriculum of schools and universities. A directive issued on March 7, 1968, ordered the PLA to begin military and political training, in order to create "a sense of organization and discipline" among school-age youth. The program, which remotely recalls the militia system of the communes, had been preceded by an experimental program after December, 1966.[25] Later in 1968, however, it was decided that the PLA would share the task of military and political education in schools and universities with representatives of the workers and peasants in the WSP teams.

The precise way in which the WSP teams supervised school operations remains unclear. The PLA's role appeared to be mainly that of training the students in military organization and discipline. The resident teams, designed to embody the spirit of the Cultural Revolution, probably supervised ideological revival sessions in each school and assisted in making reforms thought to be most beneficial to the interests of the worker and peasant classes. Their presence had the important symbolic significance of reversing the ancient tradition that "those who labor by brain shall rule; and those who labor by brawn shall be ruled." Indeed, the reversal of tradition was said to be a historic mission prescribed by Mao.[26] The importance of the task was stressed during a discussion at Futan University in Shanghai, which was attended by members of the resident "Workers' Thought of Mao Tse-tung Team," representatives of the PLA, and Red Guard leaders. One of Mao's sayings highlighted the campaign: "The lowliest are the wisest; the noblest, the stupidest."[27]

Among the reported reforms that marked a clear break with the past were: the abolition of the entrance examination system, which the Maoists condemned on the grounds that it favored children from more advantaged families; the institution of tutorial help to students from working-class and peasant families whose academic backgrounds were inadequate; greater participation by students from worker and peasant families in decisions affecting the curriculum, academic standards, and other related questions; and redirection of the curriculum toward more practical production needs.[28] Despite Maoist claims, some lowering of academic standards was probably unavoidable. Charges that faculty members retained bourgeois attitudes and ideas were often exaggerated or unwarranted. But the purpose of the reforms was clearly to admit more young people from proletarian and peasant families and to destroy the traditional "aura of authority" enjoyed by teachers. In some cases, required schooling was reduced to four years instead of six. That reduction and the lowering of academic standards made it possible to establish more schools in the communes, so that peasant students could live and work at home while going to school.[29]

Three general guidelines for educational reform were given in the Maoist press, on the basis of experiments carried out between March, 1967, and September, 1968: (1) Educational reforms must not be divorced from the needs and interests of the masses; (2) reforms must not be restricted to the revision of the curriculum but should be addressed to the entire school system; and (3) no revolution in the educational system would be possible without a prior ideological revolution.[30]

The ideological revolution was directed not only at the school system but at the intellectuals, writers, and artists. The re-education of the intelligentsia to serve the interests of the dictatorship of the proletariat and to preclude any return to capitalism was called a question of strategic importance. According to Maoists, the intellectuals had been educated under the pre-1949 "capitalist system" and had been subject to more recent "contamination" from the pernicious thought of "China's Khrushchev." For both reasons, they must be re-educated, with the help of the workers, soldiers, and peasants, so as to acquire a "proletarian *weltanschauung*." [31]

According to Maoist assertions, the purpose of re-education was to convert "negative elements" into "positive elements," not by physical punishment but by rectifying incorrect attitudes and developing a proletarian ideology. Although the tendency to accord technocrats too much prominence during Liu Shao-ch'i's administration must be corrected, members of the technocrat force must be given job opportunities, once they had fully completed the process of unity, criticism, unity. To deny them such outlets would be contrary to proletarian policies. Mao's distinction between contradictions among the people and those with the enemy was recalled, and the proletariat was reminded that only by "liberating the whole of mankind" could they "liberate" themselves. The masses must therefore help the intellectuals adopt a new work outlook and see that they gradually learned Marxism-Leninism and became one with the worker-peasant masses.[32]

The role given to the workers in re-educating the intellectuals was confirmed at the Twelfth Plenum in 1968, which announced that "the working class must lead all forms of education and must practice proletarian dictatorship in every cultural sphere of the superstructure in order to fulfill in various stages the tasks of struggle, criticism, and reform, as put forward by Chairman Mao, and to carry the Great Proletarian Cultural Revolution through to the end." [33] Lin Piao reiterated this line in Section 3 of his report to the Ninth Congress of the CCP on April 1, 1969, which was adopted by the Congress on April 14.

Reform in Arts and Letters

Appropriately enough, cultural regeneration has received a great deal of attention during the Cultural Revolution. Maoist polemics charged that Liu Shao-ch'i had intentionally disregarded the influence of arts and letters upon the ideology of the people; encouraged the retention of many pernicious plays on the grounds that their withdrawal from the repertory would render many actors jobless; objected to the banning of historical plays with questionable morals and permitted attacks on Chairman Mao in new historical plays with an anti-emperor theme; * and attempted to spread his own views of class conciliation and peaceful evolution to socialism through various cultural channels.[34]

Other attacks were directed at P'eng Chen, who before 1966 was probably second in importance only to Liu Shao-ch'i in decisions regarding arts and letters. The criticisms can be summarized as follows: First, P'eng had shown little interest in revolutionizing Chinese opera and was generally opposed to banning any plays regardless of their corrupting influence; and second, he opposed the proposal (presumably favored by Chiang Ch'ing) that the repertories of Chinese opera troupes include plays with contemporary themes and techniques. Even after Chiang Ch'ing had begun her 1964 campaign to clean up Chinese opera, ballet, and symphony music—the "most stubborn citadels" of bourgeois cul-

---

* The Maoists saw treasonable implications in the old opera *Szu-lang t'an mu* (*The Fourth Son Returns to Visit His Mother*), in which the hero, after surrendering to an alien power, marries its young princess, and an oblique attack on Mao in the new play *Hai Jui Dismissed from Office* and the new novel *Wind-Thunder*.

ture—P'eng Chen is said to have sought to evade reform by claiming that the coexistence of traditional and contemporary Chinese operas was in the spirit of the Party's "walking on two legs" policy. P'eng was also charged with the "crime" of having reversed Mao's phrase to state: "without construction, there is no destruction." [35] P'eng apparently felt that too much destruction had already taken place and that it was time to start reconstructing. In Mao's view, however, P'eng was attempting to ward off essential and radical changes.

Criticisms of other "revisionist" leaders in the cultural field generally followed the same lines, suggesting that the traditionalist aesthetic sense of such leaders would not permit them to support the drastic reforms proposed by the Maoists.

A number of Maoist works have received wide publicity in the press. One of these, a huge new oil painting, *Chairman Mao Goes to An-yüan*, portrays Mao's historic arrival, with an umbrella under one arm, at the site where he allegedly led workers in an armed struggle in the autumn of 1921, shortly after the founding of the Chinese Communist Party. The work has more political than artistic significance, in that it challenges an earlier portrait of Liu Shaoch'i as a "labor-movement leader" at An-yüan and signals Liu's political demise.[36] Mao's portrait was said to have been completed by a group of Peking students who had visited An-yüan in July, 1967, and interviewed old workers who had participated in the 1921 uprising with Mao.

Two artistic innovations are worth noting. The first is the use of the piano to accompany traditional Chinese opera. The piano was first used in July, 1968, in a new version of *Hung-teng-chi* (*Red Lantern*). The importance of the innovation was marked by the presence of Mao and Lin Piao at the first performance. The "improved" version of the opera was called a blow to the "counterrevolutionary and revisionist" line in the cultural field pursued by "China's Khrushchev." [37]

The use of the piano, credited as Chiang Ch'ing's brainchild, reflects Mao's policy of making ancient traditions serve a modern purpose, and foreign traditions a Chinese purpose. The innovation was also called an example of how people armed with the thought of Mao Tse-tung could "not only destroy the old world, but also construct one totally new." [38] Both claims suggest that the Cultural Revolution's "destruction" phase may be ending, and that a new phase of "construction" will seek to inject a new Maoist content into the vast areas of politics, social values, and popular culture. Whether the adaptation of the piano to a traditional form of art totally alien to Western music was really as successful as officially acclaimed is doubtful. But the innovation indicates that a relatively eclectic and utilitarian approach informs Maoist efforts to construct a utopian society.

Another innovation is the musical work *Sha-chia-pin* (*Shores of the Sha Village*), which "harmoniously incorporates the original characteristic melodies, instrumentation, and percussion rhythms of Chinese opera with symphony, choruses, and other forms of musical expression" borrowed from the West. Its official description as a "revolutionary symphony" is slightly misleading, since the work is not just an instrumental composition but includes arias and choruses with instrumental accompaniment. Hailed as the "first genuine symphony [opera] belonging to the world's proletariat and laboring people," the dramatic composition was said to "sing out" Mao's dictum that "political power grows out of the barrel of a gun." It is said to accord equal attention to musical harmony and the traditional Chinese emphasis on the individual words in the singing part. The work also combines the use of natural voice and falsetto. The singers who performed in the new presentation had been trained to sing Western operas, but they were said to have "overcome inhibitions and humbly made themselves pupils of Chinese opera singers in order to absorb the distinctive features of Chinese opera" that were considered worth preserving. [39]

While the *Red Lantern* remained a Chinese opera with the addition of piano accompaniment, the new composition was largely drawn from the Western operatic tradition, with features adapted from traditional Chinese conventions. In the final analysis, however, its importance lies not in the introduction of anything drastically new but in its pronounced attempt to shift the emphasis from Chinese to *Western* conventions, however modified and, to a certain extent, tortured, and to incorporate a variety of disparate elements.[40] Mao has repeatedly maintained that ideology, culture, and all forms of arts and letters have a class character and has also criticized traditional art forms for their bias in favor of the privileged classes and their neglect of the importance of the masses in historical development.[41] If superstructure reflects the quality of the society, how can the Maoists divest Western art forms of the bourgeois aspirations they reflect and adapt them to the needs of a new proletarian society?

In any event, the Chinese Communists have made concrete efforts to translate a theory of cultural value into practice. The effort is not unique in Chinese history. Nationalist China has also banned certain traditional Chinese opera-plays since 1949. One of them, *The Fourth Son Returns to Visit His Mother*, was also banned by the Maoists.[42]

In traditional thinking, arts and letters had an educational purpose that stemmed from the Confucian belief that society was a large school for the moral cultivation of its members. Social order depended not upon law (as understood in the West) but upon the preservation of "correct" human relationships. The Maoists continue to regard education and cultural expression as major components of the social order, but, as Marxists, they are highly conscious of the class character of education, and, as Leninists, they are eager to forge a new proletarian ethos through their control of education and culture. In their view, Liu Shao-ch'i and his associates were revisionists because they did not emphasize the class character of the struggle in education and culture. To realize their vision of the proletarian society, the Maoists have extended their control over all avenues of information and mass media, for the purpose of properly "educating" the population.[43]

14

ISSUES UNDERLYING
THE CULTURAL REVOLUTION—II

THE PRECEDING chapter focused primarily on the ideological, educational, and cultural issues underlying the Cultural Revolution. Those, however, are closely related to other issues of a more specifically political and economic nature. The present chapter will examine such aspects of state function as the civil administration, the role of the military, economic policy, and foreign policy. The next, and final, chapter on the Cultural Revolution will deal with the vital question of Party rebuilding under the Maoists and its significance for the future of Communist China.

The State Bureaucracy and the Military

THE CIVIL ADMINISTRATION

One of the major charges the Maoists made against the Liu Shao-ch'i administration during the Cultural Revolution was that it had permitted or encouraged an overexpansion of the state bureaucracy. The Maoists complained that the Liu group had perpetuated the ancient tradition of *tso-kuan tang-lao-yeh* ("find a career in the bureaucracy and be a revered lord"), which conferred upon its members an exclusivity that was incompatible with proletarian egalitarianism. Mao's countermeasures, known as *ching-pin chien-cheng* ("good men and simple government"), stressed the need for fewer and better personnel.[1]

Mao's concern with good government dates back to the Yenan period. His 1944 speech, "Serving the People," stressed the ideals of public service and good government, for which Mao gave credit to a contemporary non-Party member of the enlightened gentry, Li Ting-ming, who had first stressed their value.[2] Mao's opposition to bureaucratization continued after 1949. A most notable example of it was the administrative retrenchment drive launched in 1956–57.[3]

Notwithstanding criticisms during the Cultural Revolution of Liu's administration, Mao's efforts to reform the civil administration probably have a more current target. Such efforts first became evident in Mao's comments in March, 1968, on the experience of the formation of the Revolutionary Committees. As noted previously, the Committees were established between September, 1967, and September, 1968, in China's twenty-nine administrative units but, under the "three-way alliance" principle to redistribute political power, had become crowded with people needed for political, rather than administrative, reasons. It did not become clear, however, until July, 1968, when the reportedly successful retrenchment in the Revolutionary Committee of Ling-pao Hsien, Honan Province, was hailed with much fanfare, that Mao meant to streamline the civil administration.[4] Thereafter, reports of similar reform efforts elsewhere began to appear in the press.

In July, 1968, concrete steps to simplify institutions and reduce the size of the existing state bureaucracy were announced: Officials from the top-heavy bureaucracy were to be transferred to lower echelons (hsia-fang); duplicate offices and functions merged (ho-ping); superfluous agencies abolished (ch'e-hsiao); and efficiency and organization improved (ching-chien).[5] Official sources suggested that the staff of some Revolutionary Committees be cut back by as much as 80 or 90 per cent. Such overstaffing was, as always, termed a problem that had been inherited from the old (discredited) Party Committees and People's Councils (local governments) now replaced by the Revolutionary Committees.[6] A reduction in staff of that magnitude would obviously affect not only surviving bureaucrats sympathetic to the Liu line but also persons who had only recently risen to political eminence in the Revolutionary Committees. True to Mao's political style, ideological persuasion was used before organizational or staff changes were made, to show why overstaffing was against the public interest and how the reduction was a means of purging "self-seeking and revisionism." [7]

The timing of the reforms sheds considerable light on their purpose. The Maoist press issued warnings in January, 1968, against the "reactionary nature of factionalism" and, in February, against the "reactionary nature of anarchism." [8] The retrenchment drive was under way during August, 1968, when the Maoist press first issued a full blast at the Liu administration for "polycentrism." [9] That charge coincided with Maoist demands that "the working class must lead in everything." [10] It is quite possible that the administrative reforms were directed both against centrifugal tendencies in local governments and against the chaos that had resulted from the removal of many old cadres from power as a result of Red Guard attacks. Continuing clashes (factionalism) between Red Guard extremists and certain PLA forces, of which the Wuhan incident in July, 1967, was a glaring example, had made it necessary for the Maoists to stress working-class leadership (along with the peasantry) in order to control Red Guard extremists and counterbalance the military. All these events and measures were at least in part a consequence of the chaotic situation accompanying the overthrow of Liu's administration, Maoist allegations notwithstanding.

Another noteworthy feature of the Revolutionary Committee system is the new role of the mass line. Prior to the Cultural Revolution, cadres had been urged to follow the mass line, but the slogan "*from* the masses and *to* the masses" did not detract from the supremacy of the cadres. During the Cultural Revolution, however, Mao increasingly stressed "bonds with the masses" and the masses' supervision of the cadres.[11] The purpose of Mao's call for "revolutionary alliances" in February, 1967, was to use the masses to oppose "revisionism" and overstaffing in the existing bureaucracy and to dislodge the "power-holders." [12]

On the other hand, the representation of the masses, i.e., representatives of mass organizations, such as worker or peasant associations, in the Revolutionary Committees appears to have been proportionately much less than that of the PLA and the "revolutionary cadres" (those loyal to Mao).[13] Thus, Mao's concept of the mass line is not to be understood in terms of numerical representation in the political power structure. During the Cultural Revolution, the concept of the mass line seems to have had three primary emphases. First, the Revolutionary Committees were instructed to maintain close contacts with the masses (e.g., through correspondence and visits) in order to "learn with them the latest directives from Chairman Mao" and jointly to criticize the "revisionist" line of former "capitalist power-holders." [14] Second, by honoring the masses, the Maoists may have intended to provide a measure of consolation for officials who had been ousted from position either during the Cultural Revolution's seizure of power phase or during the institutional retrenchment period thereafter. Thus, "to be *lao-pai-hsing*" (common people) was given equal status with "to be *kuan*" (official).[15] Third, the role of the masses in production was stressed. Public meetings were held in production enterprises in order to boost the slackening pace of production by providing for exchanges of views between cadres and masses, by locating production bottlenecks, and by overcoming various kinds of psychological restraints on production.[16]

THE MILITARY

The important role played by the PLA in the formation of the Revolutionary Committees is well known. During the Cultural Revolution, Mao seems to have envisaged a significant but not supreme role for the military in the future as well. In the first place, a joint editorial on Army Day, August 1, 1968, in *Jen-min jih-pao, Hung-ch'i,* and *Chieh-fan chün-pao* referred specifically to Mao's 1930 statement that the Red Army must not merely fight wars but must also serve a political function, in spreading propaganda, organizing and arming the masses, assisting the masses in establishing revolutionary regimes, and even in organizing Party cells.[17] On the other hand, the editorial also referred to the resolution of the Ku-t'ien Conference of January, 1930, at which Mao had agreed to terminate the power of the soldiers' soviets and to institute a regular Political Commissariat in the Fourth Red Army (under the joint command of Mao and Chu Teh). While much mystery surrounded the Ku-t'ien Conference, it is quite certain that the event had ushered in a significant expansion of the Maoists' power, at the expense of the then Comintern-dominated Central Committee. Agreements had been reached at Ku-t'ien that allowed (Mao's) Front Committee to consolidate its control over the entire Fourth Red Army.[18] The mention of Ku-t'ien in the 1968 editorial could only be intended to re-canonize the tradition of Maoist political control of the Red Army, to the exclusion of an anti-Maoist Party machinery.

Second, the Army Day editorial described the PLA's role in the Cultural Revolution as an important one it shared with the masses. It recalled that Mao had authorized the PLA's participation in the seizure of power during the Cultural Revolution and in the formation of the Revolutionary Committees according to the "three-way alliance" principle. After paying due tribute to the PLA's successful fulfillment of its tasks (and its splendid record of "creatively learning and applying Mao's thought"), the editorial stated that the consolidation and development of the Revolutionary Committees remained a crucial task ahead. "This," it stressed, "is a common responsibility of the people in the *entire* country and an important political task confronting the People's Liberation Army" (italics added). More specifically, the editorial reasserted Mao's view that the most fundamental task in consolidating and developing the Revolutionary Committees was "to build up a leadership team that is revolutionized and united with the masses."

Although the PLA tradition of "four firsts," "three-eight working style," and "three main rules of discipline and eight points for attention" was upheld for public emulation, the PLA was reminded to unite itself with "the broad masses, the more of them the better." Mao's words were quoted: "The military is a main constituent of the political power [*cheng-chüan*, which also means government or regime] of the state." But the editorial placed an equal stress on the masses, the mass line, collective leadership, and democratic centralism. In other words, political power was not to be monopolized by the PLA. The special importance of the PLA was due not to its monopoly of brute force, however indispensable, but to its capacity to exemplify Chairman Mao's proletarian revolutionary line in helping to foster a proletarian spirit throughout the entire country.

Third, the editorial hinted that the PLA should not eclipse the Party. It stated specifically that "The honorable tradition of the People's Liberation Army *is* the honorable tradition of our Party." The list of exclamations beginning with "long live—" at the end of the editorial included both the PLA and the CCP, with the salute to the "great, honorable, and correct Chinese Communist Party" directly preceding the final salute to the "great commander Chairman Mao." [19] The order suggests that the Party ranks second only to Mao, whose thought and leadership are expected to guide it back to the correct path.

The Tasks of Production

Although Mao's Cultural Revolution caused serious disruptions in production, documentary evidence suggests that increasing production was one of his major goals in launching the Cultural Revolution. Production was given high priority in the "early ten points" (1963), the "twenty-three articles" (1965), and the "sixteen articles" (1966). Among the policy matters that came up for consideration at the Eleventh Plenum in 1966, the foremost was production.[20] According to the communiqué issued on August 12, 1966, the Eleventh Plenum considered a broad range of economic issues: (1) the "question of system and development in economic construction and national defense construction" (in other words, the proverbial "guns and butter" question); (2) "planning and arrangement for the gradual mechanization of agriculture"; (3) the question of "breaking down foreign conventions and following our own road of industrial development" (i.e., abandoning the Soviet model, which Liu was alleged to have followed, in favor of the Mao model); and (4) strategic plans concerning "preparedness against war, preparedness against natural calamities, and [preparedness to work] for the people." In this connection, the Plenum obviously had to consider the question of allocating more for military spending in anticipation of a possible expansion of the Vietnam war.

In the field of agriculture, the Plenum placed a new emphasis on mechanization. Mao had previously insisted, it was thought, that commune-level collectivization must be completed before the mechanization of agriculture. The new stress on mechanization therefore seemed to be a sharp departure from previous Maoist policy and a belated endorsement of a policy that Liu had long advocated and had pursued since September, 1959, when the Ministry of Agricultural Machinery was established. That Ministry was replaced in 1965 by a more ambitious Eighth Ministry of Machine-Building.[21] Since Mao had begun to reassert his ultimate authority in 1962 and, by 1965, had effectively reasserted control over the policy-making process, the new emphasis on agricultural mechanization probably meant that Mao had adopted and even promoted Liu's "revisionist" line in that area. Possibly to camouflage this shift, Maoist propaganda attacked Liu's handling of mechanization.[22]

A strong production bias marked the post-1962 political struggle in Peking. The establishment in 1964 of new "political departments" within the CCP Central Committee's departments for finance and trade, industry, and communications puzzled outside analysts, because their specific function was unknown. But it now appears that the purpose of the new political departments was to place Maoists in control of the various functional systems within the Party bureaucracy in order to prevent the old Liu-controlled Party committees from dominating the state bureaucracy at various levels and to halt any further drift of the nation's economy down the "capitalist road." [23] The General Political Department for Finance and Trade, for example, was established in 1964 either to supplement or to replace the Central Committee's Department of Finance and Trade. Li Hsien-nien, head of the new department, remained in the Politburo after its reorganization in August, 1966 (and again in the new Politburo, formed in April, 1969).

A strong concern for the collective economy has also characterized Mao's approach to the question of production. His "twenty-three articles" were critical of the effect of concealed lands and hidden property on the collective economy.[24] In the puritanical austerity of the Cultural Revolution, Maoists demanded that the state cease paying a 5 per cent dividend to former capitalists whose property had been taken over by the state in or before 1956.[25] There were said to be a quarter of a million such recipients in the mid-1960's. Red Guards reportedly retrieved, confiscated, or destroyed large amounts of private and hidden wealth during raids on the homes of those they suspected of capitalist leanings. One account assessed such recovered wealth at 1.2 million gold taels ($3.5 million in U.S. currency), along with the equivalent of $3.7 million in pounds sterling.[26] Maoist propaganda was sharply critical of the harm that a "revisionist" distribution system, based on the human appeal of incentives, had wrought in the state and collective economy and in the morale of individual commune members.[27] The Maoist press regularly denounced Liu Shao-ch'i, charging that he had placed "profits in command," offered material incentives, and promoted "economism" in the face of Mao's rule that "politics must take command" over purely economic or local considerations.[28]

Mao probably had not anticipated that the Red Guards' enthusiasm for the revolution and for the collective economy and their youthful unselfish spirit would inhibit productive forces. But as it turned out, the Red Guards caused serious disruptions in production [29] and finally had to be officially curbed in the summer of 1968. In an adroit maneuver, the Maoists dispatched hundreds of Red Guards and other youths from the urban centers to the countryside and as far away as sparsely populated Inner Mongolia, with the professed aim of boosting sagging production levels there.[30] By mid-January, 1969, it was reported some 15 to 20 million youths had been relocated.[31] The measure was obviously motivated as much by the desire to remove youths from urban trouble spots as by the need to reinforce the supply of labor in the countryside.

Documentary evidence, in the form of a series of public letters addressed to workers and poor and lower-middle peasants in early 1967, suggests that another central purpose of the Cultural Revolution was mobilization of the masses for another leap in production.[32] The mobilization effort differed somewhat, however, from the techniques employed during the Great Leap Forward in 1958.

In the first place, Mao's hope of a sudden economic and social transformation, which had characterized his thinking during the Great Leap period, gradually evolved into a recognition that such a transformation would require a prolonged process of nationwide and uninterrupted ideological purification, extending even beyond the socialist stage. The current mass line in production (unlike that of the Great Leap period) foresees a long period of drudgery in which it will be necessary to enforce a morality glorifying austerity, hard work, self-sacrifice, and determination to overcome obstacles. Those moral imperatives are meant to substitute for the material rewards of Liu's incentives system. They have been pressed even more forcefully than Mao's Great Leap themes of self-sacrifice, activism, and self-reliance.

In the second place, during the Great Leap period, Mao's efforts to bring about ideological self-cultivation were directed mainly at the elite. After 1960, they focused increasingly on the masses. For example, Mao's *ko-ming che-hsüeh* (revolutionary philosophy), which had been preached before primarily to the Red Army and Party cadres, was now urged upon every citizen, and to a point where a quantitative difference became a qualitative one.[33] Since the Maoists regard the worker-peasant-soldier masses as the most thoroughly steeled in the proletarian morality—much more so than the discredited Party bureaucracy—the masses are expected to supervise the ideological rebuilding of the Party, in addition to carrying out their professional and production duties.

Finally, during the Great Leap period, there was a tendency to slight technical competence and to overemphasize human will power. The current concept of the mass line, as applied in production, still places primary stress on mobilized human resources and ideological purification. But it does not neglect the importance of technical competence, as is attested by the rather awkward expression, "the three revolutionary movements of class struggle, production struggle, and scientific experiment," [34] which Mao in the post-1960 period characterized as the three main forms of man's social practice.[35]

Foreign-Policy Implications

It is difficult to clarify what policy options are under consideration in Peking at any given time and even more difficult to determine who is advocating what policy. Foreign policy was certainly one of the areas of ideological conflict during the Cultural Revolution, although it was probably less important than the internal political and economic issues to which it was related.

THE DEBATE IN 1965

Vietnam was one of several major foreign policy issues that involved relations with both the Soviet Union and the United States. The U.S. decision in 1965 to raise the level of hostilities in Vietnam had a number of repercussions. Soon afterward, the

Soviet Union approached Peking for permission to ship military hardware to North Vietnam across Chinese territory, both by air and by rail. It even requested airport facilities in South China for staging flights into Vietnam.[36] A precedent for an airlift had been established in 1960, when the Chinese Government permitted the Soviet Union to fly supplies to Laos. The new request added fuel to the continuing controversy within China about relations with the U.S.S.R. Although the precise line-up on the airport issue is not clear, Lo Jui-ch'ing, Chief of Staff of the PLA, is generally thought to have supported a more positive Chinese intervention in the Vietnam war and, hence, closer cooperation with the Soviet Union.[37] Despite the esoteric language of his article "Commemorate the Victory over German Fascism," he appeared to compare those opposing cooperation with the U.S.S.R. in a more active intervention in the Vietnam war to Daladier and Chamberlain, who had appeased Hitler at Munich. Using another dubious analogy, Lo recalled that the Soviet Union had first driven Nazi Germany from Soviet soil, then chased the Nazis out of other countries, and finally helped those other countries to set up new revolutionary regimes. The implications were that North Vietnam should undertake offensive mobile warfare in South Vietnam and that there should be all-out Chinese support for such an effort.[38]

A little more than three months later, Lin Piao outlined a different approach to the whole problem in his famous "Long Live the Victory of People's War" (see Chapter 8). A central theme of that equally esoteric article was that victory in a "people's war" depended upon self-reliance. Lin's statement implied that North Vietnam should not rely on outside support for its victory, that China should refrain from more positive action in Vietnam, and that China consequently would not ease its anti-Soviet stand in the interest of new joint Sino-Soviet efforts to support North Vietnam. Lin's reasoning was apparently based on the assumption that the United States did not plan to extend the Vietnam war to Chinese soil.[39] North Vietnam apparently understood the message: Its press commented on Lo's statement, but not Lin's.

The questions of China's policy toward Vietnam, the Soviet Union, and the United States and of the correct way to pursue a "people's war" were all thus intertwined in a debate of several years' duration. Back in 1964, Chou En-lai is known to have reported the existence in 1959–62 of widespread support, both within the Party and outside of it, for a policy line that advocated making peace with "imperialists," "reactionaries," and "modern revisionists," and the reduction of aid to foreign Communist or pro-Communist movements and to anticolonial independence movements.[40] The policy was described as the "three reconciliations and one reduction" (san-ho yi-shao) and was later attributed by Maoist propaganda to Liu Shao-ch'i.[41]

It is not yet clear whether and to what extent the foreign policy views of Lo Jui-ch'ing and Liu Shao-ch'i converged or, if so, on which issues. Maoist polemics during the Cultural Revolution consistently linked Liu and Lo together. However, if a group headed by Liu Shao-ch'i had really demanded a more relaxed foreign policy, it presumably would have favored reconciliation with the United States rather than the direct confrontation in Vietnam that Lo Jui-ch'ing had advocated. The purge of Lo during the initial stage of the Cultural Revolution and the ascendancy of Lin Piao combine to suggest that the policy Lin had advocated in his "Long Live the Victory of the People's War" was in line with Mao's own views; it was, in fact, adopted by the Eleventh Plenum in 1966.[42] The subsequent Maoist denunciation of Liu Shao-ch'i, who conceivably differed with Lo on Vietnam policy but may have shared his views on Sino-Soviet relations, suggests that the real difference between Maoists and their opponents had less to do with Vietnam than with "anti-Maoist" demands for a relaxation of China's hostility toward the Soviet Union. It is, of course, quite likely that those favoring better relations with the Soviet Union used the exigencies of the Vietnam war to support their own position.[43] It is also possible that neither Lo nor

Liu held the views for which he was denounced and purged and that we do not yet know the real reasons for their fall.

POLICY DIRECTION SINCE 1966

Any attempt to categorize the Maoists and their domestic adversaries as "doves" and "hawks," or even "hawks" and "superhawks," is an oversimplification. It is also a mistake to draw parallels between China's domestic policies and its foreign relations without taking into account the fact that domestic politics is characterized by a set of superordinate and subordinate relations that is absent in foreign relations. Although the spillover of the Cultural Revolution strained Peking's relations with many countries because of militant demonstrations by Chinese residents abroad, Red Guard humiliation of foreign envoys in Peking, and Mao's recall of Chinese envoys for ideological rectification at home,[44] it would be presumptuous to regard such incidents as a concerted attempt to export the Cultural Revolution.

Foreign policy was a high-priority item on the agenda of the Eleventh Plenum in 1966. Peking's relations with Moscow seem to have received closer attention at that session than any other issue. The communique of the Plenum declared that Mao's "open criticisms" of Soviet "revisionism" were completely correct and necessary, and it reaffirmed a series of previous CCP documents (Maoist) as the most "scientific" exposition of Marxism-Leninism. Among those documents were the "Proposals Concerning the General Line of the International Communist Movement" of June 14, 1963, written under the "personal direction of Comrade Mao Tse-tung," the nine commentaries on the CPSU Open Letter, the "Comment on the March Conference in Moscow," and Lin Piao's "Long Live the Victory of People's War."[45] The nine commentaries and the "Comment" were written jointly by the editorial staff of *Jen-min jih-pao* and *Hung-ch'i* in 1963.

The Eleventh Plenum, according to the communique, was convinced that, in order to fight "imperialism," Soviet "revisionism" had to be condemned for its capitulation to the "imperialists." Proletarian internationalism was said to be a "supreme guiding principle" of China's foreign policy. Since the Chinese call for proletarian internationalism followed Peking's condemnation of Soviet collusion with the "imperialists," it is clear that the CCP interpretation of "proletarian internationalism" differed from that of the CPSU. In CPSU usage, the principle implied Soviet primacy in the socialist bloc; to the CCP, it has become a weapon in the "anti-imperialist" struggle to rally the other socialist countries and Communist Parties in a common revolt against Soviet "modern revisionism." [46]

The Eleventh Plenum also promised "resolute support" to North Vietnam. This meant that the CCP supported without reservation Ho Chi Minh's determination to fight U.S. "imperialism" to the end, as outlined in Ho's New Year "Message to the Nation" of 1966. The session also confirmed all the measures adopted by the CCP and the Chinese Government to support North Vietnam in its fight against the United States and expressed support for further measures in the future. Soviet policy in Vietnam was called a masterpiece of duplicity, in that it feigned support but actually betrayed the North Vietnamese by its covert sellout to the "imperialists." [47]

The Plenum repeated its "anti-imperialist" attack on the United States and its "stooge," South Vietnam, and called for the formation of the "broadest possible international united front" against Washington and Saigon. The Soviet "revisionists," however, would be excluded from the alliance, because their "divisive, sabotaging, and subversive activities" directed against "international Communist movements and people's liberation movements" were carried out as a service to "American imperialism." [48] The CCP's policy of support for North Vietnam was expressed in part in a Peking-Hanoi Economic and Technical Assistance Agreement and its Protocol, which were signed in July, 1968. The official announcement of the signing of the agreement provided no details on what it contained. [49]

When Moscow and Washington signed a cultural agreement in July, 1968, Peking termed it proof of a deliberate scheme by CPSU leaders to "import American civilization" in order to satisfy "American imperialists." [50] Soviet occupation of Czechoslovakia in August was severely denounced, not out of sympathy for Dubcek's liberalization efforts, but because the act exemplified "big-nation chauvinism" of the worst kind.[51] The Soviet-Czechoslovak communique of August 27 drew further fire from Peking as a "deal under the bayonet" and as evidence of connivance by the "U.S. imperialists" and of Soviet-American "collusion" to divide the globe between them.[52]

The Twelfth Plenum of the Central Committee, which met from October 13 to October 31, 1968, was preoccupied with the same policy issues as the Eleventh Plenum. According to a communiqué issued at the end of the Twelfth Plenum, the session was even more hostile to Soviet policy than its predecessor, obviously because of Soviet intervention in Czechoslovakia. The accusation that the Soviet action had the support of "U.S. imperialists" was repeated, along with a blunt assertion that the U.S. war in Vietnam had the "tacit approval and support" of the Soviet "revisionists." Support to North Vietnam, Albania, and other "oppressed peoples" in an international "broad united front" under the principle of proletarian internationalism was reaffirmed as part of a dedicated international crusade against both "imperialism" and "revisionism." [53]

The same equation of Soviet "revisionism" with U.S. "imperialism" was expressed by Chou En-lai at a Peking rally. In a warning against complacency, Chou declared that the enemy could be expected to stage a last-ditch fight before his final defeat. He also hinted that an enemy invasion of China was possible. "If foreign enemies should dare to invade us," Chou concluded, "we will resolutely, thoroughly, and in a clean sweep destroy them all under the summons of our great leader, Chairman Mao." [54]

The "liberation" of Taiwan, a relatively muted theme after 1959, reappeared in Chinese policy statements.[55] The joint editorial in

Jen-min jih-pao and *Hung-ch'i* commemorating Army Day, August 1, 1968, concluded "We must liberate Taiwan." [56] Moreover, after September, 1968, when Revolutionary Committees had been established in all of China's twenty-nine administrative divisions, all references to the committees alluded pointedly to the unsettled status of Taiwan. For example, the Communique of the Twelfth Plenum of the Central Committee stated: "Revolutionary Committees have been established in all of China's twenty-nine provinces, metropolises, and autonomous regions, with the exception of *Taiwan* Province.[57]

Against this background, China's perspectives toward a number of interrelated foreign policy issues can be deduced. In the first place, Maoist hostility toward the Soviet Union can be expected to remain strong, both because of alleged Soviet "collusion" with the United States and because of Sino-Soviet disagreements on ideological, territorial, and other issues. Peking will also remain hostile toward the United States, both for ideological reasons and because U.S. support for South Vietnam and Taiwan poses a threat to China's own security. In Peking's view, the "collusion" between Moscow and Washington in Vietnam, Taiwan, and even Czechoslovakia is a fundamental reason for its hostility toward both major powers. At the same time, Peking will in some way continue to support North Vietnam, not only for ideological reasons but as a symbol of China's fight against Soviet-American "collusion." China will also continue to support, as a matter of doctrine, other international movements of "liberation" from "imperialist, colonial, and neocolonial" bondage. The theme of "proletarian internationalism" will be revived as a weapon against Soviet "revisionism," and the international broad united front China seeks to establish and lead will exclude the Soviet Union so long as the present Soviet leadership remains in power. Lastly, the "liberation" of Taiwan will continue to receive top priority in Peking's foreign policy thinking.

In retrospect, the Taiwan question holds the key to other questions. It is at the source of the long confrontation between

Peking and Washington and has steadily increased Peking's distrust of the Soviet Union, irrespective of ideological issues.[58] Although there is little or no evidence of substantial differences between Maoists and "anti-Maoists" on the issues of anti-imperialism and the "liberation" of Taiwan, they have probably drawn different conclusions about the evolution of Sino-Soviet relations since 1954. At least one group of "anti-Maoists" has argued in favor of reducing Sino-Soviet tensions. However, since no Chinese government is likely to want to fight two major powers on two fronts at the same time, it is likely that Peking will seek means to reduce tensions through limited negotiations with either Washington or Moscow or both.

TIME FOR A CHANGE?

At the end of 1968, there were several signs of a possible change in Peking's attitudes. In the first place, the Maoist leadership openly dropped its previous opposition to the Paris peace talks on Vietnam, although it did not regard them with any enthusiasm. On October 20, a week after the beginning of the Twelfth Plenum, the Chinese press informed the public about the talks, quoting Western news agencies.[59] The softening of Peking's stand was probably decided during the Plenum. On November 3, one day after the release of the communique of the Twelfth Plenum, *Jen-min jih-pao* published in full President Johnson's October 31 statement on the complete cessation of all U.S. aerial and naval bombardment of North Vietnam. Simultaneously, it carried the full text of an official Hanoi statement of November 2 in response to the Johnson statement.[60] Subsequently, attacks on U.S. imperialism diminished.

In late 1968, Peking also proposed that the Warsaw ambassadorial-level talks be resumed in 1969 between representatives of China and those of the new Nixon Administration in the United States. An even greater surprise was China's suggestion that the United States join in "an agreement on the five principles of peaceful coexistence." [61] Although the proposal reiterated Peking's demand for the withdrawal of U.S. forces from "China's Taiwan Province," the new initiative had considerable doctrinal importance. A key theme of the Sino-Soviet polemics has been the extent of the applicability of "peaceful coexistence." In the past, the CCP's official position was, contrary to the Soviet view, that "peaceful coexistence" was to be applied first and foremost within the socialist bloc, then to the nonaligned states, and finally to the "ordinary bourgeois" countries no longer practicing "imperialism." [62] In past Maoist doctrine, it did not extend to practicing "imperialists," even though, in practical circumstances, its *de facto* observance was not ruled out.[63] The fact that Peking subsequently cancelled the Warsaw talks, scheduled for February 20, 1969, does not lessen the importance of the apparent doctrinal change. Then, on January 20, 1970, the Sino-American talks were finally resumed, perhaps as a result of Peking's concern about its deteriorating relations with the Soviet Union.

In the light of the attacks on Liu Shao-ch'i during the Cultural Revolution for having advocated "reconciliation with the imperialists," what do the above initiatives vis-à-vis the United States mean? One possible interpretation is that the real policy differences between the Maoists and the "revisionists" were in areas other than foreign policy, such as the strategy for economic development. Another is that the most acute differences in foreign policy concern China's relations with the Soviet Union rather than the Taiwan question or "imperialism."

To Sum Up

First, although ideological differences between Maoists and those they opposed were a very real part of the momentum behind the Cultural Revolution, such differences tend to become blurred when it is recognized that Maoist words, as employed in some of the Red Guard polemics, also differed considerably from Maoist policies adopted after 1967. The Maoists did praise self-sacrifice and the virtues of frugality and accused their "revisionist" opponents of self-indulgence and even hedonism, but we do not know what justification there may have been for the charges. The Maoists also claimed that the Liu group had been responsible for the emergence of a new privileged class. Whatever truth there may have been in that claim, Mao does seem to have worked to maintain a degree of parity between the masses and the Party bureaucracy, even though his efforts to overturn the "power-holders" had other motives.

Second, improvisation marked the development of the Cultural Revolution. Much of the original planning for it had to be abandoned or altered as unexpected events rendered it obsolete. For example, the changing roles and degrees of prominence of the Party, youth, the worker-peasant class, and the PLA indicated Mao's shifting response to changing circumstances.

Third, although Liu was a convenient and almost universal scapegoat, not all corrective measures were, in fact, directed against the wrongs charged to his administration. Some, such as the administrative retrenchment measure, were prompted by anomalies that had emerged during the formation of the Revolutionary Committees after Liu's fall. The massive re-education of intellectuals and the organization of WSP teams to take over the schools appear to have been prompted by the excessive response from youth to Mao's message. Thus, the extension of the Cultural Revolution produced a qualitative transformation of the movement.

Fourth, Mao's adoption of certain policies suggests that, for all his ideological idealism, he has been forced to compromise and make necessary changes. Although he has continued to stress the need for psychic mobilization of China's masses, since 1960 he has also admitted the need for technical competence. At the same time, Mao's instant Communism strategy (the Great Leap) has given way to a more patient outlook, anticipating a protracted war on the socio-economic front, and he appears to have quietly adopted the active agricultural mechanization program originally endorsed by Liu Shao-ch'i. Such shifts may be evidence not of hypocrisy but of the practical flexibility Mao has shown on many occasions in the past. For obvious political reasons, Mao could not openly announce that he had adopted the policies of men he had accused of betraying China. Also, between 1960 and 1965, the Maoists were somewhat out of the mainstream of political decision-making. The resumption of power, with all of its responsibilities, can have a sobering effect.

Finally, although foreign policy differences also figured in the Mao-Liu schism—and these seem to have been rooted in the crucial problem of Peking's relations with Moscow—the conflict was primarily over domestic politics. In both areas, the ultimate differences between the Maoists and the "anti-Maoists" seem to boil down to differing priorities and preferences. Mao's priorities are succinctly embodied in the "four firsts": Human resources come before material ones (man over weapons); political considerations (macro-development) take precedence of economic or other considerations (micro-development); ideology has priority over politics; and the flexible application of ideology (living ideas) is more important than blind subscription to dogma (book knowledge).[64] In short, Mao's ideological leadership takes priority over everything else. The "anti-Maoists" were not necessarily determined to take the opposite course, but the Maoists appear to oppose any deviation.

The Maoists' charges against Liu Shao-ch'i were not totally groundless, nor were they totally credible. Perhaps the most profound—and often overlooked—source for Maoist opposition to domestic "revisionists" was resentment against those men for having removed the "thought of Mao Tse-tung" from the 1956 Constitution of the CCP. In drafting a new Party Constitution in 1969, the Maoists made enormous efforts to restore and even to raise the prestige conferred upon Mao's thought by the 1945 Party Constitution. In retrospect, all other issues derive from and are ancillary to this one.

15

REBUILDING THE PARTY
IN MAO'S IMAGE

FOR A time, some Western analysts thought that Mao was bent on destroying the Chinese Communist Party and ascribed such a folly to his "madness" and lust for power. Soviet polemics even made flat assertions to that effect.[1] Unquestionably, the Cultural Revolution did bring to the fore a sharp confrontation between the Maoists and the Party structure. But before analyzing Mao's intentions in regard to the Party and their ideological significance, it is important to draw these distinctions: (1) between Mao's plans for Party reform and his improvisation in response to the events of the Cultural Revolution; (2) between the "idea" of Party and its reality; (3) between *a* Party and *the* Party; and (4) between a Party as a means to an end and a Party that is an end in itself.

Chapter 12 and, to a certain degree, the subsequent two chapters dealt with the question of planning and improvisation. The other questions, to be discussed in this chapter, concern, in their essence, Mao's view of the Party and of its role in his revolution.

The Concept of Party

One essential element in the concept of Party—its function in providing national cohesion and organization—derives from the Party's historic role in the revolution and in the consolidation

of state power after 1949 in the People's Republic of China. It is
an indelible element. The total lack of cohesion threatening the
very viability of Chinese society in the first two decades of the
twentieth century led such men as Mao, Lin Piao, Ch'en Po-ta,
K'ang Sheng, Chou En-lai, and their predecessors to convert to
Communism and to adopt the Leninist mode of organization.
Even Sun Yat-sen felt it imperative to reorganize his Kuomintang
along Leninist lines in 1923 in order to maintain internal unity,
cohesion, and a central purpose.

The concept of Party also has both "ideal" and "real" elements.
The first serious sign during the Cultural Revolution that the Maoists had not forgotten the importance of the Party came approximately in May, 1968. Prominent publicity was given in the
Maoist press to an article of mysterious origin, attributed to a
"Stalin Group," described as a "revolutionary organization in the
Soviet Union that is opposed to the Khrushchevite revisionist
clique." The article castigated "Soviet revisionists' calumnies" that
the Cultural Revolution was "directed against the Chinese Communist Party." It flatly stated:

> The fact that the broadest masses of the people are taking part
> in the Cultural Revolution together with the Party *does not in
> the least impair the prestige of the Chinese Communist Party*,
> because the masses act strictly under the leadership of the Party
> and in accordance with its instructions. Participation in the
> struggle against bourgeois degeneration and opportunism only
> Bolshevizes the masses, rallies them around the Marxist core of
> the Party, educates them in the spirit of Communism and in
> revolutionary practice, that is, turns them into mighty reserves
> of the Party.
>
> The fact that the masses are actively fighting for the cause of
> the Party under the leadership of *the Party of Mao Tse-tung*
> testifies to the maturity of the Chinese Communist Party, the
> correctness of its policies, and the great unity between the Chi-
> nese Party and the people.[2]

The importance ascribed to the document's content in the Maoist press seems to outweigh the obscurity of its origin. For this

reason, some salient themes in the document, particularly in the quoted passage, deserve mention.

The allusion to "the Party of Mao Tse-tung" suggests that there may be another party within the loose boundary of the CCP. The text implicitly distinguishes between "the Marxist core" and other elements within the Party whose "bourgeois degeneration and opportunism" have led them to deviate from the "Marxist core." The assertion that massive attacks on the non-Marxist sections will "not in the least" impair the "prestige of the Chinese Communist Party" also suggests a vision of the Party as an ideal. The more restrictive term, "Party of Mao Tse-tung," seems to claim that the Maoists alone are the true carriers of Marxism, while others have become revisionists.

Thus, there can be three ways in which the word "Party" is used: (1) "the Party" in its abstract and transcendental sense; (2) "a party" made up of those within "the Party" who are responsible for its "bourgeoise degeneration"; and (3) within the Party, "a party" headed by Mao (despite the claim in "*the* Party of Mao"), which seeks to rectify the Party.

During the Cultural Revolution, Red Guard attacks so crippled the operations of the existing Party that the PLA had to assume many of its functions. In the face of that destruction, Maoists could probably argue that the devastation had been inflicted upon "a party" of "revisionists," who were undermining the ideal of "the Party." The belief that "a party" that does not live up to the expectations of "the Party" is unworthy of the name recalls the "rectification of names" urged by ancient Chinese thinkers.[3] There is a clear parallel with the ancient adage of Mencius that a king who had failed to be what a "King" should be was no longer king but a "lone person" (*yi fu*) against whom revolt was justifiable.

Mao himself never said anything against the idea of the Party. He only said that "outside a party, there exist other parties, and inside a party there exist factions; this has always been the case."[4] The English word, faction, is a conventional translation of the

Chinese term, *tsung-p'ai* (or *p'ai-hsi*) which has broader meanings. Mao was pointing out that the struggle between the Maoists and the "revisionists" was "between the proletarian party spirit and the bourgeois party spirit." [5] In seeking to rectify the "bourgeois party spirit" so as to purify the "proletarian party spirit," Mao intended not to destroy the idea of the Party but to make the reality correspond more closely with the idea. If the uninhibited attacks mounted by the Red Guards were to bare and condemn the "bourgeois party spirit," then the historical role of the PLA was to serve as a temporary repository of Party prestige and authority until a reformed Party could resume its functions.

The most important message about the role of the military came on Army Day, August 1, 1968, when a joint editorial in *Jen-min jih-pao, Hung-ch'i* and *Chieh-fang chün-pao* attributed the PLA's "honorable tradition" to the Party's traditional leadership. [6] In anticipation of their resumption of normal functions, the rectification of cadres was intensified. The massive efforts, starting in May, 1968, to send them out to perform manual labor recalled past *hsia fang* movements to shake the cadres out of their bureaucratic complacency. [7]

Dictatorship of the Proletariat

An obsessive theme in Maoist polemics during the Cultural Revolution was the "dictatorship of the proletariat," an old Marxist precept that now took on new connotations. One of the accusations against Liu Shao-ch'i was that he had betrayed the dictatorship of the proletariat in advocating "peaceful evolution" to Communism. The Maoists charged that, in the 1962 edition of his *The Self-Cultivation of a Communist,* Liu had implied that China in the socialist stage was an "all-people society," in which class struggle had ceased to have its previous significance, and had suggested that it should be governed by an "all-people dictatorship" rather than by the dictatorship of any class (even the proletariat). Liu's silence under attack was cited as evidence that he had attempted to "restore capitalism" by permitting the emergence of a new bureaucratic elite which practiced a *de facto* dictatorship over the masses.[8] In the Maoist view, under Liu's administration the Party had ceased to be the "vanguard of the proletariat"; its bureaucratization, detachment from the masses, and primary concern with its own interests constituted "repression" of the masses. This was tantamount to a "dictatorship of the bourgeoisie." Maoist polemics took pains to explain that "dictatorship of the proletariat" meant "dictatorship of the masses." "In 1962," declared an editorial signed by the Proletarian Revolutionaries of the Political Academy of the Chinese People's Liberation Army,

> Chairman Mao profoundly expounded the great significance of the exercise of *dictatorship by the masses*. . . . During the Great Proletarian Cultural Revolution, Chairman Mao pointed out again with deep wisdom that *dictatorship meant dictatorship by the masses*.[9]

The editorial recalled that in 1965 Mao had laid down as a golden rule for the Socialist Education campaign the requirement that the masses be mobilized "to supervise the *class enemies* conscientiously and remold them on the spot." [10] Mao's assertions during the Socialist Education phase and the early stage of the Cultural Revolution that the masses must "supervise" the remolding of the "cadres" in the (Liu-led) Party machine actually meant, as the editorial made clear, that a "dictatorship of the masses" must be directed against the "class enemies" who had allegedly formed a "dictatorship of the bourgeoisie." [11] It was thus necessary to retain the concept of the continued existence of classes in the socialist stage. Since the "power-holders" constituted "class enemies," the Maoists could claim justification for a "power seizure" to dislodge them, but it was necessary to revive the idea of the dictatorship of the proletariat in order to clothe the new dictatorship of the masses with Marxist legitimacy. Hence, the Maoists called for "practicing democracy toward the people and exercising dictatorship over the enemy." [12] To restore democracy among the people, dictatorship over the enemy became indispensable and justifiable.

At the same time, the meaning of the term "proletariat" was broadened to include the "interests of the proletariat *and . . .* the broad laboring masses." [13] Secondly, the power of the Party was reduced and the new dictatorship of the masses was supported by a tripod of representatives of the Party, the PLA, and the masses (including Red Guard leaders). Thirdly, the spiritual guidance of Mao's thought was to be used to dispel from people's minds the poisonous influence of the "dictatorship of the bourgeoisie." [14] The most significant of these changes was the clear shift in emphasis from the Party to the masses.

Civic Morality and the Party

During the discussion of Party rebuilding in 1968, Mao gave much thought to reviving the "three great working styles" [15] (i.e., traditions) of the CCP, one of which, its "closest ties with the masses," was said to distinguish the Communist Party from all other political parties. At the same time, Mao said that the proletariat (meaning the masses) must "liberate" not only itself but also all of mankind, if its own "liberation" was to be assured. "The entire Party and the entire people of the country," according to Lin Piao, "must be united around Chairman Mao and around Chairman Mao's thought as their center." [16] Both statements suggest a vision of something larger than the Party and the proletariat *per se*. One might call it Mao's vision of a good society or of a "general will," to be distinguished from the particular wills of any individual or group (including the Party).

In a stimulating discourse on Mao's image of civic morality, Benjamin I. Schwartz compares Mao's thinking during the Cultural Revolution to the ethical emphasis of Jean Jacques Rousseau some two centuries ago. To the extent that Mao's thought expresses a kind of general will or collective ethic, a party that is divorced from it and develops its own momentum may degenerate and become another "partial interest." [17] Schwartz notes that, whereas Rousseau's general will rejects any social hierarchy, Mao has inherited not only the Marxist concept of the "class" character of society but also the traditional Chinese notion of a social hierarchy based on intellectual and moral accomplishment, as elaborated by Mencius.[18] While Mao accepts Leninism for its organizational techniques, without adopting its concepts of Party constitutionality and legality, he recognizes that the Party is subordinate to the general will, not above it.[19] Since 1960, Mao has modified Leninist elitism (which Liu Shao-ch'i appeared to accept rather literally) by raising doubts about the Party's claim to exclusive possession of "self-consciousness." In his view, the masses must help restore the revolutionary consciousness that the elite has lost in the course of its "bourgeois degeneration."

So that the general will may prevail over the individual will, Rousseau invents the artificial device of a "legislator," as distinct from a magistrate (or prince). The former is the engineer who invents the machine, the latter merely the mechanic who sets it up and makes it go. In Rousseau's terms, the legislator is endowed with exceptional intelligence and reason "far above the range of the common herd." Being unable to appeal to either force or reason, the legislator must, according to Rousseau, "have recourse to an authority of a different order, capable of constraining without violence and persuading without convincing." [20] It is noteworthy that the emphasis on intelligence, as distinct from moral accomplishment, makes Rousseau's legislator rather alien to the Chinese. Yet, the idea has a parallel in Chinese political tradition in the concept of the sage-ruler (*hsien-che tsai-wei*) as the fountainhead of all civic morality and the contemporary repository of the cumulative wisdom of the ancient sage-kings (*hsien wang*). Their subjects basked in the grace and spirituality of the benevolent rule of a true king (*wang-tao*). A special elite of "king's men" (*chün-tzu*), whose moral and intellectual accomplishments qualified them for civil service, assisted the sage-ruler in promoting the public good under his "benign rule" (*jen cheng*).[21]

The relations between Mao and the Party bear some resemblance to both Rousseau's ideal system and the ancient Chinese ideal of the sage-ruler. Mao is halfway between Rousseau's "legislator" and Confucius's sage-ruler but, nevertheless, is supposed to be the source of all civic morality. Party members do not earn their status by their individual moral accomplishment, as understood in the Confucian sense, but the Party as a whole is expected to serve as an institutional *chün-tzu*. Its status depends on its ability to promote the public good. Its failure to live up to its mandate does not invalidate it as a conduit for the civic morality of which Mao is the source, nor does that failure reflect upon the public the Party is supposed to serve, but it does justify the rescinding of the Party's mandate until a reformed Party has again proved its worthiness.

The anger Mao has directed toward a balking Party since 1962 is quite different, in source, from the indifference Stalin displayed toward its Soviet counterpart after the 1930's. The development of European and Soviet Marxism had been influenced by St. Simon's emphasis on the importance of an industrial-scientific elite and, to a lesser extent, by Rousseau's concept of civic virtue. For Lenin, and later Stalin, the proletariat was an instrument for society's technical, economic, and moral progress, and the Party, particularly after Lenin shifted its emphasis from proletarian virtues to professional organization,[22] had a role in engineering such progress. Lenin, and Stalin after him, stressed the organizational role of the Party at the expense of its moral values. Mao, on the other hand, has found the Party insufficiently "red" rather than insufficiently "expert." Abhorring the obsessive form he believes technocracy has taken in China under the "revisionists" (after the Soviet example), Mao has stressed social and ethical, rather than technical, progress.[23]

In Mao's view, the future of the Communist revolution in China depends not so much on the skill of the Party as on the acceptance, both within China and abroad, of the Maoist concept of civic virtue. Without using the term "social contract" (which appears to reflect the Western mercantile tradition, unknown in agrarian China), Mao's vision embodies the general will and, in Rousseau's words, Sovereign Power. Very much like Rousseau, Mao believes that the Sovereign ought to be capable of changing human nature, in pursuance of civic virtue, and of altering man's constitution for the purpose of strengthening it. The Party is an agency to help realize civic virtue but is not a substitute for it; nor can the Party impose virtue on the masses. In short, the Party is a means to a Maoist end, not an end in itself.

The Task Ahead

Although Party rebuilding was cited as a major task for 1968 in a New Year's Day editorial in the *People's Daily*, the preparatory work for the convening of the Ninth Party Congress took more than a year to complete. Generally chaotic conditions and the difficulties involved in "democratizing" the surviving Party cadres were among the many reasons for the delay. The reconstruction of the Party required the resolution of several key issues: (1) the language of the draft Party Constitution to be presented for adoption at the Ninth Party Congress; (2) the relationship between the Party and the PLA, in which the Party apparatus within the PLA would presumably play a critical role; (3) the future political role of Red Guard youth; (4) the streamlining of the Party bureaucracy; and (5) the balance among Party, army, and Red Guard activists on the Revolutionary Committees.

Possibly as an interim measure, pending the convening of the long-delayed Ninth Party Congress, the Central Committee held its Twelfth Plenum between October 13 and October 31. It was packed with Maoists brought in from outside the Committee's membership. The session officially confirmed the ouster of the Liu "anti-Party" and "traitor" group. It affirmed the correctness of Mao's line from the Great Leap Forward through the Cultural Revolution and fomally endorsed the policy shifts introduced since the Eleventh Plenum in 1966, most of which have been discussed in the two preceding chapters. Regarding the future of the Party, the Twelfth Plenum adopted the slogan: "Exhaling the stale and absorbing the fresh" (*t'u-ku na-hsin*).[24]

The New CCP Constitution

A draft Party Constitution circulated in late 1968 and early 1969 was adopted, with some changes, by the Ninth Party Congress, which met in Peking from April 1 to April 24, 1969.[25] Some of the changes are rather significant from the ideological point of view and also suggest the configuration of forces within the new Party leadership. The Constitution is the most important single document to emerge from the Cultural Revolution; it is expected to guide the Party and the entire nation for the foreseeable future. The major provisions of this document are outlined below.

(1) According to the new Constitution, the "basic program" of the CCP calls for the "*complete* overthrow of the bourgeoisie and all other exploiting classes, the establishment of the dictatorship of the proletariat in place of the dictatorship of the bourgeoisie and the triumph of socialism over capitalism." "The *ultimate* aim," it is declared, "is the realization of Communism." (Emphasis added.) In the 1968 draft, only the "complete overthrow of the bourgeoisie" was mentioned. The text, as adopted, added "and all other exploiting classes." The admission that the bourgeoisie, along with other exploiting classes, had not been completely overthrown seems to conflict with contrary claims made in the 1956 Party Constitution. In that earlier document, it was stated that, following the overthrow in 1949 of the rule of imperialism, feudalism, and bureaucratic capitalism, the Party-led democratic revolution" had been *accomplished*, resulting in the establishment of a socialist society. The use of the phrase "complete overthrow" in the 1969 Constitution confirms Mao's post-1956 belief that bourgeois remnants may persist even during the socialist stage. In Mao's view, it follows that continued strug-

gle against the bourgeois remnants will be necessary, since it is much harder to erase bourgeois ideas and traditions from people's minds than it is to overthrow the social structure. The word "complete" also suggests Mao's feeling that "revisionists" have prevented or delayed the establishment of the dictatorship of the proletariat. In point of fact, the incomplete overthrow of the bourgeoisie could have been a result of Mao's own four-class coalition under his "new democracy" program, in which he envisaged the continued coexistence of the national and urban petty bourgeoisie under joint peasant-worker leadership. But it was never anticipated, of course, that the bourgeoisie would be anything more than a silent junior partner in the coalition. The denunciation of the "dictatorship of the bourgeoisie" is clearly a reference to the Liu Shao-ch'i administration.

The assertion that the realization of Communism remains the "ultimate" aim of the Party constitutes another doctrinal concession. Contrary to Mao's claims during the Great Leap Forward, it admits that China has yet to enter the Communist stage of development. Moreover, the new Constitution openly admits that the period of transition from socialism to Communism is a "fairly long historical period." This note of realism confirms that Mao has retreated from his earlier efforts to achieve instant Communism.

(2) The Constitution formally sanctifies the Cultural Revolution as "a great political revolution carried out under conditions of socialism by the proletariat against the bourgeoisie and all other exploiting classes." It states that "throughout this historical period, there are classes, class contradictions, and class struggle; there is the struggle between the socialist road and the capitalist road . . . the danger of capitalist restoration, and . . . the threat of subversion and aggression by imperialism and modern revisionism." Having reaffirmed Mao's ideas on continued revolution and contrived class struggle, the Constitution justifies the Cultural Revolution as one phase of a ceaseless ideological struggle leading into the future. Its language no doubt reflects Mao's personal reaction to events in China between 1959 and 1965,

but its bearing on the course of events after Mao's lifetime is questionable.

(3) The CCP, according to the new document, is "composed of the advanced elements of the proletariat; it is a vigorous vanguard organization leading the proletariat and the revolutionary masses in the fight against the class enemy." The Constitution repeats in broad outline the Leninist notion of the Party, thus restoring weight to the Party's leadership and playing down the "leadership of the masses"—a major slogan of the Cultural Revolution, especially after mid-August, 1968.

(4) The new Constitution supports several Maoist attitudes toward China's foreign policy. It "upholds proletarian internationalism" in alliance with "the genuine Marxist-Leninist Parties and groups the world over" and with "the proletariat, the oppressed people and nations of the whole world." Their common cause is the struggle against "imperialism headed by the United States, modern revisionism with the Soviet revisionist renegade clique as its center, and the reactionaries of all countries." It has been suggested earlier that Mao feared Moscow was exploiting the principle of "proletarian internationalism" to justify Soviet primacy within the Communist bloc.[26] Since mid-1968, Chinese foreign policy statements have called for a different kind of "proletarian internationalism" that would rally support for a broad international united front that excludes the Soviet Union. This new militant strategy emerged from Maoist opposition to the policy of "three reconciliations and one reduction," which Liu Shao-ch'i had allegedly followed.

(5) The original draft of the preamble to the new Constitution rather prominently featured the slogan "exhaling the stale and absorbing the fresh," which had been formally adopted at the Twelfth Plenum as a fundamental principle of Party rebuilding. Its inclusion suggests that the author of the Twelfth Plenum resolutions may also have drafted the preamble of the Constitution. In the Constitution as adopted, however, the phrase has been shifted from the preamble to the last paragraph of the last

article, which deals with the organization of the primary-level Party apparatus. The juxtaposition makes it clear that the infusion of new blood is to be effected at the lower levels of the Party rather than at the center.

The shift may also show a renewed interest among a more self-confident top leadership in routinization at the upper levels of the Party. On the other hand, the shift may be due to a compromise between such rising stars as Lin Piao and the surviving senior members of the top Party leadership, with the former seeking to justify the final ouster of the Liu group and their own meteoric rise, and the latter concerned about maintaining their power. If the shift was, in fact, due to a compromise, Lin Piao's leadership position may be less certain than it now appears to be.

(6) The Party's long-standing policy of opposing both rightist and leftist opportunism is reiterated in the 1969 Constitution. Unlike the 1956 Constitution, the new document is explicit about Mao's personal importance: "The Communist Party of China, with Comrade Mao Tse-tung as its leader, is a great, glorious, and correct Party and is the core of leadership of the Chinese people." Although Mao's person is glorified, the intention is not the simple service of a personality cult. As suggested earlier, Mao never intended to let the prestige of the Party be destroyed, although Red Guard attacks on the Party severely damaged its structure. Throughout the Cultural Revolution, Mao maintained the distinction between a degenerate machine under the "revisionists" and the Party under his effective leadership. The new Constitution reaffirms that the Party under Mao is still the "great, glorious, and correct Party" that should lead the nation.

The importance of Mao is not personal but ideological. The 1969 Constitution restores his thought to the pre-eminent position it held in the 1945 Party Constitution. The earlier document, however, refers to Mao's thought as the synthesis *par excellence* of Marxist theory and the practical experience of the Chinese revolution. In the 1969 charter, Mao's thought is described as a new historical contribution in the continuum extending from Marxism and Leninism into the future and is granted the same ideological importance. Mao's thought is defined as "Marxism-Leninism of the era in which imperialism is heading for total collapse and socialism is advancing to worldwide victory." Mao has thus *developed* Marxism-Leninism and brought it to a "higher and completely new stage." As for the Party, it "takes Marxism-Leninism–Mao Tsetung Thought * as the theoretical basis guiding its thinking [*szu-hsiang*]." Allegiance to Mao's thought has become the supreme criterion for Party leadership. The Constitution names Lin Piao as Mao's successor, because he "has consistently held high the great red banner of Mao Tsetung Thought and has most loyally and resolutely carried out and defended Comrade Mao Tsetung's proletarian revolutionary line."

(7) All Party members must, according to the new document, "dedicate their lives to the struggle for Communism . . . be resolute, fear no sacrifice, and surmount every difficulty to win victory." The provision echoes Maoist exhortations to the public during the Cultural Revolution to reject the hedonistic philosophy ascribed to Liu and adopt a revolutionary philosophy of austerity and self-sacrifice. Although the 1956 Constitution specified that Party members were expected to "place the Party's interests above personal interests," the 1969 Constitution sets even higher standards for Party members.

The authors of the original draft of the new Constitution pointedly praised the austere traditions developed by the PLA and recommended that the Party's primary-level organizations adopt the PLA's "four firsts" and "three-eight working style." [27] These references do not appear in the adopted text, however, and have been replaced with an allusion to the three great working styles of the Party, i.e., "integrating theory with practice, main-

---

* The hyphen in Tse-tung, Mao's given name, was dropped in all English-language literature from Peking in 1969 to form one word as it appears here, in order to simplify the linkage of Mao Tsetung thought to Marxism-Leninism. There is no similar problem in Chinese, since Chinese ideographs can be arranged in close proximity without the use of hyphens.

taining close ties with the masses of the people, and practicing criticism and self-criticism." Thus, in the long run, Party traditions may be expected to prevail over PLA traditions.

(8) Qualifications for Party membership are spelled out more explicitly than before. In the 1956 Constitution, membership was open to "any Chinese citizen who works and does not exploit the labor of others," provided that he accepted the Party's program and worked for it. In Article 1 of the new document, an explicit class character is stipulated. Among other things, a member must be a "worker, poor peasant, lower-middle peasant, revolutionary army man [serviceman], or any other revolutionary element who has reached the age of eighteen and who accepts the Constitution of the Party." The minimum age requirement, carried over from the previous Constitution, appears to exclude many Red Guards, since most of them were under eighteen.

Article 3 adopts the five criteria, which were originally outlined by Lin Piao as the test for the succeeding leadership generation,[28] as the standard qualifications for Party membership. In comparison to the 1956 Constitution, the 1969 document appears to establish stricter procedures for disciplining Party members who have violated the Party's spirit or directives. According to the degree of discipline required, a Party member may be warned, removed from his Party posts, placed on probation, or expelled, and those expelled are barred from rejoining the Party later. The 1956 document was more cautious on expulsion. Under the new Constitution, however, individuals may be permitted to withdraw from Party membership. The measure is obviously designed to cope with the kind of situation that confronted the Party after the failure of the Great Leap Forward, when, as the "Lienchiang Documents" have revealed, many cadres actually wanted to resign.[29] Voluntary withdrawals may obviate the need for more violent forms of Party purification.

(9) Another feature that signals the revival of the Party is the reaffirmation in Article 5 of democratic centralism, which means that individuals obey the Party organization, lower levels

of the Party obey superior levels, the minority obeys the majority, and the whole Party obeys the center (under Mao Tsetung). This article confirms the victory of the Maoists over opposition elements within the Party. Mao's argument in the Sixteen Articles of August 8, 1966, that the "correct" voice of the minority must be heeded suggests that his was a minority position at that time. Again in a dominant position in 1969, the Maoists could benefit from democratic centralism.

The new Constitution does provide a procedure for safeguarding minority views, but it seems to have been a subject of constitutional debate. The draft Constitution had specified that dissenting views were to be transmitted directly to the Central Committee and Chairman Mao, bypassing all intermediate levels. The measure bore a remote resemblance to the practice in imperial China of directly memorializing the emperor.[30] The final provision in the Constitution as adopted states: "If a Party member holds different views with regard to the decision or directives of the Party organization, he is allowed to reserve his view and has the right to bypass the intermediate leadership and report directly to higher levels, up to and including the Central Committee and the Chairman of the Central Committee." The modification may be due to pressure from provincial Party cadres who did not wish to be excluded from all opportunity to hear primary-level disagreements and grievances. Or it may indicate that Mao and the new Central Committee felt that their position was now strong enough to share some authority with intermediate Party levels. In any case, the previous lack of channels for the communication of dissenting views had resulted in widespread dysfunction in Party organization in the past. The practice of apparent compliance and covert opposition had been graphically described during the Cultural Revolution as "raising the red flag to oppose the red flag." The new channels are also a sign that Mao intends to keep in direct touch with the masses and to prevent the development of new bureaucratic bottlenecks.

(10) The provisions of the 1969 Constitution dealing with

the structure of the Party are somewhat simpler than those of the 1956 Constitution. They reflect the imprint of Mao's anti-formalism and antipathy to excessive bureaucracy. Apart from the following exceptions, the new Constitution does not make any significant changes in the structure of the Party. First, the 1956 Constitution provided for several Vice Chairmen of the Party; Article 9 of the 1969 Constitution specifies a single Vice Chairman. Second, the 1956 Constitution established the office of Honorary Chairman of the Party, which has been abolished in the 1969 Constitution. The deletion tends to confirm the speculation that the Honorary Chairmanship was a device by which Mao's opponents hoped to remove him from effective power. Third, the 1956 Constitution provided that Party congresses at various levels should meet at certain intervals but made no provision for postponement. In the 1969 Constitution, Article 8 specifies that the National Party Congress shall meet every five years, Article 10 provides that PLA Party congresses above the regimental level and Party congresses above the *hsien* level shall meet every three years, and Article 11 stipulates that basic-level meetings shall be held each year, but it also provides that, "under special circumstances," a congress may be advanced or postponed. This language reflects the long delays experienced in convening the Ninth Party Congress in 1969; it should have met in 1961. Fourth, the 1969 Constitution makes no specific reference to the Secretariat of the Central Committee, whereas, in 1956, the status of the Secretariat seemed almost equivalent to that of the Politburo and its Standing Committee, both of which were elected by the Central Committee, although the Secretariat functioned under Politburo direction. The omission may reflect opposition to the Secretariat's accretion of power under Teng Hsiao-p'ing, a chief aide of Liu Shao-ch'i. The new document merely provides that the Central Committee may establish "necessary organs," in conformity with "compact and efficient" principles, to discharge the day-to-day functions of "the Party, the Government, and the Army." Finally, the 1969 Constitution does not explicitly state that the Party is ultimately responsible for the People's Liberation Army. Under the 1956 Constitution, Party control over the PLA was extended through the General Political Department of the PLA, although, in practice, that control was exercised by the Central Committee's own powerful—and extra-legal—Military Affairs Commission (MAC).* Both the Secretariat and the MAC continue to exist today, as part of the "necessary organs" of the Central Committee.

Although the 1969 Constitution is relatively less concerned with formal structure than the 1956 Constitution, its Article 12 devotes greater attention to the continuance of the militant—and defiant—revolutionary spirit that characterized the Cultural Revolution. Primary-level Party cells and cadres must not only lead and educate the masses, as was emphasized in 1956, but must lead in the learning and creative application of Mao's thought, must conduct education in class struggle, and must "maintain close ties with the masses." The new Constitution does not re-iterate the 1968 slogan that "the worker class must lead in every-thing," but it is clear that cadres must no longer dominate the masses but must engage in a constant dialogue with them.

(11) The 1969 Constitution provides unmistakable evidence that the Maoist leadership intends to restore Party supremacy in China. Article 5 stipulates, among other things, that "the organs of state power of the dictatorship of the proletariat, the People's Liberation Army, the Communist Youth League, and all revolutionary mass organizations, such as those of the workers, the poor and lower-middle peasants, and the Red Guards, must all accept the *Party's leadership*." (Emphasis added.) Evidently, the Revolutionary Committees, which are functioning as govern-ments at different levels, fall under the category of "organs of state power of the dictatorship of the proletariat." The reference to the Communist Youth League means that that organization,

---

* There is reason to suspect today that Mao may have created the MAC, subsequent to the passage of the 1956 Constitution, to bypass a Liu-controlled Party machine, but there is no way to document such a supposition.

defunct during the Cultural Revolution, has been revived. The draft Constitution did not mention the Red Guards—an indication that the Communist Youth League, instead of the Red Guards, would represent and control China's youth. The fact that both the League and the Red Guards are mentioned in the final document may indicate that a concession was made to Red Guard leaders at the Party Congress.

To sum up, the 1969 Party Constitution obviously represents a victory for the Maoists, but it also contains significant compromises, suggesting that the Maoists did not win every point. In the case of the role of Mao's thought, the Party, under the new Constitution, "takes Marxism-Leninism–Mao Tsetung Thought as the theoretical basis guiding its thinking." [31] Although the reference to Mao's thought has been restored in the 1969 Constitution, the language is far more restrained than, for example, that of the Eleventh Plenum, which, on August 12, 1966, termed Mao's thought *"the* guiding principle for all the work of our Party and country." [32] It is not impossible that some veteran Party leaders before and at the Ninth Party Congress opposed the elevation of Mao's thought at the expense of that of Marx and Lenin. The earlier, more exuberant praise of Mao's thought had originated in the PLA, under Lin Piao's leadership. The new Constitution confirmed Lin's selection as Mao's successor and describes his credentials in terms that are distinctly Maoist, not just Marxist-Leninist. He "has consistently held high the great red banner of Mao Tsetung Thought and . . . defended Comrade Mao Tsetung's proletarian revolutionary line." Should Lin move too forcefully to increase his power as Mao's designated successor, he might conceivably face opposition from those responsible for maintaining parity between Marxism-Leninism and "Mao Tsetung Thought" in the new Constitution.

Under the new Constitution, vast responsibilities have been assigned to the reconstituted Party. These include "carrying out the three great revolutionary movements of class struggle, the struggle for production, and scientific experiment," "strengthening and consolidating the dictatorship of the proletariat," and "building socialism . . . through self-reliance and by going all out, aiming high, and achieving greater, faster, better, and more economical results." As noted earlier, the inclusion of "scientific experiment" among the "three great revolutionary movements" constituted a tacit admission on Mao's part that he had overemphasized human will power during the Great Leap Forward. The fact that the three movements appear before other slogans bearing the imprint of the Great Leap era suggests that Mao does not envisage a new Great Leap of 1958 dimensions. At the same time, the vast scope of the tasks assigned to the Party implies that Mao is still very much at the helm. These and other provisions of the new CCP Constitution embody Mao's concept of the role that ideology and Party must play in order to realize his vision of the good society.

16

CONCLUDING REMARKS

Chinese and Communist?

ONE MUST judge Mao in the light of China's long history, its sociopolitical legacy, and the dictates of its modernization,[1] as well as its Communist ideology. In all of those areas, there are salient points that are unique to China, in contrast to the experience of the West.

The first important point of departure is the absence or weakness, throughout China's long history, of an institutionally enforced normative system, such as, in Western societies, law or the Church. As a result, traditional Chinese society was characterized by an internalized moral code, the Confucian *li*. There was no institutionalized Confucian Church, as it were, with the power to exercise sanctions to enforce the code. The conscious self-discipline of the individual was essential for social order and stability. Through this process of internalization, every Chinese was quite deeply Confucianized. At the same time, the internalized code defined the duties of the individual in relation to a firm hierarchy of loyalties and relationships, both within the family and within the state. As a result, there has been no sharp separation in China between the moral and religious spheres of life, on the one hand, and the social and political, on the other. Modernization, however, implied the need for a new system of values, social relationships, and loyalties. To change the society, it was therefore necessary to change the mentality of the people.

In contrast, modern Western history has been characterized by the development of two distinct spheres, the sacred and the secular, or the private and the public. Political and social change has emerged from a process of dialogue between them.

Another legacy with relevance to politics in China today is the unique division of labor in Chinese society, in which political responsibility is delegated to a professional political elite. The underlyng belief is that, since not everyone is endowed with equal political acumen, politics is a special profession unto itself for those of proven quality. In the past, the elite's claim to leadership was based on the moral and intellectual accomplishments of its members. The legitimacy of its counterpart in Communist China, the CCP, is justified by its vision of the good society and its professed ability to lead the nation in translating that vision into reality. In both cases, the function of the political elite is to see that a proper normative code is understood, accepted, and internalized by every Chinese.

Furthermore, China as a sociopolitical unit traditionally encompassed two polities that merged into one at the *hsien* (county) level. At the top was the bureaucratic state in which the Confucian elite held exclusive political responsibility. At the bottom was a kinship-centered society. The magistrate, the lowest-level appointee of the emperor, represented the imperial, bureaucratic state in negotiating with the family elders and village headmen, who, in their own right, were the emperor's counterparts in the kinship-centered polity at the bottom. Excessive checks and balances within the state bureaucracy and between the two polities often impeded effective central control and political integration. As a result of that circumstance and of ineffectual communication channels, the kinship-based society retained in many spheres a residual degree of autonomy that was inimical to state control. The need for accommodation between central authority and local autonomy, and between the central political elite and the other professional elites (such as the technocrats), lies at the origin of the practice of what is known as "consultation" politics (*hsieh-shang*) in China.

In Communist China prior to the Cultural Revolution, primary-level Party cadres were subject to similar kinds of pressures from the center, on the one hand, to maintain order and produce certain revenues or goods, and from the people, on the other, who wished to retain as large a share as possible of their production. In formulating policy, the Chinese Communist elite has had to take such pressures from the masses into account. Similarly, it has had to accommodate and absorb the non-Party elites ("experts") into the new system, ideally at no cost to the Party's monopoly of political authority. At the same time, the Communist elite benefits from modern means of communication and transportation, which permit it to exercise a greater degree of control over every individual and over the kinship structure. In actuality, its control is not total and is subject to pressures from the population in at least the minimal form of apathy or fatigue. The pattern of alternating pressure and liberalization that has characterized Chinese economic policy since the mid-1950's probably in part reflects Communist China's rather special form of "consultation" politics.

The legacy of the consultation process entails informal, sometimes invisible, but nevertheless real give-and-take, at least to an extent greater than our Western conceptualization of "totalitarian regimes" would have us believe. It is different from the "inputs" (interest articulation, interest aggregation, political recruitment, and political communication) and "outputs" (rules-making, implementation, and adjudication) known to Western political processes. Yet, the consultation process serves to ensure some circularity in the sociopolitical processes of the system. Part of our difficulty in comprehending politics in Communist China stems from our lack of information on the rather subtle processes of consultation and accommodation as such. I shall deal with this problem in greater depth elsewhere.[2] Here, suffice it to say that Communist China has inherited, with obvious modifications, the political legacies outlined above. Because of the fusion of social and political responsibility, all of Chinese society is, as before, envisioned as a huge school in which the citizenry at large is the pupils, and the professional political elite is their teachers. Here is rooted the crux of the whole question of ideology. Contrary to its counterpart in the West, ideology is not the self-interest of any particular group but is supposed to be the fountainhead of collective wisdom for the entire society. Politics, in this context, is defined in terms not so much of "power" as of "authority"—i.e., the authority to lead the society by foresight and judicious judgment.

In order to change the attitudes and sentiments of the people, consonant with the dictates of modernization, the Maoist leadership has prescribed a new ideology and moral code and has endeavored, by ubiquitous inculcation and organization, to have the Chinese people internalize that code and practice it in their daily lives. The content of the new iedology is Marxist, but the belief about the role of ideology has its traditional roots.

Mao not only prescribes the goals and values for the new society in the making but also strives to overcome public lethargy and to mobilize all the human and material resources needed to achieve these goals and values. China under Mao and the Maoists cannot be understood apart from their belief that the realization of their vision of the good society requires the creation of a new Communist man.

Paradoxes in Mao's Thought

The Maoists assert that the thought of Mao is the "microscope and telescope" [3] of their revolutionary cause—the instrument for analyzing the problems of the present and for marking the path to the great future to come. Indeed, for some fifty years, Mao has sought to overcome China's chronic economic and social problems by an all-out assault on their sources. The very force of his attack is a measure of the implacable nature of those problems. In the 1920's, Mao urged China to develop nationalism in order to fight "imperialism," scientific culture to eradicate superstition, and mass organization to arouse the people to overthrow the power of the traditional gentry-literati class. Practice was stressed precisely because Chinese intellectuals had indulged in an ivory-tower intellectualism that despised everything but book knowledge.

In his concern for China's future, Mao shared some of the aspirations of other revolutionary nationalists of the 1920's. Like his early Communist peers, he wanted to industrialize China by adopting Western technology, but, unlike some of his more "revisionist" colleagues in recent years, he has grown seriously worried about the danger of succumbing to the evils of modern technology and Western capitalism. The Marxist theory of alienation has struck a responsive chord in Mao's thought. It has also justified the need for a working-class revolution and Leninist organizational techniques. Although their goals were different, both Sun Yat-sen and Mao owed an intellectual debt to Leninism. In fact, Sun, not Mao, was the first to perceive that a Leninist elite organization might succeed in arousing the masses. Yet, the very fact of revolutionary victory in 1949 has posed a new set of problems for the Maoist leadership: how to build a modern state and still perpetuate the egalitarian nature and dynamic thrust of the Communist revolution. Efforts to solve that fundamental problem have resulted in a number of paradoxes.

The first paradox has roots in Mao's experience in Yenan during the 1930's. Those years of revolutionary comradeship, defiance of material hardship, and successful guerrilla warfare seem to have marked Mao deeply. Although the situation of a beleaguered Communist force in a primitive area of Yenan is vastly different from that of a Communist government exercising authority over the entire Chinese mainland, Mao's experience in Yenan led him to seek to revive the "spirit of Yenan" to deal with contemporary problems and to revere a past whose relevance to the present is at best questionable. Moreover, any such reverence for the past would seem to compromise the Communist belief in Marxism's promise that historical redemption lies in the future.

Mao's successes in assuming Party leadership in 1935 and in conquering China in 1949 were largely due to his relative realism about the strength of various social forces in China and about the direction of Communist policy during different phases of the revolutionary struggle. He steered clear of the pitfalls of Comintern-imposed dogma. His independent line of thought appealed to China's vast peasantry, as well as to its minute urban proletariat and the more radical segment of the intelligentsia. Between 1950 and 1954, the People's Republic was able to achieve a large measure of postwar recovery and some economic growth primarily because its policies remained realistic. Although stringent measures were directed against the bourgeoisie, their impact was more than offset by the redistribution of land among a grateful peasantry. The sacrifices demanded of the masses were accompanied by measures to eliminate capitalist exploitation. Between 1955 and 1958, however, Mao's realism gradually gave way to a belief that the mobilization of human will power would permit the rapid creation of a Communist society. The Great Leap Forward failed, however, because the contradiction between maximum sacrifice and minimum incentive proved irreconcilable. Although Mao had previously attacked the "commandism" of his CCP colleagues, his coercive ideological indoctrination also constituted a form of commandism. Confronted by intractable problems, Mao's present outlook has perhaps best been captured by one of the graffiti on the walls of Paris in May, 1968: "Be realistic, ask the impossible." [4]

In Mao's view, however, what he is asking is not impossible. As Robert J. Lifton has observed, the thought of Mao is a "Way" (*Tao*), a call to a particular mode of being on behalf of a transcendent purpose. This "Way" is based on a number of psychological assumptions, which, although long prominent in Mao's thought, were expressed most eloquently during the Cultural Revolution. The first, according to Lifton's analysis, is an image of the human mind as infinitely malleable and capable of being reformed and spiritually expanded beyond the world of the common man. The second is a related vision of the human will, once rectified, as all-powerful, even to the extent that ."the subjective creates the objective." [5] The two assumptions of Mao have been compared in earlier chapters of this book to similar assumptions in neo-Confucianism regarding *hsin*, the potentially great human will. Acting on his assumptions, Mao has sought to use spiritual indoctrination to mobilize the masses to overcome China's problems. His indoctrination has emphasized the values of austerity and puritanism, continuous study, and class struggle.

A recent visitor to China, Alberto Moravia, found that purposive poverty had become a way of life, a basic virtue, a religious dogma.[6] Certainly, until Mao's ideal society of collective contentment can be created, he wants to liberate the masses and elite alike from the bondage of acquisitive self-interest. Puritanism, in other words, is a means to an end, a necessary stage in a long process of construction, and a strategy for development. After the failure of the Great Leap Forward, there appeared to be two alternative developmental strategies: One would authorize material incentives to raise production; the other would stress ideological incentives and demand private austerity. The Liu group apparently opted for the first and, for that reason, was condemned as "revisionist." The more relentless Maoists chose the latter alternative. Although Mao has had to slow the pace of his developmental strategy since 1959, it is paradoxical that his continuing commitment to an ascetic ideal, stressing macro-development at the expense of the consumer economy for the immediate future, has meant that any former exploitation of the masses by the bourgeoisie has given way to a new kind of ideological exploitation, defined in terms of Communist goals, which also obliges the ordinary Chinese to dispense with personal comforts and wants.

"Ceaseless study" or the "continuous remolding of thought"

has been a major element of Mao's indoctrination of the Chinese masses, particularly prior to 1959, as he sought to transform human character and to eradicate those frailities he considered obstacles to socialist progress. In his essays "On the Correct Handling of Contradictions Among the People" and "On the Historical Experience of the Dictatorship of the Proletariat," Mao urged that the corrective for internal dissension within the Party was a "gentle breeze" of rectification, carried out by means of correct study. But when severe dissension developed within the Party after 1959, Mao's corrective measure was to mobilize elements outside the Party, such as the Red Guards, and to overthrow the entrenched Party hierarchy by means of the vast social movement of the Cultural Revolution. Still, in comparison to Stalin, he has rarely resorted to execution of his enemies; his usual response to intransigent critics is excommunication or exile from Peking. Quite typically, however, the central role of Mao's thought was one of the major issues of the Cultural Revolution. This was made unequivocally clear by the *People's Daily* in an editorial of May 7, 1967, entitled "To Make the Entire Country a Huge School of Mao Tsetung Thought." The inculcation of Mao's thought is to be both constant and extensive.

Another element of Mao's indoctrination, particularly since 1959, has been class struggle. Alarmed by developments in Soviet society, Mao has become increasingly aware of the persistence of inherited bourgeois ideas and habits under socialism and has prescribed continuing class struggle as the key remedy. Class struggle is defined as a fight against both the handful of leaders "taking the capitalist road" and the private wants and aspirations of the ordinary Chinese. The standard techniques of criticism and self-criticism have been intensified to accelerate this form of indoctrination. Efforts have also been made to place the masses on a par with Party cadres, both to humble the overbearing cadres and to reduce the size of a top-heavy Party bureaucracy. While such efforts do make for some democratization, the ordinary Chinese (if not some Party leaders as well) must sometimes wonder why his modest individual interests and aspirations are given so little weight alongside Mao's vision of the Communist man.

Mao's present mood is averse to routinization, lest his revolution be sacrificed again. In 1966, he hinted that "a few cultural revolutions" might be in store for the future.[7] For Mao, "permanent revolution" seems to be like a live fuse connecting a series of bombs of different sizes that are designed to set off periodic explosions. If so, there is some irony in this. The Communist revolution in China began in the 1920's as a means to an end; it now appears to have become an end in itself, at least in the short run.

Inciting the masses to revolt in order to overthrow the ruling class and create a proletarian regime is one thing. Perpetuating the spirit of that revolution—and controlling it—is another. Increasingly, because of disputes within the Party hierarchy, Mao turned toward youth as the true bearer of the revolutionary torch. There is, however, a qualitative difference between Mao's generation and younger ones. Since 1937, China's youth has grown up without firm roots in earlier traditions and has become attuned to the turmoil of the twentieth century. At the same time, the generations born since 1949 are numerically important; by the late 1960's, it was estimated that 40 per cent of China's population was under seventeen years of age.[8] These younger people—and indeed the entire nation—have been subjected to some of the most systematic indoctrination known in human history. In such a context, the mass hysteria of the Great Leap Forward campaign is hardly surprising. The prolonged cultivation of young Maoist revolutionaries bore fruit during the initial period of the Cultural Revolution, when they committed acts of often violent and useless destruction. Their suppression in mid-1968 must have been a source of widespread disillusionment among youth. Mao bears the major responsibility for the creation and repression of this colossal genie. Yet, China's future belongs to them. It remains to be seen whether the suppression of the Red Guard movement will leave any residue of cynicism about the methods and goals of Mao's revolution, and whether the thought of Mao will long survive Mao himself. Nor is it certain that Mao's immediate successors, who lack his history of revolutionary leadership and charismatic appeal, can maintain the intensity of ideological indoctrination that has characterized Mao's efforts to mobilize China's people for the enormous task of modernizing the Chinese nation.

Nevertheless, it may be argued that, if future leaders are to reduce the present level of intensity of ideological inculcation, it does not necessarily follow that the tradition of ideological leadership will be altogether abandoned. That tradition is a corollary to the Chinese division of labor, which, as noted above, delegates political leadership to a special elite. The ideal of a political elite, ruling by correct ideology, has been perpetuated for at least two millenniums, and there are no signs of its early demise. Unless this indigenous division of labor is abandoned, the role of ideology, as well as the prominence of the political elite, will continue. The specific interpretation of ideology, and the intensity of indoctrination, may change from time to time, depending upon the attitudes of the prevailing political elite. But the traditional Chinese deductive approach to social and political problems, proceeding from whole to part and from general to specific, is likely to continue. By applying ideology to concrete conditions and by further enriching ideology through experience, Chinese Communism will likewise continue to evolve. It is on this ceaseless process of self-renewal that the viability of Chinese Communism depends.

NOTES

Abbreviations Used in the Notes and Bibliography

AS	*Asian Survey*
CB	*Current Background*
CFCP	*Chieh-fang chün-pao: Liberation Army Daily,* organ of the Ministry of Defense and the People's Liberation Army, People's Republic of China
CQ	*China Quarterly*
CS	*Current Scene,* published in Hongkong
HC	*Hsüan-chi: Selected Works* of Mao Tse-tung (in Chinese)
IASP	International Arts and Sciences Press, White Plains, N. Y., publisher of *Chinese Law and Government*
JAS	*Journal of Asian Studies*
JMJP	*Jen-min Jih-pao: People's Daily,* organ of the Central Committee of the Chinese Communist Party
NCNA	New China (Hsinhua) News Agency
PR	*Peking Review,* English-language monthly published in Peking
SCMM	*Survey of China Mainland Magazines* (U.S. Consulate General, Hongkong)
SCMP	*Survey of China Mainland Press* (U.S. Consulate General, Hongkong)
SW	*Selected Works* of Mao, English-language edition of HC
TWKH	*Chung-hua jen-min kung-ho-kuo tui-wai kuan-hsi wen-chien chi: Collection of Documents Relating to the Foreign Relations of the People's Republic of China,* published in Peking

Introduction

1. In David E. Apter, ed., *Ideology and Discontent* (Glencoe, Ill.: Free Press, 1964), pp. 206–62.
2. Robert E. Lane, *Political Ideology* (Glencoe, Ill.: Free Press, 1962), p. 15.
3. Richard M. Merelman, "The Development of Political Ideology: A Framework for the Analysis of Political Socialization," *American Political Science Review* 63, No. 3 (September, 1969), 750 ff.
4. Franz Schurmann, *Ideology and Organization in Communist China*, 2d ed. (Berkeley: University of California Press, 1969), p. 18.
5. Yehudi A. Cohen, *Man in Adaptation: The Cultural Present* (Chicago: Aldine, 1968), p. 1.

Chapter 1

1. The division follows roughly that of Dennis Doolin in his introduction to O. Briere, S. J., *Fifty Years of Chinese Philosophy, 1898–1948* (New York: Praeger Publishers, 1965), p. 1,
2. G. Robina Quale, *Eastern Civilizations* (New York: Appleton-Century-Crofts, 1966), pp. 281–87; and Wm. Theodore de Bary, Jr., *et al.*, eds., *Sources of Chinese Tradition*, 2 vols. (New York: Columbia University Press, 1960), 1:1–33.
3. George Lichtheim, in *Marxism: An Historical and Critical Study* (New York: Praeger Publishers, 1961), made the following statement (p. 142) regarding the process of history in Marx: "For his own purpose it was essential that the pattern of events should display the kind of internal logic where each successive stage is seen to arise as a matter of *necessity*, and not just of fact. Thus processes such as the development of feudalism out of primitive tribalism, or the growth of bourgeois society within the feudal system, had to be related to changes inherent in the logic of the anterior stage." See also Donald M. Lowe, *The Function of "China" in Marx, Lenin, and Mao* (Berkeley: University of California Press, 1966), p. 6.
4. Karl Marx, *The Eastern Question* (London, 1897), p. 21.
5. Mao Tse-tung, *Chung-kuo ko-ming yü chung-kuo kung-ch'an-tang* (*The Chinese Revolution and the Communist Party of China*) (n.p., 1939) p. 6, stated, among other things: "By the mid-nineteenth century, only with the invasion of foreign capital did a fundamental transformation within this [Chinese] society occur." In the 1951 edition of the *HC*, 2:620, however, the passage was revised to read: "It was not until the mid-nineteenth century, with the penetration of foreign capitalism, that great changes occurred within this society."
6. Cf. Wing-tsit Chan, *A Source Book in Chinese Philosophy* (Princeton, N.J.: Princeton University Press, 1963), pp. 14–48 and *passim*; and Fung Yu-lan, *A Short History of Chinese Philosophy*, ed. by Derk Bodde (New York: Macmillan, 1948), pp. 38–48.
7. De Bary, *et al.*, eds., *Sources of Chinese Tradition*, 1:157–83.

8. Chan, *Source Book in Chinese Philosophy*, pp. 272 ff.

9. Cf. Johanna Menzel, *The Chinese Civil Service* (Boston: D. C. Heath, 1963).

10. Y. C. Wang, "Western Impact and Social Mobility in China," *American Sociological Review* 25 (1950): 854.

11. O. Edmund Clubb, "'Plus ça change . . .' in China?" *Far Eastern Survey* 22 (January 28, 1953): 18–19. For more insights into the traditional normative order, see Derk Bodde and Clarence Morris, *Law in Imperial China* (Cambridge, Mass.: Harvard University Press, 1967).

12. Briere, *Fifty Years of Chinese Philosophy*; and Y. C. Wang, *Chinese Intellectuals and the West: 1872–1949* (Chapel Hill: University of North Carolina Press, 1966), pp. 1–192.

13. Ssu-yu Teng and John K. Fairbank, *China's Response to the West* (Cambridge, Mass.: Harvard University Press, 1954), pp. 61–108, 147–87.

14. Lowe, *Function of "China,"* p. 86.

15. Chow Tse-tsung, *The May Fourth Movement* (Cambridge, Mass.: Harvard University Press, 1960), pp. 84–170.

16. Ch'en Tu-hsiu, "Tung-hsi min-tsu ken-pen ssu-hsiang chih ch'a-yi" ("The Basic Differences in the Thought of the Eastern and Western Peoples"), in *Tu-hsiu wen-ts'un (Collection of Works by Ch'en Tu-hsiu)* (Shanghai: Ya-tung, 1922), 1:35–40.

17. See *Hu-shih wen-hsuan (Selected Works of Hu Shih)* (Shanghai: Ya-tung, 1930), p. 154 ff.

18. Lu Hsün, "Feng-jen jih-chi" ("The Madman's Diary"), *Hsin ch'ing-nien* (*New Youth,* Peking), April, 1918; English translation in *Selected Works of Lu Hsün* (Peking: Foreign Language Press, 1956), 1:8–21.

19. Lowe, *Function of "China" in Marx*, p. 91.

20. Joseph R. Levenson, *Confucian China and Its Modern Fate,* 3 vols. (Berkeley: University of California Press, 1966), 1:95 ff., and John K. Fairbank, *The United States and China,* new ed. (New York: Viking Press, 1958), pp. 140, 164.

21. See Mao Tse-tung, "On People's Democratic Dictatorship," *SW,* 4 (Peking: Foreign Language Press, 1961): 413.

22. Chang Chih-tung, *China's Only Hope,* trans. by S. I. Woodbridge (New York, 1900), pp. 93–94; and K'ang Yu-wei, "Memorial on Promoting the Translation of Japanese Books and the Establishment of a Translation Bureau at the Capital" (1898), in Chang Ching-lu, ed., *Chung-kuo ch'u-pan shih-liao pu-pien (Supplement to a Collection of Materials on the History of Publishing in China)* (Peking, 1957), p. 50.

23. Shih Chün, ed., *Chung-kuo chin-tai ssu-hsiang shih ts'an-k'ao tzu-liao chien-pien (A Brief Collection of Reference Materials on the History of Modern Chinese Thought)* (Peking, 1957), pp. 665, 559.

24. Maurice Meisner, *Li Ta-chao and the Origins of Chinese Marxism* (Cambridge, Mass.: Harvard University Press, 1967), p. 55; and Benjamin I. Schwartz, *Chinese Communism and the Rise of Mao* (Cambridge, Mass.: Harvard University Press, 1951), pp. 10–11.

25. Meisner, *Li Ta-chao and Origins of Chinese Marxism*, pp. 56–70; and Schwartz, *Chinese Communism and Rise of Mao*, pp. 14–16.

26. Chow, *May Fourth Movement*, pp. 84–116.

27. Li Ta-chao, "Kuo-chi-p'ai te yin-hsien" ("The Fuse of Internationalism [Bolshevism]"), *Li Ta-chao hsüan-chi (Selected Works of Li Ta-chao.)* (Pe-

king: Jen-min, 1959), p. 152. See discussion in Meisner, *Li Ta-chao and Origins of Chinese Marxism*, p. 95.

28. Ch'en Tu-hsiu, "O-kuo ko-ming yü Chung-kuo jen-min" ("The Russian Revolution and the Chinese People"), *Hsin Ch'ing-nien* (*New Youth*), April, 1917.

29. Schwartz, *Chinese Communism and Rise of Mao*, p. 21; Robert C. North, *Moscow and Chinese Communists*, 2d ed. (Stanford, Calif.: Stanford University Press, 1963), pp. 42–52.

30. Schwartz, *Chinese Communism and Rise of Mao*, p. 15; and North, *Moscow and Chinese Communists*, pp. 42 ff.

31. Meisner, *Li Ta-chao and Origins of Chinese Marxism*, pp. 94–104 and 112–14; and Schwartz, *Chinese Communism and Rise of Mao*, pp. 22–23.

32. Stuart Schram, *The Political Thought of Mao Tse-tung* (New York: Praeger Publishers, 1963), pp. 7–21, 103–10.

33. Li Jui, *Mao Tse-tung t'ung-chih te ch'u-ch'i ko-ming huo-tung* (*The Revolutionary Activities in the Initial Period of Comrade Mao Tse-tung*) (Peking: Chung-kuo ch'ing-nien, 1957), pp. 40–44, trans. in Schram, *Political Thought of Mao Tse-tung*, p. 12.

34. Schram, *Political Thought of Mao Tse-tung*, pp. 103, 105 ff., and *passim*.

35. Edgar Snow, *Red Star Over China* (New York: Random House, 1944), p. 157.

Chapter 2

1. Hu Shih, "Tuo yen-chiu hsieh wen-t'i, shao t'an hsieh chu-yi" ("More Study of Problems and Less Talk About Isms"), *Me-chou p'ing-lun* (*Weekly Commentary*), July 20, 1919, reprinted in *Hu Shih wen-ts'un* (*Collected Essays by Hu Shih*) (Shanghai, 1926), 2:147–53.

2. Maurice Meisner, *Li Ta-chao and the Origins of Chinese Marxism* (Cambridge, Mass.: Harvard University Press, 1967), pp. 107–8.

3. *Ibid.*, pp. 109–11.

4. Emile Durkheim, *Socialism and Saint-Simon*, ed. by Alvin W. Gouldner (Yellow Springs, Ohio: Antioch Press, 1968), p. 7; see further discussion in W. G. Runciman, *Social Science and Political Theory* (Cambridge, England: Cambridge University Press, 1965), p. 47.

5. Mao Tse-tung, "On People's Democratic Dictatorship" (1949), SW 4:413.

6. Meisner, *Li Ta-chao and Origins of Chinese Marxism*, pp. 107–8.

7. *Ibid.*

8. Cf. Hajime Nakamura, *Ways of Thinking of Eastern Peoples* (Honolulu: East-West Center Press, 1964), pp. 256 and 180; and Chang Tung-sun, "Ts'ung Chung-kuo yen-yü kou-tsao shang k'an Chung-kuo che-hsüeh" ("See Chinese Philosophy from Chinese Language Structure"), *Tung-fang tsa-chih* (*Eastern Miscellany* [Peking])33, No. 7 (1929): 97. See also my "Chinese Ways of Thinking and Chinese Language," in *Journal of the Chinese Language Teachers Association* 4, No. 2 (May, 1969): 41–54, at 47.

9. Arnold Brecht, *Political Theory: The Foundations of Twentieth-Century Political Thought* (Princeton, N.J.: Princeton University Press, 1959), pp. 187 ff.

10. Cf. Karl Marx, *Economic and Philosophical Manuscripts* (of 1844), trans. by T. B. Bottomore in Erich Fromm, *Marx's Concept of Man* (New York: Frederick Unger, 1961), p. 96.

11. Marx, *Theses on Feuerbach*, in Karl Marx and Frederick Engels, *The German Ideology* (New York: International Publishers, 1947), p. 199. See also Marx, "Economic and Philosophic Manuscripts," trans. by T. B. Bottomore, in Fromm, *Marx's Concept of Man*, p. 96; and "Preface to a Contribution to the Critique of Political Economy" in Marx and Engels, *Selected Works*, 1:363.

12. Lenin, "What Is to Be Done?" (1902), in V. I. Lenin, *Selected Works* (Moscow, 1952), 1:203–409.

13. Mu Fu-sheng, *The Wilting of the Hundred Flowers* (New York: Praeger Publishers, 1962), p. 127.

14. A pathetic description of how a "square peg," a scholar trained in the Confucian tradition, could not fit in the "round hole" of the changing society of early-twentieth-century China can be found in the *K'ung Yi-chi* by Lu Hsün, written in January, 1919. In this vivid writing, the hero personified an impoverished old-time scholar reduced to drinking and thievery, always appearing in his only dirty old gown, which had not been washed or repaired for years. K'ung Yi-chi's self-defense for his plight and demoralization consisted in his pretense to classical learning, which was no longer useful to new demands, and his badge of gentility, which inhibited him from taking jobs beneath his dignity.

15. Franklin Houn, *A Short History of Chinese Communism* (Englewood Cliffs, N.J.: Prentice-Hall, 1967), p. 1.

16. Lu Hsün, Preface to *Cheers from the Sidelines*, in *Lu Hsün ch'üan-chi* (*Complete Works of Lu Hsün*) (Peking, 1956).

17. In "On New Democracy," written in 1940, a little over three years after Lu Hsün's death, Mao Tse-tung eulogized him as "the greatest and the most militant standard-bearer" of the new cultural force released in the May Fourth Movement. *SW*, 2, p. 372.

18. See *Commemorating Lu Hsün—Our Forerunner in the Cultural Revolution* (Peking: Foreign Language Press, 1967).

19. John Rue, *Mao Tse-tung in Opposition: 1927–1935* (Stanford, Calif.: Stanford University Press, 1966), pp. 24–30.

20. Cf. Harold Isaac, *The Tragedy of the Chinese Revolution*, 2d rev. ed. (Stanford, Calif.: Stanford University Press, 1961); Shanti Swarup, *A Study of the Chinese Communist Movement, 1927–1934* (New York and London: Oxford University Press, 1966); Hsiao Tso-liang, *Power Relations Within the Chinese Communist Movement, 1930–1934* (Seattle: University of Washington Press, 1961); C. P. Fitzgerald, *The Birth of Communist China* (Baltimore, Md.: Penguin, 1964); Robert C. North, *Moscow and Chinese Communists*, 2d ed. (Stanford, Calif.: Stanford University Press, 1962); Franklin Houn, *op. cit.*, n. 15 above, etc.; Professor James P. Harrison, of Hunter College (New York City), is currently working on a comprehensive history of the Chinese Communist Party, to be published by Praeger.

21. Karl Marx and Friedrich Engels, *Gesamtausgabe*, Section I, 6 (Berlin: Marx-Engels Verlag, 1932): 397–98; see discussion in Arthur A. Cohen, *The Communism of Mao Tse-tung* (Chicago: University of Chicago Press, 1964), pp. 34–35.

22. Contrast Lenin's *Two Tactics in the Democratic Revolution* (June–

July, 1905) (New York: International Publishers, 1935) with his *Agrarian Program of Social Democracy* (November–December, 1907), in Lenin, *Selected Works*, 3 (New York: International Publishers, n.d.): 258. The quote is taken from the latter.

23. "Lenin, Democracy, and Narodism in China (July 1922)," in *The National Liberation Movement in the East: Lenin* (Moscow: Foreign Languages Publishing House, 1957), pp. 43–44.

24. "Preliminary Draft of Some Theses on the National and Colonial Questions," The Second (Comintern) Congress, *Proceedings*, pp. 570–79, quoted in North, *Moscow and Chinese Communists*, pp. 19–20.

25. Conrad Brandt, Benjamin I. Schwartz, and John K. Fairbank, *A Documentary History of Chinese Communism* (New York: Atheneum, 1966), p. 62.

26. *Ibid.*, p. 164.

27. *Ibid.*, pp. 71–72, 74–77.

28. *Ibid.*, pp. 70–71.

29. *Ibid.*, pp. 93–97.

30. "Resolution on the Chinese Question," *International Press Correspondence*, June 16, 1927, p. 737, quoted in North, *Moscow and Chinese Communists*, pp. 98–99.

31. Brandt *et al.*, *Documentary History of Chinese Communism*, p. 122.

32. Benjamin I. Schwartz, *Chinese Communism and the Rise of Mao* (Cambridge, Mass.: Harvard University Press, 1951), p. 102, gave September 19, 1927, as the date for the Comintern authorization to the CCP on establishing soviets and organizing armed revolts by peasant militias. The November, 1927, plenum of the Central Committee of the CCP repeated the Moscow line and declared unequivocally that "a decidedly revolutionary situation" now existed in China. "Resolution of the November Plenum" (of the Chinese Central Committee), in P. Mif, *Kitaiskaia kommunisticheskaia partiia v kriticheskie dni (The Chinese Communist Party in the Critical Days)*, pp. 239–71, cited in North, *Moscow and Chinese Communists*, p. 117n.

33. "Resolution on the Chinese Question," *International Press Correspondence*, March 15, 1928, pp. 321–22, quoted in North, *Moscow and Chinese Communists*, p. 120.

34. Jane Degras, ed., *The Communist International: Documents, 1919–1943*, 3 vols. (London and New York: Oxford University Press, 1956–60), 2:437–38.

35. Brandt *et al.*, *Documentary History of Chinese Communism*, pp. 130–31.

36. James P. Harrison, "Li Li-san and the CCP in 1930," *China Quarterly* (London), No. 14 (April–June, 1963), pp. 178 ff.

37. Brandt *et al.*, *Documentary History of Chinese Communism*, p. 211. The Resolution of the Enlarged Fourth Plenum of the Central Committee of the CCP, January, 1931, declared, among other things, "Li substituted Trotsky's point of view, denying the place of the bourgeois-democratic stage of the revolution in Lenin's theory of the transformation of the revolution . . . the Li-san line is contradictory to the line of the Comintern, a policy of opportunism under the camouflage of 'leftist phrases,' and an opportunistic passivism in regard to the task of organizing the masses in a practical and

revolutionary way. The historical root of the Li-san line is the opportunism and the putschism. . . ." *Ibid.*

38. North, *Moscow and Chinese Communists*, p. 64.

39. Brandt *et al.*, *Documentary History of Chinese Communism*, p. 75. Italics added.

40. Schwartz, *Chinese Communism and Rise of Mao*, p. 43.

41. *Ibid.*, p. 29.

42. "The economically and culturally backward countries," Ch'en asserted in 1923, "are not injured by the development of capitalism but rather by the lack of capitalist development." Ch'en Tu-hsiu, "Chung-kuo kuo-min ko-ming yü she-hui ko-chieh-chi" ("The Chinese National Revolution and the Various Social Classes") originally published in *Ch'ien-feng* (*Vanguard*), No. 2, and included in *Chung-kuo ko-ming wen-t'i lun-wen chi* (*A Collection of Essays on Problems of the Chinese Revolution*) (Shanghai, 1927). Cf. Meisner, *Li Ta-chao and Origins of Chinese Marxism*, p. 231.

43. Schwartz, *Chinese Communism and Rise of Mao*, pp. 61–62.

44. Ch'en Tu-hsiu *et al.*, Wo-men te cheng-chih yi-chien shu (*Our Political Platform*) (n.p., n.d.), pp. 1–2 and 8, cited in Donald M. Lowe, *The Function of "China" in Marx, Lenin, and Mao* (Berkeley: University of California Press, 1966), p. 104.

45. Meisner, *Li Ta-chao and Origins of Chinese Marxism*, pp. 80–89; 237–41.

46. *Ibid.*, pp. 233, 237.

47. Li Ta-chao, "T'u-ti yü nung-min" ("Land and Peasants"), *Li Ta-chao hsüan-chi*, pp. 523–36, quoted in Meisner, *Li-Ta-chao and Origins of Chinese Marxism*, p. 239. This essay was written in three parts between December 30, 1925, and February 3, 1926. Italics added.

48. Meisner, *Li Ta-chao and Origins of Chinese Marxism*, pp. 255–56.

Chapter 3

1. John Rue, *Mao Tse-tung in Opposition: 1927–1935* (Stanford, Calif.: Hoover Institution, 1966), pp. 8–9.

2. *Ibid.*, p. 9.

3. Published in *Hsiang-chiang p'ing-lun* (*Hsiang River Review*), founded by Mao, issue of July–August, 1919; English translation in Stuart Schram, *The Political Thought of Mao Tse-tung* (New York: Praeger Publishers, 1963), pp. 94–97, 170.

4. This periodization is adopted from Donald Lowe, *Function of "China" in Marx, Lenin, and Mao* (Berkeley: University of California Press, 1966), pp. 107 ff.

5. Published in *Hunan tzu-liao* (*Hunan Material*), No. 9 (1959); trans. in excerpts in Schram, *Political Thought of Mao Tse-tung*, pp. 214–16.

6. "The Peking Coup d'État and the Merchants," published in *Hsiang-tao* (*Guide*), Nos. 31–32 (July 11, 1923), pp. 233–34; trans. in excerpts in Schram, *Political Thought of Mao Tse-tung*, pp. 139–42.

7. Cf. the original text in *Chung-kuo nung-min* (*Chinese Peasants*), No. 2 (February, 1926), pp. 1–13, with revised text in Mao Tse-tung, *HC*, 1951 edition, 1:3–9.

8. *Chung-kuo nung-min, loc. cit.* Cf. Schram's discussion of this point, *Political Thought of Mao Tse-tung,* p. 29.

9. *Chung-kuo nung-min, loc. cit.*

10. *Ibid.,* p. 2. The passage was deleted, however, from the 1951 edition of *HC.*

11. *Hsiang-tao (Guide),* No. 191 (March 12, 1927), trans. in Conrad Brandt, Benjamin I. Schwartz, John K. Fairbank, *A Documentary History of Chinese Communism* (New York: Atheneum, 1966), pp. 80–93. Although written in February, 1927, Mao's report was not published until March.

12. M. N. Roy, *Revolution and Counter-revolution in China* (Calcutta: Renaissance Publishers, 1946), pp. 481–84, 516–21, 548–49.

13. *International Press Correspondence,* 7, No. 11:231, quoted in Brandt *et al., Documentary History of Chinese Communism,* p. 78.

14. Brandt *et al., Documentary History of Chinese Communism,* p. 79.

15. Mao Tse-tung, "Letter of the Front Committee for the Central Committee of the CCP," quoted in "Kei Lin-piao t'ung-chih te hsin" ("A Letter to Comrade Lin Piao"), *HC* (1947), Supp. (December, 1947), p. 94. See also Shanti Swarup, *A Study of the Chinese Communist Movement, 1927–1934* (New York and London: Oxford University Press, 1966), pp. 80–81.

16. Brandt *et al., Documentary History of Chinese Communism,* p. 79.

17. Communist Party of China, "Chung-kung (pa-ch'i) hui-yi kao ch'üan-tang tang-yuan shu" ("A Letter from the August 7 Party Conference to All Members of the Party"), in Hu Hua, ed., *Chung-kuo hsin min-chu chu-yi ko-ming-shih ts'an-k'ao tzu-liao (Reference Materials on the History of the Chinese New-Democratic Revolution)* (Peking: Chung-kuo, 1951), p. 197. Italics added. See discussion in Swarup, *Study of Chinese Communist Movement,* pp. 81–82.

18. *HC* (1951), 1:4–5.

19. Stalin, "Results of the Work of the Fourteenth Conference of the Russian Communist Party (B): Immediate Tasks of the Communist Elements in the Colonial and Dependent Countries" (May 9, 1925), *Collected Works* (Moscow: Foreign Languages Publishing House, 1952–55), 7:108–9. Stalin's view in turn followed that of Lenin made in 1906, "The Stages, Trends and Prospects of Revolution," *Selected Works* (New York: International Publishers, n.d.), 3:134.

20. Mao, "Hu-kan pien-chieh ko hsien tang ti-erh-tz'u tai-piao ta-hui chüeh-yi-an" ("Resolutions of the Second Congress of Delegates of the CCP in the Various Hsien Along the Hunan-Kiangsi Border") (October 5, 1928), *HC* (1947), Supp. (December, 1947), p. 101; and "Ching-kang-shan ch'ien-wei tui chung-yang te pao-kao" ("Report from the Chingkang Mountain Front Committee to the Central Committee"), *HC* (1947), Supp. (December, 1947), p. 82. These were published in the 1951 edition of the *HC* as: "Chung-kuo hung-se cheng-ch'üan wei shen-mo neng-kou ts'un-tsai" ("Why the Red Regime Can Exist in China") (October 5, 1928), and "Ching-kang shan shang te tou-cheng" ("Struggle on the Chingkang Mountain").

21. Cf. Boyd Compton, *Mao's China; Party Reform Documents, 1942–44* (Seattle: University of Washington Press, 1952), p. 245.

22. Cf. Swarup, *Study of Chinese Communist Movement,* p. 86, n. 2.

23. This resolution was later published as "Why Can the Chinese Red Regime Exist?" *HC* (1947), Supp. (December, 1947), pp. 103–5. Wording was slightly changed in the 1951 edition of *HC*, 1:50–52.

24. *HC* (1947), Supp., p. 54. Wording in the 1951 edition of *HC*, 1:59, is somewhat different.

25. *HC* (1947), Supp., p. 91. Cf. the modifications in the 1951 edition of *HC*, 1:104–5. Italics added. Like many Chinese, Mao often used the terms *chu-kuan* and *k'e-kuan* (translated here as revolutionary and counterrevolutionary). In Chinese, they have a number of connotations, depending on context: "we" versus "they"; "consciousness" as against material conditions unknown to the actor; the speaker's viewpoint versus that of the audience; subjective and objective; positive and negative (recalling the *yin-yang* antinomy); will power as against material force, etc. Here Mao was talking about "we," the revolutionary forces, against "them," the counterrevolutionary forces.

Chapter 4

1. Mao Tse-tung, "Chung-kuo ko-ming chang-cheng te chang-lüeh wen-t'i" ("Strategic Problems of China's Revolutionary War"), (December 1936), *HC* (1966), 1:154–225.

2. Mao, "Lun hsin chieh-tuan" ("On the New Stage") (October, 1938) (Yenan: Chieh-fang she, 1939), pp. 34–35. It was Mao's report to the Sixth Plenum of the Sixth Central Committee. Chapter 7 of it was republished as "Chung-kuo kung-ch'an-tang tsai min-tsu chan-cheng chung te ti-wei" ("The Place of the CCP in the National War"), *HC* (1951). In the new version, however, the original passage delineating China's difference from the industrial countries was deleted. Whereas Russia was not named in the original passage, a new paragraph inserted in its place included Russia among Western countries whose revolutionary experience, moving from the cities to the countryside, was contrasted to China's, moving in the opposite direction. *HC*, 2:529–30.

3. Mao's reference to Ethiopia is found in "Lun ch'ih-chiu chan" ("On Protracted War"), *HC* (1966), pp. 409, 419–22. In Mao Tse-tung *et al.*, *K'ang-jih yu-chi chan-cheng te yi-pan wen-t'i* (Yenan, 1938), p. 11, a similar differentiation was made by him between China and Morocco.

4. Mao, "Lun hsin chieh-tuan," p. 102.

5. Arthur A. Cohen, *The Communism of Mao Tse-tung* (Chicago: University of Chicago Press, 1964), pp. 8, 14, thinks Mao's "On Practice" was published in 1950 rather than 1937 as the Chinese Communists claimed; similarly, Mao's "On Contradiction" was published for the first time in 1952, though Peking spoke of it as a republication.

6. Mao, "Lun hsin chieh-tuan"; excerpts in English translation in Stuart Schram, *The Political Thought of Mao Tse-tung* (New York: Praeger Publishers, 1963), p. 113. This section was altered in the 1951 edition of *HC*, 2:522. Italics added.

7. Mao, "Lun hsin chieh-tuan."

8. Donald Lowe, *The Function of "China" in Marx, Lenin, and Mao* (Berkeley: University of California Press, 1966), p. 128.

9. Mao, *Chung-kuo ko-ming yü chung-kuo kung-ch'an-tang* (n.p., 1939), pp. 23 ff.; also *HC* (1966), 2:608.

10. Mao, "Lun hsin min-chu chu-yi" ("On New Democracy") (1940), *HC* (1966), 2:636.

11. Cf. comments in Brandt *et al.*, *A Documentary History of Chinese Communism* (New York: Atheneum, 1967), p. 262.

12. Mao, "Dialectical Materialism," excerpts in English in Schram, *Political Thought of Mao Tse-tung*, pp. 120–28. This article is not included in *HC*.

13. *Ibid.*, p. 121. Italics added.

14. Schram's commentary, *ibid.*, p. 112.

15. Cf. David Nivison, " 'Knowledge' and 'Action' in Chinese Thought Since Wang Yang-ming," in Arthur Wright, ed., *Studies in Chinese Thought* (Chicago: University of Chicago Press, 1953), p. 140.

16. Robert C. North, *Moscow and Chinese Communists*, 2d ed. (Stanford, Calif.: Stanford University Press, 1962), p. 174.

17. *HC* (1966), 3:747.

18. Mao, "Kai-tsao wo-men te hsüeh-hsi" ("Reform Our Studies") (May, 1941), *HC* (1966), 3:753–61.

19. Mao, "Cheng-tun tang te tso-feng" ("Rectify the Party's Working Style") (February 1, 1942) and "Fan-tui tang pa-ku" ("Oppose the Party's Formalism") (February 8, 1942), in *HC* (1966), 3:769–86 and 787–803. For an analytical study of the interrelatedness of "subjectivism," "sectarianism," and "formalism," see David Nivison, *Communist Ethics and Chinese Tradition* (Cambridge, Mass.: Center for International Studies, Massachusetts Institute of Technology, 1954), pp. 22 ff.

20. Mao, "Cheng-tun tang te tso-feng" and "Fan-tui tang pa-ku."

21. *Cheng-feng wen-hsien* (*Literature on the Rectification Campaign*), rev. ed. (Kalgan: Hsin-hua, 1946), p. 2, cited in Brandt *et al.*, *Documentary History of Chinese Communism*, p. 374.

22. Central Committee of the CCP, "Decision on Methods of Leadership" (June 1, 1943), *Cheng-feng wen-hsien*, p. 262, cited in Brandt *et al.*, *Documentary History of Chinese Communism*, p. 375.

23. *Cheng-feng wen-hsien*, pp. 145–46, quoted in Brandt *et al.*, *loc. cit.*

24. Mao, "Yen-an wen-yi chiang-tso" ("Talks at the Yenan Forum on Literature and Arts") (May, 1942), in *HC* (1966), pp. 804–35.

25. *Loc. cit.* English trans. of the passage in Schram, *Political Thought of Mao Tse-tung*, p. 223. The passage does not appear in *HC*. Italics added.

26. Mao, "Lun lien-ho cheng-fu" (Kalgan, 1945), p. 42, quoted in Lowe, *Function of "China*," p. 167, n. 112. The entire paragraph was deleted from *HC* (1951), 3:1063.

27. Mao, "Lun lien-ho cheng-fu," p. 34, quoted in Lowe, *Function of "China*," p. 134. Italics added.

28. *HC* (1951), 3:1056.

29. Mary C. Wright, *The Last Stand of Chinese Conservatism* (New York: Atheneum, 1967), p. 303.

30. Mao, "Ho Mei-kuo chi-cheh An-na Lu-yi-szu Szu-t'e-lang te t'an-hua" ("Talks with American Correspondent Anna Louise Strong"), *HC* (1951), 4:1191.

31. Mao, "Ying-chieh Chung-kuo ko-ming te hsin kao-ch'ao" ("Greet the

New High Tide of the Chinese Revolution") (1947), *HC* (1951), 4:1210–11.

32. Mao, "Wei-hsin li-shih-kuan te p'o-ch'an" ("The Bankruptcy of the Idealist Conception of History") (1949), *HC* (1966), pp. 1449–52.

Chapter 5

1. Chalmers Johnson, *Revolution and the Social System* (Stanford, Calif.: Hoover Institution, Stanford University, 1964), pp. 1–22.

2. Mao Tse-tung, "Investigation of the Peasant Movement in Hunan," *HC* (1966), 1:28. Italics added.

3. Mao, "China Is Poor and Blank" (April 15, 1958), *Hung Ch'i* (*Red Flag*), June 1, 1958, pp. 3–4; English excerpts in Stuart Schram, *Political Thought of Mao Tse-tung* (New York: Praeger Publishers, 1963), p. 252. Italics added.

4. Crane Brinton, *An Anatomy of Revolution*, rev. and expanded ed. (New York: Vintage, 1965), esp. Ch. 9.

5. Franklin Houn, *A Short History of Chinese Communism* (Englewood Cliffs, N. J.: Prentice-Hall, 1967), pp. 6–7; also Albert Feuerwerker, "China's 19th-Century Industrialization," in C. D. Cowan, ed., *The Economic Development of China and Japan* (New York: Praeger Publishers, 1964), p. 102.

6. Brinton, *Anatomy of Revolution*, pp. 221–25.

7. Adam Ulam, *The Unfinished Revolution* (New York: Random House, 1960), *passim*.

8. Cf. David Wilson, "Nation-Building and Revolutionary War," in Karl W. Deutsch and William A. Folz, eds., *Nation-Building* (New York: Atherton, 1966), pp. 85 ff.

9. This formulation of the destruction of premodern social fabrics and the subsequent reintegration during the process of social mobilization finds substantiation in a macro-study on the topic by Karl Deutsch. A leading commentator on social mobilization, Deutsch finds two distinct stages to the process in general: "(1) the stage of uprooting or breaking away from old settings, habits, commitments; and (2) the induction of the mobilized persons into some relatively stable new patterns of group membership, organizational commitment." "Social Mobilization and Political Development," *American Political Science Review* 55 (1961): 494.

10. My translation. *HC*, 3:759. Italics added.

11. Chalmers Johnson, *Peasant Nationalism and Communist Power: The Emergence of Revolutionary China, 1937–45* (Stanford, Calif.: Stanford University Press, 1962), p. ix. Italics added.

12. Mao, "Lun hsin min-chu chu-yi" ("On New Democracy"), *HC* (1966), 3:535. Italics added.

13. Mao, "Lun jen-min min-chu chuan-cheng" ("On People's Democratic Dictatorship"), *HC* (1966), 4:1416.

14. Liu Shao-ch'i, *On the Party* (Peking: Foreign Language Press, 1950), p. 53; and Tu Ching, "Kung-ch'an tang-yuan ying-kai shih jen-min ch'ün-chung te chung-shih tai-piao" ("A Communist Should Be a Genuine Representative of the Masses of the People"), *Hung-Ch'i*, No. 6, 1962, p. 2.

15. James Townsend, *Political Participation in Communist China* (Berkeley: University of California Press, 1967), pp. 67–68.

16. Hannah Arendt, *On Revolution* (New York: Viking, 1965), p. 84f. Italics added.

17. Lu Ting-yi, *Let Flowers of Many Kinds Blossom, Diverse Schools of Thought Contend* (Peking, 1959), pp. 15–16.

18. Mao, "On Coalition," English translation in Conrad Brandt *et al.*, *A Documentary History of Chinese Communism* (New York: Atheneum, 1966), p. 296.

19. Excerpts of the two editorials in Schram, *Political Thought of Mao Tse-tung*, pp. 277, 278.

20. *HC* (1966), 4:1375.

21. Mao, "Lun jen-min min-chu chuan-cheng" ("On People's Democratic Dictatorship") (1949), *HC* (1951), 4:1480–82.

22. Benjamin I. Schwartz, "Modernization and the Maoist Vision: Some Reflections on Chinese Communist Goals," *CQ*, No. 21 (January–March, 1965), p. 4.

23. *Ibid.*, p. 5.

24. Some of these categories are offered in John W. Lewis, *Leadership in Communist China* (Ithaca, N.Y.: Cornell University Press, 1963), Chs. 8, 2, and 3; and A. Doak Barnett, *Cadres, Bureaucracy, and Political Power in Communist China* (New York: Columbia University Press, 1967), esp. p. 429, and *passim*. See also CCP Constitution of 1956, in Theodore H. E. Chen, ed., *The Chinese Communist Regime* (New York: Praeger Publishers, 1967), p. 128. For a discussion of the problems of modernization during the nation-building process, see Lucian W. Pye, *Politics, Personality, and Nation-Building* (New Haven, Conn.: Yale University Press, 1962), pp. 3–54.

25. Cf. Betty B. Burch, "The Role of Goals in the Communist Systems," in Andrew Gyorgy, ed., *Issues of World Communism* (Princeton, N.J.: Van Nostrand, 1966), pp. 245–58.

26. "Proposal Concerning the General Line of the International Communist Movement," *PR*, No. 30 (July 26, 1963), p. 16.

27. *PR*, May 10, 1968, p. 3.

28. V. I. Lenin, *Philosophical Notebooks, 1914–1918* (Moscow, 1947), p. 192 ff.

29. *HC* (1966), 1:297.

30. *HC* (1966), 1:302.

31. Arthur A. Cohen, *The Communism of Mao Tse-tung* (Chicago: University of Chicago Press, 1964), p. 17.

32. *HC* (1966), 1:302. See also the last part of Chapter 1 above for the influence of *yin-yang* upon Mao's thinking in his pre-Marxist years.

33. "On Correct Handling of Contradictions Among the People," English translation available in *Communist China, 1955–1959* (Cambridge, Mass.: Harvard University Press, 1965), at 292.

34. Robert Jay Lifton, *Revolutionary Immortality* (New York: Random House, 1968).

35. Stuart Kirby, "The Framework of the Crisis in Communist China," *CS* 6, No. 2 (February 1, 1968): 2.

36. For a comparative study of the Maoist and the Soviet strategies for development, see Nicholas Spulber, "Contrasting Economic Patterns: Chinese and Soviet Development Strategies," *Soviet Studies* 15, No. 1 (July, 1963): 1–16; reprinted in Andrew Gyorgy, ed., *Issues of World Communism* (Princeton, N.J.: Van Nostrand, 1966), pp. 171–84.

Chapter 6

1. Mu Fu-sheng, *The Wilting of the Hundred Flowers* (New York: Praeger Publishers, 1962), p. 117.
2. "Resolutions of the Central Committee of the Communist Party of China on the Education of Cadres" (February 28, 1942), trans. in Boyd Compton, *Mao's China* (Seattle: University of Washington Press, 1952), p. 80.
3. Mu, *Wilting of the Hundred Flowers*, p. 128.
4. Stuart Schram, *Mao Tse-tung* (Baltimore, Md.: Penguin, 1967), p. 265. An-ying's mother, Mao's first wife, was Yang K'ai-hui, the daughter of his teacher. She was executed by the Nationalists in 1930.
5. For standard works see, for example, Franz Schurmann, *Ideology and Organization in Communist China* (Berkeley: University of California Press, 1966); John W. Lewis, *Leadership in Communist China* (Ithaca, N.Y.: Cornell University Press, 1963); Arthur A. Cohen, *The Communism of Mao Tse-tung* (Chicago: Chicago University Press, 1964); Roderick MacFarquhar, ed., *China Under Mao* (Cambridge, Mass.: MIT Press, 1966); Theodore Chen, *Thought Reform of the Chinese Intellectuals* (London and New York: Oxford University Press, 1960); Franklin Houn, *To Change a Nation* (Glencoe, Ill.: Free Press, 1961); Frederick Yu, *Mass Persuasion in Communist China* (New York: Praeger Publishers, 1964); Robert Lifton, *Thought Reform and the Psychology of Totalism* (New York: W. W. Norton, 1963); A. Doak Barnett, *Cadres, Bureaucracy, and Political Power in Communist China* (New York: Columbia University Press, 1967).
6. See Schurmann, *Ideology and Organization*, pp. 7 ff.; Luke Lee, "Chinese Communist Law: Its Background and Development," *Michigan Law Review*, February 2, 1962; and Mu, *Wilting of the Hundred Flowers*, pp. 116–18.
7. Mao Tse-tung, "Proclamation of the Central People's Government of the People's Republic of China," read at a Peking rally on October 1, 1949; reprinted in Theodore H. E. Chen, ed., *The Chinese Communist Regime* (New York: Praeger Publishers, 1967), p. 33.
8. Mao, "On Contradiction," *SW* (Peking: Foreign Language Press, 1960), 1:312. Italics added.
9. *Ibid.*, 1:314. Italics added.
10. Mao, "On Practice," *SW* 1:295. The words in parentheses—"material production, class struggle, or scientific experiment"—were not in the original text but were added in the 1960 edition. Italics added.
11. Cf. Feng Yu-lan, "Mao Tse-tung's 'On Practice' and Chinese Philosophy," *People's China*, November 16, 1951.
12. Preamble of the Constitution of the People's Republic of China (CPR) of 1954; also the preamble of the Common Program of 1949; both reprinted in Chen, ed., *Chinese Communist Regime*, pp. 76 and 35.
13. CPR Constitution, esp. Articles 1, 4, 11, 12, 15, 17, and 19, and Chapter 3.
14. CPR Constitution, see esp. Article 5, text in Chen, ed., *Chinese Communist Regime*, p. 65.
15. CPR Constitution, Article 1, in Chen, *Chinese Communist Regime*, p. 270.

16. "Revolutionary Theory Is the Guide of Action: On the Dictatorship of the Proletariat," *Izvestia* (Moscow), May 17, 1964, pp. 3–4.

17. Mao, "On New Democracy," *SW*, 2:380 and *passim*.

18. "Chairman Mao's March 7 Directive Guides Victorious Advance of the Great Cultural Revolution in Peking Schools," *PR*, No. 11, March 15, 1968, p. 10.

19. Tung Chi-ping, *Thought Revolution* (New York: Coward-McCann, 1966), p. 160.

20. *Ibid.*

21. *Kung-tso t'ung-hsün* (*Bulletin of Activities*, captured Chinese Communist Army documents, released by the U.S. Department of State), No. 29 (August 1, 1961), p. 3; see discussion in John W. Lewis, "China's Military Papers: 'Continuities' and 'Revelations,' " in MacFarquhar, ed., *China Under Mao*, p. 59.

22. For an interesting description of the practice, see Andrew L. March, "An Appreciation of Chinese Geomancy" *JAS* 27, No. 2 (February, 1968), pp. 253–67.

23. C. K. Yang, *A Chinese Village in Early Communist Transition* (Cambridge, Mass.: MIT Press, 1959), pp. 179–80. Italics added.

24. Article 1 of the Agrarian Reform Law of 1950, English text in Chen, ed., *Chinese Communist Regime*, p. 196.

25. "Who Is Our Enemy and Who Is Our Friend," *JMJP*, March 25, 1963.

26. No systematic study has been made of the ills of *shih-ta-fu hsi-ch'i*, perhaps because Chinese scholars avoid self-incrimination and Westerners do not want to affront the sensibilities of the Chinese and, besides, lack sufficient data in available published sources. But plenty of piecemeal information can be obtained through reading modern Chinese novels, especially those written by "leftist" writers in the post-1912 era. A ready example is Lu Hsün, *Our Story of Ah Q*. Another is *Mr. Almost* by Hu Shih. Some cogent arguments regarding the value system are found in T'ang Yüeh, "A Few Weak Points in Our Habit of Thought," *Tung-fang tsa-chih* (*Eastern Miscellany*) (Peking), 20:7. An older volume on the characteristics (and weaknesses) of the Chinese in general is Arthur H. Smith, *Chinese Characteristics*, 2d ed., (New York: F. H. Revell, 1894). See also Howard L. Boorman and Scott A. Boorman, "Strategy and National Psychology in China," *The Annals of the American Academy of Political and Social Science*, March, 1967 (section headed "National Character in the Perspective of the Social Sciences"), 143–55.

27. The lasting effect of the "habit and aura of the gentry-literati" is surprising. A former student told me of a personal experience she had had while teaching in a school in Hongkong. One day, after the scheduled opening time of a meeting had long passed, students were still milling in the hall, waiting for the janitor to put up the chairs. No student would even lift one finger to put up the chairs in the meantime, because it would be beneath the dignity of a student and put him in an embarrassing position open to the laughter of the others. I still remember that before the Communists took the China mainland many male members of the "long-gowned" (Chinese equivalent to "white-collar") families purposely raised long fingernails, not for beauty, but for ostentatiously showing their status of not having to work with their hands.

28. F. T. Mits, in "The Wanderer," *Current Scene* (Hongkong) 5, No. 13

(August 15, 1967), 2, has even gone so far as to suggest a "hippie-Maoist" trend.

29. "What Is Party Spirit? Why Is Revolutionary Vigilance a Noble Quality? Why Is Lethargic Mentality a Rightist Trend?" *Hsüeh-hsi* (*Study*), No. 8, 1955, trans. in *SCMM*, No. 11 (October 24, 1955).

30. See further discussion in Chapter 8.

31. Schurmann, *Ideology and Organization*, pp. 58–68. In an analysis of official and less official national and local newspapers, Schurmann found that published materials fell into six broad categories, and, particularly, the first four of these categories: (1) policy decisions, (2) discussions of experiences in policy implementation, (3) general principles, (4) criticisms, (5) propaganda, and (6) "public information."

32. Mao, "On People's Democratic Dictatorship," *SW*, 4:415.

33. Mu, *Wilting of the Hundred Flowers*, pp. 134–35.

34. Richard Solomon, "Communications Patterns and the Chinese Revolution," *CQ*, No. 32 (October–December, 1967), pp. 101–4.

35. For the text of Chou Yang's speech, see *Hung-ch'i*, No. 24, 1963.

36. "Talks by Comrade Lin Pao at the Central Committee Meeting on Its Work" (November 23, 1966?), printed in *ta-tzu-pao* (wall poster) form by the Mao Tse-tungism Corps of the Peking Institute of Physical Education for Workers, Peasants, and Soldiers, the Jui-chin Combat Contingent, and the Thorough Revolutionary Combat Contingent. The copy was distributed in Xerox reproduction by the Harvard-Yenching Library, Cambridge, Mass., in 1967.

Chapter 7

1. See discussion in the preceding chapters, esp. Chapter 5. Cf. also the views of Stuart Schram, Joseph R. Levenson, and Benjamin I. Schwartz, in "Maoism: A Symposium," *Problems of Communism*, September–October, 1966, pp. 1–7, 17–18, 20–22.

2. Alfred North Whitehead, *Adventures of Ideas* (New York: Macmillan, 1933), Ch. 9.

3. See generally Oswald Spengler, *The Decline of the West*, abridged edition, ed. by Helmut Werner (New York: Knopf, 1962).

4. Cf. Victor F. Lenzen, *The Nature of Physical Theory* (New York: John Wiley and Sons, 1931); and Joseph H. Woodger, *The Axiomatic Method in Biology* (Cambridge, England: Cambridge University Press, 1937).

5. *HC* (1966), 1:262; 2:624, 655.

6. *HC*, 1:275 ff.

7. Mao Tse-tung, "On Practice," *HC*, 1:261.

8. Franz Schurmann, *Ideology and Organization in Communist China* (Berkeley: University of California Press, 1966), pp. 21 ff.

9. *JMJP* editorial, November 11, 1960. Italics added.

10. See, for example, the view offered by Harold Hinton in his review of *The Communism of Mao Tse-tung* by Arthur Cohen, in *JAS* 25, No. 2 (February, 1966): 335.

11. Scores of other examples of translated terms in which *chu-yi* is used for

"ism" are found in frequent usage, such as in anarchism, Kautsky-Marxism, totalitarianism, militarism, Physiocratism, Pan-Moslemism, Pan-Germanism, Pan-Americanism, anti-Semitism, Fabianism, feudalism, legalism, vanguardism, realism, patriotism, humanism, Kantianism, Classicism, revisionism, Nihilism, humanitarianism, Keynesianism, Marxism, Leninism, Bonhommieism, and so forth. Cf. *Standard Translation of Chinese Communist Terms*, JPRS Handbook (Washington: U.S. Department of Commerce, Joint Publications Research Service, 1962), pp. 32–39.

12. Other terms include: *cheng-pan chu-yi*, punitivism; *chiao-t'iao chu-yi*, dogmatism; *ching-yen chu-yi*, empiricism; *chu-kuan chu-yi*, subjectivism; *ko-jen chu-yi*, individualism; *mao-hsien chu-yi*, adventurism; *pao-fu chu-yi*, revengeism; *pen-wei chu-yi*, particularism; *shan-t'ou chu-yi*, mountaintop-ism; *shen-mi chu-yi*, mysticism; *t'iao-ho chu-yi*, compromise-ism; *wen-tu chu-yi*, documentism, etc. *Standard Translation of Chinese Communist Terms*, JPRS Handbook.

13. There are not many words in this group. A few other examples are: *yi-shu chih-shang chu-yi*, art-for-art's-sake-ism; *jen-chung chu-yi*, racism; *kai-liang chu-yi*, reformism; *Nung-yeh she-hui, chu-yi*, agricultural socialism (absolute egalitarianism based on small-farm economy), etc. Many of these, obviously, are translations or semitranslations. *Standard Translation of Chinese Communist Terms*. JPRS Handbook.

14. Mao, *HC* (1966), 4:1407; *SW* (1960), 4:413.

15. John W. Lewis, *Leadership in Communist China* (Ithaca, N.Y.: Cornell University Press, 1963), pp. 38–39.

16. My own translation. Italics added.

17. Its preamble stated, in words reminiscent of those of Mao: "Marxism-Leninism is not a dogma, but a guide to action. It demands that in striving to build socialism and Communism we should proceed from reality, apply the principles of Marxism-Leninism in a flexible and creative way for the solution of various problems arising out of the actual struggle, and thus continuously develop the theory of Marxism-Leninism. Consequently, the Party in its activities upholds the principle of integrating the universal truths of Marxism-Leninism with the actual practice of China's revolutionary struggle, and combats all doctrinaire or empiricist deviations." English text of the CCP Constitution of 1956 in Theodore H. E. Chen, ed., *The Chinese Communist Regime* (New York: Praeger Publishers, 1967), p. 127.

18. *JMJP*, April 5, 1956; English trans. in *Communist China: 1955–1959* (Cambridge, Mass.: Center of International Affairs and East Asian Research Center, Harvard University, 1965), p. 144.

19. *JMJP* on March 30, 1956, carried a translation of a March 28, 1956, article in *Pravda*: "Why the Cult of the Individual Is Alien to Marxism-Leninism." This was the first Chinese reaction to Khrushchev's revelations in his speech to the Twentieth Party Congress in February of that year. *JMJP* on June 16, 1956, published a "Collection of Criticisms on the Stalin Issue" made by foreign Communist Parties. See *SCMP*, No. 1332.

20. "The 'Wicked' History of P'eng Te-huai," *CB*, No. 851 (April 26, 1968). See also Red Guard tabloid "Fan-ko-ming hsiu-cheng fen-tzu Liu Shao-ch'i shih ta tsui-chuang" ("Ten Flagrant Crimes of Liu Shao-ch'i, the Counterrevolutionary Revisionist"), put out originally by the Red Guard unit of Tsinghua University and reproduced by the Hsin Peita (New Peking University) Red Guard Combat Corps; copy available in the collection of Red Guard

tabloids reproduced for U.S. distribution by the Harvard-Yenching Library, Cambridge, Mass.

21. English translation by *SCMP*, August 17, 1966, No. 3762; reprinted in A. Doak Barnett, *China After Mao* (Princeton, N.J.: Princeton University Press, 1967), p. 285. Italics added.

22. Cf. Arthur A. Cohen, *The Communism of Mao Tse-tung* (Chicago: University of Chicago Press, 1964).

23. Franklin Houn, *A Short History of Chinese Communism* (Englewood Cliffs, N.J.: Prentice-Hall, 1967), p. 82.

24. Marx and Engels, *The German Ideology* (New York: International Publishers, 1947). Italics added.

25. Marx, *Theses on Feuerbach*, in *Selected Works*, 1:471.

26. Lenin, *Philosophical Notebooks* (1914–1918) (Moscow, 1947), p. 156.

27. *Ibid.*, p. 146.

28. *Ibid.*, p. 174.

29. *HC* (1966), 3:832, my translation. Italics added.

30. *Communist China, 1955–1959*, p. 281.

31. "Hold High the Great Red Banner of the Thought of Mao Tse-tung . . .," *CFCP*, April 18, 1966. Italics added.

32. *Hsüeh-hsi Mao Tse-tung te szu-hsiang fang-fa ho kung-tso fang-fa (Learn from Mao Tse-tung's Ways of Thinking and Ways of Working)* (Peking: Chung-kuo ch'ing-nien, 1958), p. 73; English translation in Schram, *Mao Tse-tung*, p. 295. Italics added.

33. Schram, *Mao Tse-tung, loc. cit.*

34. *Ibid.*

35. Mao, *HC* (1966), 2:437, 462; the translation is mine and differs from that of the official English edition. In the official translation, *hsin* in the two instances came out as "morale" and "mother wit," respectively.

36. *Chu-tzu ch'üan-shu (Collected Works of Chu Hsi)*, 44:1b–13b; English translation in William Theodore de Bary, *Sources of Chinese Tradition* (New York: Columbia University Press, 1964), 1:496.

37. The contrast of "human heart" and "moral heart" is derived from the *Shu-ching (Book of History)*, *Counsels of the Great Yü*. Whereas the former is in a precarious position because it is liable to mistakes, the latter always follows that which is right.

38. De Bary, *Sources of Chinese Tradition*, 1:480.

39. *Ibid.*, 1:515.

40. David Nivison, "The Problem of 'Knowledge' and 'Action' in Chinese Thought Since Wang Yang-ming," in Arthur Wright, ed., *Studies in Chinese Thought* (Chicago: University of Chicago Press, 1953), pp. 112–45.

41. Cf. Wing-tsit Chan, *A Source Book in Chinese Philosophy* (Princeton, N.J.: Princeton University Press, 1963), p. 655.

42. *Hsüeh-hsi Mao Tse-tung te szu-hsiang fang-fa ho kung-tso fang-fa (Learn from Mao Tse-tung's Ways of Thinking and Ways of Working)* (Peking: Chung-kuo ch'ing-nien, 1958), p. 40.

43. Ch'en Po-ta, *Jen-hsing, tang-hsing, ko-hsing (Human Nature, Party Character, and Personal Character)* (Ch'ao-hsi she [Yenan], 1947), p. 7.

44. David Nivison, *Communist Ethics and Chinese Tradition* (Cambridge, Mass.: Center for International Studies, Massachusetts Institute of Technology, 1954), p. 39.

45. Filmer S. C. Northrop, "The Complementary Emphases of Eastern In-tuition Philosophy and Western Scientific Philosophy," in Charles A. Moore, ed., *Philosophy, East and West* (Princeton, N.J.: Princeton University Press, 1946), p. 187. Also F. S. C. Northrop, *Meeting of East and West* (New York: Macmillan, 1946), pp. 312 ff.

46. Northrop, *Meeting of East and West*, p. 205.

47. Fung Yu-lan, *A Short History of Chinese Philosophy*, ed. by Derk Bodde (New York: Macmillan, 1948), pp. 24–25.

48. Cf. de Bary, *Sources of Chinese Tradition*, 1:6.

49. *Ibid.*, 1:15–33, 86–97.

50. *Ibid.*, 1:37, 47. Also, Hsiao Kung-ch'üan, *Chung-kuo cheng-chih szu-hsiang shih* (*A History of Chinese Political Thought*) (Taipei, Taiwan: Chinese Cultural Publications, 1954), 1:132.

51. De Bary, *Sources of Chinese Tradition*, 1:55–57.

52. *Ibid.*, 1:101.

53. *Ibid.*, 1:132; and Chan, *Source Book in Chinese Philosophy*, p. 256.

54. Chang Tung-sun, "Thought, Language and Culture," *She-hui-hsüeh chieh* (*The World of Sociology*, Peking), 10:32, 41.

55. Chan, *Source Book in Chinese Philosophy*, p. 257.

Chapter 8

1. David Nivison, *Communist Ethics and Chinese Tradition* (Cambridge, Mass.: Center for International Studies, Massachusetts Institute of Technology, 1954), pp. 58–59.

2. Mao Tse-tung, SW (1965), 1:11. Italics added.

3. Otto B. Van der Sprankel, Robert Guillain, and Michael Lindsay, *New China: Three Views* (London: Turnstile Press, 1950), p. 130.

4. Theodore Chen, *The Chinese Communist Regime* (New York: Praeger Publishers, 1967), p. 12.

5. Stuart Schram, *Mao Tse-tung* (Baltimore: Penguin, 1967), p. 293.

6. Proclamation No. 1 of the Central Executive Committee of the Chinese Soviet Republic, December 1, 1931, in *Hung-se Chung-hua* (*Red China*), No. 1 (December 11, 1931), p. 2, available in *Shih-sou tzu-liao-shih kung-fei tzu-liao* (a microfilmed collection of documents from the files of the late Vice-President Ch'en Ch'eng of Nationalist China).

7. Cf. Conrad Brandt *et al.*, *A Documentary History of Chinese Communism* (New York: Atheneum, 1966), p. 320. See also discussion in Chapter 7 above.

8. K. S. Karol, *China: The Other Communism* (New York: Hill and Wang, 1967), p. 183.

9. V. I. Lenin, *Selected Works* (Moscow: Progress Publishers, 1965), xxxix: 389; emphasis in the original.

10. J. V. Stalin, *Problems of Leninism*, 11th ed. (Moscow: Foreign Languages Publishing House, 1953), p. 317.

11. David E. Powell, "Mao and Stalin's Mantle," *Problems of Communism*, March–April, 1968, pp. 21–30.

12. Khrushchev's "secret speech" at the Twentieth CPSU Congress of 1956, in *The Anti-Stalin Campaign and International Communism* (New York: Columbia University Press, 1956), pp. 28–29. Also see Khrushchev's remarks

to the 1961 Twenty-Second CPSU Congress, *Pravda*, October 18, 1961, p. 5.

13. CPSU Party Program, approved by the Twenty-Second Party Congress, in Charlotte Saikowski and Leo Gruliow, eds., *Current Soviet Policies IV* (New York: Columbia University Press, 1962), p. 23.

14. Khrushchev, "On the Program of the Communist Party of the Soviet Union," in *Road to Communism: Documents of the 22nd Congress of the CPSU, October 17–31, 1961* (Moscow: Foreign Languages Publishing House, 1961), pp. 187–96. Italics added.

15. *The New York Times*, May 29, 1957.

16. CPSU Party Program, in Saikowski and Gruliow, eds., *Current Soviet Policies IV*, p. 23. Italics added.

17. Cf. Chapter 6 above and bibliography given in n. 5 in that chapter.

18. Robert Jay Lifton, *Thought Reform and the Psychology of Totalism* (New York: W. W. Norton, 1963), pp. 419–37 and *passim*.

19. Mao, "Tsai Yen-an wen-yi tso-t'an-hui-shang te t'an-hua" ("Talks at the Yenan Forum of Arts & Literature"), *HC* (1966), 3:832; English text in *SW* (1960), 3:94.

20. Mao's talk was reprinted in a factory newsletter, *Hung hsien-pan (Red Line Edition)*, December 19, 1966; English translation in *Chinese Law and Government: A Journal of Translations* (White Plains, N.Y.: International Arts and Sciences Press), Spring, 1968 (inaugural issue), pp. 7–12.

21. The view that Peking's foreign policy has been Mao's policy was shared by O. Edmund Clubb, in a talk on "Sino-Soviet Border Relations," at a luncheon of the East Asian Institute, Columbia University, March 15, 1968.

22. Richard Lowenthal, "Soviet and Chinese Communist World View," in Donald Treadgold, ed., *Soviet and Chinese Communism* (Seattle: University of Washington Press, 1967), pp. 380 ff.

23. Donald Zagoria, "Russia, China, and the New States," in Treadgold, ed., *Soviet and Chinese Communism*, pp. 405–7; and John H. Kautsky, ed., *Political Change in Underdeveloped Countries* (New York: John Wiley, 1962), pp. 70 ff.

24. I have dealt with this point in greater detail in "China's Foreign Policy: The Interplay of Ideology, Practical Interests, and Polemics," in William Richardson, ed., *China Today* (Maryknoll, N.Y.: Maryknoll Publications, 1969), pp. 25-55.

25. Franz Schurmann and Orville Schell, *The China Reader*, 3 (*Communist China*) (New York: Random House, 1967): 614; and Harold Hinton, in his contribution in Richardson, ed., *China Today*.

26. Anna Louise Strong, *Letter from China* (Peking), No. 56 (February 22, 1968), p. 4.

27. Lin Piao, *Long Live the Victory of the People's War* (Peking: Foreign Language Press, 1965).

28. *PR*, April 12, 1968, pp. 18–20.

29. Donald Zagoria, "China and the Non-Western World," *Diplomat*, September, 1966, p. 55. Italics added.

30. Quoted in Isaac Deutscher, *The Prophet Armed: Trotsky, 1879–1921* (London and New York: Oxford University Press, 1954), p. 238.

31. Cf. Mao's statement on race relations in the United States, August 8, 1963, in *SCMP*, No. 3038 (August 13, 1963).

32. *JMJP*, August 23, 1968; *The New York Times*, August 23, 1968, p. 1.

33. NCNA, August 23, 1968; *The New York Times*, August 25, 1968.
34. NCNA, August 23, 1968.

Chapter 9

1. Franz Schurmann, "Politics and Economics in China and Russia," in Donald Treadgold, ed., *Soviet and Chinese Communism* (Seattle: University of Washington Press, 1967), p. 298.
2. Some writers still believe that the intra-party disagreements did not arise until after the failure of the Great Leap. See, for example, Tang Tsou, "The Cultural Revolution and the Chinese Political System," *CQ*, No. 38 (April–June, 1960), p. 75. I would argue, however, that a careful examination of the record of the pre-1959 period indicates that many disagreements already existed, although it was still possible then to compose them.
3. Zbigniew Brzezinski, *The Soviet Bloc*, revised and enlarged edition (Cambridge, Mass.: Harvard University Press, 1967), pp. 130, 133.
4. Mao's speech to the Tenth Plenum of the Eighth Central Committee of the CCP, which met in Peking on September 28, 1962. A summary of the speech was taken from a wall poster in Peking by the Japanese correspondent Takada, whose dispatch was published in *Mainichi Shimbun* (Tokyo) on March 9, 1967. Text was reproduced in *Chinese Law and Government* (White Plains, N.Y.: International Arts and Science Press), 1, No. 1 (Spring, 1968): 6.
5. Based on my own interviews with Chinese ex-POW's from the Korean War who were repatriated to Taiwan.
6. *JMJP*, July 14, 1957.
7. The Central Committee's position regarding the Kao-Jao "anti-Party bloc" can be seen in the February 10, 1954, resolution adopted by the Fourth Plenum of the Seventh Party Congress, which denounced leaders who "exaggerated the role of the individual" and ran their departments like "separate kingdoms." See discussion in Franz Schurmann, *Ideology and Organization in Communist China* (Berkeley: University of California Press, 1966), pp. 267 ff; and John Lewis, "Revolutionary Struggle and the Second Generation in Communist China," *CQ*, No. 21 (January–March, 1965), pp. 132 ff.
8. NCNA, August 1, 1949.
9. Liu Po-ch'eng's speech before the Second Session of the First National People's Congress (NPC), July 21, 1955, NCNA (Peking), July 21, 1955, in *CB*, No. 347 (August 23, 1955), p. 27; Yeh Chien-ying's speech, at the same session, *CB*, No. 347, pp. 29–31.
10. Alice Hsieh, *Communist China's Strategy in the Nuclear Era* (Englewood Cliffs, N.J.: Prentice-Hall, 1962), p. 41.
11. *Ibid.*, pp. 35–38, 41, 43, 46, 53.
12. *Ibid.*, p. 23.
13. See P'eng's "confession" (December 28, 1966–January 5, 1967) in *Tsu-kuo chou-k'an* (*Fatherland Weekly*, Hongkong), No. 5 (May, 1968), p. 40; English translation in *CB*, No. 851 (April 16, 1968), p. 17.
14. Chang Wen-t'ien, "Ssu-shih nien wei-le ho-p'ing" ("Forty Years for Peace"), *JMJP*, November 2, 1957.

15. Li Hsien-nien's report to the Fourth Session of the First NPC, June 29, 1957, *CB*, No. 464 (July 5, 1957), p. 15; Hsieh, *Communist China's Strategy*, pp. 61–62.

16. Mao Tse-tung, "More on the Experience of the Dictatorship of the Proletariat," *JMJP*, December 29, 1956. See also Mao's "On Correct Handling of Contradictions Among the People," *JMJP*, June 19, 1957. Note the sequence of Mao's two comments on war: "First, we are against it; second, we are not afraid of it." Mao's view regarding the extent to which peaceful coexistence should be applied changed over the years, but his main difference with Khrushchev was his belief that peaceful coexistence should not apply to relations with the "imperialists." Cf. Tang Tsou, "Mao Tse-tung and Peaceful Coexistence," *Orbis*, 8, No. 1 (Spring, 1964): 36–51.

17. *CFCP*, January 7, 1956.

18. *Hsin-hua pan-yüeh-k'an (New China Bimonthly)*, No. 21, 1956; also Ellis Joffe, *Party and Army* (Cambridge, Mass.: Harvard East Asian Research Center, 1967), pp. 48–84.

19. A. Doak Barnett, *Communist China and Asia* (New York: Harper, 1961), pp. 87–100, 105.

20. V. P. Dutt, *China and the World* (New York: Praeger Publishers, 1964), p. 21 ff.; and Barnett, *loc. cit.*

21. Kao's speech before a meeting of cadres in Inner Mongolia in August, 1948, Shih Chia-ling, *Chung-kung kao-jao shih-chien mien-mien kuan (The Case of Kao-Jao Viewed from Various Angles)* (Hongkong: Freedom Press, 1955), p. 7.

22. *Kuo-chi chu-yi yü min-tsu chu-yi (Internationalism and Nationalism)* (Peking: Chieh-fang she, 1949). It is interesting that the same volume contains a selection from Mao entitled "All the World's Revolutionary Forces Unite to Fight Imperialist Aggression."

23. The year 1954 was probably the earliest beginning of the current Sino-Soviet split, in the sense that Peking was already demanding greater autonomy and less subordination to the Moscow-centered hierarchy. I have dealt with this thesis in my article in William Richardson, ed., *China Today, loc. cit. supra*, Chapter 8, n. 24, and in another book on Communist China's international behavior to be published under the auspices of the East Asian Institute, Columbia University. For that reason, I shall refrain from elaborating my arguments. I shall merely note that, in Peking's usage since 1954, "internationalism" or "proletarian internationalism" has always been associated with an unexpressed fear of Soviet dominance; for, during the Stalin era, the concept was employed to justify satellite subordination to Moscow, allegedly to defend the socialist bloc against the "imperialist" camp in an asserted bipolar contention. Cf. Brzezinski, *The Soviet Bloc*, pp. 105 ff.

24. Liu Shao-ch'i in 1964 was indirectly accused of advocating the policy of "three reconciliations and one reduction" *(san-ho yi-shao)*, including reconciliation with the Soviet Union. In his 1966 "confession," Liu admitted to this, though rather vaguely.

25. In a comment on the Soviet statement of October 31, 1956, clarifying the Soviet position on its relations with other Communist states in the wake of the Hungarian Revolution, Peking on November 1 declared: "The People's Republic of China *has always believed* [*yi-hsiang jen-wei*] that the Five Prin-

ciples of mutual respect for sovereignty and territorial integrity, mutual non-aggression, mutual noninterference in internal affairs, equality and mutual benefit, and peaceful coexistence should become the uniform norms [chun-tse] for the establishment and development of mutual relations among *all* nations in the world. Socialist countries are all independent and sovereign nations and at the same time are bound together by the common ideal of socialism and the spirit of proletarian internationalism. For this reason, interrelations between socialist nations should *all the more* be structured on the basis of the Five Principles. *Only in this way* can socialist nations bring about brotherly friendship and unity and realize their common aspirations for economic advancement through mutual cooperation." Italics added. Text in *TWKH*, 4 (1956–57): 149.

26. I have devoted two chapters to this point in my forthcoming book mentioned in note 23 above. I shall merely suggest here that the priority given in the Chinese comment of November 1, 1956, cited above, to independence and sovereignty of socialist nations before "proletarian internationalism" is typical of Peking's position ever since 1954.

27. Mao-Khrushchev communiqué of October 12, 1954, defined Sino-Soviet relations as guided by the principles of "equality, mutual benefit, and mutual respect for sovereignty and territorial integrity." *TWKH*, 3:176. In another communiqué issued by Mao and Khrushchev in 1958, relations between the two countries were said to be built "on the basis of full equality and comradely mutual assistance." *TWKH*, 5:147.

28. During the CCP purge of Kao Kang and Jao Shu-shih in 1954, "collective leadership" was stressed to combat the "small separate kingdoms" alleged to have existed under the Kao-Jao "anti-Party bloc." While to Mao "collective leadership" meant the elimination of regional power pockets, there is evidence that among some other CCP leaders it represented a muffled discontent with Mao's own "cult of the individual." See, for example, P'eng Te-huai's "confession," n. 13 above.

29. *JMJP* on March 30, 1956 published a translation of the *Pravda* editorial of March 28, "Why the Cult of the Individual Is Alien to Marxism-Leninism." In "On the Dictatorship of the Proletariat" (*JMJP*, April 5, 1956), Mao did not conceal his true thinking about Stalin's "mistakes" but promptly pointed out that the "mark of a good leader" was not his infallibility but that "he takes mistakes seriously."

30. P'eng Te-huai, in his "confession," note 13 above, admitted: "At the 1956 Eighth Party Congress I suggested removing the 'thought of Mao Tse-tung' [from the Party's Constitution]. As soon as I made the suggestion, Liu Shao-ch'i agreed. He said: 'We'd better cross it out.' I am opposed to the cult of the individual."

31. *JMJP*, December 29, 1956.

32. *JMJP*, June 19, 1957. Relevant parts are reproduced in *TMKH*, 4:303.

33. Cf. Audrey Donnithorne, *China's Economic System* (New York: Praeger Publishers, 1967); Chao Kuo-chun, *Agrarian Policies of Mainland China: A Documentary Study* (1949–1956) (Cambridge, Mass.: Harvard East Asian Research Center, 1957); Alexander Eckstein, *Communist China's Economic Growth and Foreign Trade* (New York: McGraw-Hill, 1966); W. W. Hollister, *China's Gross National Product and Social Accounts 1950–1957* (Glen-

coe, Ill.: The Free Press, 1958); T. J. Hughes and D. E. T. Luard, *The Economic Development of Communist China*, 2d ed. (London and New York: Oxford University Press, 1961); Choh-ming Li, *Economic Development of Communist China* (Berkeley: University of California Press, 1959); Ta-chung Liu and Kung-chia Yeh, *The Economy of the Chinese Mainland*, 2 vols. (Santa Monica, Calif.: The RAND Corp., 1963); L. A. Orleans, *Professional Manpower and Education in Communist China* (Washington, D.C.: GPO, 1961); Yuan-li Wu, *An Economic Survey of Communist China* (New York: Bookman Associates, 1956); and Schurmann, *Ideology and Organization*.

34. See, for example, Schurmann, in Treadgold, ed., *Soviet and Chinese Communism.*

35. See Teng's "Report to the Rural Work Conference . . . New Democratic League, July 15, 1954," reprinted in Chao, *Agrarian Policies of Mainland China*, pp. 70–79. As late as July 5 and 6, in a report to the Second Session of the First NPC, Li Fu-ch'un was still following the gradualist policy. He gave the establishment of one million cooperatives by 1957 as a target of the state's First Five-Year Plan. Li, *Report on the First Five-Year Plan for the Development of the National Economy of the People's Republic of China in 1953–1957* (Peking: Foreign Language Press, 1955). Three weeks later, however, Mao in a speech raised the target number of cooperatives to 1.3 million by October, 1956, representing a 100 per cent increase in 14 months. Mao hoped that by the spring of 1958 about half the peasant population, roughly 55 million households, would be in cooperatives of the "semi-socialist" (elementary) type. By 1960, according to Mao, the other half would have joined the elementary cooperatives, and some of those already formed would have been transformed into advanced "socialist" cooperatives (collectives). Mao, *The Question of Agricultural Cooperation* (July 31, 1955) (Peking: Foreign Language Press, 1956). Both Li's and Mao's reports are reprinted in *Communist China 1955–1959: Policy Documents with Analysis* (Cambridge, Mass.: Harvard University, Center for International Affairs and East Asian Research Center, 1965), pp. 43–91, 94–105.

36. The fact that Mao chose to announce his plan for accelerating the rate of agricultural cooperativization to an unprecedented conference of provincial-level Party secretaries (in late July, 1955), which had questionable "legality" under the existing Party Constitution, was probably an indication that he had run into trouble in the Central Committee. It was only after its adoption at this conference that the plan was approved by the Central Committee in October. Ch'en Yi's remark, in *JMJP*, November 13, 1955, translated in *SCMP*, No. 1177, seems to support this speculation. Italics added.

37. Mao, *Socialist Upsurge in the Countryside* (Peking: Foreign Language Press, 1957), pp. 159–60.

38. E.g., "Sweep Away All Monsters," *JMJP* editorial, June 1, 1966; the denunciation of "monsters" and "demons" pervaded Yao Wen-yuan's article "On the 'Three-Family Village,'" *Chieh-fang pao* (*Liberation Daily*, Shanghai) and *Wen hui pao* (Shanghai), on May 10, 1966.

39. "Struggle in China's Countryside Between the Two Roads," simultaneously published in *JMJP, Hung-ch'i*, and *CFCP*, November 23, 1967; English translation in *SCMP*, No. 4068 (November 28, 1967). Cf. Parris

Chang, "Struggle Between the Two Roads in China's Countryside," *CS* 6, No. 3 (February 15, 1968).
    40. *SCMP*, Nos. 1183 and 1179.

Chapter 10

1. Ch'i Pen-yü, "Ai-kuo chu-yi hai-shih mai-kuo chu-yi," ("Patriotism or National Betrayal") *Hung-ch'i*, No. 5, 1967; *PR*, April 7, 1967.
2. "Statement by the Spokesman of the Chinese Government: A Comment on the Soviet Government Statement of August 3" (August 15, 1963), in *PR*, August 16, 1963.
3. Mao reportedly told the Tenth Plenum of the CCP Central Committee, in September, 1962, that "in the second half of 1958 Khrushchev brought up a plan for a Sino-Soviet joint fleet and, by this plan, tried to place the coasts of China under Soviet control and to blockade China." See *Mainichi shimbun* (Tokyo), March 9, 1967, and John Gittings, *Survey of the Sino-Soviet Dispute, 1963–1967* (London and New York: Oxford University Press, 1968), p. 103, n. 3.
4. These points were raised in Gittings, *Survey of Sino-Soviet Dispute*, p. 103.
5. M. I. Sladkovsky, ed., *Leninskaya politika SSSR v otnoshenii kitaya* (Moscow: Nauka, 1968). I am indebted to Harrison E. Salisbury, Assistant Managing Editor of *The New York Times*, for this information. See also Salisbury's article: "The Urgent Question Dominating the Asian Heartland Is: Will There Be War Between Russia and China?" *The New York Times Magazine*, July 27, 1969, p. 56.
6. Tang Tsou, "The Cultural Revolution and the Chinese Political System," *CQ*, No. 38 (April–June, 1969), p. 70.
7. Franz Schurmann, "Politics and Economics in China and Russia," in Donald Treadgold, ed., *Soviet and Chinese Communism* (Seattle: University of Washington Press, 1967), at 305; *idem, Ideology and Organization in Communist China* (Berkeley: University of California Press, 1966), p. 195.
8. Soviet credits to China appear to have been exhausted in 1957. No further credits emerged following Mao's Moscow visit in November of that year, although it was not impossible that Mao, in his over-all dissatisfaction with the nature of the Soviet alliance, resisted the terms of further Soviet aid. Cf. Gittings, *Survey of Sino-Soviet Dispute*, p. 93.
9. Schurmann, *Ideology and Organization*, pp. 198 ff.
10. Alexander Eckstein, *Communist China's Economic Growth and Foreign Trade* (New York: McGraw-Hill, 1966), pp. 31 ff.
11. See Gittings, *Survey of Sino-Soviet Dispute*.
12. Cf. Dwight H. Perkins, "Centralization and Decentralization in Mainland China's Agriculture, 1949–1962," *Quarterly Journal of Economics* 77 (May, 1964): 208–37; and *idem,* "Centralization and Decentralization in Mainland China and Soviet Union," *Annals* (American Academy of Political and Social Sciences), 349 (September, 1963): 70–80. A useful discussion on industrial "verticalization" is in Audrey Donnithorne, *China's Economic System* (New York: Praeger Publishers, 1967), pp. 168–70.

13. Yuan-li Wu, "Economics, Ideology and the Cultural Revolution," *AS* 8, No. 3 (March, 1968): 226–28.

14. See Chapters 7 and 8 above. Lucian Pye has also dealt with will power and morality as Communist China's "dynamics of action" in *The Spirit of Chinese Politics* (Cambridge, Mass.: MIT Press, 1968), pp. 125 ff.

15. Li Fu-ch'un's report to the National People's Congress in April, 1959; cf. Peter S. Tang and Joan M. Maloney, *Communist China: The Domestic Scene, 1949–1967* (South Orange, N.J.: Seton Hall University Press, 1967), p. 399.

16. Tang and Maloney, *Communist China*, p. 338. See also George Jan, "Failure of the Chinese Commune Experiment," in George Jan, ed., *Government of Communist China* (San Francisco, Calif.: Chandler, 1966), pp. 453–74.

17. Han Suyin, *China in the Year 2001* (New York: Basic Books, 1967), p. 77.

18. Although Mao may not be conscious of the analogy, his instant Communism strategy recalls the "subitist" school of Buddhism, which believed in the instant salvation of the faithful. Cf. Arthur Wright, *Buddhism in Chinese History* (New York: Atheneum, 1965), pp. 47, 92.

19. P'eng's July 14, 1959, letter to Mao; English translation in *CB*, No. 851.

20. "Resolution on Some Questions Concerning the People's Communes" (Wuhan Resolution), adopted by the Eighth Central Committee at its Sixth Plenum, December 10, 1958 (issued on December 17); English translation in *Communist China, 1949–1959: Policy Documents and Analysis* (Cambridge, Mass.: Harvard University Press, 1965), pp. 502–3.

21. *CB*, No. 851. My attention to the intricate case of P'eng was called by Richard Sorich of the East Asian Institute, Columbia University.

22. This was the view taken by, for example, John Gittings in *The Role of the Chinese Army* (London and New York: Oxford University Press, 1967), pp. 225–34. In his later work, *Survey of the Sino-Soviet Dispute*, Gittings slightly modified his position (p. 105, n. 2).

23. I agree with William Dorrill, *Power, Policy and Ideology in the Making of China's 'Cultural Revolution'* (Santa Monica, Calif.: The RAND Corp., 1968), p. 33, that P'eng's disagreements were broader than on military policy alone. This same view was also expressed by David Charles in "The Dismissal of Marshal P'eng Te-huai," *CQ*, No. 8 (October–December, 1961), pp. 65, 67.

24. *CB*, No. 851, pp. 24–26. Emphasis added.

25. *CB, loc. cit.*

26. Cf. Oleg Hoeffding, "Sino-Soviet Economic Relations in Recent Years," in Kurt London, ed., *Unity and Contradiction* (New York: Praeger Publishers, 1962); and Gittings, *Role of the Chinese Army*, pp. 234 ff.

27. Liu Shao-ch'i was accused of having said in 1961 that "those who held views similar to those of P'eng Te-huai [opposed to Mao's policies] can be rehabilitated, so long as there are no implications involving any foreign country." Liu's remark at an "expanded work conference" in 1961 was quoted in *Chingkang Mountain*, a Red Guard bulletin, on February 8, 1967; reprinted in *Liu chu-hsi yü-lu* (*Quotations from Chairman Liu*, compiled and published by the Tzu-lien Publishers, Hongkong, 1967), p. 110. This incident was

confirmed in a *Hung-ch'i* editorial, which claimed that P'eng had acted "with the support and shelter of the bourgeois headquarters headed by China's Khrushchev [Liu Shao-ch'i]; text in *PR*, August 18, 1967. Liu's remark, therefore, indirectly confirms that P'eng's disgrace was due to his relations with Soviet leaders.

28. I do not believe that P'eng Te-huai was the leader, as the later Maoist polemics were to charge, of an "anti-Party" group in the Politburo—if that should mean a personal power struggle—but I doubt if P'eng's criticisms were really as shocking to the other CCP leaders at the 1959 Lushan Conference as David A. Charles suggested in "Dismissal of Marshal P'eng," *loc. cit.* n. 23 *supra*, p. 67. P'eng took a bold initiative in openly condemning Mao's policy, and he may have taken the other CCP leaders aback; but it does not mean that the substance of his criticisms was totally shocking to them. The very fact that a few other prominent Party leaders, including Huang K'e-ch'eng and Chang Wen-t'ien, were likewise disgraced indicates the relative prevalence of a common dissent at the time. The silence of the others did not mean that they totally approved of Mao's policy; nor does it mean, as later events proved, that they would not express their disagreements in other ways in attempting to modify the excesses of Mao's programs. In this sense, I think William Dorrill painted too sanguine a picture of the support Mao enjoyed at the Lushan Conference. Dorrill stated that the Lushan Resolution (presumably that of August 16, 1959) "reaffirmed the absolute correctness of the Party line." In his view, the Lushan Conference rejected P'eng's criticisms without compromise and condemned him for factional activity—specifically, for going beyond permissible expression of dissent in the Politburo to lobby within the Central Committee. Dorrill, *Power, Policy and Ideology*, at 33.

29. Communiqué of the Eighth Plenum, issued on August 26, 1959; and its Resolution on Developing the Campaign for Increasing Production and Practicing Economy, August 16, 1959 (issued on August 26). Both texts in English appear in *The Eighth Plenary Session of the Eighth Central Committee of the Communist Party of China* (Peking, Foreign Language Press, 1959).

30. "The Great Call," *Hung-ch'i*, September 1, 1959; for English translation, see *CB*, No. 590.

31. *Nun-ts'un jen-min kung-she kung-tso tiao-li ts'ao-an* (*Sixty Articles on the Activities in Rural Communes* [Preliminary]) (1961). A summary in Chinese was made by the Union Research Institute, Hongkong, handwritten copy, 21 pp.

32. H. F. Schurmann, "China's 'New Economic Policy'—Transition or Change?" originally published in *CQ* and reprinted in Roderick MacFarquhar, ed., *China Under Mao* (Cambridge, Mass.: MIT Press, 1966), pp. 211–37.

33. Party reorganization was an absolute necessity in view of the widespread low morale afflicting the primary-level cadres, many of whom complained that the rewards were not commensurate with the burdens and tensions of office and even wished to resign. Misappropriation of public funds and other forms of corruption among the cadres were prevalent. Revelations such as these are found in *Fan-kung yu-chi t'u-chi lien-chiang lu-huo fei-fang wen-chien hui-pien* (*Collected Documents Captured During an Anti-Communist Commando Raid in Lienchiang Hsien, Fukien*), generally known as the "Lienchiang Docu-

ments" (Taipei, Taiwan: Ministry of National Defense, Bureau of Intelligence, March, 1964).

34. *Tsu-kuo chou-k'an* (*Fatherland Weekly*, Hongkong), No. 467 (1961), pp. 269–70; *Nan-fang jih-pao* (Canton), November 26, 1960, in *SCMP*, No. 2416, p. 1; October 7, 1960, in *SCMP*, No. 2380, p. 12; and *JMJP*, March 4, 1961, in *SCMP*, No. 2455, p. 10. Cf. Charles Neuhauser, "The Chinese Communist Party in the 1960's: Prelude to the Cultural Revolution," *CQ*, No. 32 (October–December, 1967), pp. 8–9; and Richard Baum and Frederick C. Teiwes, "Liu Shao-ch'i and the Cadre Question," *AS*, VIII, 4 (April, 1968), pp. 232–345.

35. Neuhauser, "Chinese Communist Party in the 1960's," pp. 14 ff.

36. "Before and After the Counterrevolutionary Incident of 'Chang Kuan Lou'," *Tung-fang Hung* (*East is Red*, a Red Guard publication), April 20, 1967. More on Liu's organizational leadership approach will come up for discussion in Chapter 11.

37. *Nan-fang jih-pao*, January 10, 1962, in *SCMP*, No. 2699, p. 1; also Neuhauser, "Chinese Communist Party in the 1960's," p. 15.

38. Neuhauser, "Chinese Communist Party in the 1960's," pp. 9–10.

39. Liu's "self-criticism," dated November 23, 1966, which appeared in Red Guard posters; English translation in *Atlas* (New York), April, 1967, and *SCMP*, No. 4037 (October 9, 1967).

40. *Yang-ch'eng wan-pao* (Canton), May 3, 1966, in *SCMP*, No. 3698, p. 5.

41. Liu's remark at an "enlarged work conference" in 1961, quoted in *Chingkangshan* (Ch'inghua University, a Red Guard bulletin), February 8, 1967; reprinted in *Liu chu-hsi yü-lu* (*Quotations from Chairman Liu*, compiled and published by Tzulien Publishers, Hongkong, 1967), p. 110.

42. At a meeting of philosophers and social scientists in 1963, quoted in *Chingkangshan*, February 1, 1967; reprinted in *Liu chu-hsi yü-lu*, p. 110.

43. "Thoroughly Smash the Counterrevolutionary and Revertive Conspiracy of Liu Shao-ch'i," *Chingkangshan*, February 8, 1967.

44. Cf. Benjamin I. Schwartz, "The Reign of Virtue: Some Broad Perspectives on Leader and Party in the Cultural Revolution," *CQ*, No. 35 (July–September, 1968). Also see my discussion of the rebuilding of the Party in Mao's image in Chapter 15 below.

45. Tang Tsou, "Cultural Revolution and Chinese Political System."

Chapter 11

1. "Struggle in China's Countryside Between Two Roads," published on November 23, 1967, in *JMJP*, *Hung-ch'i*, and *CFCP*; English translation in *SCMP*, No. 4068 (November 28, 1967), p. 8.

2. The "early ten points," written by Mao personally, Sec. III. Trans. in Richard Baum and Frederick C. Teiwes, *Ssu-Ch'ing: The Socialist Education Movement of 1962–1966* (Berkeley: Center for Chinese Studies, University of California, 1968).

3. *CB*, No. 691, p. 1; Charles Neuhauser, "The Chinese Communist Party

in the 1960's: Prelude to the Cultural Revolution," *CQ*, No. 32, October–December, 1967, p. 17.

4. Mao's "Talk at a Central Work Conference" (October 25, 1962), reprinted in a factory newsletter *Hung-hsien-pan (Red-line Edition)*, on December 19, 1966; English translation in *Chinese Law and Government*, Spring, 1968, pp. 7 ff.

5. Unfortunately, no single work has appeared that gives comprehensive coverage to all the related campaigns. See general works cited in Chapter 6, n. 5, above. Many important documents are contained in *The Great Cultural Revolution in China* (Tokyo, and Rutland, Vt.: Charles E. Tuttle, 1968), and in *Chung-kung wen-hua ta ko-ming tzu-liao hui-pien (Collected Documents on the Chinese Communist Great Cultural Revolution)* (Hongkong: Ming Pao Bimonthly, 1967).

6. The documents referred to appear in English in Baum and Teiwes, *Ssu-Ch'ing*, Appendixes B, C, E, and F.

7. *JMJP*, August 14, 1966.

8. Though Maoist allegations attributed the "later ten points" to Liu Shao-ch'i, it was most possibly the work by P'eng Chen. See Liu's "Self-Criticism" of October 23, 1967, which appeared in English in *Atlas* magazine, April, 1967.

9. See, for example, the "early ten points," Section IV.

10. Mao's "Talk Before the Tenth Plenum of the Central Committee," taken from a dispatch by the Japanese journalist Takada, published in *Mainichi Shimbun* on March 9, 1967. Takada relied upon a wall poster that had appeared in Peking the previous day. Text is reprinted in *Chinese Law and Government*, Spring, 1968, p. 4.

11. Communiqué of the Tenth Plenum of the Central Committee of the CCP, quoted in the "early ten points," Section II.

12. The "early ten points," Sec. VI.

13. The "early ten points," Sections IV, VII, and VIII.

14. The "early ten points," Section IX.

15. "Cadres' Participation in Collective Production Labor Is a Matter of Fundamental Importance to the Socialist System," *Hung-ch'i*, July 10, 1963.

16. Mao's directive quoted in the "first ten points," Section X.

17. The "later ten points (revised)," Section I. Italics added.

18. *Tsao-fan yu-li pao (There Is Reason to Rebel,* a Red Guard publication), February 12, 1967.

19. The "twenty-three articles," Section I.

20. The "later ten points," Section V. Italics added.

21. The "revised later ten points," Section II.

22. The "twenty-three articles," Section III.

23. The "twenty-three articles," Sections V, VII, and XIV.

24. See *Tsao-fan yu-li pao*, February 12, 1967.

25. The "twenty-three articles," Section X. Italics supplied.

26. See *Tsao-fan yu-li pao*, February 12, 1967.

27. The "twenty-three articles," Section V.

28. Liu Shao-ch'i, *"Lun tang-nei tou-cheng"* ("On Intra-Party Struggle") (July 12, 1941), reprinted in *Liu Shao-ch'i hsüan-chi (Selected Writings by Liu Shao-ch'i)* (Tokyo: Chinese Culture Service Publications, 1967), p. 94.

29. *Ibid.*, pp. 79, 98 ff.

30. See Chapters 6 and 8 above.

31. Liu, "*Lun Hsiu-yang*" ("On Cultivation") (1939), in *Liu Shao-ch'i hsüan-chi*, pp. 7–76.

32. Mao's "Talk Before the Tenth Plenum of the Central Committee."

33. In his *On Contradiction*, Mao assigned an equal weight to the "identity" (unity) and "struggle" between contradictions. In the years following the Great Leap failure, Mao seemed increasingly to stress "struggle" over "identity."

34. "New Polemic on the Philosophic Front," *Hung-ch'i*, No. 12, 1964.

35. Article by Ai Heng-wu and Liu Ch'ing-shan in *Kuang-ming jih-pao*, May 29, 1964, reprinted in *JMJP*, July 17, 1964, together with critiques by orthodox authors holding the "one splitting into two" view. Cf. John W. Lewis, "Revolutionary Struggle and the Second Generation in Communist China," *CQ*, No. 21, January–March, 1965, p. 142.

36. See "New Polemic on the Philosophic Front," *Hung-ch'i*, No. 12, 1964.

37. *Ta kung pao*, September 6, 1964, and *Hung-ch'i*, No. 16, 1964.

38. The "twenty-three articles," Section II.

39. "Uncover a Grand Plot for the Restoration of Capitalism," *Wen hui pao*, April 29, 1967, p. 3.

40. Yang Chien-pai, "The Problem of National Economic Equilibrium and 'Production Price,'" *Ching-chi yen-chiu (Economic Research)*, No. 12 (December, 1963), 40–56; and Ho Chien-chang and Chang Ling, "A Tentative Discussion on 'Production Price' in the Socialist Economy," *Ching-chi yen-chiu*, No. 5 (May, 1964), 10–20.

41. Meng Kuei and Hsiao Lin, "On Sun Ye-fang's Reactionary Political Stand and Economic Program," *PR*, October 21, 1966, pp. 21–25.

42. Cf. Audrey Donnithorne, *China's Economic System* (New York: Praeger Publishers, 1967), pp. 162 ff., 480 ff.

43. See a report on the work of the Communist Youth League by Ho Yang-pang on June 11, 1964, in *Great Cultural Revolution in China*, pp. 63–82, and "Bring up Heirs to the Revolution," *PR*, No. 30, 1964.

44. See Chapter 9 above for an account of P'eng's removal.

45. Hsiao Hua, Director of the General Political Department of the PLA, in *JMJP*, January 25, 1966.

46. Communiqué of the Eleventh Plenum of the CC, August 12, 1966, in *JMJP*, August 14, 1966.

47. "In the Field of Art and Literature, Modern Revisionism Follows in the Footsteps of the Declining Bourgeoisie," *Hung-ch'i*, No. 21, 1962.

48. K. S. Karol, *China: The Other Communism* (New York: Hill and Wang, 1967), pp. 257–58.

49. *Introduction to Rent Collection Courtyard* (Peking: Foreign Language Press, 1965). My attention was called to the work by Nancy Thompson Price, a Ph.D. candidate specializing in Chinese art at New York University, who now teaches at Vassar College.

50. Chün-tu Hsüen, "The Cultural Revolution and Leadership Crisis in Communist China," *Political Science Quarterly* 82:2 (June, 1967).

51. Mao's "December [1963] Instructions," cited in Ting Wang, *Wen-hua ta ko-ming p'ing-lun chi (Collection of Commentaries on the Great Cultural Revolution)* (Hongkong: Contemporary China Research Institute, 1967), p. 69.

Chapter 12

1. William F. Dorrill, *Power, Policy, and Ideology in the Making of China's "Cultural Revolution"* (Santa Monica, Calif.: RAND Corporation, 1968), p. 85 ff.

2. According to information made available in 1967, Mao made the demands at an enlarged session of the Politburo Standing Committee on September 10, 1965. The session itself, which ran into October, was attended by members of the CCP's regional bureaus as well. *Mainichi Shimbum* (Tokyo), April 27, 1967, based on a Peking wall poster.

3. Some Red Guard sources reported that Mao had asked his colleagues point-blank what they would do if revisionism appeared in the Central Committee and had suggested that this would happen. See, for example, Mao's talk at a Central Work Conference on October 25, 1966, reprinted in a factory newsletter, *Hung-hsien-pan* (*Red-line Edition*), December 19, 1966; English trans. in *Chinese Law and Government* 1, No. 1 (Spring, 1968): 8.

4. "Circular" of the Central Committee, dated May 16, 1966, printed in *JMJP*, May 17, 1966.

5. Mao's talk at the CC Work Conference, October 25, 1966, English trans. in *Chinese Law and Government* 1, No. 1:8. The assertion was confirmed by Yao Wen-yuan, a principal spokesman for Mao during the Cultural Revolution, in "The Worker Class Must Lead," *JMJP*, August 26, 1968, p. 1.

6. See n. 4 above; English trans. in *China Reconstructs* (Peking), June, 1967.

7. *JMJP*, May 18, 1968.

8. "P'eng Chen Is the Deadly Enemy of the Great Proletarian Cultural Revolution," *JMJP*, August 23, 1968, p. 5.

9. We rely on what is given in the "Circular" of the Central Committee, *JMJP*, May 17, 1966.

10. "Equality before truth" was condemned as a "bourgeois slogan" in an article by Ch'in Chung-szu in *Chung-kuo ch'ing-nien* (*Chinese Youth*), June 16, 1966. Actually, in my opinion, it presented a direct challenge to the *primacy* of the thought of Mao, if primacy negates equality.

11. "Circular" of the Central Committee, *JMJP*, May 17, 1966.

12. "Thoroughly Criticize Our Institute's Work Team in Carrying out the Bourgeois Movement on the Cadre Question," *Cheng-fa kung-she*, April 6, 1967, quoted in Charles Neuhauser, "The Impact of the Cultural Revolution on the Chinese Communist Party Machine," *AS* 8, No. 6 (June, 1968): 470, n. 7.

13. See Mao's October 25, 1966, talk, translated in *Chinese Law and Government* 1, No. 1. The second anniversary of the issuance of Mao's "Bombard the Command Headquarters" was officially celebrated by a front-page editorial in *JMJP*, August 5, 1968.

14. P'an Fu-sheng, "Resolutely Stand Together with the Proletarian Revolutionary Faction," *Hung-ch'i*, No. 6, 1967, p. 36; *JMJP* editorial, February 2, 1967; "The Basic Experience of the Heilungkiang Red Rebels in the Struggle of Seizing Power," in *JMJP*, February 10, 1967, and *Hung-ch'i*, No. 4, 1967; and Parris Chang, "The Revolutionary Committee in China: Two Case Studies—Heilungkiang and Honan," *CS* 6, No. 9 (June 1, 1968): 2–3.

15. The full title of the Sixteen Articles is "The Decision of the Central Committee of the Communist Party of China on the Great Proletarian Cultural Revolution," adopted on August 8, 1966, and published in *JMJP*, August 9, 1966. According to the Communique of the Twelfth Plenum, dated October 31, 1968, the Sixteen Articles were formulated "in person" by Chairman Mao (*JMJP*, November 2, 1968, p. 1). Under Mao's personal chairmanship, the Eleventh Plenum met between August 1 and August 12, 1966, in Peking. It was attended by not only the full and alternate members of the CC but also representatives from the CC's regional bureaus and from Party committees at the provincial, municipal, and autonomous-region levels; members of the Cultural Revolution Group; comrades of the CC departments concerned; and "revolutionary representatives" of the faculty and student bodies at institutions of higher education in Peking. This composition indicated two probabilities: first, that Mao attempted to pack the meeting (which ordinarily would have been attended exclusively by the full and alternate members of the CC) with "outsiders" in whom he had greater trust; and second, that the *original* thrust of the Cultural Revolution had been more purely cultural-educational, as attested by the presence of college faculty and student representatives.

According to the communique issued at the end of the plenum, policies of a far more lasting nature than the Cultural Revolution were under consideration. "The plenary session," the communique declared, "fully approves the series of brilliant policies of decisive and fundamental import put forward by Comrade Mao Tse-tung over the past four years [1962–66]." The affirmation of Mao's policies indicated the triumph of his thought over the alternative line or lines of thought. The plenum lauded the "great victories" scored in the "three great revolutionary campaigns" (class struggle, production craze, and scientific advancement), under Mao's General Line of *tuo k'uai hao sheng* (more, faster, better, and more economical production), first introduced during the Great Leap. It mentioned the three nuclear tests as evidence of success. Noting the "unprecedented" Cultural Revolution, the communique declared that the "masses of workers, peasants, and soldiers, the revolutionary intellectuals, and the great body of cadres" were participating in a "mass movement for creatively learning and applying the thought of Mao Tse-tung." In doing so, they were ushering in a "new era" in which "the laboring people directly master and apply Marxism-Leninism." The communiqué further noted Mao's speech at the plenum, which reasserted his view regarding the continued existence of "contradictions, classes, and class struggle in a socialist society." *JMJP*, August 14, 1968.

16. Article 2 of the Sixteen Articles.

17. Central Directive V (January 21, 1967), printed in *Tung-fang hung* (*East Is Red*, a Red Guard publication) on January 31, 1967.

18. *The New York Times*, September 1, 1968.

19. Articles 3 and 4 of the Sixteen Articles.

20. Article 7.

21. Article 5.

22. Article 8.

23. Article 6.

24. Article 5.

25. Article 6.

26. The letter was sent in the name of students of Senior III and IV of

Peking's First Girls' Middle School, made public by NCNA, Peking, June 17, 1966. It is not impossible that the letter had had Mao's prior blessings.

27. Article 10 of the Sixteen Articles.

28. Donald MacInnis, "Maoism: The Religious Analogy," *Christian Century*, January 10, 1968, p. 41.

29. Sec. III of the "twenty-three articles."

30. Article 13 of the Sixteen Articles.

31. Article 12.

32. Article 13.

33. Article 9.

34. According to the May 16, 1966, "Circular," *JMJP*, May 17, 1966.

35. Article 11 of the Sixteen Articles.

36. Neuhauser, "Impact of the Cultural Revolution," AS 8, No. 6:475.

37. While the Party was being remolded, the PLA would provide stability, which was the role it played after February, 1967, when military control commissions were set up in every province to take over civil administration. The temporary nature of the PLA role can be seen from the fact that, between early 1967 and September, 1968, revolutionary committees, a new institution, were formed in every province. Although the PLA was particularly active between September, 1967, and May, 1968, the formation of revolutionary committees advanced the most rapidly between May and September, 1968. The last four of the twenty-nine sprang up in less than four weeks. Just as the gradual reduction of PLA influence in civil administration corresponded with the swift completion of the revolutionary committees, the latter are probably another transitional step toward the eventual resumption of functions by the Party, presumably after a period of rebuilding.

38. More detailed accounts of the Red Guard movement and the Cultural Revolution can be found in: Philip Bridgham, "Mao's Cultural Revolution: Origin and Development," CQ, No. 33 (January–March, 1967), pp. 1–35; "Mao's Cultural Revolution in 1967: The Struggle to Seize Power," CQ, No. 34 (April–June, 1968), pp. 6–37; British Foreign Office, *Mao's Cultural Revolution* (London: December, 1967); Theodore H. E. Chen, "A Nation in Agony," in *Problems of Communism*, November–December, 1966, pp. 14–20; Chün-tu Hsüeh, "The Cultural Revolution and Leadership Crisis in Communist China," *Political Science Quarterly* 82, No. 2 (June, 1967): 1–20; Chalmers Johnson, "China: The Cultural Revolution in Structural Perspective," AS 8, No. 1 (January, 1968): 1–15; Richard Lowenthal, "Mao's Revolution: The Chinese Handwriting on the Wall," *Encounter*, April, 1967, pp. 3–9; Charles Neuhauser, "The Chinese Communist Party in the 1960's: Prelude to the Cultural Revolution," CQ, No. 32 (October–December, 1967), pp. 3–36; Benjamin Schwartz, "Upheaval in China," *Commentary*, February, 1967, pp. 55–62; and Yuan-li Wu, "Economics, Ideology, and the Cultural Revolution," AS 8, No. 3 (March, 1968): 223–35; Tang Tsou, "The Cultural Revolution and the Chinese Political System," CQ, No. 38 (April–June, 1969), pp. 63–91.

39. Neuhauser, "Impact of the Cultural Revolution," AS 8, No. 6:475; see also Hans Granqvist, *The Red Guard*, translated by Erik J. Friis (New York: David McKay, 1968).

40. "Central Directive V (January 21, 1967)," *Tung-fang hung*, January 31, 1967.

41. Wang Li was said to have demanded that Red Guard extremists be armed so as to seize weapons, ammunition, and material from the PLA. He was also alleged to have advanced the slogan "drag out the handful of people from the PLA." He was responsible for the formation of the mysterious "May 16 Corps," an extreme Red Guard unit later disbanded by Mao himself in September, 1967. Between late June and early July, Wang Li, Kuan Feng, and Liu Chieh reportedly convened a "First Congress of the May 16 Corps in the Capital," which adopted a resolution attacking Chou En-lai. Wang also delivered a sensational "August 7" speech at the Foreign Ministry in a Red Guard struggle session aimed at Ch'en Yi. Confession by Lo Feng, a member of the defunct "May 16 Corps," made available in Red Guard sources. "Chiang Ch'ing," CS 7, No. 1 (January 6, 1969): 10. This source suggests that Chiang Ch'ing was the "backstage boss" of the "extreme left" Red Guards, but Wang Li was purged as a scapegoat.

42. "Central Directive of September 5, 1967," in SCMP, No. 4026, p. 1.

43. Chang, "Revolutionary Committee in China," CS 6, No. 9; The New York Times, September 7, 1968; and "Revolutionary Committee Leadership," CS 6, No. 18 (October 18, 1968). Revolutionary Committees were formed at the hsien level as well.

44. JMJP, November 2, 1968. See further discussions on this in Chapter 15, below.

45. NCNA, Peking, March 26, 1968. The near-simultaneous purges of Ch'i, a prominent member of the Central Cultural Revolution Group, and of Yang, Acting Chief of Staff of the PLA, were believed to be a political trade-off to resolve differences between Chiang Ch'ing's forces and the PLA. Cf. "Chiang Ch'ing," CS 7, No. 1 (January 6, 1968): 11.

46. JMJP, August 15, 1968; "The Red Guards Should Join Hands with the Workers, Peasants and Soldiers," JMJP editorial, August 18, 1968.

47. Yao Wen-yüan, "The Worker Class Must Lead," JMJP, August 26, 1968; and Hung-ch'i, No. 2, 1968.

Chapter 13

1. Article 13 of the Sixteen Articles, published as "The Decision of the Central Committee of the Communist Party of China on the Great Proletarian Cultural Revolution" in JMJP, August 9, 1966. See discussion in Chapter 12 above.

2. See discussion in Chapter 11, under "Liu's 'Revisionism.'"

3. "Che-hsüeh chan-hsien shang te hsin cheng-lun" ("New Polemics on the Philosophical Front"), Hung-ch'i, No. 12, 1964.

4. "Po-ch'ih yi-nien chih ch'a te mai-kuo lo-chi" ("Refute the Traitor Logic of Conceptual Differential"), JMJP, June 12, 1968, p. 4.

5. Ibid.

6. "Chung-kuo he-lu-hsiao-fu te huo-ming che-hsüeh shih mai-kuo-che-hsüeh" ("The Huo-ming Philosophy of China's Khrushchev Is the Philosophy of a Traitor"), ibid., p. 4. Cf. Mao's own writing on the topic, "Wei jen-min fu-wu" ("Serving the People"), HC, 3:954.

7. "The Revolutionary Great Criticisms Are Splendid," JMJP, June 15, 1968, p. 1.

8. A Red Guard poster of the Middle School of Tsinghua University declared its determination to wipe out *wen-ch'ing* (literally, "warm sentiments" or "human affection," but referring to a Chinese tradition of particularism based on affective relations). The militant spirit of Mao's class struggle was recaptured in the following: "There are also some persons who are scared to death at the thought of revolution and rebellion. You submit to conventions, always answer in assent, and hide yourselves in the shell of revisionism. . . . We want to be rough! How can we be sentimental toward revisionism?" Quoted in Donald MacInnis, "Maoism: The Religious Analogy," *Christian Century*, January 10, 1968.

9. Cf. Chapters 6 and 8 above.

10. See discussion in Chapter 8, fourth paragraph under heading "Szu-hsiang and Social Structure," and notes 22 and 23 below.

11. *JMJP*, August 14, 1966.

12. *Ibid.*, and "The Masses Armed with the Thought of Mao Tse-tung Are Full of Creative Power," *JMJP*, June 30, 1968, p. 4.

13. On the sending of Red Guards to production duties, see "Peking's Red Guards Are New Herdsmen on the Grassland," *JMJP*, June 20, 1968, p. 3. *The New York Times*, January 19, 1969, p. 9, reported that some 15 to 20 million people, including former Red Guards, were being sent off from cities to the countryside. On the WSP teams, see *The New York Times*, July 8, 1968, and September 3, 1968; and Yao Wen-yüan, "The Worker Class Must Lead," *JMJP*, August 26, 1968, and *Hung-ch'i*, No. 2, 1968.

14. *The New York Times*, October 27, 1968, p. 9.

15. "To Carry Through Struggle, Criticism, and Reform in the Schools under the Leadership of the Worker Class," *JMJP*, August 23, 1968; "Persist in the High Tides of Struggle, Criticism, and Reform Aroused by the Worker Leadership," *JMJP*, August 28, 1968, p. 3; "The Worker Class Must Run the Universities and Will Do Well," *JMJP*, August 31, 1968, p. 3; "Persist in the Stationing in the Schools of the Workers' Thought of Mao Tse-tung Teams," *JMJP*, September 2, 1968, p. 1; and "Entry by Workers, Peasants, and Soldiers into the Schools," *JMJP*, September 2, 1968, p. 2.

16. Yao, "Worker Class Must Lead." "Mountaintop-ism" is a kind of "sectarianism" in which the individual creates his own little world. Mao used the terms in "Hsüeh-hsi shih-chü" ("Learn Current Affairs"), written on April 12, 1944, and published in *HC*, 3:894, n. 7.

17. "Unite under the Leadership of the Proletarian Command Headed by Mao Tse-tung," *JMJP*, August 5, 1968; "Defend the Proletarian Command Headed by Chairman Mao: Resolutely Criticize the Reactionaries' 'Polycentrism,' " *JMJP*, August 15, 1968, p. 3. The first all-out Maoist attack on such centrifugal tendencies appeared in "On the Reactionary Nature of Factionalism," *Wen-hui Pao*, January 12, 1968.

18. Yao, "Worker Class Must Lead."

19. Quoted in Yao, *ibid.*

20. *Ibid.*

21. *JMJP* editorial, July 29, 1966.

22. "Comrade Lin Piao's Talk at a Work Session of the Central Committee (November 23, 1966 [?])," reprinted by the Mao Tse-tung Corps of the Peking Athletic Institute for Workers, Peasants, and Soldiers, *et al.*, December 20, 1966.

23. *Ibid.*

24. *Wen-hui pao*, July 10, 1967.

25. "Notice on Short-Term Military Training for Revolutionary Faculty and Students in Universities and Middle Schools," *Chingkang Mountain*, January 11, 1967.

26. "Workers Must Run Universities," *JMJP*, August 31, 1968, p. 3.

27. See a report bearing that title, *Ibid.*

28. *JMJP*, September 5, 1968, pp. 1–2; and *Hung-ch'i*, No. 3, 1968, pp. 7–13.

29. "Rural Education Must Rely on the Poor and Lower-Middle Peasants," *Hung-ch'i*, No. 3, 1968, pp. 27–31.

30. *Ibid.*, and *The New York Times*, November 10, 1968.

31. "On the Re-education of the Intellectuals," *Hung-ch'i*, No. 3, 1968, at 3.

32. *Ibid.* For a Maoist condemnation of Liu's reverence of "technocracy" and "experts," see *JMJP*, November 3, 1968, p. 6, and October 12, 1968, p. 4.

33. Communiqué of the Twelfth Plenum, August 31, 1968, in *JMJP*, November 2, 1968, p. 2.

34. "China's Khrushchev Is the Path-Blocking Tiger in the Revolution in Peking Opera," JMJP, August 19, 1968, p. 4; "The Circumstances Surrounding the Appearance of the Reactionary Novel *Wind-Thunder*," *JMJP*, July 10, 1968, p. 3; "To See the Reactionary Novel *Wind-Thunder* from T'ao-yüan," *JMJP*, July 17, 1968, p. 4.

35. "P'eng Chen Is the Deadly Enemy of the Proletarian Revolution in Arts and Letters," *JMJP*, August 23, 1968, p. 5. The phrase attributed to P'eng was said to date from a 1965 conference of provincial cultural commissars.

36. "A Glorious Blossom in Arts Born of the Great Proletarian Cultural Revolution," *JMJP*, July 9, 1968, p. 1.

37. "A New Victory of Chairman Mao's Policy of 'Ancient Tradition for Modern Purpose, and Foreign Tradition for Chinese Purpose,'" *JMJP*, July 12, 1968, p. 1; and "A New Blossom Nurtured by Sunshine and Rainfall," *JMJP*, July 4, 1968, p. 3.

38. *Ibid.* (both articles).

39. "An Illuminating Model for 'Foreign Tradition for Chinese Purpose,'" *JMJP*, August 14, 1968, p. 5.

40. Chinese used to traditional Peking opera will find it difficult to accept the new mixture of disparate elements taken from both Chinese and Western traditions. However, the attempt may be viewed as a first step toward progress.

41. Mao, "Talks at the Yenan Forum" (May 2, 1942), *HC*, 3:804 ff.; also "Glorious Blossom in Arts," *JMJP*, July 9, 1968, p. 1.

42. *Szu-lang t'an-mu* (*Fourth Son Returns to Visit His Mother*), one of the most popular Chinese opera-plays until 1949, was probably intended by the Manchu rulers to preach ties between different races, in order to portray themselves (the Manchus were aliens at the time of their conquest) in a better light. But after 1949, it was banned in Taiwan under the Nationalists (until it wan drastically rewritten) as well as in mainland China.

43. "Carry Through the Great Revolution in the Mass Media to the End," *JMJP*, September 1, 1968; and *Hung-ch'i*, No. 2, 1968, p. 8.

Chapter 14

1. *Hung-ch'i*, No. 4, 1968, p. 32.
2. Mao Tse-tung, "Serving the People" (September 8, 1944), *HC* 3:954.
3. Franz Schurmann, *Ideology and Organization in Communist China* (Berkeley: University of California Press, 1966), pp. 195 ff.
4. *JMJP*, July 11, 1968.
5. *Hung-ch'i*, No. 4, 1968, p. 32.
6. *Ibid.*
7. "Following the Words of Chairman Mao; Resolutely Take the Road of 'Good Men and Simple Government,'" *JMJP*, July 14, 1968, p. 1.
8. *Wen-hui Pao*, January 12, 1968; and February 6, 1968.
9. *JMJP*, August 5, 1968.
10. *JMJP*, August 15, 1968; also Yao Wen-yüan, "The Worker Class Must Lead," August 26, 1968, and *Hung-ch'i*, No. 2, 1968, pp. 3–7.
11. Cf. Article Ten of the "twenty-three articles." See discussion of the "twenty-three articles" under "Liu's 'Revisionism'" in Chapter 11 above, at note reference 25, and *Kuang-ming jih-pao*, July 3, 1966.
12. Chou En-lai, *Chi-kuan hung-sze t'ung-hsin* (*Bulletin of the Red Apparatus of Offices*), No. 4, January 9, 1967.
13. Cf. *CS* 6, No. 9 (June 1, 1968), No. 18 (October 18, 1968), and No. 21 (December 6, 1968).
14. *JMJP*, June 20, 1968.
15. *Ibid.*
16. For example, the experience of the Hsin-hua (New China) Printing Plant in Kiangsi, *JMJP*, April 7, 1968; also that of K'ai-luan Coal Mine, *JMJP*, May 14, 1968.
17. "The Firm Pillar of the Dictatorship of the Proletariat," *JMJP*, August 1, 1968.
18. Agnes Smedley, *The Great Road* (New York: Monthly Review Press, 1956), p. 267; John Rue, *Mao Tse-tung in Opposition, 1927–1935* (Stanford, Calif.: Stanford University Press, 1966), pp. 171 ff.
19. Slogan-shouting like this is common in CCP documents for public consumption, especially those in commemoration of special occasions. The list of "long lives" at the end usually follows a climactic order.
20. *JMJP*, August 14, 1966.
21. Audrey Donnithorne, *China's Economic System* (New York: Praeger Publishers, 1967), pp. 112, 150.
22. "China's Khrushchev's Crime of Thwarting the Farm Tool Renovation Movement Must Be Thoroughly Reckoned With," *Agricultural Machinery Techniques*, No. 3, 1968, in *SCMM*, No. 624 (August 27, 1968); and "The Conflict Between Mao Tse-tung and Liu Shao-ch'i over Agricultural Mechanization in Communist China," *CS* 6, No. 17 (October 1, 1968): 18.
23. For a discussion of the various "functional systems" in the CCP bureaucracy, see A. Doak Barnett, *Cadres, Bureaucracy, and Political Power in Communist China* (New York: Columbia University Press, 1967), pp. 6 ff.
24. Article 12 of the "twenty-three articles."
25. These interests were supposed to terminate in 1962 but were extended

for three more years, after which their continuance was to be considered anew. *PR*, April 20, 1962, p. 6. While nominally constant at 5 per cent a year, the rate of interest was probably lowered to 3⅓ per cent in 1957, possibly by reassessing the capital stock values downward and nominally leaving the 5 per cent unchanged. Donnithorne, *China's Economic System*, p. 147.

26. "The Economic Side of the Chinese Communist Great Cultural Revolution," *Keizai gakujin (Economist*, Tokyo), February 7, 1967.

27. "Hoist High the Great Red Banner of the Thought of Mao Tse-tung: Relentlessly Criticize the Revisionist Black Wares of China's Khrushchev on the Question of Distribution," *JMJP*, June 15, 1968.

28. See article by the self-styled "Proletarian Revolutionary Committee" of the State Economic Commission in *JMJP*, July 9, 1968, p. 4.

29. Cf. "Communist China: Economy at Mid-Year, 1968," *CS* 6, No. 12 (July, 1968).

30. "Peking's Red Guards Are New Herdsmen on the Grassland," *JMJP*, June 20, 1968.

31. *The New York Times*, January 19, 1969, p. 9.

32. "Notice by the Central Committee of the CCP on Opposition to Economism" (January 11, 1967), "A Letter from the Central Committee of the CCP to the Poor and Lower-Middle Peasants in China" (February 20, 1967), and "A Letter to the Workers of the Country from the Central Committee of the CCP" (March 18, 1967), reprinted in *Chung-kung wen-hua ta ko-ming tzu-liao hui-pien* (*Collected Materials on the Chinese Communist Great Cultural Revolution*) (Hongkong: Ming Pao Monthly, 1968), pp. 43–47.

33. See fourth paragraph under "A Philosophy of Selfless Struggle" in Chapter 13.

34. E.g., Yao, "Worker Class Must Lead," *JMJP*, August 26, 1968.

35. These were added to the new editions of Mao's earlier writings, e.g., "On Practice," *SW* (Peking: Foreign Languages Press, 1965), p. 296.

36. Harold Hinton, "China and Vietnam," in William Richardson, ed., *China Today* (Maryknoll, N.Y.: Maryknoll Publications, 1969), pp. 133 ff.; also, Donald Zagoria, *Vietnam Triangle* (New York: Pegasus, 1967), p. 95.

37. Hinton, "China and Vietnam," p. 134.

38. Lo Jui-ch'ing, "Commemorate the Victory over German Fascism," *PR*, May 14, 1965, pp. 7–15, reprinted in Richardson, ed., *China Today*, pp. 203 ff.

39. Hinton, "China and Vietnam," p. 135n.

40. Chou's report at the First Session of the Third National People's Congress, December 22, 1964, in *Main Documents of the First Session of the Third National People's Congress* (Peking: Foreign Language Press, 1965), p. 28.

41. Liu admitted to this in his self-criticism of 1966.

42. Communique of the Eleventh Plenum of the Central Committee, *JMJP*, August 14, 1966.

43. In fact, this interpretation was favored by some analysts, e.g., Uri Ra'anan, "Rooting for Mao," *The New Leader*, March 13, 1967.

44. Peking's relations with Burma were strained because of the spillover, *The New York Times*, July 8, 1967, p. 3; July 12, 1967, p. 10; and November 1, 1967, p. 1. Cf. Robert Scalapino, "The Cultural Revolution and Chinese Foreign Policy," *CS* 6, No. 13 (August 1, 1968).

45. *JMJP*, August 14, 1966.
46. In December, 1968, Peking sent a military delegation to Albania, headed by Huang Yung-sheng, Chief of Staff of the PLA. *PR*, December 13, 1968, pp. 3 ff.
47. *Ibid.*
48. *Ibid.*
49. *JMJP*, July 25, 1968, p. 4.
50. *JMJP*, July 17, 1968, p. 6.
51. *JMJP* editorial, August 23, 1968, and Chou En-lai's speech at Rumanian National Day reception in Peking, *PR*, Supp., August 23, 1968.
52. *JMJP*, August 30, 1968; *PR*, September 6, 1968, p. 8.
53. *JMJP*, November 12, 1968, p. 2.
54. Chou's speech of September 7, 1968, in *Hung-ch'i*, No. 3, 1968, at 17.
55. According to a Nationalist Chinese source, Peking's shelling across the Taiwan Strait in 1958 was Mao's policy, about which P'eng Te-huai apparently was not enthusiastic. See *Chin-jih ta-lu* (*Today's Mainland*), No. 1367, (1967), p. 2. According to the journal, the article was written with the assistance of Sung Ta-lou, a defected Communist.
56. *JMJP*, August 1, 1968, at 2.
57. *JMJP*, November 2, 1968, p. 1. Italics added.
58. See my article in Richardson, ed., *China Today*. For the Chinese Communist leaders' views on Peking-Moscow relations over Taiwan, see Ch'en Yi's address of December 7, 1958, in *TWKH* 5:210–14; and Chou En-lai's report, *TWKH* 5:20–21.
59. "Western News Agencies Report One After Another That 'Vietnam-U.S. Paris Talks' Are Entering a 'Delicate Stage,'" *JMJP*, October 20, 1968, p. 1.
60. *JMJP*, November 3, 1968, p. 5. No comment was offered by Peking.
61. *The New York Times*, November 27, 1968. For President Nixon's favorable response, see *The New York Times*, November 28, 1968, p. 1.
62. "Peaceful Coexistence—Two Diametrically Opposed Policies: Comment on the Open Letter of the Central Committee of the CPSU (VI) by the Editorial Departments of *JMJP* and *Hung-ch'i*, December 12, 1963" (Peking: Foreign Language Press, 1963), p. 16.
63. Chou En-lai has repeatedly claimed that Peking desires some sort of an understanding even with the United States on the basis of "peaceful coexistence" over the question of Taiwan. See Chou's reply of Sept. 6, 1958, to a statement by Secretary Dulles made on Sept. 4. English text in *PR*, No. 28 (September 9, 1958), pp. 15–16. Cf. James C. Hsiung, "Communist China's Conception of World Public Order: An Attitudinal and Pragmatic Analysis of Some Basic Issue of International Law" (doctoral dessertation, Columbia University, 1967), p. 59.
64. See the last part of Chapter 6.

Chapter 15

1. "On the Establishment of a Military Bureaucratic Dictatorship in China," *Narody Asii i Afriki* (*Peoples of Asia and Africa*), No. 1, 1968, cited in Benjamin I. Schwartz, "The Reign of Virtue: Some Broad Perspectives on Leader

and Party in the Cultural Revolution," *CQ*, No. 35 (July–September, 1968), p. 3, n. 7.

2. " 'Stalin Group' in the Soviet Union Acclaims China's Great Cultural Revolution," *PR*, No. 20, May 17, 1968, at 23.

3. See discussion at reference for n. 54 in Chapter 7 above.

4. "Make a Class Analysis of Factionalism," by a *Hung-ch'i* "Commentator," *PR*, No. 19, May 10, 1968, p. 1.

5. *Ibid.*

6. *JMJP*, August 1, 1968, p. 2.

7. *PR*, October 11, 1968, p. 23; and October 18, 1968, p. 8. See also discussion in Chapter 11, at references for nn. 15 and 16.

8. "Betrayal of the Proletarian Dictatorship Is the Heart of the Book on 'Self-Cultivation,' " Editorial Departments of *JMJP* and *Hung-ch'i*, May 8, 1967 English translation by Foreign Languages Press, 1967.

9. *Ibid.*, p. 16. Italics added.

10. *Ibid.* Italics added.

11. Cf. the "twenty-three articles" and discussion in Chapter 11.

12. See "Betrayal of Proletarian Dictatorship," n. 8 above, p. 15.

13. See "Make Class Analysis of Factionalism," *PR*, No. 19, 1968, p. 3. Italics added.

14. Cf. discussion at reference for n. 8 in Chapter 8 above.

15. "Greatly Revive the Party's Three Great Working Styles," *CFCP* editorial, reprinted in *JMJP*, September 23, 1968.

16. *Ibid.*

17. Schwartz, "Reign of Virtue," *CQ*, No. 35, p. 13.

18. *Ibid.*, p. 15.

19. *Ibid.*, p. 16.

20. Jean-Jacques Rousseau, *The Social Contract*, Book II, Ch. 7.

21. Cf., e.g., *The Mencius*, Book II, Ch. 6 and 2.

22. Schwartz, "Reign of Virtue," *CQ*, No. 35, pp. 11–13.

23. Cf. Maoist criticisms of Liu's "technocracy" cited in n. 32, Chapter 13 above. In fact, blind worship of technology at the expense of art, social science, and humanities in general has been a rather serious problem among Chinese in the mid-twentieth century. Because China's weakness since the nineteenth century has often been laid to its lack of technology, many young people seek to identify themselves with something or someone in the technical field on the general assumption that science and technology can solve all social, economic, philosophical, and aesthetic problems. Scattered evidence suggests that a similar attitude prevailed under Liu's administration. Whereas Mao looks more to the "human" resources in agricultural development, Liu appears to have focused on mechanization. Cf. "The Conflict Between Mao Tse-tung and Liu Shao-ch'i over Agricultural Mechanization in Communist China," *CS* 6, No. 17 (October 1, 1968).

24. *JMJP*, November 2, 1968, p. 2.

25. English trans. of the draft in *The New York Times*, January 8, 1969. Text of the new Constitution as finally adopted by the Ninth Party Congress appears in *Hung-ch'i*, No. 5, 1969; English trans. in *PR*, April 30, 1969.

26. Cf. discussion at reference for n. 46, Chapter 14. The 1956 Party Constitution only referred to "internationalism" and did so in a rather cautious way: "The Party . . . educates its members and the Chinese people in

the spirit of internationalism, as expressed in the slogan 'Proletarians of all lands, unite.' " English text available in Theodore H. E. Chen, *The Chinese Communist Regime* (New York: Praeger Publishers, 1967), pp. 129–30. Curiously, it did not expressly use "proletarian internationalism."

27. See discussion at reference for n. 6 in Chapter 13 and "Greatly Revive the Party's Three Working Styles," *JMJP*, September 23, 1968. For a definition of the "four firsts" see the last section of Chapter 6 above. The "three-eight working style" adopted from the PLA tradition refers to Mao's three phrases and eight additional characters meaning: firm, correct political orientation; a plain, hard-working style; flexibility in strategy and tactics; and unity, alertness, earnestness, and liveliness.

28. See n. 22 in Chapter 13 above.

29. *Fan-kung yu-chi-tui t'u-chi fu-chien lien-chiang lu-huo fei-fang wen-chien hui-pien* (*A Compilation of Communist Documents Captured by the Anti-Communist Guerrilla Team in a Raid on Lienchiang, Fukien*) (Taipei, 1964), available on microfilm, Hoover Institution, Stanford University, Palo Alto, Calif. See a discussion in Pi-chao Chen, "Individual Farming After the Great Leap: As Revealed by the Lien-kiang [Lienchiang] Documents," *AS* 8, No. 9 (September, 1968): 775.

30. Cf. Ssu-yu Teng and John K. Fairbank, *China's Response to the West* (Cambridge, Mass.: Harvard University Press, 1954), p. 6.

31. This probably constitutes the most important section in Chapter I of the new Constitution.

32. Communiqué of the Eleventh Plenum, *JMJP*, August 14, 1966. Italics added. See discussion at reference to note 21, Chapter 7, regarding the Maoist claims about the contribution of the thought of Mao Tse-tung to Marxist ideology.

Chapter 16

1. I shall devote another volume to a comparative study of the modernization of China and Japan, to be published by Holt, Rinehart, and Winston.

2. In a book scheduled for publication in 1973, I shall seek to adapt to the Chinese Communist system the theoretical framework developed by functionalists, such as Gabriel A. Almond and G. Bingham Powell, Jr. in *Comparative Politics: A Developmental Approach* (Boston: Little, Brown, 1966). Since their analysis was based on empirical data drawn from the experience of Western democracies, it will need considerable adaptation to apply to Communist China.

3. *CFCP* editorial, June 6, 1968.

4. *The New York Times*, June 18, 1968, in a dispatch from Paris by Gloria Emerson. These lines from the walls of Paris have been published in *The Walls Speak* (Paris: Claude Tchou, 1968).

5. Robert Jay Lifton, *Revolutionary Immortality* (New York: Random House, 1968), p. 70. This question was discussed in some detail in Chapters 7 and 8 above.

6. Alberto Moravia, *The Red Book and the Great Wall* (New York: Farrar, Straus, and Giroux, 1968), pp. 63, 82–87.

7. Mao's talk before the Central Work Conference of the Central Committee, October 25, 1966, cited in n. 3, Chapter 12, above.

8. Cf. Ping-ti Ho, "Salient Aspects of China's Heritage," in Ping-ti Ho and Tang Tsou, eds., *China in Crisis* 1, Book One (Chicago: University of Chicago Press, 1968): 9.

BIBLIOGRAPHY

Mainly sources in English.

Methodological and Reference Aids

BOORMAN, HOWARD L. "The Study of Contemporary Chinese Politics: Some Remarks on Retarded Development," *World Politics* 7, No. 4 (July, 1960): 585–99.

FAIRBANK, JOHN K., and KWANG-CHING LIU. *Modern China: A Bibliographical Guide to Chinese Works, 1898–1937.* Cambridge, Mass.: Harvard University Press, 1950.

GENTZLER, J. MASON. *A Syllabus of Chinese Civilization.* New York: Columbia University Press, 1968.

HALPERN, ABRAHAM. "Contemporary China as a Problem of Political Science," *World Politics* 15, No. 3 (April, 1963): 361–76.

HSÜEH, CHÜN-TU. *The Chinese Communist Movement, 1921–1937.* Stanford, Calif.: Hoover Institution, Stanford University, 1960.

————. *The Chinese Communist Movement, 1937–1949.* Stanford, Calif.: Hoover Institution, Stanford University, 1962.

HUCKER, CHARLES O. *China, a Critical Bibliography.* Tucson: University of Arizona Press, 1962.

JOHNSON, CHALMERS. "The Role of Social Science in China Scholarship," *World Politics* 17, No. 2 (January, 1965): 256–71.

TENG, SSU-YÜ, and JOHN K. FAIRBANK. *China's Response to the West: A Documentary Survey, 1839–1923.* Cambridge, Mass.: Harvard University Press, 1954.

TENG, SSU-YÜ, and JOHN K. FAIRBANK. *Research Guide for China's Response to the West: A Documentary Survey, 1839–1923.* Cambridge, Mass.: Harvard University Press, 1954.

YUAN, TÛNG-LI. *China in Western Literature.* New Haven, Conn.: Far Eastern Publications, 1958.

Documentary Sources

ASIA RESEARCH CENTER, comp. and ed. *The Great Cultural Revolution in China.* Rutland, Vermont and Tokyo, Japan: Charles E. Tuttle, 1968.

BAUM, RICHARD, and FREDERICK C. TEIWES. *Ssu-ch'iang: The Socialist Education Movement of 1962–1966,* with appended documents. Research Monograph No. 2 of Center for Chinese Studies, University of California, Berkeley, 1968.

BRANDT, CONRAD, BENJAMIN I. SCHWARTZ, and JOHN K. FAIRBANK. *A Documentary History of Chinese Communism.* Cambridge, Mass.: Harvard University Press, 1952.

CENTER FOR INTERNATIONAL AFFAIRS and EAST ASIAN RESEARCH CENTER, Harvard University. *Communist China, 1955–1959: Policy Documents with Analysis.* Cambridge, Mass.: Harvard University Press, 1965.

Chung-kung wen-hua ta ko-ming tzu-liao hui-pien (Collection of Materials Concerning the Chinese Communist Great Cultural Revolution). Hongkong: Ming Pao Monthly, 1968.

COMPTON, BOYD. *Mao's China: Party Reform Documents, 1942–1944.* Seattle: University of Washington Press, 1952.

FAN, K. H., ed. *The Chinese Cultural Revolution: Selected Documents.* New York: Grove Press, 1968.

HARVARD-YENCHING LIBRARY. *Reproductions from Red Guard Tatzupao.* Cambridge, Mass.: Harvard University, 1967.

Liu Chu-hsi yü-lu (Quotations from Chairman Liu, compiled by independent sources in Hongkong). Hongkong: Tzulien Publishers, 1967.

Liu-Shao-ch'i Hsüan-chi (*Collected Writings of Liu Shao-ch'i*). Tokyo: Chinese Culture Service Publications, 1967.

MAO TSE-TUNG, translations of recent documents:

(a) Sino-Soviet Dispute

Speech at the Tenth Plenary Session of the Eighth Central Committee (September 24, 1962)—*Chinese Law and Government* (a journal of translations). White Plains, N.Y.: International Arts and Sciences Press. Vol. I, No. 4 (Winter, 1968–69), pp. 85–93.

(b) Great Leap Forward

Speech at the Supreme State Conference (January 28, 1958)—*ibid.*, pp. 10–14.

Speech at the Lushan Conference (July 23, 1959)—*ibid.*, pp. 27–43.

(c) Mao at Work

"On Ten Major Relationships" (April, 1956)—*ibid.*, pp. 21–34.

A Letter on the Writing of Poetry (January 12, 1957)—CB, No. 891, p. 23.

"Sixty Work Methods (Draft)" (February 19, 1958)—CB, No. 892 (October 21, 1969), pp. 1–14.

Comments on Li Chung-yun's Letter of Opinion (July 26, 1959) [Li is a former deputy director of a bureau in the State Planning Commission]—*ibid.*, pp. 47–51.

Instruction (September 7, 1966)—*ibid.*, p. 69.

Speech at a Report Meeting (October 24, 1966)—CB, No. 891 (October 8, 1969), pp. 70–73.

Talk on the Question of Democratic Centralism (January 30, 1962)—CB, No. 891, p. 37.

Instructions on Public Health Work (June 25, 1965)—JPRS, No. 49826, p. 24.

(d) Attitude Toward the Masses

Talk with Mao Yüan-hsin [Mao's nephew] (February, 1966)—JPRS, No. 49826 (February 12, 1970), pp. 29–30.

(e) Mao's Ideal Society

Letter to Comrade Lin Piao [which now forms the basis for a series of May 7 cadre schools throughout the Chinese People's Republic] (May 7, 1966)—CB, No. 891, pp. 56–57.

(f) On Education

Speech at the Ch'engtu Conference (March 22, 1958)— JPRS, No. 49826, pp. 45–52.

Instructions Given at the Spring Festival Concerning Educational Work (February 13, 1964)—CB, No. 891, pp. 42–44.

(g) On Bureaucracy

Twenty Manifestations of Bureaucracy (undated but probably from 1966)—JPRS, No. 49826, pp. 40–43.

(h) On the Cultural Revolution

Instructions (July 13, 1966)—JPRS, No. 49826, pp. 22–23.

Talks to Central Committee Leaders (believed to be in the summer of 1966)—*ibid.*, pp. 31–32.

Address to Regional Secretaries and Members of the Cultural Revolution Group (July 21, 1966)—CB, No. 891, pp. 60–62.

A Talk Before the Central Committee Work Conference (August 23, 1966)—*ibid.*, p. 68.

Speech at a Report Meeting (October 24, 1966)—*ibid.*, pp. 70–73.

Letter to Chou En-lai (February 1, 1967)—JPRS, No. 49826, p. 22.

Quotations from Chairman Mao Tse-tung. Peking: Foreign Language Press, 1967. (Reprinted in paperback in New York: Bantam, 1967. Known as the "Little Red Book.")

Selected Works of Mao Tse-tung, 4 vols. Peking: Foreign Language Press, 1965.

Books and Monographs

APTER, DAVID E. *Ideology and Discontent.* New York: Free Press, 1964.

BARNETT, A. DOAK. *Cadres, Bureaucracy, and Political Power in Communist China.* New York: Columbia University Press, 1967.

———. *China After Mao: With Selected Documents.* Princeton, N.J.: Princeton University Press, 1967.

———. *Chinese Communist Politics in Action.* Seattle: University of Washington Press, 1969.

———, ed. *Communist Strategies in Asia: A Comparative Analysis of Governments and Parties.* New York: Praeger Publishers, 1963.

BIGGERSTAFF, KNIGHT. *The Earliest Modern Government Schools in China, 1861–1894.* Ithaca, N.Y.: Cornell University Press, 1961.

BOARDMAN, E. P. *Christian Influence upon the Ideology of the Taiping Rebellion, 1851–1864.* Madison: University of Wisconsin Press, 1952.

BODDE, DERK. *China's Cultural Tradition: What and Whither?* New York: Holt, Rinehart & Winston, 1966.

BRIERE, O. *Fifty Years of Chinese Philosophy.* Translated by LAWRENCE G. THOMPSON, with an introduction by DENNIS J. DOOLIN. New York: Praeger Publishers, 1965.

CHAN, WING-TSIT. *A Source Book in Chinese Philosophy.* Princeton, N.J.: Princeton University Press, 1963.

———. *Chinese Philosophy, 1949–1963: An Annotated Bibliography of Mainland China Publications.* Honolulu: East-West Center, 1967.

CH'EN, JEROME. *Mao and the Chinese Revolution.* London and New York: Oxford University Press, 1965.

CHEN, THEODORE H. E. *The Chinese Communist Regime: Documents and Commentary.* New York: Praeger Publishers, 1967.

———. *Thought Reform of the Chinese Intellectuals.* London and Hongkong: Oxford University Press, 1960.

CHENG, CHESTER, ed. *Politics in the Chinese Red Army.* Stanford, Calif.: Hoover Institution, Stanford University, 1966.

CHOW, TSE-TSUNG. *The May Fourth Movement*. Stanford, Calif.: Stanford University Press, 1960.

CLUBB, O. EDMUND. *Twentieth Century China*. New York: Columbia University Press, 1964.

COHEN, ARTHUR A. *The Communism of Mao Tse-tung*. Chicago: University of Chicago Press, 1964.

COHEN, JEROME ALAN. *The Criminal Process in the People's Republic of China, 1949–1963*. Cambridge, Mass.: Harvard University Press, 1968.

CROIZIER, RALPH C. *China's Cultural Legacy and Communism*. New York: Praeger Publishers, 1970.

DE BARY, WM. THEODORE, *et al.*, eds. *Sources of Chinese Tradition*, 2 vols. New York: Columbia University Press, 1964.

DONNITHORNE, AUDREY. *The Chinese Economic System*. New York: Praeger Publishers, 1967.

ECKSTEIN, ALEXANDER. *Communist China's Economic Growth and Foreign Trade: Implications for U.S. Policy*. New York: McGraw-Hill, 1966.

FAIRBANK, JOHN KING. *China: The People's Middle Kingdom and the U.S.A.* Cambridge, Mass.: Harvard University Press, 1967.

————. *The United States and China*, rev. ed. Cambridge, Mass.: Harvard University Press, 1958.

————, ed. *The Chinese World Order*. Cambridge, Mass.: Harvard University Press, 1968.

FEUERWERKER, ALBERT, ed. *History in Communist China*. Cambridge, Mass.: M.I.T. Press, 1968.

FUNG, YU-LAN. *A Short History of Chinese Philosophy*. Edited by DERK BODDE. New York: Macmillan, 1948.

GITTINGS, JOHN. *Survey of the Sino-Soviet Dispute: A Commentary and Extracts from the Recent Polemics, 1963–1967*. London, New York, and Toronto: Oxford University Press, 1969.

GOLDMAN, MERLE R. *Literary Dissent in Communist China*. Cambridge, Mass.: Harvard University Press, 1967.

GRAY, JACK, ed. *Modern China's Search for a Political Form*. London, New York, and Toronto: Oxford University Press, 1969.

HARRISON, JAMES P. *The Communists and Chinese Peasant Rebellions.* New York: Atheneum, 1969.

HINTON, HAROLD C. *Communist China in World Politics.* Boston: Houghton Mifflin, 1966.

HINTON, WILLIAM. *Fansen, A Documentary of Revolution in a Chinese Village.* New York: Random House, 1966.

HO, PING-TI. *Studies on the Population of China, 1368–1953.* Cambridge, Mass.: Harvard University Press, 1959.

HO, PING-TI, and TANG TSOU, eds. *China in Crisis,* 2 vols. Chicago, Ill.: University of Chicago Press, 1968.

HSIA, C. T. *A History of Modern Chinese Fiction, 1917–1957.* New Haven, Conn.: Yale University Press, 1961.

HSIAO, TSO-LIANG. *Power Relations within the Chinese Communist Movement, 1930–1934: A Study of Documents.* Seattle: University of Washington Press, 1961.

HSÜEH, CHÜN-TU. *Huang Hsing and the Chinese Revolution.* Stanford, Calif.: Stanford University Press, 1961.

ISAACS, HAROLD R. *The Tragedy of the Chinese Revolution,* 2d rev. ed. Stanford, Calif.: Stanford University Press, 1966.

JOHNSON, CHALMERS A. *Peasant Nationalism and Communist Power: The Emergence of Revolutionary China, 1937–1945.* Stanford, Calif.: Stanford University Press, 1962.

KAROL, K. S. *China: The Other Communism.* New York: Hill & Wang, 1967.

LEVENSON, JOSEPH R. *Confucian China and Its Modern Fate,* 3 vols. Vol. 1: *The Problem of Intellectual Continuity;* Vol. 2: *The Problem of Monarchical Decay;* Vol. 3: *The Problem of Historical Significance.* Berkeley and Los Angeles: University of California Press, 1958, 1964, 1965.

———. *Liang Ch'i-ch'ao and the Mind of Modern China.* Cambridge, Mass.: Harvard University Press, 1959.

LEVY, MARION J. *The Family Revolution in Modern China.* Cambridge, Mass.: Harvard University Press, 1949.

LEWIS, JOHN W. *Leadership in Communist China.* Ithaca, N.Y.: Cornell University Press, 1964.

————, ed. *Major Doctrines of Communist China.* New York: W. W. Norton, 1964.

LIFTON, ROBERT J. *Revolutionary Immortality: Mao Tse-tung and the Chinese Cultural Revolution.* New York: Vintage Books, 1968.

————. *Thought Reform and the Psychology of Totalism.* New York: W. W. Norton, 1961.

LOWE, DONALD M. *The Function of "China" in Marx, Lenin, and Mao.* Berkeley and Los Angeles: University of California Press, 1966.

MACFARQUHAR, RODERICK. *China Under Mao.* Cambridge, Mass.: M.I.T. Press, 1966.

————. *The Hundred Flowers Campaign and the Chinese Intellectuals.* Epilogue by G. F. HUDSON. New York: Praeger Publishers, 1960.

MANNHEIM, KARL. *Ideology and Utopia.* New York: Harcourt, Brace & World, 1937.

MEISNER, MAURICE J. *Li Ta-chao and the Origins of Chinese Marxism.* Cambridge, Mass.: Harvard University Press, 1967.

MU FU-SHENG. *The Wilting of the Hundred Flowers: The Chinese Intelligentsia Under Mao.* New York: Praeger Publishers, 1963.

MUNRO, DONALD J. *The Concept of Man in Early China.* Stanford, Calif.: Stanford University Press, 1969.

MYRDAL, JAN. *Report from a Chinese Village.* New York: Pantheon, 1965.

NAKAMURA, HAJIME. *Ways of Thinking of Eastern Peoples: India, China, Tibet, and Japan.* Edited by P. P. WIENER. Honolulu: East-West Center, 1964.

NIVISON, DAVID S. *Communist Ethics and Chinese Tradition.* Cambridge, Mass.: Center for International Studies, Massachusetts Institute of Technology, 1954.

NORTH, ROBERT C. *Moscow and the Chinese Communists,* 2d ed. Stanford, Calif.: Stanford University Press, 1963.

NORTHROP, FILMER S.: *The Meeting of East and West: An Inquiry Concerning World Understanding*. New York: Macmillan, 1946.

PERKINS, DWIGHT H. *Agricultural Development in China, 1366–1968*. Chicago: Aldine, 1969.

PYE, LUCIAN W. *The Spirit of Chinese Politics: A Psychocultural Study of the Authority Crisis in Political Development*. Cambridge, Mass.: MIT Press, 1968.

RICHARDSON, WILLIAM, ed. *China Today*. Maryknoll, N.Y.: Maryknoll Publications, 1969.

RUE, JOHN E. *Mao Tse-tung in Opposition, 1927–1935*. Stanford, Calif.: Stanford University Press, 1966.

SCALAPINO, ROBERT A., and GEORGE T. YU. *The Chinese Anarchist Movement*. Berkeley: University of California Institute of International Studies, Center for Chinese Studies, 1961.

SCHRAM, STUART R. *Mao Tse-tung*. Baltimore: Penguin, 1966.

———, ed. *The Political Thought of Mao Tse-tung*, rev. ed. New York: Praeger Publishers, 1970.

SCHURMANN, FRANZ. *Ideology and Organization in Communist China*, 2d ed. Berkeley and Los Angeles: University of California Press, 1968.

SCHWARTZ, BENJAMIN I. *Chinese Communism and the Rise of Mao*. Cambridge, Mass.: Harvard University Press, 1964.

———. *Communism and China: Ideology in Flux*. Cambridge, Mass.: Harvard University Press, 1968.

SNOW, EDGAR. *Red Star over China*. New York: Random House, 1933 and 1948.

———. *The Other Side of the River*. New York: Random House, 1961.

SWARUP, SHANTI. *A Study of the Chinese Communist Movement, 1927–1934*. London and New York: Oxford University Press, 1966.

TAN, CHESTER C. *The Boxer Catastrophe*. New York: Columbia University Press, 1955.

TENG, SSU-YÜ, and JOHN K. FAIRBANK. *China's Response to the West*. Cambridge, Mass.: Harvard University Press, 1954.

THORNTON, RICHARD. *The Comintern and the Chinese Communists, 1928–1931*. Seattle: University of Washington Press, 1969.

TOWNSEND, JAMES R. *Political Participation in Communist China*. Berkeley and Los Angeles: University of California Press, 1967.

TREADGOLD, DONALD W., ed. *Soviet and Chinese Communism: Similarities and Differences*. Seattle: University of Washington Press, 1967.

WANG, YI C. *Chinese Intellectuals and the West, 1872–1949*. Chapel Hill: University of North Carolina Press, 1966.

WILBUR, C. MARTIN, and JULIE LIEN-YING HOW, eds. *Documents on Communism, Nationalism, and Soviet Advisers in China, 1918–1927*. New York: Columbia University Press, 1956.

WITTFOGEL, KARL A. *Oriental Despotism: A Comparative Study of Total Power*. New Haven, Conn.: Yale University Press, 1957.

WRIGHT, ARTHUR, F., ed. *Confucianism and Chinese Civilization*. Stanford, Calif.: Stanford University Press, 1964. New York: Atheneum, 1965.

———, ed. *Studies in Chinese Thought*. Chicago: University of Chicago Press, 1953.

WRIGHT, MARY CLABAUGH, ed. *China in Revolution: The First Phase, 1900–1913*. With an introduction by the editor. New Haven, Conn.: Yale University Press, 1968.

———, ed. *The Last Stand of Chinese Conservatism: The T'ung-chih Restoration, 1862–1875*. Stanford, Calif.: Stanford University Press, 1957.

YANG, C. K. *A Chinese Village in Early Communist Transition*. Cambridge, Mass.: MIT Press, 1959.

YU, FREDERICK T. C. *Mass Persuasion in Communist China*. New York: Praeger Publishers, 1964.

Articles

BOORMAN, HOWARD. "How to Be a Good Communist: The Political Ethics of Liu Shao-ch'i." *Asian Survey* 3, No. 8 (August, 1963): 372–83.

BOORMAN, HOWARD, and SCOTT BOORMAN. "Strategy and National Psychology in China." *The Annals* (American Academy of Political and Social Science) 370 (March, 1967): 143–55.

BRIDGHAM, PHILIP. "Mao's Cultural Revolution: Origin and Development." *China Quarterly* No. 29 (January–March, 1967), pp. 1–35.

———. "Mao's Cultural Revolution in 1967: The Struggle to Seize Power." *China Quarterly* No. 34 (April–June, 1968), pp. 6–37.

———. "Mao's Cultural Revolution: The Struggle to Seize Power." *China Quarterly* No. 41 (January–March, 1970), pp. 1–25.

CHEN, THODORE H. E. "A Nation in Agony." *Problems of Communism*, November–December, 1966, pp. 14–20.

CHENG, CHESTER. "Problems of Chinese Communist Leadership as Seen in the Secret Military Papers." *Asian Survey* 4, No. 6 (June, 1964): 861–72.

HSÜEH, CHÜN-TU. "The Cultural Revolution and Leadership Crisis in Communist China." *Political Science Quarterly* 82, No. 2 (June, 1967): 1–20.

JOHNSON, CHALMERS A. "China, the Cultural Revolution in Structural Perspective." *Asian Survey* 8, No. 1 (January, 1968): 1–15.

LEVENSON, JOSEPH, et al. "Twentieth Anniversary of the Chinese People's Republic." *China Quarterly* No. 39 (July–September, 1969), pp. 1–116.

LOWENTHAL, RICHARD. "Mao's Revolution: The Chinese Handwriting on the Wall." *Encounter*, April, 1967, pp. 3–9.

MACINNIS, DONALD. "Maoism: The Religious Analogy." *Christian Century*, January 10, 1968, pp. 39–42.

NEUHAUSER, CHARLES. "The Chinese Communist Party in the 1960's: Prelude to the Cultural Revolution." *China Quarterly* No. 32 (October–December, 1967), pp. 3–36.

OKSENBERG, MICHEL. "The Institutionalization of the Chinese Communist Revolution: The Ladder of Success on the Eve of the Cultural Revolution." *China Quarterly* No. 36 (October–December, 1968), pp. 61–92.

POWELL, RALPH L. "The Increasing Power of Lin Piao and the Party Soldiers, 1959–1966." *China Quarterly* No. 34 (April–June, 1968), pp. 38–65.

SCHRAM, STUART R. "The Party in Chinese Communist Ideology." *China Quarterly* No. 38 (April–June, 1969), pp. 1–26.

SCHWARTZ, BENJAMIN I. "The Reign of Virtue: Some Broad Perspectives on Leader and Party in the Cultural Revolution." *China Quarterly* No. 35 (July–September, 1968), pp. 1–17.

————. "Upheaval in China." *Commentary*, February, 1967, pp. 56–62.

SIMMONS, J. D. "P'eng Te-huai: A Chronological Re-Examination." *China Quarterly* No. 37 (January–March, 1969), pp. 120–138.

TSOU, TANG. "The Cultural Revolution and the Chinese Political System." *China Quarterly* No. 38 (April–June, 1969), pp. 63–91.

UNITED KINGDOM, FOREIGN OFFICE. "Mao's Cultural Revolution." London: December, 1967.

WU, YUAN-LI. "Economics, Ideology, and the Cultural Revolution." *Asian Survey* 8, No. 3 (March, 1968): 223–35.

INDEX